Contagion and Enclaves

Tropical Medicine in Colonial India

Postcolonialism across the Disciplines 10

Postcolonialism across the Disciplines

Series Editors
Graham Huggan, University of Leeds
Andrew Thompson, University of Leeds

Postcolonialism across the Disciplines showcases alternative directions for postcolonial studies. It is in part an attempt to counteract the dominance in colonial and postcolonial studies of one particular discipline – English literary/cultural studies – and to make the case for a combination of disciplinary knowledges as the basis for contemporary postcolonial critique. Edited by leading scholars, the series aims to be a seminal contribution to the field, spanning the traditional range of disciplines represented in postcolonial studies but also those less acknowledged. It will also embrace new critical paradigms and examine the relationship between the transnational/cultural, the global and the postcolonial.

Contagion and Enclaves

Tropical Medicine in Colonial India

Nandini Bhattacharya

Liverpool University Press

First published 2012 by
Liverpool University Press
4 Cambridge Street
Liverpool L69 7ZU

Copyright © 2012 Nandini Bhattacharya

The right of Nandini Bhattacharya to be identified as the author of this book has been asserted by her in accordance with the Copyright, Design and Patents Act 1988.

All rights reserved. No part of this book may be reproduced, stored in a retrieval system, or transmitted, in any form or by any means, electronic, mechanical, photocopying, recording, or otherwise, without the prior written permission of the publisher.

British Library Cataloguing-in-Publication data
A British Library CIP record is available

ISBN 978-1-84631-829-0 cased

Typeset in Amerigo by Koinonia, Manchester
Printed and bound in the United States of America

To Pratik

Contents

List of Illustrations viii
List of Tables ix
Acknowledgements x
List of Abbreviations xii

1 Disease and Colonial Enclaves   1
2 The Sanatorium of Darjeeling: European Health in a Tropical Enclave   18
3 Pioneering Years in Plantation and Medicine in Darjeeling, Terai
   and Duars   53
4 The Sanatorium Enclave: Climate and Class in Colonial Darjeeling   84
5 Contending Visions of Health Care in the Plantation Enclaves   99
6 The Plantation Enclave, the Colonial State and Labour Health Care   119
7 Tropical Medicine in Its 'Field': Malaria, Hookworm and the Rhetoric
   of the 'Local'   149
8 Habitation and Health in Colonial Enclaves: The Hill-station and
   the Tea Plantations   184

Bibliography 194
Index 210

List of illustrations

2.1	View of Jalapahar, Darjeeling. Author's personal postcard collection.	23
2.2	Street Map of Darjeeling town, nineteenth century.	28
2.3	Scenic Darjeeling. Author's personal postcard collection.	49
3.1	Production of Tea, Ging Tea Estate, Darjeeling. Author's personal print collection.	61
4.1	View of bazaar, Darjeeling. Author's personal postcard collection.	89
7.1	Malaria Experiments at Meenglas Estate. Taken from *Report of the malaria survey of the Jalpaiguri Duars*, Government of Bengal, Public Health Department (Calcutta: Bengal Government Press, 1926), first page. With permission from the Wellcome Library, London.	163

List of tables

3.1	Expansion of tea gardens in Darjeeling.	59
3.2	Expansion of tea gardens in the Duars.	66
3.3	Ailments and their cures.	69
6.1	Vital statistics in the tea estates of Duars, Jalpaiguri district and Bengal.	123
7.1	Spleen index of tea estates in Mal tea district of Duars in 1926.	166
7.2	Spleen index of tea estates in Nagrakata tea district of Duars in 1926.	166

Acknowledgements

I have accumulated many debts in the course of writing this book, which is a revised version of my doctoral thesis at the Wellcome Trust Centre for History of Medicine at University College London. I wish to thank the Wellcome Trust for awarding me the Roy Porter Memorial studentship to pursue my doctoral thesis. The UCL Centre was a vibrant platform for a young researcher, and I am grateful to the many scholars with whom I had the privilege of discussing my work there. I am indebted to my supervisor, Anne Hardy, who advised me with rigour, clarity and unfailing courtesy and has always been most generous with her time and expertise. Janet Browne, who was formerly the graduate tutor at the Centre, initiated me into the norms of British academia with kindness and great tolerance. I would like to thank H.J. Cook, Christopher Lawrence, Roger Cooter and Helga Satzinger for their support.

I am particularly grateful to Mark Harrison who took the trouble to read and comment on some of my drafts. I am also grateful to David Arnold whose insightful comments, I hope, have enriched this work and to David Hardiman who patiently read my doctoral thesis and provided invaluable advice. While writing this book I have been employed at various places where I could share my work with wonderful scholars of imperial history and the history of medicine. I am grateful to Sarah Hodges, Guy Attewell, Frank Snowden, Naomi Rogers, John Warner, Deepak Kumar, Claudia Stein, Roy Macleod, Alex Mackay and Prashant Kidambi for their comments at various stages of this work. I also wish to thank Simon Gunn, Steven King and Roey Sweet for their constant support to me here at the School of Historical Studies, University of Leicester. I would also like to thank Alison Welsby of Liverpool University Press for her patience throughout the preparation of the manuscript.

In my field trips to northern Bengal, I was hosted by my cousin, Dr Nivedita Chakraborty. Scholarly discussions with her enriched my understanding of the region. I am grateful to her, my aunt Chinmoyee Devi, and Tutun and Rana for

Acknowledgements

their love and generosity. Dr Ashoke Ganguly was especially helpful with his wide knowledge of the history of tea gardens in northern Bengal. I am indebted to the various people who made my visits to the tea estates successful, including Dr S. Bol, Dr D.N. Chatterjee, Krishan Aggarwal, U.B. Das, Ishwar Aggarwal, A.K. Chatterjee, P.K. Bhattacharjee, Dr Krishna Dasgupta, Satya Dasgupta, Paromita and Shoma Chakraborty, Rathin Bose, P. Dutta and Sister Dr Regina for their help and particularly to the management and workers of Hasimara, Banarhat, and Pahargoomia tea estates for sharing their stories of life on the tea plantations. On my trips to the Darjeeling, Terai and Duars I recorded several interviews with Indian planters and doctors, which were generally rather than specifically useful. I met tea workers, including *bhagats* (spirit-ousters and healers) and managers as well as doctors, nurses and compounders. At their request, I have not named or quoted many of them. I am very grateful to the many employees of tea estates who gave me their time and shared memories of their daily lives and experiences; even more so because at this time they were experiencing lock-outs and consequent impoverishment in many tea estates of northern Bengal. I am especially thankful to Sujit Naskar, who accompanied me on my trips to the tea estates and was my guide, counsellor and chivalrous companion.

At UCL the camaraderie and intellectual stimulation provided by my friends sustained me while this work was in progress. My friends and colleagues Candice Delisle, Stephen Casper and Akinobu Takabayashi challenged me intellectually and simultaneously indulged my emotional excesses. The companionship and discussions with my friends Aparna Vaidik, Samira Sheikh, Sanchari Dutta, Rochana Bajpai, Leela Sami, Katrina Gatley, Jorge Varanda, Karen Buckle, Richard Barnett, Liew KK and Christos Papadopoulous were invaluable. I wish to particularly thank Bhavani Raman for a long and intense discussion of the book.

I owe my engagement with history to my former teachers and my friends at Jawaharlal Nehru University, New Delhi, as well as at the M.S. University of Baroda, and take this opportunity to thank them, particularly Dilbagh Singh, Seema Alavi and S. Hassan Mahmood. I am indebted to my former professor and old friend Iftikhar Ahmad Khan, who taught me that nothing is sacred, and my friend the late Bhavana Krishnamoorthy, who showed me, with great compassion, that it is possible to question everything.

I would especially like to thank Mr Hugh Rayner of the Pagoda Tree Press for kindly permitting me to publish the map of Darjeeling from his collection.

I also thank my parents-in-law and uncle and aunt who hospitably shared their homes with me in Calcutta. I am grateful to my parents, especially to my father who inspired me to value intellectual pursuits, and to my brother Biswanath who has looked on my academic life with bemused tolerance, but loyally supported me nevertheless. I have shared my life and work with Pratik for many years, and I hope that this book, which is dedicated to him, will be an adequate tribute to his love.

List of Abbreviations

APAC	Asia, Pacific and Africa Collections, British Library
BMA	British Medical Association
BMJ	*British Medical Journal*
CSTM	Calcutta School of Tropical Medicine
DPA	Dooars Planters' Association
DPAAR	*Dooars Planters' Association Annual Report*
ICS	Indian Civil Service
IMG	*Indian Medical Gazette*
IMS	Indian Medical Service
ITA	Indian Tea Association
ITAAR	*Indian Tea Association Annual Report*
ITPA	Indian Tea Planters' Association
JLA	Jalpaiguri Labour Act
JLAAR	*Jalpaiguri Labour Act Annual Report*
LMINA	Lady Minto Indian Nursing Association
PLA	Plantation Labour Act
RCLI	*Report of the Royal Commission on Labour in India*
TTPA	Terai Tea Planters' Association

CHAPTER 1

Disease and Colonial Enclaves

This book is about the interaction between Tropical Medicine, the colonial state and colonial enclaves. The epistemologies and therapeutics of Western science and medicine informed the practices of colonialism in the tropical world from the eighteenth to the twentieth century. The European conquest and colonization of the non-European world was imbued with the dread of 'tropical diseases' and simultaneously sustained by the practices of settlement in these tropical colonies. In analysing these two processes together, this book investigates the links between Tropical Medicine and colonial enclaves.

The perception of the 'tropics' itself changed from the abundant and the paradisiacal in the sixteenth century to dark, dank territories that generated 'putrefaction', disease and death by the mid-eighteenth century.[1] In eighteenth-century European writing, the status of the Indian subcontinent as a distinctively tropical zone was ambivalent due to its vastness and diversity and the prevalence of different 'climatic zones' within.[2] This gradual transformation in the idea of the tropics was the consequence of prolonged European interaction with, and experience of, the tropics. Along with these ideas and experiences of the tropics, from the eighteenth century, European traders, sailors and armies built their own commercial, military and social spaces in the tropics. In the Indian subcontinent, initially these were factories (in their eighteenth-century sense factories were European warehouses), fortresses, churches, barracks and white towns that were located near ports and harbours.[3] Through the eighteenth and

---

1 David Arnold, *The Tropics and the Traveling Gaze: India, Landscape, and Science, 1800–1850* (Delhi, Permanent Black, 2006); Nancy Stepan, *Picturing Tropical Nature* (Ithaca, NY, Cornell University Press, 2001).
2 Mark Harrison, *Climates and Constitutions: Health, Race, Environment and British Imperialism in India, 1600–1850* (Delhi, Oxford University Press, 1999).
3 Susan M. Neilds-Basu, 'Colonial Urbanism: The Development of Madras City in the Eighteenth and Nineteenth Centuries', *Modern Asian Studies*, 13 (1979), pp. 217–46;

the nineteenth centuries, as European commercial and revenue interests after territorial expansion became more intensive, the establishment and maintenance of enclaves within colonial society became vital. These European enclaves within tropical colonies served various purposes: as cantonments for the army, plantations for large-scale capitalist cultivation of cash crops with resident planters and labourers; as hill-stations for British civilian and official residence during the summer, and as exclusive 'civil lines' within larger, densely populated towns and cities. Colonialism in modern India was marked by the relationship between the enclaves and the tropical world beyond; these enclaves, therefore, were permeated with the movement of labourers, commodities, soldiers, prostitutes, markets and traders as well as pathogens. This book traces the history of the colonization of the Darjeeling hills in north Bengal as one of the inter-relationships between colonial enclaves and the tropical world; a relationship that, from the late nineteenth century, was imbued with the optimism and momentum provided by Tropical Medicine.

Colonialism and Tropical Medicine

In the late-nineteenth century, the ambivalence in medical discourse about the suitability of tropical climates for European bodies gave way to a hardening of racial categories. The effects of British imperialism gradually produced more strident views about tropical disease; places like Bengal were now considered the 'home' of cholera and diseases such as malaria, cholera and dysentery acquired specifically tropical characteristics. The institutionalization of 'Tropical Medicine', a medical specialism that was distinguished by laboratory medicine energized by the insect-vector theories of filaria, malaria, sleeping sickness and affirmed by the final conquest of Africa and most of Asia, also established the links between 'tropical' diseases and the environment, parasites, insect hosts and partly immune 'native' populations. This reinforced the links between tropical colonies and disease. Although a new specialism, Tropical Medicine appropriated its therapeutics from older bodies of knowledge and practices of survival and fitness of Europeans in the tropics. From the years of the maritime expansion of Western European powers into Asia and Africa, thousands of European sailors, soldiers, merchants and adventurers died in the course of conquest, exploration and the settlement and administration of tropical colonies. Simultaneously, there developed a knowledge and practice of 'medicine of warm climates'. The 'medicine of warm climates' was a heterogeneous, substantial body of knowledge; a selection of scattered observations and therapies by European medical practitioners in tropical colonies, largely from practical experience.[4] These empirical observations continued to inform medical

---

Partha Mitter, 'The Early British Port Cities of India: Their Planning and Architecture, Circa 1640–1757', *The Journal of the Society of Architectural Historians*, 45 (1986), pp. 95–114.

4 David Arnold (ed.), *Warm Climates and Western Medicine: The Emergence of Tropical Medicine,*

practice in the tropical colonies. As Philip Curtin has pointed out, the decrease in European mortality and morbidity figures in nineteenth-century Africa, the Caribbean and parts of South Asia was the consequence of access to greater sanitary facilities and enforcement of a regime of behaviour that included the older precepts of 'tropical hygiene' – a regime of careful control of the influence of environment on the European body through specific clothing, diet, exercise and sexual behaviour.[5] Including, heterogeneously, tropical hygiene and the myriad influence of environment on insect-vectors and depending on fieldwork for its cognitive content, Tropical Medicine was virtually synonymous with colonial medicine and relied on the agencies of the colonial state or the patronage of imperial commercial networks for its sustenance.

For medical researchers in the British Empire, Tropical Medicine represented opportunities for advancement through new discoveries and challenges, glamour and the lure of exotic field locations in which to practise their science. Among colonial officials and the public in Britain it produced optimism about controlling epidemic disease within European colonies through carefully managed programmes of containment or eradication.[6] Its practices were sponsored by the colonial states or by private entrepreneurs who had commercial interest in specific areas and diseases.[7] Researchers conceived of and pursued Tropical Medicine through imperial and international networks of knowledge.[8] Patrick Manson discovered the transmission of the filaria parasite through the mosquito after years of medical practice among the Chinese, but the proclaimed 'father' of Tropical Medicine achieved his ambitions and institutional recognition in metropolitan London. Ronald Ross established his school at Liverpool and, despite his knighthood and the Nobel Prize, spent his later years regretting his perceived lack of acclaim within the British establishment. David Bruce similarly pursued his research in Africa and recognition and rewards

---

1500–1900 (Amsterdam, Rodopi, 1996), pp. 1–19. Empirical observations continued to inform discourses on the healthiest and most suitable clothes and accessories for white men and women in 'tropical Africa' in the twentieth century. See Ryan Johnson, 'European Cloth and "Tropical" Skin: Clothing Material and British Ideas of Health and Hygiene in Tropical Climates', *Bulletin of the History of Medicine*, 83 (2009), pp. 530–60.

5 P.D. Curtin, *Death by Migration: Europe's Encounter with the Tropical World in the Nineteenth Century* (Cambridge, Cambridge University Press, 1989).

6 David N. Livingstone, 'Tropical Climate and Moral Hygiene: Anatomy of a Debate', *The British Journal for the History of Science*, 32 (1999), pp. 93–110; Warwick Anderson, 'Immunities of Empire: Race, Disease, and the New Tropical Medicine, 1900–1920', *Bulletin of the History of Medicine*, 70 (1996), pp. 94–118.

7 Douglas M. Haynes, *Imperial Medicine: Patrick Manson and the Conquest of Tropical Disease* (Philadelphia, PA, Penn, 2001); Helen J. Power, *Tropical Medicine in the Twentieth Century: A History of the Liverpool School* (London and New York, Kegan Paul International, 1998); John Farley, *Bilharzia: A History of Imperial Tropical Medicine* (Cambridge and New York, Cambridge University Press, 1991), pp. 1–30.

8 Michael Worboys, 'Manson, Ross, and Colonial Medical Policy: Tropical Medicine in London and Liverpool, 1899–1914', in Roy MacLeod and Milton Lewis (eds), *Disease, Medicine, and Empire: Perspectives on Western Medicine and the Experience of European Expansion* (London and New York, Routledge, 1988), pp. 21–37; Haynes, *Imperial Medicine*.

Contagion and Enclaves

from metropolitan institutions. International medical conferences and medical journals in the early twentieth century registered the research conducted by experts in Tropical Medicine who corresponded with each other, compared their theories and conclusions and validated new research in the discipline. The above processes of the institutionalization of Tropical Medicine occurred in the high imperial age, and its context was the consolidation of colonialism itself.[9] Colonial experiences generated the need for tropical hygiene and eventually Tropical Medicine. Colonial realities informed, modified and occasionally challenged metropolitan sciences; social contexts often formed an integral part of the 'ecology' of imperial science, none more so than Tropical Medicine.[10] Ronald Ross compared the advances in Tropical Medicine in treating malaria, sleeping sickness and yellow fever to Columbus's 'god-like gift' and speculated that these would mean 'civilization and prosperity for vast possessions in the tropics'.[11] Yellow fever and trypanosomiasis extended beyond local outbreaks to continent-wide epidemics in the Caribbean and Africa respectively as a consequence of the large-scale migration of people and livestock in response to a range of colonial economic and military policies, as did malaria within South and Southeast Asia. To understand Tropical Medicine, therefore, we must situate its history firmly within the political and economic contexts of colonialism itself.

Colonialism and Medicine in India

Within the British Empire in Africa and South Asia, colonial states exercised varying degrees of control over its territories. Particularly within the areas of 'indirect control' British policy left day-to-day administration to 'native rulers'. British administration in colonies delegated great civil, military and judicial powers to its local administrating official, the man on the spot. Colonial governments were also responsible to the British Parliament at home and sensitive to political and cultural resistances to many of its policies within the colonies. The hegemony of colonial rule, particularly in South Asia, has been questioned by historians;[12] the role of the colonial state in institutionalizing Western therapeutics is similarly a contentious point.

9 Michael Worboys, 'The Emergence of Tropical Medicine: A Study in the Establishment of A Scientific Speciality', in Gerald Lemaineet al. (eds), *Perspectives on the Emergence of Scientific Disciplines* (Hague and Paris, Mouton, 1976), pp. 76–98.
10 P. Palladino and M. Worboys, 'Science and Imperialism', *Isis*, 84 (1993), pp. 91–102.
11 Ronald Ross, 'Medical Science and the Tropics', *Bulletin of the American Geographical Society*, 45 (1913), pp. 435–38.
12 C.A. Bayly, *Indian Society and the Making of the British Empire* (Cambridge, Cambridge University Press, 1988), and his *Empire and Information: Intelligence Gathering and Social Communication in India, 1780–1870* (Cambridge, Cambridge University Press, 1996); D.A. Washbrook, 'Progress and Problems: South Asian Economic and Social History c.1720–1860', *Modern Asian Studies*, 22 (1988), pp. 57–96; William R. Pinch, 'Same Difference in India and Europe', *History and Theory,* 38 (1999), pp. 389–407.

Historians have long debated interventions of 'Western' therapeutics and preventive strategies within colonial South Asia and 'colonial medicine' is itself a contested term.[13] As Shula Marks has pointed out, the distinctions between colonial medicine and the colonizing aspects of biomedicine that transformed the European and North American metropolises were most evident in debates on race and eugenics and in the long-term persistence of health inequalities in modern 'developing' nations.[14] Among historians of South Asia, the debates initially centred on the intent and praxis of Western therapeutics and preventive medicine; and whether or not they were limited to the relatively narrow group of British soldiers and Anglo-Indian civilians within the Raj.[15] It has been argued by R. Ramasubban that the dissemination of Western medicine was indicative of colonial priorities and the benefits of Western medicine and sanitary provisions were only fitfully applied to the greater Indian population. In her narrative of public health in Bengal, for instance, Kabita Ray has argued that the transfer of the pecuniary burden of controlling epidemic disease and providing medical facilities to the impoverished municipalities and district boards was indicative of a systematic neglect of public health on the part of the colonial government.[16] Mridula Ramanna, in another regional study in Bombay, has argued for a more qualified view, but generally believes that the colonial state limited its extent of intervention in wider public health measures in colonial Bombay.[17] Others have argued that the relationship between the colonial state and public health in British India was multifarious and often tortuous. David Arnold has evoked the ambiguities of this relationship between the colonial state and public health.[18] In his discussion of state policies and indigenous responses to the management of three epidemic diseases – smallpox, cholera and plague – he has argued that the 'corporeality of colonialism' was not simply the conse-

13 Mark Harrison, *Public Health in British India: Anglo-Indian Preventive Medicine, 1859–1914* (Cambridge, New York, Cambridge University Press, 1994); Margaret Jones, *Health Policy in Britain's Model Colony: Ceylon (1900–1948)* (Hyderabad, Orient Longman, 2004).
14 Shula Marks, 'What is Colonial about Colonial Medicine? And What Has Happened to Imperialism and Health?', *Social History of Medicine*, 10 (1997), pp. 205–19.
15 Radhika Ramasubban, 'Imperial Health in British India, 1857–1900', in Roy Macleod and Milton Lewis (eds), *Disease, Medicine, and Empire: Perspectives on Western Medicine and the Experience of European Expansion* (London and New York, Routledge, 1988), pp. 38–60.
16 Kabita Ray, *History of Public Health: Colonial Bengal 1921–1947* (Calcutta, K.P. Bagchi and Co., 1998), p. 346. Deepak Kumar has similarly emphasized the point of 'neglect' by the colonial state and the bureaucratic 'tangles' and financial constraints to the full implementation of public health policies such as vaccination against smallpox and the control of cholera in colonial India. See Deepak Kumar, 'Perceptions of Public Health: A Study in British India', in Amiya Kumar Bagchi and Krishna Soman (eds), *Maladies, Preventives and Curatives: Debates in Public Health in India* (New Delhi, Tulika Books, 2005), pp. 44–59. See also David Arnold, 'Medical Priorities and Practice in Nineteenth Century British India', *South Asia Research*, 5 (1985), pp. 167–83.
17 Mridula Ramanna, *Western Medicine and Public Health in Colonial Bombay 1845–1895* (Hyderabad, Orient Longman, 2002), pp. 83–122.
18 David Arnold, *Colonizing the Body: State Medicine and Epidemic Disease in Nineteenth-Century India* (Berkeley, Los Angeles, London, University of California Press, 1993), p. 7.

quence, however broad-based, of the intent to protect the British in India, but rather encompassed the benevolence and hegemony of Western epistemology and therapeutic praxis in colonial India. He has nevertheless pointed out that colonial realities modified this aspiration to the hegemonic domination of state medicine, and that Indian cultural and social resistance to vaccination and militaristic sanitation regimes often subverted state medical policy. Mark Harrison and others have pointed out that the ambivalence of medical policy and administrative commitment towards control of smallpox and cholera was also associated with the financial constraints and political expediency of the Indian Empire.[19] Harrison has also noted that the constraints of political expediency and the limitations of colonial administration informed medical policy in colonial India and that the relatively marginal status of the Indian Medical Service (IMS), as compared to the Indian Civil Service, in Anglo-Indian society, the 'pervasive anti-intellectualism' and general 'institutional inertia' contributed to an active resistance on the part of its officials to medical trends from the metropolis.[20] Moreover, post-1857 anxieties continued to inform the gradualism that characterized government public health provisions, which outside of the cantonments (where they were most efficacious) were concentrated more on sanitary education and promotion of charitable dispensaries.[21] Meanwhile, when there was some devolution of power to local government after 1885, the Indian elites' lack of interest in Western sanitary models undermined limited attempts to initiate rural sanitation.[22] These constraints and an episodic symbiosis of nationalist protest and cultural resistance were projected sharply into relief when the Bombay government sought to enforce quarantine policy during the plague epidemic in Pune at the turn of the century, a resistance that was reflected in many other parts of India, including the capital, Calcutta.[23] The civil administration remained generally tentative in pushing unpopular sanitary agendas on the larger Indian population. The government suspended this hesitancy briefly during the plague in Bombay, but it re-emerged as the dominant official discourse of public medicine in colonial India.

Despite the qualifications above, historians have most frequently and usefully associated Western sanitary models and therapeutics with colonialism in the non-European world. Public health systems, however imperfect or limited, were initiated by colonial states in tropical Asia and Africa, sometimes in coercive forms such as sanitary cordons; on other occasions in the form of vaccination

---

19 Harrison, *Public Health in British India*, pp. 139–226. See also, Sanjoy Bhattacharya, M. Harrison and M. Worboys, *Fractured States: Smallpox, Public Health and Vaccination Policy in British India, 1800–1947* (New Delhi, Orient Longman, 2005), p. 7.
20 Harrison, *Public Health in British India*, pp. 34–35.
21 Harrison, *Public Health in British India*, pp. 87–98.
22 Harrison, *Public Health in British India*, p. 200.
23 Harrison, *Public Health in British India*, pp. 211–26. On the contradictory plague policies of the Bombay, Calcutta and Punjab governments, see I.J. Catanach, 'Plague and the Tensions of Empire: India 1896–1918', in D. Arnold (ed.), *Imperial Medicine and Indigenous Societies* (Manchester and New York, Manchester University Press, 1988), pp. 149–71.

or public health education programmes to an often bewildered or resentful colonized population.[24] In the places where state medicine was inadequate or impossibly stretched or even absent, medical missions stepped in to provide everyday moral and physical succour to the sick and the marginalized within indigenous societies.[25] From the nineteenth century, further, the epistemologies of indigenous medicine were systematically undermined by British officials and missionaries.

The dissemination of concepts and mechanisms for public health, therefore, were undoubtedly within the remit, however loosely defined, of the state in colonial India and indeed, in most parts of the British Empire. In India, these included not only medical interventions but political and institutional ones: the establishment of local government with responsibility for sanitary measures at the district level, partial vaccination and occasional vector-control programmes, encouragement of voluntary and charitable hospitals and dispensaries with contributions from the local elite, the attempt, through medical schools, of creating an independent medical profession in India. These co-existed with government-aided hospitals, military hospitals and special asylums, and the monopoly of the cadres of the IMS within the government medical and research institutions. These processes also changed indigenous medicine in the long term, because Ayurveda and Unani practitioners responded to the challenges of the state support for Western therapeutics and its gradual but steady dissemination by re-inventing and modernizing many of their own therapeutic practices for the modern medical marketplace.[26]

Colonial Enclaves and the Practices of Settlement

Colonial rule actively introduced and enriched Western therapeutics and epistemologies in colonial India. These were realized most effectively where colonial power could be exercised relatively easily, that is, within colonial enclaves. It is within demarcated colonial enclaves that were of economic or political importance that the colonial state and Tropical Medicine first tried out vaccination

24 For instance, see Lenore Manderson, *Sickness and the State: Health and Illness in Colonial Malaya 1870–1940* (Cambridge, Cambridge University Press, 1996); W. Anderson, *Colonial Pathologies: American Tropical Medicine, Race and Hygiene in the Philippines* (Durham, NC and London, Duke University Press, 2006); Maryinez Lyons, *The Colonial Disease: A Social History of Sleeping Sickness in Northern Zaire, 1900–1940* (Cambridge and New York, Cambridge University Press, 1992); Myron Echenberg, *Black Death, White Medicine: Bubonic Plague and Public Health in Colonial Senegal, 1914–1945* (Portsmouth, NH, Heinemann, 2002).
25 Megan Vaughan, *Curing Their Ills: Colonial Power and African Illness* (Oxford, Polity Press, 1991); David Hardiman, *Missionaries and Their Medicine: A Christian Modernity for Tribal India* (Manchester, Manchester University Press, 2008).
26 Kavita Sivaramakrishnan, *Old Potions, New Bottles: Recasting Indigenous Medicine in Colonial Punjab 1850–1945* (Hyderabad, India, Orient Longman, 2006); Guy Attewell, *Refiguring Unani Tibb: Plural Healing in Late Colonial India* (Hyderabad, India, Orient Longman, 2007); Seema Alavi, *Islam and Healing: Loss and Recovery of an Indo-Muslim Medical Tradition, 1600–1900* (Basingstoke, Palgrave Macmillan, 2008).

campaigns, established sanitary infrastructure, initiated and sustained control of venereal diseases, and in triumphant partnership with Tropical Medicine, implemented vector- and parasite-control programmes. Such measures were usually focused at particular sites because they were of paramount political or economic interest to colonial governance; and it was always easier to conceive of and implement expensive medical and sanitary programmes at small, easily manageable sites. Arnold has suggested that the most significant sites were the cantonments and the jails.[27] He therefore identifies the role of medicine in such enclaves as unique and distinct from that in civil society in colonial India.

But although cantonments and jails were the enclaves where preventive health measures were often initiated, colonial enclaves need a wider definition. It is my view that colonial enclaves were not confined to institutions of regimentation and confinement. They were an essential part of colonial civil society and economy and at the same time designed as special and distinct zones of colonial habitation, power and productivity. The control of disease and the maintenance of hygiene and sanitation were essential to the sustenance of such zones of special interest. This book studies disease control as a mode of colonial power, governance and intervention in areas of productivity and attempts to protect their social and political exclusivity. The creation and sustenance of special zones of economic interest and social habitation was an essential aspect of British colonialism. The beginnings of British enclaves in tropical colonies can be traced in the 'white towns' of the port cities like Calcutta, Madras and Bombay in the eighteenth century; or in the plantation complexes of the West Indies and Southeast Asia. The establishment of civil lines, exclusive social clubs and hill-stations in the nineteenth century in India, Ceylon and Malaya borrowed from eighteenth-century traditions of creating exclusive spaces for European habitation and commerce in the colonies. Through their architectural, racial and aesthetic distinctions, these spaces also represented colonial power. With the integration of colonial India into the global economy in the nineteenth century, the colonial state encouraged economic enclaves such as mines and plantations (tea, coffee, cinchona, rubber etc.) developed as isolated units of industrial and agricultural production in the colonies. The plantation system in India marked a break from the erstwhile agrarian policies and practices of the government of India where it had concentrated on the collection of agrarian revenue from peasants or landlord-proprietors. They were not exclusive to India; partially or fully segregated civil enclaves for European populations were sustained in parts of the British Empire in South Africa, Malaya and Tanzania, as well as the Belgian Congo, French Senegal and Dutch Indonesia. These are distinct from 'settler societies', which were defined by the will to keep out non-white populations in imperial dominions.[28] This book therefore posits

---

27 Arnold, *Colonizing the Body*, p. 61.
28 For an examination of the complicity of scientific racism and politics in creating and sustaining a white settler colony, see W. Anderson, *Cultivation of Whiteness: Science, Health and Racial Destiny in Australia* (Carlton South, Victoria, Melbourne University Press, 2002).

colonial enclaves as distinctive sites of the articulation of colonial power and economic priorities. Despite the richness of recent historiography on public health and Tropical Medicine in colonial India, historians have not analysed the discourses and praxis of medicine within colonial enclaves and the communities they engendered. The result has been the imposition of ideas and experiences of nineteenth-century British public health (characterized by sanitation, vaccination movements, role of local municipality etc.) on the Indian subcontinent. This book argues that public health in colonial India needs to identify and engage with the peculiar institutions of the colonial society and economy. By studying the social history of disease within two such enclaves, the hill-station of Darjeeling and the plantation enclave in its neighbourhood in colonial north Bengal, this book argues that disease and its control was linked to the essential modes of colonial functioning, in practices of settlement, governance and in economic productivity.

Plantation and Sanatoriums as Colonial Enclaves

This book suggests that the plantations and sanatoriums of the Darjeeling hill-station were coterminous enclaves. This was for a variety of reasons: similarities in colonization processes and colonial investments; geographical proximity, patterns and experiences of settlements (both among the white planters and entrepreneurs and the immigrant labourers); the political economy of colonization and trade in timber, tea and an emergent leisure economy that linked both the plantation and the hill-station; and finally, their simultaneous absorption within the colonial and imperial economy.

One part of this book is an exploration of colonial governance through the control of disease in an economic enclave: the tea plantations of north Bengal. In the late nineteenth century, English and Dutch entrepreneurs established tea, coffee, rubber and cinchona plantations in colonies in Asia: Malaya, Java, Sumatra, Ceylon and parts of eastern and southern India.[29] Situated in remote locations several miles from the nearest town and appropriating vast tracts of land leased at nominal rates from the government, the plantations were isolated habitations that housed immigrant labourers and the management within them, in barrack-like residences for the labourers and bungalows for the management. Colonial plantations have generally been characterized as peripheral enclosed spaces. In his study of the plantation economy of east Sumatra, Jan Breman has pointed out that its determining characteristics were 'the region's peripheral situation within the colonial domain, the rapid rise of plantation agriculture as a predominant factor and, in principle, the temporary presence of both employers and employees'.[30] The most prominent feature

---

29 Abhijeet Mukherjee, 'The Peruvian Bark Revisited: A Critique of British Cinchona Policy in Colonial India', *Bengal Past and Present*, 117 (1998), pp. 81–102.
30 Jan Breman, *Taming the Coolie Beast: Plantation Society and the Colonial Order in Southeast Asia* (Delhi and Oxford, Oxford University Press, 1989), p. 176.

Contagion and Enclaves

of the enclaves, the hegemony enjoyed by the planters, was an integral part of the frontier settlement zones where the plantations were located. Breman identified Ceylon, India (Nilgiris and Assam), French Indo-China, Malaya and the Philippines as regions where similar plantation systems emerged in the mid- to late nineteenth century. These were distinct from the classical plantation societies of Latin America and the Caribbean regions of the eighteenth century. Breman argued that the nineteenth-century plantations were characterized by large-scale immigrant labour.[31] A distinctive feature of the plantation system in tropical Asia was the great authority exercised by the planters within the system, and the enclosed aspect of the plantations evident in the restrictions on mobility, the residence of most of the labourers within the plantations and a general non-interference of the local government within the tea estates. The new plantations in Asia and Africa, although different in character from the large American and Caribbean plantation-complexes of the eighteenth century, also shared many of their characteristics. Such as labour-intensive operations, European management, a belief in white racial superiority and 'ideas about labor discipline and concepts of a proper social order'.[32] In practice, the plantations, like other colonial enclaves, were permeable to some extent and exposed to immigrant labourers, pathogens and commodities. As a feature of colonial capitalism, these plantations produced principally for the export market were dominated by white capital and enjoyed a close but ambivalent relationship with the state, which allowed the planters great civil and informal policing powers within their estates but intervened in crises such as epidemics and political riots. It is in the plantations as well that Tropical Medicine achieved progress in researching and conducting anti-vector and anti-parasite programmes. The Liverpool School, the Calcutta School of Tropical Medicine (CSTM) and the Ross Institute (Putney, London) sought the patronage of the planters in India, Malaya and Ceylon and their experts argued that in order to sustain the productivity of the labouring population in the plantations where malaria, hookworm and dysentery ravaged the immigrant labouring population, the planters needed to invest in Tropical Medicine. Therefore, the plantations regularly carried out studies on blackwater fever and anti-malarial sanitation, and conducted hookworm eradication programmes and anti-cholera sanitary measures with the aid of government grants and the expertise of Tropical Medicine.

The other part of this study is the practices of settlement and medicine in the sanatorium enclave of Darjeeling. The British built 'hill-stations' at selected mountain sites in most tropical colonies. They were originally conceived as mountain sanatoriums (similar to those in Switzerland and Germany in the nineteenth century), but were distinctively colonial, because the British articulated them as sites for 'Europeans' (whites) to rejuvenate themselves away

---

31 Breman, *Taming the Coolie Beast*, p. 178.
32 P.D. Curtin, 'Readjustments in the Nineteenth Century', in idem, *The Rise and Fall of the Plantation Complex: Essays in Atlantic History* (Cambridge, Cambridge University Press, 1990), p. 179.

from the heat, dust and germs of the tropical plains. Like many other colonial institutions of privilege, hill-stations changed in character, and in India became contested territories between the Indian elite and the British. Anthony D. King identified the city of New Delhi, built by the British in 1911 near the old Mughal capital, the army cantonments and the hill-stations in colonial India as sites that reflected 'the effect of power relationships on urban structure and particularly, urban social structure, planning, race relations', and argued that the above also represented, in postcolonial societies, the problems of development and modernization.[33] Dane Kennedy has studied the various hill-stations of colonial India as 'places where the British endeavoured at one and the same time to engage with and to disengage from the dominion they ruled'.[34] Kennedy argues that over the nineteenth century, in the absence of medical unanimity on the healthiness of all hill-stations, there was a shift in British perceptions of hill-stations 'from clinical assessment of climatic disease to a more socially resonant understanding of the effects of the tropics on the European'.[35] His conclusion is that the hill-stations could not be retained as exclusively British institutions in colonial India. The Indian elite – native princes as well as the middle classes – staked a claim to the hill-stations. The consequent 'intrusion of the other', also evident in the huge number of servants and minor clerks necessitated by British domestic life and civil administration, subverted the idyll of Edenic sanctuaries in the hill-stations. Other historians have studied particular hill-stations. In her study of colonial Simla, Pamela Kanwar has also outlined the Indian presence, comprising not of only the princes (who could be kept out by diplomatic means), but others (who could not) – rich Indians who bought up the hill-side bungalows, commission agents and merchants who occupied the lower bazaar and controlled the supply of provisions to the town as well as the 'labouring classes' such as the rickshaw pullers and nightsoil men.[36] These incursions had political consequences: Kanwar has concluded that even in the quintessentially European town, the Indian merchants, low-level clerks and labourers were to some extent politicized by the nationalist movement in the twentieth century.[37] In her study of Ootacamund (Ooty) in the Nilgiri hills, Judith T. Kenny has noted that 'the practice of British authority and the hill-station were inextricably linked'.[38] In the hill-station 'social rank was closely matched with elevation'.[39] Kenny emphasized, like the authors above, that the

---

33 Anthony D. King, *Colonial Urban Development: Culture, Social Power and Environment* (London, Henley and Boston, 1976), p. 2.
34 Dane Kennedy, *The Magic Mountains: Hill-stations and the British Raj* (Berkeley and London, University of California Press, 1996), p. 1.
35 Kennedy, *The Magic Mountains*, p. 30.
36 Pamela Kanwar, *Imperial Simla: The Political Culture of the Raj* (Delhi and Oxford, Oxford University Press, 1990) pp. 146–89.
37 Kanwar, *Imperial Simla*, pp. 202–14.
38 Judith T. Kenny, 'Climate, Race, and Imperial Authority: The Symbolic Landscape of the British Hill-station in India', *Annals of the Association of American Geographers*, 85 (1995), pp. 694–714.
39 Kenny, 'Climate, Race, and Imperial Authority', p. 706.

Contagion and Enclaves

presence of large numbers of Indians in various subordinate capacities, as well as prosperous visitors, contributed to the subversion of the idyllic European enclave of Ootacamund. She similarly concluded that after the First World War, 'growing Indian nationalism inspired by new campaigns of civil disobedience could not be ignored even in the hills'.[40]

The studies above have variously emphasized the political importance of hill-stations in British India. They were built as exclusive social spaces for the British, but paradoxically became crowded urban spaces filled with Indians in various capacities. Many postcolonial accounts of hill-stations have rued the contamination of the previously idyllic hill-stations, principally through overcrowding.[41] Overcrowding and pollution in the hill-stations in colonial medical and public discourse has to be understood in the context of the struggle for social exclusivity. Historians, particularly Kennedy, have not questioned contemporary colonial accounts of pollution and congestion that supposedly marred the idyllic, beautiful hill-stations in the late colonial decades. It is more useful to see the hill-stations as colonial enclaves that were constantly breached by unwanted social elements, but nevertheless sustained due to political and social reasons, and it is undeniable that they provided social exclusivity and municipal infrastructure not available to the Indian cities elsewhere. Apart from symbolizing the power of the state and emphasizing the cultural and racial distance of the ruling elite from the masses, the locations of the various hill-stations in the Himalayas had great strategic and economic importance.[42] Shimla, the imperial summer capital, overlooked Kashmir and beyond to Central Asia. Darjeeling bordered on trade routes to Nepal and Tibet. Their establishment facilitated the colonization and economic and administrative integration of remote areas to the globalized imperial economy through demographic changes, entrepreneurship and a range of horticultural and botanical experiments that expanded to orchards and plantations producing exotic fruit and plantation crops in vast areas.[43] There was a constant tension, therefore, between the social and political exclusivity of the hill-station enclaves and their permeability due to their integration within the imperial political economy. To implement exclusive civic sanitation (always an exception in colonial India), maintain privileged municipal and medical infrastructure and sustain disease control within the hill-stations remained a challenge to colonial authorities. Nationalist Indians resented and contested the racial exclusivity of the hill-stations, but not their special

---

40 Kenny, 'Climate, Race, and Imperial Authority', p. 710.
41 Mollie Panter-Downes, *Ooty Preserved: A Victorian Hill-station* (London, H. Hamilton, 1967).
42 In the 1880s, military strategists such as Major General David Newall argued that the hill-stations should become the bases for 'reserve circles' of troops to protect the Empire as well as form loyal bastions of European troops near border and frontline zones. See Aditi Chatterjee, *The Changing Landscapes of the Indian Hill-stations: Power, Culture and Tradition* (Calcutta, Prabasi Press, 1997), pp. 42–44.
43 Daniel R. Headrick, *The Tentacles of Progress: Technology Transfer in the Age of Imperialism, 1850–1940* (New York and Oxford, Oxford University Press, 1988); Lucile Brockway, *Science and Colonial Expansion: The Role of the Royal Botanic Gardens* (New Haven and London, Yale University Press, 2002).

municipal identity and medical infrastructure. The hill-station of Darjeeling, therefore, comprises one part of this study: to study how and if disease could be controlled and 'European' health sustained in mountain sanatoriums that provided refuge to people tired of the disease and filth in the tropical plains. In the process, colonial medical discourse invented new 'local' diseases such as hill-diarrhoea to distinguish the disease environment of the hill-stations from that of the tropical plains.

Plantations, Sanatoriums and Tropical Medicine

While the hill-station of Darjeeling and the plantations around it had distinctive spatial and political organizations, they were colonial enclaves that experienced focused and strategic implementation of medical and sanitary programmes due to their political, economic and strategic importance to the colonial economy. The establishment of the hill-station of Darjeeling facilitated the colonization of the surrounding areas and the government actively encouraged plantation enclaves. The hill-stations and the plantations changed drastically the ecology, demography and economy of the entire region. It also put the region on the medical map of colonial India, first because of its unique disease environment and then because of the availability and economic and political need of the plantations and the hill-station for research in Tropical Medicine.

Both the hill-station and the tea plantations marked distinct colonial interventions within the social and economic history of nineteenth-century India. The former was defined by colonial power and its forms of governance; the latter, the plantations, by a typically colonial form of production. For that reason, they were also important sites of medical attention and intervention. This book studies how the colonial control of and concern for disease reflected the essential mode of functioning of these enclaves. A study of the social history of disease in the two different enclaves in north Bengal is therefore a study of colonial governance through disease control and health policies. This book approaches colonial governance within a broad framework, which includes policies initiated by the mostly British-owned plantations as well the British civilian population of Darjeeling. Although there were conflicts in policy and practice between the government and planters and British residents throughout our period, control and prevention of disease was negotiated within modes of intervention and assertions of autonomy.

The Darjeeling hills and their neighbouring tea plantations comprised the administrative districts of Darjeeling and Jalpaiguri, both frontier areas with sparse population that were colonized and settled from the mid-nineteenth century. The hill-station of Darjeeling was established in 1839, and the district's first tea plantations began producing commercially from 1856. Thirty years later, in 1869, the district of Jalpaiguri was formed, incorporating newly annexed areas from neighbouring Bhutan. Within these two administrative districts, Darjeeling and Jalpaiguri, there were three tea-producing regions – in official terminology known as 'tea districts'. These were Darjeeling, which comprised the hills around and below the town of Darjeeling, its foothills known as the Darjeeling Terai and Western Duars, located in Jalpaiguri district. By the turn of the century, the tea districts produced about a quarter of the annual export of tea from India. The region as a whole encompassed a peculiar duality. The hill-station of Darjeeling was established as a sanatorium town, and used as a convalescent station for British troops in India as well as being the summer capital of Bengal. Government officials, soldiers and travellers meanwhile characterized the Darjeeling Terai and the neighbouring Western Duars as particularly unhealthy regions. These raise important questions about public health and medical practice in the two distinct regions. Colonial commercialization of agriculture and development of plantation agriculture in the northern Bengal districts of Jalpaiguri and Darjeeling were initiated by 'the kind of commercialization closely associated with increased accumulation, giving rise to expansion of productive scale based on managerial farming or plantation agriculture'.[44] The tea plantations and the extension of commercial cultivation of rice and jute in north Bengal represented broadly the constitution of the region's absorption within the colonial political economy.[45] The socio-economic processes that accompanied the commercialization of agriculture in the entire district and the establishment of the plantation system in Western Duars included demographic changes and the transformation of a hitherto unsettled, frontier region into a settled agrarian revenue-producing region. This settlement was effected in the context of the marginalization of the indigenous Meches and Garos, the creation of a standardized set of agrarian rights in the land and the appearance of sub-infeudation of rights and agrarian production, with several layers of differentiation among the peasantry.[46]

Throughout the late nineteenth and early twentieth centuries, all three tracts experienced demographic change through massive immigration. In the case of the town of Darjeeling, this entailed the establishment and rapid expansion of the hill-station. Like other hill-stations in colonial India, Darjeeling was originally meant to accommodate principally white bodies: Europeans. British experience in the region from the time of its incorporation into British India and its settlement was also different. Joseph Dalton Hooker, the son of William Hooker, the Director of Kew Gardens who later succeeded his father in that position, made botanical expeditions in Sikkim and Bhutan in the eastern Himalayas in the mid-nineteenth century. During this time he was based in Darjeeling, a hill-station newly built on a tract of land first leased from the Raja of Sikkim in 1839. He proclaimed Darjeeling as an excellent sanatorium for

---

44 Sugata Bose, *Peasant Labour and Colonial Capital: Rural Bengal Since 1770* (Cambridge, Cambridge University Press, 1993), p. 41.
45 For a focused history of the commercialization of agriculture and its consequence in one district, see Ranajit Das Gupta, *Economy, Society, and Politics in Bengal: Jalpaiguri 1869–1947* (Delhi and Oxford, Oxford University Press, 1992).
46 Subhajyoti Ray, *Transformations on the Bengal Frontier: Jalpaiguri 1765–1948* (London, Routledge, 2002).

Europeans in the tropics, contrasting the rosy cheeks of European children in the hills with the pale, weak countenances of those in the hot tropical plains. Just below the Himalayan sanatorium of Darjeeling were the foothills known as the Terai; covered in forests, dank and miasmatic. A stretch of the Terai was claimed from Sikkim in 1850. Travellers to the hill-station of Darjeeling were advised to cross the Terai as quickly as possible to avoid its unhealthy miasma. When Lady Canning, wife of the Viceroy Lord Canning, stopped in the Terai for a day to paint the landscape, she contracted a fever from which she died. Just as Hooker's comment on the rosy cheeks of European children in Darjeeling was quoted countless times in all the travel guides to Darjeeling, so the incident of Lady Canning's death served as warning on the unhealthiness of the Terai to all prospective passers-by on the road to Darjeeling.[47] Next to the Terai was the Duars, annexed to British India from Bhutan after the war of 1865–66, and sparsely populated by the indigenous tribal population who cultivated cotton and rice and tended buffaloes. Duars, too, was a febrile land, only the Meches, its original inhabitants, were reputedly able to survive there.

At the edges of the hill-station, the tea plantations expanded from the mid-nineteenth century, encouraged by government grants of land at nominal prices. The consequent settlement scheme for the entire area was therefore complex. It included the hill-station of Darjeeling, originally intended to be a European retreat from the plains; the tea estates, where large numbers of migrant labourers resided alongside the European management; and after 1850, a tract of land around Kalimpong which was settled with Nepali immigrants cultivating maize and potatoes. There was also, within the Jalpaiguri district, an older, settled tract which had formed part of the Company's territory for almost one hundred years. The newly incorporated Western Duars tract, acquired after the Anglo–Bhutan war in 1865, was the land between the rivers Torsha and the Teesta, mostly given over to tea plantations and reserved forest interspersed with villages of peasant cultivation of rice and jute. The tea estates were enclosed territories within which resided the plantation's managerial staff and workers.

Practices of Settlement, Medicine and the Tea Economy

Suggesting that the two enclaves of the hill-station and the tea plantations were coterminous, I pose the question, how did they provide a different problem and scope for the rhetoric and practice of colonial medicine? Mountain sanatoriums were supposedly refuges from quintessentially tropical diseases like cholera and malaria. Hence the need for British administration of mountain towns away from the plains, coyly termed 'hill-stations' in the tropical colonies.[48] The irony

---

47 L.S.S. O'Malley, *Bengal District Gazetteers: Darjeeling* (Calcutta, The Bengal Secretariat Book Depot, 1907), p. 68.
48 Kennedy has pointed out that the nomenclature was an effort etymologically to 'tame' awesome large mountains. See Kennedy, *The Magic Mountains*, p. 46.

was that it was precisely when optimism about white settlement in the tropics was eclipsed that the Indian Empire was at its zenith.[49] Therefore, they also functioned as social and political 'homelands' of the British Raj. The question here is, what were the perceived rejuvenating properties of the hill-stations for the Europeans in nineteenth- and twentieth-century India? What provided economic vitality to the hill-station? How did medical discourses and institutions accommodate the hills–plains duality of British India in the context of Europeans suffering from disease at the hill-station? The hill-stations of colonial India were conceived of as European sanatoriums. The presence of natives of every class in the hill-stations rendered their characteristic as exclusive enclaves doubtful. How was the presence of the Bengalis accommodated in medical discourses on acclimatization and institutionality in the sanatoriums of Darjeeling?

Acclimatization theories were on the wane from the mid-nineteenth century, the point at which this book begins. Yet, the accommodation of Indians in Darjeeling (and possibly in other hill-stations) altered medical perceptions on acclimatization. In the twentieth century, the Bengali elite negotiated the appropriation of hill-stations, and this book will examine that process. The tea plantations, being sites of private enterprise, presented public health problems of a different kind. They were sites where large numbers of immigrant labourers resided in coolie lines (huts), as did the management in bungalows. Labourers often migrated with entire families and resided in coolie lines located at one end of the tea estates. Due to their residence within the plantations and their work regime, they were more easily controlled than any other working population. Initially situated in remote territory, with only the plantation doctor and dispensary or the medicine box of the planter as therapeutic aids, the plantations in the twentieth century were also where specialized medical research took place, particularly in hookworm, kala-azar and malaria. With a crucial difference from colonial enclaves: the plantations were sites of private enterprise. Government intervention and public health policies within the plantations were limited and always under negotiation. Managerial and occasionally official discourse posited that the aim of rationalized productivity of labour led to greater investment for medical therapeutics as well as research within the plantations, which were supposedly far superior to the health care available in the rural areas. However, a history of public health policies within the plantations requires an examination of the structure and exigencies of the plantation economy and its specific medical imperatives. I have attempted to situate the relationship of the plantation estates with the colonial state and with the sites of peasant agricultural production outside the boundaries of the tea estates. How did the tea estates negotiate medical practice and preventive health in the tea estates vis-à-vis the areas of peasant production with which they had a 'symbiotic' relationship, and how did the colonial state mediate such negotiation? This leads to the question of the logistics of the plantation economy: What was the structure of the medical economy of the tea plantations?

49 Harrison, *Climates and Constitutions*.

A fundamental problem for the medical history of plantation enclaves is their function as sites of experimentation in Tropical Medicine. Arnold has argued that it was the colonial enclaves of jails and barracks that represented the clearest triumphs of Western medicine in colonial India, being the spaces where this medicine could be practised relatively independently; without the cultural and political constraints that characterized its reception in civilian society in India. Simultaneously, the sites of the jails or the army barracks and the cantonments came to be, in Anglo-Indian medical perception and to some extent in official policy, representative of the patterns that might occur at other sites of indigenous health and disease. Their inmates replicated, in their persons, the prototype of the Indian physique (at least, that of the Indian labouring classes) as demonstrated, examined and articulated upon in the jails or the barracks.[50]

Yet the practices of Tropical Medicine were not limited to jails and cantonments; official policy extended them to selected areas. These included parts of the large ports and capital cities, industrial sites such as harbours, mines, railway 'colonies' and plantations. Particularly from the interwar years, medical researchers focused on disease in the plantations due to the ease of conducting 'experiments' at the relatively segregated sites, and because often in addition to government grants, entrepreneurial patronage facilitated the research. In the interwar years a great deal of research on hookworm and malaria as well as nutritional deficiencies used the tea plantations for study. Arnold has pointed out that the 'perceived importance of India as a scientific laboratory' was prevalent for more than a century before Tropical Medicine was established.[51] But it acquired new dimensions with the institutionalization of Tropical Medicine in the twentieth century, and the plantations and other industrial locations became identified as sites which would have to minimize the occurrence of disease to generate productive labour.

Research in Tropical Medicine in the area had two distinct trends – first, research on hookworm or nutritional diseases, and reproductive health that focused on the physique of the plantation labourers. Second, the ecology and environment of the area provided a site for research on malaria studies. The particular perception of India as a unique disease environment persisted long after the discoveries of Pasteur and Koch. In the nineteenth century the Darjeeling Terai and Duars were perceived as febrile terrain; in the twentieth century a great deal of malaria research was conducted in the tea districts of Terai and Duars. To what extent did the particular location and ecology of the hill-station and the plantations contribute to the knowledge of Tropical Medicine? This book makes a case for the examination of medical research in terms of the political economy.

50 Arnold, *Colonizing the Body*, p. 114.
51 Arnold, 'The Discovery of Malnutrition and Diet in Colonial India', *Indian Economic and Social History Review*, 31 (1994), pp. 1–26.

CHAPTER 2

The Sanatorium of Darjeeling: European Health in a Tropical Enclave

There were many ideological, political, military and medical reasons for hill-stations in tropical colonies. The urgency of the question of the Europeans' long-term survival in the tropics engaged medical discourses in Britain as well as in the tropical colonies in the seventeenth and eighteenth centuries.[1] The eighteenth century represented a period of optimism about acclimatization and it had been generally a period when racial categorizations had not assumed absolute rigidity.[2] By the third decade of the nineteenth century acclimatization theories were eclipsed and there were serious doubts about the survival of the Englishman in India over a few generations. The contrast between the disease-ridden, crowded, unsanitary plains and the pure and healthy air of the 'hills' therefore came to be a familiar trope of official as well as medical discourses in colonial India. The hill-stations provided one means of establishing comfortable, familiar surroundings for the British in the tropics: their climate was supposedly *not tropical*.[3] The logic of the development of hill-stations was their climatic opposition to the plains. The hill-station was a uniquely colonial phenomenon, and although best known in India, was institutionalized in many tropical

---

1   The point has been made by David Arnold, 'Introduction', in idem (ed.), *Warm Climates and Western Medicine: The Emergence of Tropical Medicine, 1500–1900* (Amsterdam, Rodopi, 1996), pp. 1–19.
2   Mark Harrison, '"The Tender Frame of Man": Disease, Climate, and Racial Difference in India and the West Indies, 1760–1860', *Bulletin of the History of Medicine*, 70 (1996), pp. 68–93.
3   Harrison has further argued that until the nineteenth century European medical perceptions regarded India's difference with Europe, in climate as well as in civilizational terms, as one of degree rather than of kind. See Harrison, *Climates and Constitutions*, p. 119. Arnold has also argued that there was ambivalence regarding the recognition in European scientific and travel accounts of India's topography as 'tropical' and that such a recognition was a historical process that continued to the mid-nineteenth century; Arnold (2006), pp. 110–42.

colonies. The British built hill-stations in Asia in the Ceylon and the Malay Straits – in fact the earliest 'hill-station' was at Penang in Malaya, which was occupied by the English East India Company (EEIC) in 1786 and by the early 1800s served as a site for recuperation for civil and military officials.[4] In late nineteenth- and early twentieth-century Africa, social segregation followed closely on the heels of sanitation in the British colonies, and hill-stations facilitated the creation of exclusive, clean and secure social space for white Europeans.[5]

Empire in the Tropics, Recess in the 'Hills': The Hill–Plains Dichotomy in Colonial India

Historians of colonial India have seen the establishment, evolution and historical trajectory of hill-stations as determined by racial distinctions and a value system which favoured the hills over the plains.[6] The explorations in the Himalayas, the slow but sure penetration of British influence in the areas bordering the mountains on the north, north-east and the north-west of India took place in the first two decades of the nineteenth century. As Kennedy has pointed out, the nomenclature was deceptive.[7] Most of the 'stations' were located not on hills, but on high mountains, usually from 4000 to 6000 feet above sea level. Such were the hill-stations of Simla, Mussoorie, Landour and Darjeeling. Like many other colonial institutions the hill-station developed multiple nuances and spread geographically. For instance, the Bombay government, lacking access to high mountains, resorted to various hill tops in the Mahabaleshwar over the relatively modest Satpura and Aravalli ranges where several hill-stations sprang up to accommodate a seasonal population. Similarly Ootacamund in the Nilgiri range emerged as a notable hill-station in southern India. Initially established to ensure the recuperation of European troops in tropical colonies from eighteenth-century tropical diseases like cholera and dysentery, they evolved to become the seats of government and foci of elite social activity in colonial India.

4   S. Robert Aiken, 'Early Penang Hill-station', *Geographical Review*, 77 (1987), pp. 421–39.
5   For an overview of white segregation within African cities, see Maynard Swanson, 'The Sanitation Syndrome: Bubonic Plague and Urban Native Policy in the Cape Colony, 1900–1909', *Journal of African History*, 38 (1977), pp. 387–410. For a comparison of segregated colonial town-planning in Africa between the French and the British empires, see Odile Goerg, 'From Hill-station (Freetown) to Downtown Conakry (First Ward): Comparing French and British Approaches to Segregation in Colonial Cities at the Beginning of the Twentieth Century', *Canadian Journal of African Studies/Revue canadienne des études africaines*, 32 (1998), pp. 1–31. See also P.D. Curtin, 'Medical Knowledge and Urban Planning in Tropical Africa', *The American Historical Review*, 90 (1985), pp. 594–613.
6   Kennedy, *The Magic Mountains*, pp. 1–14; King, *Colonial Urban Development*, pp. 165–76. See also Judith T. Kenny, 'Climate, Race, and Imperial Authority: The Symbolic Landscape of the British Hill-station in India', *Annals of the Association of American Geographers*, 85 (1995), pp. 694–714, and Queeny Pradhan, 'Empire in the Hills: The Making of Hill-stations in Colonial India', *Studies in History*, 23 (2007), pp. 33–91.
7   Kennedy (1997), pp. 46–47.

The numbers of European troops in India increased under the drastically changed concerns after the revolt of 1857 and this lent greater urgency to the problem of high mortality among European troops in the tropics. Although their flora and fauna were often unique both in the Himalayas and in the Nilgiri, Satpura and Aravalli ranges, some hill-stations provided sites conducive to the introduction of flora from colder climates. And most importantly, they promised the space for an alternative world where the European (as a racial category) could feel comfortable and the Englishman recreate in some measure the cosy, even intimate, atmosphere of 'home' within the tropical colonies. Apart from their natural and scenic advantages, hill-stations also afforded to the British in India opportunities for architectural distinctiveness, the advantages of sewerage, clean water and social spaces such as the Mall, a promenade that excluded Indians except in manual capacities. British rule established municipal governance in all parts of urban India, but the governance of hill-stations remained in the control of colonial officials and therefore beyond the interventions of Indian nationalists whose priorities in local government rarely extended to conservancy and sanitation.

As historians and indeed contemporary residents in late colonial Indian hill-stations have argued, the hill-stations did not remain exclusive European enclaves, overrun as they were by multitudes of lower-class Indians in menial and subordinate positions within households as well as in civilian administration. Since they are supposed to have collapsed under their own weight, can we then see a hill-station as a colonial enclave at all? I would argue here that the enclaves maintained a balance between permeability and exclusivity; that the *raison d'être* of the hill-station was the integration of their respective areas within the colonial political economy. Therefore it was immaterial whether or not the hill station was truly a healthy climatic resort. Diseases could and often did make their presence felt in chronic and epidemic forms in the hill resorts. Colonial governance was administered through the control of epidemics and the sustenance of an exclusive social and political space through modes that included the invention of a distinct disease environment for the 'hills' from that of the Indian plains. Similarly, the hill-stations actively encouraged migrant populations, and at the same time administrators attempted to limit their social and cultural influence within the limits of the town. In this chapter I have analysed the sustenance of Darjeeling as a site of medicalized leisure for Europeans. While hill-stations were sites of rejuvenation of white, European bodies in tropical climates, the very concept of rejuvenation of white bodies in the tropics was problematic. The British had seen tropical climate as the cause of their ill health and in that it was not just the hill-stations, but the hills themselves that were British colonial constructions. The hills–plains duality was constructed in terms of medical discourse and climatic theories of disease. This chapter shows that the hills–plains dichotomy was a false one, and was sustained through medical discourse and practice through the institutionalization of the hill-stations themselves. The hill-station of Darjeeling itself was sustained through its absorption into the larger colonial economy through the development of the tea plantations in the surrounding regions. Once established, the Indian elite formulated their own medicalized rationale for staking their claims on the hill-station.

The Expansion of Darjeeling

The area of Darjeeling and indeed the tracts where most of the Himalayan hill-stations were located had been part of the growing Gorkha Kingdom of Nepal in the late eighteenth century. From the late eighteenth century the Gorkha Kingdom, formerly a small principality in Nepal, had militarized itself and taken over the more prosperous kingdoms in the Kathmandu valley.[8] It next eyed the Himalayan principalities of Kumaon, Garhwal and Sikkim. The rapid conquest of the hill principalities in Garhwal and Kumaon, as well as British ambitions in the trans-Tibetan trade which would have to pass through Nepal, put Nepal into direct conflict with the EEI Company.[9] The consequence was a bloody war in which it took two years for the Company's army to decisively defeat Nepal. Under the treaty of Sagauli (1816) between India and Nepal, a large section of the western Himalayan Terai was taken from Nepal and annexed by the East India Company.[10] This was the tract where Mussoorie and Simla were later built. The area of Darjeeling, further, under a separate agreement (Treaty of Titalya, 1817) was given over to the King of Sikkim as part of the ring-fence policy, to create a buffer state between Nepal and India.[11]

Captain G.A. Lloyd and J.W. Grant, the Commercial Resident at Maldah in northern Bengal, visited the area to settle border disputes between Nepal and Sikkim. Later they arrived at Chongtung near Darjeeling and first thought of a sanatorium at the site in 1828.[12] In 1829 the Government of India sent Captain J.D. Herbert, Deputy Surveyor General, to the site to explore possibilities for the establishment of a sanatorium for the use of European troops in India. His report was wholly favourable and his first assumption was to link health with climate: 'The first point to be considered in the establishment of a station of

---

8 Kumar Pradhan, *The Gorkha Conquests: The Process and Consequences of the Unification of Nepal, with Particular Reference to Eastern Nepal* (Calcutta and Oxford, Oxford University Press, 1991), pp. 89–105.

9 D.R. Regmi, *Modern Nepal: Rise and Growth in the Eighteenth Century* (Calcutta, Firma KLM, 1975), pp. 332–417.

10 John Pemble, *The Invasion of Nepal: John Company at War* (Oxford, Clarendon Press, 1971), pp. 344–48.

11 For British policy in the princely states of colonial India, see Michael Fisher, *Indirect Rule in India: Residents and the Residency System, 1764–1857* (Delhi, Oxford University Press, 1998). For a brief overview of British recruitment of various Nepali communities in Darjeeling, see Atis Dasgupta, 'Ethnic Problems and Movements for Autonomy in Darjeeling', *Social Scientist*, 27 (1999), pp. 47–68.

12 E.C. Dozey, *A Concise History of the Darjeeling District with a Complete Itinerary of Tours in Sikkim and the District* (2nd edn, Calcutta Art Press, 1922), pp. 2–3.

health is obviously climate.'[13] Besides, he considered the logistics: new roads and maintenance of a supply line. To that end it was also essential to have permanent and settled British-ruled administrative centres relatively close, and Herbert found Darjeeling more convenient than other hill-stations for British troops in north India from Allahabad:

> To give a better idea of the nature of the approach to Dargeeling, I would say that it is very nearly as promising as that to Semla, it is much more so than that to Dehra, and between it and the Almorah one, there can be no comparison whatsoever ...[14]

In 1835, Captain Lloyd negotiated with the King of Sikkim for the cession of the land on which the sanatorium of Darjeeling was to be situated. Faced with the intent of the British government in India, the king, initially reluctant, finally leased the area in 1835 for an annual payment of Rs 3000.[15] In the true tradition of the man in the field, Lloyd did not wait for instructions from the Governor General before pushing for and obtaining the lease.[16] There were supposedly around a hundred inhabitants at the site, who were mainly the indigenous Lepchas.[17] After he successfully secured the lease and organized the labour for building the road to Darjeeling, the government replaced Lloyd with another official, Archibald Campbell.[18] In 1839, Surgeon Major Campbell who had formerly served at the Residence in Nepal, was posted to Darjeeling. He was vested with wide-ranging fiscal, civil and judicial powers. For the next 22 years Campbell served as the Superintendent of Darjeeling and oversaw its settlement and steady expansion.[19]

Archibald Campbell, a postgraduate surgeon from Edinburgh, had joined the EEIC in 1827. He was posted to Kathmandu.[20] Campbell served for eight years in Nepal. He, along with Brian Hodgson, the Resident at Nepal, was a keen Orientalist as well as naturalist. Like most old India-hands, his local knowledge included knowledge of local flora and fauna as well as the inhabitants of the region. The British residency at Kathmandu had an uneasy relationship with the Court, but Campbell used his local knowledge to good effect and wrote several papers on the economic, social and cultural aspects of the country and of the inhabitants of Nepal during his tenure. This knowledge served him later

---

13 *Report on Dargeeling: A Place in the Sikkim Mountains, Proposed as a Sanitarium, or Station of Health* (Calcutta, Baptist Mission Press, 1830), p. 3.
14 *Report on Dargeeling*, p. 6.
15 Joseph Dalton Hooker, *Himalayan Journals: Notes of a Naturalist in Bengal Sikkim and Nepal Himalayas etc.* (New Delhi, 1999, first pub. 1854), vol. 1, p. 110.
16 Fred Pinn, *The Road of Destiny: Darjeeling Letters, 1839* (Calcutta and Oxford, Oxford University Press, 1986), pp. 119–29.
17 O'Malley, *Bengal District Gazetteer*, p. 22.
18 Pinn, *The Road of Destiny*, pp. 174–75.
19 R.D. O'Brien, *Darjeeling: The Sanitarium of Bengal and Its Surroundings* (Calcutta, W. Newman & Co.,1883), pp. 14–15.
20 *Memorandum of the Services of Dr A. Campbell, Bengal Medical Services...* (Hastings, Osborne, 1856), p. 1.

The Sanatorium of Darjeeling

Figure 2.1 View of Jalapahar, Darjeeling

when he developed the town of Darjeeling by encouraging Nepali immigration. Campbell's first task on becoming Superintendent was to attend to the construction of the basic administrative infrastructure. In the next ten years he made allotments of land to private individuals. The Army established a 'convalescent depot' for British troops at Jalapahar near Darjeeling. Around the nucleus of a church, bazaar, the administrative *cutchery* and a few houses the hill-station gradually came to be well known and often frequented by seasonal visitors.[21]

Initially, Darjeeling was a frontier zone that offered various opportunities to enterprising Europeans. A group of such were the Wernicke-Stolke family, who had initially arrived in 1841 as Moravian missionaries.[22] They established their mission at Tukvar, a few miles below the town.[23] After his mission shut down, Johann Andreas Wernicke engaged in contract work for the government in Darjeeling, which involved supplying timber and brick for the construction of public buildings and roads. Two of the three Moravian families found reasons to stay on, and Wernicke went on to build several shops in the town, having received contracts from the government and acquired land within the town as well. 'At this time ... the East India Company were ready to make grants of land to persons who were willing and capable of helping in the development of Darjeeling as a station.'[24] Three of his sons went into the flourishing tea industry in the 1870s. The family owned several tea gardens in the Darjeeling area, as well as several buildings, in fact a part of an entire street. His grandson

21 *The Dorjeeling Guide: Including a Description of the Country, and of Its Climate, Soil and Productions, with Travelling Directions etc.* (Calcutta, Samuel Smith, 1845), p. 43.
22 Typescript titled 'The Wernicke-Stolke Story', Mss Photo Eur 421, APAC, p. 4.
23 'The Wernicke-Stolke Story', p. 4.
24 'The Wernicke-Stolke Story', p. 4.

Frank was sent 'home' to England where he and his siblings received an expensive public school education.[25] Later he joined the IMS and changed his name to the anglicized Warwick.[26]

Within a decade of the lease, Darjeeling was a fast-growing town with opportunities for enterprise and commerce, ready to receive European convalescents. When the botanist Joseph Dalton Hooker visited in 1848 he found it a pleasant hill-station with a small resident European population that attracted several seasonal visitors. He could at the end of an eventful two-year visit compare the growth of Darjeeling to an Australian colony, 'not only in amount of building, but in the accession of native families from the surrounding countries'.[27] While it was evidently proving popular with Europeans who needed to convalesce, the efforts of Campbell further established its position as a trading centre for the people of the surrounding areas:

> At the former period there was no trade whatsoever; there is now a very considerable one, in musk, salt, gold dust, borax, soda, woollen cloths, and especially in ponies ... The trade has been greatly increased by the annual fair which Dr Campbell has established at the foot of the hills, to which many thousands of natives flock from all quarters, and which exercises a most beneficial influence throughout the neighbouring territories. At this, prizes are given for agricultural implements and produce, stock, etc, by the originator and a few friends, a measure attended with eminent success.[28]

The establishment of Darjeeling, the colonization and the settlement of the neighbouring areas, and the expansion of its trade was achieved through a steady poaching of territories from Sikkim and Bhutan. This formed part of the strategy of securing the border of British India with its supposedly recalcitrant neighbours. The first annexation was from Sikkim. During his visit, J.D. Hooker went on several botanizing trips in the eastern Himalayas, to the borders of Sikkim and Tibet.[29] Consent for his expeditions was reluctantly forthcoming, and in one of the expeditions in Sikkim he and Campbell were held hostage by a faction of the Sikkim court. Their six-week captivity ended when the British government sent extra troops to Darjeeling and threatened an invasion. The entire episode resulted in cessation of the annual payment of Rs 6000 (it was doubled from Rs 3000 in 1846) and the annexation of the Sikkim Terai and of 640 square miles to British territory at the frontier.[30] In 1860–61 following further

---

25 'The Wernicke-Stolke Story', p. 4.
26 D.G. Crawford, *Roll of the Indian Medical Service 1615–1930* (London, London Stamp Exchange, 1986), p. 538.
27 Hooker, *Himalayan Journals*, vol. 1, pp. 108–9.
28 Hooker, *Himalayan Journals*, vol. 1, p. 109.
29 Hooker represented India, particularly the eastern Himalayas, as a decisively tropical region, despite the variations in temperature and the existence of fauna typically found in temperate regions in the area. See Arnold (2006), pp. 199–201.
30 O'Malley, *Bengal District Gazetteers*, pp. 29–31. See also Dozey, *A Concise History*, p. 4, and Hooker, *Himalayan Journals*, vol. 1, pp. 302–3, and A. Campbell, 'On the Lepchas', *The Journal of the Ethnological Society of London*, 1 (1869), pp. 143–57.

battles with Sikkim a new treaty 'guaranteed the opening out of the country to trade, and the removal of all restrictions on travellers and merchants ... fixed the minimum rates of transit duties to be levied on goods between British India and Tibet'.[31] Thereafter, the efforts of Campbell resulted in making the area (through Kalimpong) the centre of the trans-Tibet trade and also encouraged immigration from Nepal.[32] In 1866 the British territories in the Darjeeling hills area were further expanded by the annexation of Kalimpong from the King of Bhutan. The Anglo–Bhutan war, too, was occasioned by 'lawlessness' in Bhutan and periodic raids from the Bhutan frontiers.[33]

Darjeeling and Colonial Economy

British policy enabled immigration from eastern Nepal who settled in the area and provided the crucial labour needed to establish the sanatorium town with its cantonment and fledgling commerce and industry. It also encouraged trade between the borders and even fuelled dreams of a trans-Tibetan trade, the subject of many treaties with Nepal as well as Tibet. That, and strategic considerations regarding both Nepal and Tibet, make it difficult to assume that the Edenic hill sanatoriums were 'uncontaminated' spaces in the perspective of the British administrators. At first many Nepalis crossed the border to work for a season and went back to their villages.[34] Gradually many settled in Darjeeling. Nepali immigration proved particularly useful when the tea plantations, an enormously labour-intensive industry, took off commercially. My contention is that the Edenic sanctuary was always a part of the colonial economy, not just a refuge from the ills of the tropics. The Darjeeling plantations, unlike the first tea plantations in neighbouring Assam, did not have to resort to indentured labour because Campbell actively encouraged the migration of labourers from eastern Nepal. The example of Darjeeling reveals many more motives in the establishment of enclaves for European health, their settlement and occupation. The indigenous Lepchas were pushed out of the area by the more enterprising Paharia (Nepali) immigrants 'partly due to their inability to stand Paharia competition for land and partly due to the daily increase in population of the place.'[35] The Lepchas, like the Meches of the Terai, practised *jhum* (shifting) cultivation, a practice always looked upon with suspicion and disdain by the

---

31 O'Malley, *Bengal District Gazetteers*, p. 32.
32 For immigration to the Darjeeling district, see Tanka Bahadur Subba, *The Quiet Hills: A Study of the Agrarian Relations in Hill Darjeeling* (Bangalore, ISPCK, 1985), pp. 10–17. See also by same author, *Dynamics of a Hill Society: The Nepalis in Darjeeling and Sikkim Himalayas* (Delhi, Mittal Publications, 1989), pp. 120–21.
33 Subhajyoti Ray has argued that Bhutanese raids were not attacks on the property of peasants, but a means of 'enforcing collection of tribute'. See Ray, *Transformations on the Bengal Frontier*, p. 28.
34 See O'Malley, *Bengal District Gazetteers*, p. 317.
35 Memorandum of Manager, Government Estate, to Deputy Commissioner, Darjeeling, 20 June 1898, General Department, collection G, file no. 32 (Record Room, Darjeeling).

colonial officials, whose attempt was to generally settle the land with permanent rent-paying cultivators. But even those Lepchas who tried to cultivate permanent fields were driven out by the Paharia moneylenders who usurped their land by the turn of the century.

Campbell introduced tea to Darjeeling, the product that would contribute most to the transformation of the economic base and geographical space of the entire Darjeeling hills. He reported his first experiments in tea cultivation to the Agri-Horticultural Society in 1847. He first attempted to grow tea from seeds from the Kumaon, which he procured from Nathaniel Wallich, Director of the Botanical Garden at Calcutta, in November 1841. In 1846 he obtained seeds from Assam, in order to 'give an extended trial to the plant'.[36] The next year he reported the failure of his seedlings, which did not survive the winter snow. The *Journal* advised that, similar results having been obtained in Mussoorie, the tea plant would thrive up to the altitude of 6500 feet.[37] In the ensuing years he distributed seedlings to various settlers in the Darjeeling hill region, and several of them succeeded in growing tea.[38]

Campbell moreover attempted to establish local industry by introducing the manufacture of coarse paper by importing artisans from Nepal and local materials.[39] He also (unsuccessfully) tried to grow cotton in the region.[40] There were also plans to establish cinchona plantations through private enterprise in the Darjeeling hill area after the success of the tea plantations.[41] Besides the commercial plantations, large sections of the land in Darjeeling were taken over by government as 'reserve forests', where forest management and the supply of timber and other commodities from the forest provided the government with revenues. It moreover restricted access to forests resources for the local population. The sanatorium town as well as the entire Darjeeling district became a part of the colonial economy.

Therefore Campbell's initiatives, exercised through the powerful office of the Superintendent of Darjeeling, contributed greatly to the colonization and settlement of the Darjeeling hill area in the first decades of the foundation of

---

36 A. Campbell, 'Note on the Culture of the Tea Plant at Darjeeling', *Journal of the Agri-Horticultural Society of India*, 6 (1848), pp. 123–24.
37 *Journal of the Agri-Horticultural Society of India*, 7 (1850), p. 31.
38 J.A. Crommelin, 'A Brief Account of the Experiments That Have Been Made with a View to the Introduction of the Tea Plant at Darjeeling', *Journal of the Agri Horticultural Society of India*, 8 (1852), pp. 91–95.
39 *Journal of the Agri-Horticultural Society of India*, 1 (1842), pp. 210–21.
40 A. Campbell, 'On the Cultivation of Cotton in the Darjeeling Morung; and the Capabilities of That Tract for the Extensive Growth of Superior Cottons', *Journal of the Agri-Horticultural Society of India*, 7 (1850), p. 287. The cultivation of the superior variety of cottons in India was a very crucial component of scientific agronomy in colonial India. Reports of attempts to cultivate cotton (and tea) in India were published regularly in the volumes of the *India Review and Journal of Foreign Science Arts* from 1838 to 1848 as well as in the publications of the *Journal of Agri-Horticultural Society of India* between 1842 and 1852.
41 J.A.H. Louis, *Gates of Thibet: A Bird's Eye View of Independent Sikkhim, British Bhootan and the Dooars as a Doorga Poojah Trip* (Delhi, Vivek Publishing House, 1972, first pub. 1894), p. 8.

the hill resort. A few years after he retired, at a meeting of the Ethnological Society of London, Campbell reminded his audience, 'People flocked from all sides, and we rapidly acquired a thriving population. When I took charge there were not more than fifty families in the whole tract ... In 1861, when I left Darjeeling, the total population was estimated at 60,000.'[42]

David Rennie, an IMS surgeon, found Darjeeling a bustling town, accommodating two companies of the British army at its cantonment at Jalapahar in 1865.[43] Besides the tea plantations, in the late nineteenth century the Government of India established a cinchona plantation in Mungpoo in the Darjeeling hill area near Kalimpong.[44] By 1871, when the production of tea in Darjeeling exceeded three million pounds, and tea plantations extended to the foot of the Terai, the *Journal of Society of Arts* in London (which promoted commercial agriculture in the colonies) noted that 'The great drawback now is a line of railway, to connect Darjeeling with the East Indian Railway at Sahibgunge or Rajmahal.'[45] The Darjeeling Himalayan Railway, which ran from the foothills of the Terai up to the hill town, was completed in 1881.[46] This facilitated the bulk transportation of tea. It also reduced the travelling time for seasonal visitors. In 1882, the first sanatorium in the town, the Eden Sanitarium, exclusively for Europeans, was established. The large increase in the population of the town was partly due to the regular summer shift of the entire administration of the government of Bengal from Calcutta to Darjeeling. The overall dramatic rise in the population of the Darjeeling hill area is evident from the census over the years: it rose from 94,996 in 1872 to 249,117 in 1901.[47]

We have noted above the military, strategic and commercial background of the gradual British annexations into the area that finally formed the district of Darjeeling. This was not only the site of the idyllic retreat of an Edenic sanctuary from the over-populated, clamorous plains. Kennedy has empha-

42 A. Campbell, 'On the Tribes around Darjeeling', *Transactions of the Ethnological Society of London*, 7 (1869), pp. 144–59.
43 David Field Rennie, *Bhotan and the Story of the Dooar War: Including a Three Months Residence in the Himalayas etc.* (London, John Murray, 1866), pp. 272–74.
44 Abhijit Mukherjee, 'The Peruvian Bark Revisited: A Critique of British Cinchona Policy in Colonial India', *Bengal Past and Present*, 117 (1998), pp. 81–102. Cinchona plantations were also established in the Nilgiris in south India. Kavita Philip has made a distinction between the government-owned cinchona plantations in the Nilgiris and the privately owned and managed tea, coffee and rubber plantations, because the cinchona plantations were supposed to have 'occupied a romanticised ecological space in the colonial imagination, unlike the economic and managerial conceptions of the plains landscapes'. See Kavita Philip, *Civilising Natures: Race, Resources And Modernity in Colonial South India* (Hyderabad, India, Orient Longman, 2003), p. 255. In Darjeeling, where the landscapes were romanticized in the tea plantation areas as much as anywhere else, Philip's argument is not acceptable.
45 'Darjeeling Tea Crop', *Journal of the Society of Arts*, 20 (1871), p. 94.
46 *Darjeeling and Its Mountain Railway: A Guide and Souvenir* (Calcutta, Caledonian Printing Co., 1921), pp. 13–14.
47 *Imperial Gazetteer of India, Provincial Series, Bengal*, vol. 2 (Calcutta, Superintendent of Government Printing, 1909), p. 197.

Contagion and Enclaves

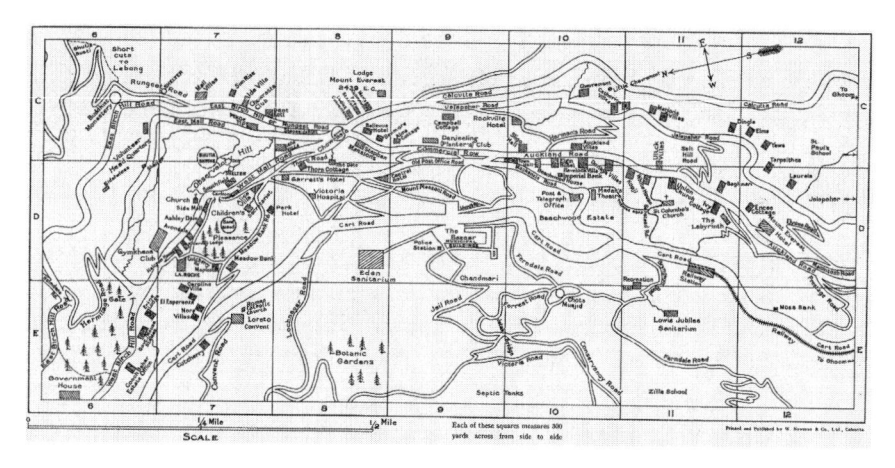

Figure 2.2 Street Map of Darjeeling town, nineteenth century

sized the Edenic sanctuary aspect of the hill-station, arguing that the British understood the Lepchas, the indigenous people, as the 'guardians' of the Edenic sanctuary because they did not militarily confront annexation to British India.[48] But the demography of the entire Darjeeling hill area changed drastically after its annexation to British India. The Nepali immigration into Darjeeling was the result of a conscious policy initiated by Campbell in order to populate and settle the entire region, as well as to provide much of the labour necessary to sustain the European habitation of the town itself. The hill-station of Darjeeling was indeed a colonial enclave, but its sustenance was the consequence of military, strategic and economic considerations as well as debates over climate and health in tropical colonies.

Sanatorium Darjeeling

The unhealthiness of the hot and humid Indian plains, and especially the plains of Bengal, was an all too familiar convention of medical discourse in nineteenth-century colonial India.[49] The mountains were posited in opposition. Harrison has pointed out that until the 1830s, the acclimatization theories were both optimistic and heterogeneous; this, together with the fact that the implications, mostly derogatory, of the word 'tropics' were not explicit until

---

48 Kennedy, *The Magic Mountains*, pp. 63–87. Campbell himself had thought that the Lepchas were 'the most interesting and pleasing of all the tribes around Darjeeling' ('On the Lepchas', p. 145). This was so because, he pointed out, 'They were the first to join us on our arrival there, and have always continued to be the most liked by Europeans, and to be the most disposed to mix freely with them' (p. 145). Hooker noted that 'In their relations with us, they are conspicuous for their honesty ... Kindness and good humour soon attach them to your person and service.' Hooker, *Himalayan Journals*, vol. 1, p. 136.

49 Harrison, *Climates and Constitutions*, p. 19. See also, Arnold (2006), pp. 42–54.

the 1830s, meant that the quest for survival of Europeans in India was located within the parameters of the Indian experience itself. Therefore, medical texts often advised borrowing from Indian dietary habits and Indian clothing, and borrowed, for example, from the Mughal customs of leaving the hottest places in the peak of the summer for more salubrious ones.[50] The hill-stations were built and sustained also to retain, in physical as well as in metaphorical terms, the distance between the rulers and the ruled.[51] This distancing was articulated in the location of the stations themselves, away from the mainstreams of the Indian population in the plains. It was reinforced in the architecture and the social life of the British in India. When J.D. Herbert wrote his survey of the site that was to become the sanatorium of Darjeeling, he recommended it as a station of health for European troops, mainly for its cold climate, so pleasant and different from the plains. The Governor General's note on his survey carried the opinion of one Dr Jeffrey, who validated the efficacy of a mountainous climate: 'Of the healthiness of Darjeeling ... Dr Jeffrey I believe mentions that fever and ague disappears amongst these mountains at an elevation of 6000 feet, and if he is correct Dargeeling will be exempt'.[52]

Although the forests of the Terai at the foothills of Darjeeling were infamous for fevers, the elevation of the hill-station was to secure Darjeeling from most diseases. It was not only free of disease, its air was supposed to help European invalids effect miraculous recoveries. All writing on Darjeeling, whether medical texts or informative tourist guides, invariably contributed to the construction of a narrative of the healing mountains. J.T. Pearson, the army official who stayed there in 1839, commented,

> There is an elasticity of the air in these mountains, and a freshness, which impart a feeling of positive enjoyment ... You are then cold, but not chilly; and exercise gives all the pleasant glow of an English walk on a frosty morning. In the day you are warm, but not hot; the sunshine is pleasant.[53]

Pearson was convinced of the prospects of Darjeeling as a hill-station: 'there have been ... very few cases of bad health even in the natives; and those were generally found to have been contracted in the morning, in the plains'.[54] There are two significant points to his testimony. The first is the clear assumption of the distinction on the very constitutions between the 'natives' and the others, the non-natives. The non-natives were the white Europeans; possibly the English who would identify with the 'pleasant glow of an English walk' – and for them the mountain air would prove bracing and healthy. The second is the assumption that whatever diseases did prevail in the mountains were somehow contracted in the plains. Both assumptions persisted in medical as well as non-medical texts on Darjeeling over the next century. The essential

50   Harrison, *Climates and Constitutions*, p. 52.
51   Kennedy, *The Magic Mountains*, p. 149 and Kenny, 'Climate, Race, and Imperial Authority'.
52   Kennedy, *The Magic Mountains*, pp. 18–19.
53   Pearson, *Note on Darjeeling*, pp. 11–12.
54   Pearson, *Note on Darjeeling*, p. 12.

rhetoric rested on the concept of the healthy, active, muscular English constitution for which 'corporeal exertion' was supposed to be a joyful activity and a natural state of being.[55] The tropical plains had divested the English constitution of its natural self. The mountains were posited to restore it, or at least in some measure. Pearson went on to describe the European's life in Darjeeling in typological terms: 'Europeans soon lose their dyspeptic symptoms, regain their appetite, and feel an aptitude and desire for corporeal exertion.'[56] Brian Hodgson, formerly the British Resident at Kathmandu (who retired to a villa in Darjeeling), extended the hill-plains dichotomy with reference to cholera, the scourge of the plains:

> The fearful epidemics of the plains seldom penetrate the Himalayas, which, moreover, seem to have a positive exemption from endemic diseases. For forty years cholera has ravaged the plains continually ... But in all that period Nepal has been visited only twice and Darjeeling scarcely at all.[57]

Hooker, who spent several months at Hodgson's home in Darjeeling between his botanizing expeditions, endorsed the rejuvenating qualities of Darjeeling for Europeans;

> When estimating in a sanatory point of view the value of any health-station ... I have seen prejudiced individuals rapidly recovering, in spite of themselves, and all the while complaining in unmeasured terms of the climate of Dorjiling, and abusing it as killing them. With respect to its suitability to the European constitution I feel satisfied, and that much saving of life, health, and money would be effected were European troops drafted thither on their arrival in Bengal, instead of being stationed in Calcutta, exposed to disease, and temptation to those vices which prove fatal to so many hundreds.[58]

As the comments above make clear, the construct of the healthy hill-station Darjeeling was under way from its outset, and this discourse denied or glossed over unsavoury British experience with the climate. Hooker's comment on the healthiness of the climate of Darjeeling endured and received wide circulation in official and non-official histories of Darjeeling.[59]

55 On the rise of a culture of sport in Victorian England and its association with health, see Bruce Haley, *The Healthy Body and Victorian Culture* (Cambridge, MA, and London, Harvard University Press, 1978), especially pp. 95–140. On the construction of the muscular English gentleman and the conflation of Social Darwinist and Christian values among this class, see J.A. Mangan, *Athleticism in the Victorian and Edwardian Public School: The Emergence and Consolidation of an Educational Ideology* (London and Portland, OR, Frank Cass, 2000), especially pp. 122–40.
56 Pearson, *Note on Darjeeling*, p. 12.
57 Brian Hodgson, 'On the Colonization, Commerce, Physical Geography etc. of the Himalaya Mountains and Nepal', *Selections from Records of Government of Bengal*, 27–32, National Archives of India, New Delhi (hereafter NAI), p. 15.
58 Hooker, *Himalayan Journals*, vol. 1, p. 110.
59 *The Dorjeeling Guide*, p. 47. Also Mary H. Avery, *'Up in the Clouds': or Darjeeling and Its Surroundings, Historical and Descriptive* (Calcutta, W. Newman and Co., 1878), p. 35; K.C. Bhanja, *The Wonders of Darjeeling and the Sikkim Himalaya* (Darjeeling, 1943).

The mountain air was not an isolated prescription. Commentators usually qualified their enthusiasm, especially when they considered the prevalence of dysentery in the hill-stations. The moist mountain air, so fresh and bracing to Victorian constitutions, could cause a range of 'respiratory diseases'. Hooker, whose remark on the healthy rosiness evident in the cheeks of the European children was quoted in almost every guide book to Darjeeling over the next seventy years, also pointed out that

> There are however disorders to which the climate (in common with all damp ones) is not at all suited; such are especially dysentery, bowel and liver complaints of long standing; which are not benefited by a residence on these hills, though how much worse they ... might have become in the plains is not known. I cannot hear that the climate aggravates, but it certainly does not remove them.[60]

The dampness of Darjeeling and its effects on European constitutions engendered several theories and disputes in the medical discourse of colonial India. Moreover, acclimatization was not only a problem for European bodies. In the mid-nineteenth century, Hooker pointed out the difficulties of native Bengali existence in Darjeeling: 'Natives from the low country, and especially Bengalees, are far from enjoying the climate as Europeans do, being liable to sharp attacks of fever and ague, from which the poorly clad natives are not exempt'.[61]

The dampness of Darjeeling qualified its idyllic elevation to some extent. In the early twentieth century, the problem persisted, and a long-term resident noted that 'The population of the higher levels, or temperate zone, suffer from chills, fevers; bowel complaints, and for rheumatism, and phthisis '.[62] That people suffering from diseases of the lung like tuberculosis could not benefit to any great extent from a stay at Darjeeling was apparent by the early twentieth century.[63] The climate interfered malignantly with the treatments.[64] For most of the year, the enjoyment of fresh ozone-rich air so elaborately described in many handbooks and confirmed by medical opinion, was an impossibility:

> From the beginning of June till the middle of October there are heavy rains with mist and absolute saturation of the air with moisture. There is not much sunshine, and exercise out of doors is curtailed. To keep out the mist and the damp, rooms have to be shut up ... unsuitable for all classes of cases.[65]

---

60 Hooker, *Himalayan Journals*, vol. 1, p. 111.
61 Hooker, *Himalayan Journals*, vol. 1, p. 111.
62 Dozey, *A Concise History*, p. 84.
63 The discovery of the tuberculosis bacillus by Koch did not immediately do away with climatic cures for lung diseases. 'Fresh air' sanatoriums were built in Germany and in the UK in the early twentieth century as well. See Linda Bryder, *Below the Magic Mountain: A Social History of Tuberculosis in Twentieth-Century Britain* (Oxford, Clarendon, 1988), pp. 46–48.
64 J.T. Calvert, 'Note on Darjeeling Climate in the Treatment of Pthisis', *Indian Medical Gazette*, 44 (1909), p. 2.
65 Calvert, 'Note on Darjeeling Climate', p. 2.

Contagion and Enclaves

British Troops in the Tropical Mountains

The inclement climate of Darjeeling affected the health of the British Indian troops in the cantonments as well. The Jalapahar convalescent depot was built in 1848 and sited on a narrow ridge (the Jalapahar) above the Mall.[66] In 1859 the buildings consisted of five barracks, including two married quarters. There was a hospital and officers' accommodation.[67] The medical officer in charge, one G. Maclean, reported that it was the climate of Darjeeling, 'wet, foggy and cold', especially the rain, that made his charges ill and unhappy.[68]

He therefore questioned the very climate of Darjeeling that was meant to regenerate invalided British soldiers from the diseases and debility experienced in the plains. Besides the cold, he complained of the monsoons when it rained heavily and interminably and pointed out that with the exception of two months in the year, there was little sunshine; moreover, the barracks were built in the style of those in the plains, which excluded sunlight. A smaller cantonment for British troops was located at Senchal nearby at a height of 8000 feet, even higher than Jalapahar. It accommodated invalided soldiers from 1844 even before barracks were properly built in 1858.[69] Of Senchal he said, 'If in their construction has intended to exclude light and deprive almost completely their inmates of the benefits of ventilation the result could be hardly more satisfactory'.[70]

Faulty planning, universal and rigid rules for institutional architecture, and a lack of responsiveness to local situations may be characteristics of any bureaucratic structure, and the British army in India was plainly not exempt from such rigidities. What is interesting in this instance is the particular combination of the lack of attention to details that would help modify the buildings to the climate and at the same time, the recognition by the medical men on the spot that the corrections to the architecture addressed only part of the problem. Essentially the problem of the convalescent depot was its location and its climate, which was too close to that of the home country for comfort. What does this tell us of Maclean's understanding of British constitutions and acclimatization? The troops who had been in India for a period were unused to the extreme cold and dampness; their health had deteriorated and they had not the physical resilience, it is presumed, to be able to recoup in the heights of Darjeeling, where the cold and damp were extreme. On the one hand this was an endorsement and reaffirmation of the logic of physical weakening of the white man in the tropics: but the solution did not appear to lie in an absolute acceptance of the reversal of climatic zones; indeed, such was hardly possible. In fact, Maclean's report indicates that he thought that the British troops underwent a certain

---

66 Dozey, *A Concise History*, p. 30.
67 'Report of G. Maclean, Assistant Surgeon 42nd Royal Hussars, in Charge of Darjeeling Sanitary Depot', 334/171/WO/PRO, p. 1. The National Archives, Kew.
68 'Report of G. Maclean', p. 2.
69 Dozey, *A Concise History*, p. 151.
70 'Report of G. Maclean', p. 8.

kind of acclimatization in the plains, so that they had to re-accustom themselves to a cooler temperate climate in Darjeeling.

However crystallized the racial categories and the hardening of attitudes might have become in the post-1858 situation, the oppositional constructs between the hills and the plains did not resolve all problems of health among the British troops. A too-literal interpretation of the hill–plains duality posed problems that the medical officers in the army had to confront in convalescent depots like Jalapahar. The happy prospects envisaged by Herbert seem exaggerated when confronted with the complaints of Maclean. And yet, troops suffering from fever, ague and diarrhoea as well as dysentery, bronchitis and phthisis were sent there regularly.[71] Maclean thought that Senchal was even more unsuitable for the troops than Jalapahar at Darjeeling. He described it as 'too harsh and too exposed for the British soldier, well or ill'.[72] Maclean believed that the very elevation and locations of both convalescent depots could actually increase the mortality rates of the European troops. He was not isolated – all his predecessors were of the same opinion and appear to have sent voluminous quarterly and annual reports to the same effect.[73]

David Rennie, whose regiment was stationed at Darjeeling at the time of the Anglo–Bhutan war in 1865, also had little favourable to say about the convalescent depots.[74] From his observations of the trends of fever among the troops located at Senchal and Jalapahar, he attributed fever and ague to the 'atmospheric climate' rather than miasmatic causes.[75] If the miasmatic explanation was not acceptable, how could the troops be secured from malaria? Not, certainly, by establishment of hill sanatoriums for them. Rennie's rejection of a miasmatic explanation of fever and ague, and exposition of atmospheric conditions as causing fever are indicative of a heterogeneity of understandings regarding disease causation. It differed from the opposing construction of the tropical air of the plains versus the purity of the mountains. He did not specify the 'morbific agent'; hence the mountains and the plains could both easily be affected and prove ruinous to the health of his troops.

Rennie, like McLean, dwelled on the fog and the dampness at the cantonments of Darjeeling, and noted the fevers and ague prevalent among the British troops, although their understanding of the causes for the illnesses differed. Rennie's explanation linked disease and immunity from fevers with race. He confirmed his observations after his visit to Duars where he saw the indigenous Meches who appeared to be immune from fevers, although they lived in marshy lands infamous for malaria.[76] The differentials in race, however, did not prompt advocacy of mountain sanatoriums for the British troops in India. Rennie's analysis of the health of the Meches verged towards racial understanding of

---

71 'Report of G. Maclean', p. 3.
72 'Report of G. Maclean', p. 7.
73 'Report of G. Maclean', p. 6.
74 Rennie, *Bhotan*, p. 349.
75 Rennie, *Bhotan*, pp. 302–3.
76 Rennie, *Bhotan*, p. 347.

disease but also looked back to the older conception of 'seasoning' that still appears to have prevailed to some extent in the second half of the nineteenth century. Rennie contested the miasmatic theories of fever and announced a robust contempt for the 'sanitarians'.[77] This was a significant deviation from the prevalent miasmatic theories. Besides miasmatic theories which were attributed to the physical conditions of life, and by logical extension, the lack of hygienic practices among the natives which were familiar conventions of medical commentary, there was another pattern of explanation of fever: the racial immunity and native-land explanation. I would argue for a multiplicity of etiological understandings of tropical diseases even in the second half of the nineteenth century, which in turn informed the form and content of Tropical Medicine in the twentieth century.

At the time, condemnation of some of the cantonment sites around Darjeeling by medical officials in the army had limited effect. The cantonment at Senchal, which occupied the highest elevation of all the stations around Darjeeling at 8163 feet, was abandoned in 1867 and transferred to Jalapahar, located at 7701 feet, among rumours of several suicides by soldiers stationed there 'owing to the excessive isolation and bitter cold'.[78] The fact that the cantonment at Jalapahar survived demonstrates the tenacity of the influence of the hills–plains dichotomy in official discourse despite the lack of medical evidence that the 'hills' were healthier for British soldiers. Meanwhile the graveyard at the abandoned Senchal cemetery was a grim reminder of the limitations of mountain sites as convalescent depots in British India.

Multiple Constructions of a Social Space

> A Welcome
> When you feel, below, dead-beat,
> Overpowered by trying heat,
> Worn by day, at night no rest;
> Then, 'tis surely manifest,
> That you should at once take train;
> Come above, and health regain!
> Here, in Flora's grove be instant;
> Prospect beauteous near and distant .
> Ferns and orchids in their prime,
> Scented blossoms sweet as thyme.
> Pleasant Mall, Chowrusta clear;
> Tempting resting place is here!
> See, the Snows' celestial wreath!
> Search, the deep ravines beneath.
> Hear, the torrents' raging wrath
> Thundering down each rocky path,

---

77 Rennie, *Bhotan*, pp. 302–3.
78 Dozey, *A Concise History*, p. 151.

> Leaping, frantic, mad with glee,
> Bounding, foaming to the sea.
> Come! Darjeeling, Queen of Health!
> Cedes to all, her precious wealth;
> Vigour, spirit, bloom, desire,
> Strength, and impulse to admire
> Scenes, that sentient souls uplift.
> Great Creator, Thine the gift!
> Mountain breezes, from the Snow,
> Pure, invigorating blow.
> Respite here, from heat and strife,
> Gives a new-born lease of life!
> Health's Queen pleading, from her throne,
> Bids you welcome to her Home![79]

The above verse was written by one Captain J.A. Keble, who also wrote several other similarly undistinguished verses on various aspects of European life in Darjeeling. The final stanza is both the declaration of the resurrection – 'Gives a new-born lease of life!' – and an invitation to experience a similar rebirth. The verses above represent the various meanings that Europeans could ascribe to Darjeeling articulated within a discourse of health and rejuvenation. Unfavourable experience and medical comment from military officials did not significantly affect the reputation of sanatorium Darjeeling as a hill-station or indeed as a resort for convalescence and cure. How is it possible to understand the phenomenal growth of Darjeeling as a hill-station in the context of the inconsistencies in the medical discourses of the hill-station? The first assumption of course is that there are always differences in medical discourses under any circumstances. Official policy was not always accommodating of dissent from medical experts, particularly in British India. That apart, Kennedy argues that the rush for the hill-stations in the nineteenth century reflected the need to carve out a social space that was particularly Europeanized as well as sanitized, as the plains of India increasingly came to be identified with dirt and filth, and the sanitarian perspectives of IMS officials assumed prominence in medical discourse as diseases came to be increasingly identified with filth. A distancing was prominent between Indians and Europeans in the hill-stations: the native bazaars were always located separately, and at a lower elevation from the European habitations. Physical distance was expressive of social distance, achieved with forethought and supposed to be scrupulously maintained. While I agree with Kennedy that there was deliberation in the location of European habitations in Darjeeling and that they created a social space, my point is that the hill-stations were carrying forward a tradition of civil stations and European enclaves from the plains themselves. They were not unique to the mountains.

The older colonial ports, such as Madras and Calcutta and to an extent Bombay, from the seventeenth century generally retained distinctions between

---

79 J.A. Keble, *Darjeeling Ditties and Other Poems: A Souvenir* (Calcutta, Calcutta General Print Co., 1908), p. 14.

the Indian and the European residential parts of the town.[80] In the decades after the revolt of 1857, the cityscape of many Indian towns was deliberately marked out into the native part of the town and the European enclave. Thus the civil lines, cantonments, wide roads and sanitary regimes of colonial Lucknow were so self-consciously different from the maze of old lanes and crowded bazaars of *nawabi* Lucknow.[81] A multitude of symbolic, cultural, sanitary and medical values were associated with the construction of the new colonial Lucknow. Nor was Lucknow the only instance of such an assertion. There was a similarity to Kanpur, for instance, where there was a European settlement due to the Company's cantonment from the eighteenth century. When the various European-owned industries in Kanpur took off in the nineteenth century, their owners and managers lived in houses that were secluded and airy, next to the river, and grew in their kitchen gardens all sorts of English vegetables for their tables.[82] Thus they created minor enclaves, clearly marked-out European residential areas in Kanpur. Similarly, in nineteenth-century Benaras, British officials as well as non-officials stayed two miles away from the crowded old town in a new suburb where they built sprawling bungalows open on four sides to let the air in.[83] The British settlement in Darjeeling created an enclave for themselves; but it was a settlement that eventually, with the consolidation of the tea industry, assumed commercial importance, not an Edenic sanctuary that was gradually disrupted. The British associated the hill-stations particularly with the rejuvenation of European constitutions. However, the mountain sanatoriums were *one* of several such strategies of creating enclaves and attempting to adapt to the particularities of the country and of the environment.

In the final decades of the nineteenth century and over the early years of the twentieth century substantial medical opinion, although occasionally ambivalent, nevertheless endorsed the air, the climate and the physical aspects of Darjeeling as being suitable for European rest and recuperation in the tropics. A plethora of guidebooks and other forms of tourist literature, often containing additional favourable opinions by European medical men, were printed throughout this period with the European visitor in mind. The travel guides of the period both contributed to the construction of a mountain sanatorium and

---

80 Meera Kosambi and John E. Brush, 'Three Colonial Port Cities in India', *Geographical Review*, 78 (1988), pp. 32–47. P.J. Marshall has argued that 'Although they never achieved the kind of segregation that Europeans later established in some Indian towns by withdrawing to cantonments and civil lines, the British in Calcutta always aimed to live in their own town and were largely successful in this aim. A considerable part of Calcutta came to be known as 'the white town'. 'The White Town of Calcutta under the Rule of the East India Company', *Modern Asian Studies*, 34 (2000), pp. 307–31.

81 Veena Oldenburg, *The Making of Colonial Lucknow, 1856–1877* (Princeton, Guildford, Princeton University Press), 1984.

82 Chitra Joshi, *Lost Worlds: Indian Labour and Its Forgotten Histories* (Delhi, Permanent Black, 2003).

83 Bernard S. Cohn, 'The British in Benares: A Nineteenth Century Colonial Society', in idem, *An Anthropologist among the Historians and Other Essays* (Delhi, Oxford, Oxford University Press, 1987), pp. 422–62.

served to medicalize a retreat that evoked, to the British, memories of home. Even when it sometimes appeared, and it happened soon after its establishment, that Darjeeling was not really free of illness or disease, most ailments that occurred there were either held to occur in a milder form or straightaway attributed to the 'plains'. One guide noted in 1845 that

> Fevers in Dorjeeling, as in most other places, form the great bulk of Indian diseases. They are believed to be, for the most part, contracted below ... It is said that malaria does not ascend to above 2,500 ft ... he has never seen a case in the well-fed European, which could not be traced to below.[84]

It claimed that the diseases contracted in Darjeeling could be compared favourably even in relation to Europe, even in diseases such as rheumatism.[85] And invariably so in relation to the 'plains': 'When contracted below, it would be relieved by removal to this climate.'[86] For sickness and debility, for general breakdown of the European constitution, a stay in Darjeeling came to be endorsed as the perfect remedy. A few weeks in Darjeeling could induce cures for many vague and incomprehensible dissatisfactions of being: 'The appetite becomes improved; hypochondrial symptoms disappear; and the aptitude to exercise returns with all the activity felt at home.'[87] The travel guides constructed and nurtured the association of England with Darjeeling; except for details of porters' wages, availability of local servants and ayahs, fresh poultry, and occasionally, the picturesqueness of the native Lepchas. The summer transfer of the provincial administration to the town lent its social space glamour and urgency.

The shift of capital to Darjeeling occurred in the quest for a location away from the harmful miasma of the plains of Bengal in the summer. Such miraculous recoveries of the body and spirit evoked with deliberation memories, real or re-constructed, of the English way of life in the Victorian age: 'Ladies who, in the plains, rose and took a constitutional drive by prescription, get up early in the morning, and take a long walk; while gardening, and other out of door work, affords agreeable employment for the day.'[88] Thus recovery of good health was a family affair: 'Children, of all others, are benefited by a change to this climate. They are not long here, before the thin, pallid, playing on the carpet, peevish child, becomes fat and rosy ... regaining his health and strength, and playing about as merry as an English child.'[89] European constitutions and the familiar pleasures of outdoor bourgeois English life – walks, gardening – and the prospect of their children, sickly and unhealthy in the plains, transformed into rosy-cheeked energetic English boys and girls, were evoked in the guidebooks. Although they referred to the English climate and topography as a measure of comparison, the guide also provided adequate information about

84 *The Dorjeeling Guide*, p. 35.
85 *The Dorjeeling Guide*, p. 35.
86 *The Dorjeeling Guide*, p. 35.
87 *The Dorjeeling Guide*, p. 35.
88 *The Dorjeeling Guide*, pp. 36–37.
89 *The Dorjeeling Guide*, p. 37.

the availability of native servants and ayahs for the children.

The early optimism about Darjeeling as a sanatorium survived. Much of the expansion of the town of Darjeeling in the next few years was owed to its reputation as a sanatorium. Invariably its distinction was set down with relation to the 'plains'. A guidebook on the hill-station in 1883 articulated the distinction of Darjeeling as a site for rejuvenation of health:

> On account of its elevation Darjeeling is above the reach of malaria, and its equable, though moist climate renders it an excellent sanitarium for Europeans. The mountain air is charged with ozone, and at almost every inspiration the visitor, whose health has suffered from a long residence in the plains of Bengal, feels as if he were adding days to his life.[90]

Hooker's description of Darjeeling, particularly his comment that the faces of children in Darjeeling indicate the healthiness of the place, was quoted and elaborated upon:

> The children born and reared in Darjeeling are quite as chubby, bright, active and happy as could be seen in the most favoured spots of Europe, while children brought up from the plains of Bengal suffering from anaemia, flabby, pale, fretful ... soon become models of health and cheerfulness, and run their parents' Butchers' bill up in an astonishing way.[91]

When fevers occurred they were attributed to the 'plains'.[92] The virtues of the climate and situation of Darjeeling were sometimes even held to surpass that of Europe: 'unlike towns at home, scarlatina is absolutely unknown, and so are most infantile maladies that one has to be prepared for in the old country'.[93] Discourses of illness and health were expressed in racial terms. English constitutions, and indeed disease, were indistinguishable from European ones, and the 'old country' and 'home' and 'Europe' were used indiscriminately. The commonality among or uniformity of the European body appears, at this juncture, to have been a given fact. It was juxtaposed with the native bodies and the diseases associated with the 'plains': 'no case is on record of a European, whether child or adult, ever having been attacked with cholera in Darjeeling ... Enlargement of the spleen is always much improved by a stay at Darjeeling, as are all other diseases traceable to malarial poisoning.'[94]

In the 1880s, there were some qualifications regarding the good effects of Darjeeling: 'But the visitor, more or less broken down in constitution, must

---

90 O'Brien, *Darjeeling*, pp. 22–23.
91 O'Brien, *Darjeeling*, p. 24.
92 S.O. Bishop, *Medical Hints for the Hills* (Darjeeling, Scotch Mission Orphanage Press, 1888), p. 64.
93 O'Brien, *Darjeeling*, p. 24.
94 O'Brien, *Darjeeling*, p. 24. Arnold has argued that the sudden death induced by cholera greatly contributed to the representation of the 'tropical deathscape' of the plains of India in European imagery. Arnold (2006), pp. 45–46. The plains of lower Bengal were known as the 'home of cholera'. Harrison, *Climates and Constitutions*, p. 19.

be cautious if he wants the change of climate to do him good.'[95] Still, as its expansion and the glut of seasonal visitors testified, the town retained some reputation as a health sanatorium; in fact the Eden Sanitarium and Hospital was founded in 1882 to cater exclusively to Europeans and the Lowis Jubilee Sanatorium for Indians was set up within five years, in 1887, with initiatives from the rajahs of Cooch Behar and Burdwan.[96] Both possessed palaces in Darjeeling.

It is remarkable how much of the travel and medical literature agreed on the efficacy of Darjeeling as a hill-station. The travel guides were aimed generally at comfortable middle-class civilian and non-official Europeans, invalids and escapees from the oppressive heat of the plains in the summer. Darjeeling, like Ootacamund and Simla, hosted the official civil servant class as well as non-officials, alongside the European troops in the British army in India who lodged in a somewhat different mode in the convalescent depots at Jalapahar.

The guidebooks evoked an idyllic hill-station. But it came at a price. In Darjeeling, as in Simla and Ootacamund, houses were expensive and difficult to obtain. In Darjeeling particularly, all foodstuffs had to be carried over from the plains by train or road and were very expensive.[97] To those who could afford it, Darjeeling had many pleasant distractions to offer besides the climate and the scenery. Keble's celebration of such amusements lacks in literary appeal but not in detail and zest:

> 'Darjeelingisticism'! …
> 'Tis from *it* we catch our bright, social, fine shine.
> Then our *kala jagas*, set back in the dark!
> So arranged, for heated pair-dancers to lark.
> 'Virtue traps'! so named, 'most disgraceful, closed things';
> 'Tis from these our scandalous scandal most springs! …
> The Amusement Club and the Medical Ball,
> Civil Service dances, *et cetra*, near all;
> Garland in *kala jaga e'en under the stairs!*
> 'Shameful, hidden, dark places', screened off for fond pairs.
> Should official ones' wives interweave up places!
> And so favour foul scandal's invented disgraces![98]

Stolen kisses under the stairs, a schoolboyish glee at creating scandals, the excitements of a cosmopolitan life without undue intrusion of natives – such were the attractions of Darjeeling to Europeans. For instance, to planters and civil servants in the tea districts of northern Bengal, even a brief sojourn at

---

95 Harrison, *Climates and Constitutions*, p. 23
96 O'Malley, *Bengal District Gazetteers*, p. 188.
97 Pamela Kanwar has stated that it was so expensive to rent suitable bungalows in Simla that only the upper echelons of the military and civilian officials could afford to do so. See Kanwar, 'The Changing Profile of the Summer Capital of British India: Simla 1864–1947', *Modern Asian Studies*, 18 (1984), pp. 215–36.
98 Keble, *Darjeeling Ditties*, p. 89.

Contagion and Enclaves

Darjeeling offered a respite from the daily monotony of their lives in the plains. John Tyson, who was posted at Jalpaiguri in the 1920s, described his return to Jalpaiguri from a trip to Darjeeling: 'back among the punkahs and mosquito-curtains: or, what is worse, back among chocolate coloured Bengalis and a pile of law-books'.[99] W.M. Fraser, a planter in Terai, spent more than a month in Darjeeling after an attack of malarial fever. When he briefly contemplated emigration from the Terai, he was even offered a position in a tea plantation from Andrew Wernicke.[100]

'Hill-Diarrhoea': The Making of Diseases Specific to the Hills

One of the peculiarities of the uncontaminated-hills discourse was the formulation of certain diseases that were supposed to be unique to the 'hills'. Certain diseases were identified and prospective visitors were advised on precautionary measures. A form of diarrhoea was 'discovered': hill-diarrhoea. This appears to have been a general aspect of mountain sanatoriums all over the tropics. There were various debates about its nature in contemporary medical journals and in 1892 the aetiology and cures for hill-diarrhoea were still being debated.[101] It was perceived to be a mild form of diarrhoea, not particularly damaging to the patient, so that 'the days grow into weeks and months before the patient seeks advice so little physical deterioration does the disease cause'.[102]

Hill-diarrhoea, curiously, was supposed to occur not only in the Indian mountain sanatoriums, but also in Natal and Hong Kong. James Cantlie, a doctor at Hong Kong, speculated that one thing common between the mountain sanatoriums of India, Natal, and the rocky height of Hong Kong had to be the elevation, even though Hong Kong did not rise above 1700 feet. Significantly, the European habitation in Hong Kong was in the highest part of the island.[103] Cantlie rejected a climatic explanation and tentatively attributed the diarrhoea to drinking the water.

The nomenclature and diagnosis of hill-diarrhoea seem merely descriptive. Indeed, it was common to name diseases after places in the colonial tropics:

99 Letter from John Tyson, 29/10/1920, Mss Eur E 341/2 (APAC).
100 W.M. Fraser, *The Recollections of a Tea Planter* (London, Tea and Rubber Mail, 1935), pp. 75–81.
101 Scrapbook compiled by James Cantile, The Wellcome Library MS. 6933, p. 54.
102 Scrapbook compiled by James Cantile.
103 Any residence on an elevated space, even a mound, was preferable to the flat earth anywhere in the 'tropics'. At the turn of the century G.M. Giles wrote, 'For a single house, no better position can be selected than the summit of a mound, whether natural or artificial; and such situations are generally to be preferred to the slope of a hill... good examples of which are to be found in Chittagong, where nearly every European residence has its own little hill,...and it is doubtless to this ....that the comparative healthiness of the European population of the town ...is mainly due '. G.M. Giles, *Climate and Health in Hot Countries And The Outlines of Tropical Climatology: A Popular Treatise on Personal Hygiene in the Hotter Parts of the World, and on the Climates that will be with within them* (London, J. Bale, sons & Danielsson,1904), p. 2.

'Pali plague', 'Burdwan fever' or 'Simla trots', the last a colloquial term for diarrhoea in Simla, are examples of this form of nomenclature. Nonetheless, 'hill-diarrhoea' (and its variants, such as Simla trots) also indicated a tendency to construct particularly 'hill' diseases because it was unacceptable that simple diarrhoea, an affliction sadly pervasive in the plains, should also invade the mountains. Eluding a strict definition, but indisputably present in every hill-station, 'hill-diarrhoea' simultaneously subverted the idyll of the uncontaminated hill-station and served to keep the disease environment of the hills distinct from that of the plains.

Yet, the consequence of 'hill-diarrhoea' could imitate the aftermath of that tropical malady Europeans were fleeing – a general debility of the body. One medical author attributed the onset of debility once hill-diarrhoea progressed to its 'Cachectic' third stage.[104] Ironically, he concluded that it could be permanently cured or improved 'only on change of climate'! Another contemplated an 'upper limit to the diarrhoea region', and recommended escape to heights above 12,000 feet to avoid hill-diarrhoea.[105]

The aetiology of hill-diarrhoea in Darjeeling was confusing but by the nineteenth century experts settled causation on the levels of mica in the water supply. Therefore, a sanitary explanation was acceptable; the fact that it was seen chronologically in the case of Darjeeling, which was earlier free of 'hill-diarrhoea', means also that the idea of gradual contamination of the pure mountains to some extent resolved the apparent paradox of the occurrence of 'hill-diarrhoea'. As a physician with an active practice in the Darjeeling hills wrote, 'Dr R. Lidderdale, the Sanitary Commissioner of Bengal, informs me, that he can recollect the time when Darjeeling claimed that it was the only hill-station free from it.'[106] However, it appears to have been endemic from around 1874. The Sanitary Commissioner's theory was that 'it has followed the opening out of the country by destruction of forests, increase of population, and attendant evils'.[107] This was disputed by our author who favoured the idea that it was caused by a malfunction of the liver and therefore prescribed 'bland nourishment' as its cure.[108] That 'hill-diarrhoea' continued to trouble Europeans in Darjeeling is evident, for the district gazetteer noted a few years later, 'The chief danger is of having hill diarrhoea, owing to the great difference of climatic conditions and carelessness regarding diet, clothing, and exercise.'[109] It became an accepted fact that most European visitors to Darjeeling would be susceptible to an attack of 'hill-diarrhoea'. A history of Darjeeling, first published in 1916,

---

104 W.G. Macpherson, 'Memorandum on Hill Diarrhoea and Its Treatment by Perchloride of Mercury', *Indian Medical Gazette*, 22 (1887), pp. 193–94.
105 'The Relation of Elevation to Hill Diarrhoea', *Indian Medical Gazette* (August 1892), p. 254.
106 Bishop, *Medical Hints*, p. 20.
107 Bishop, *Medical Hints*, p. 21. See also, 'Report of the Sanitary Commissioner of Bengal for 1886', Government of Bengal Proceedings, Sanitary Department, Dec. 1887, nos 16–18, IOR/ P/2947 (APAC), p. 11.
108 Bishop, *Medical Hints*, pp. 21–24.
109 O'Malley, *Bengal District Gazetteers*, p. 54.

concluded that the chief and probably the only ailment suffered by the British in Darjeeling was hill-diarrhoea, and blamed it on the mica in the drinking water.[110] There was never an established aetiology of hill-diarrhoea. As late as 1947 the district gazetteer disputed the mica theory and instead attributed the causation of hill-diarrhoea to 'changes of climate and diet and more particularly to the error of overeating into which visitors are prone to fall due to the unaccustomed cold'.[111]

Medicalized Leisure in a Colonial Enclave: The Eden Sanitarium and Hospital

The Eden Sanitarium was built in 1882, although it did not begin to function until 1884.[112] It was named after the governor of Bengal, Sir Ashley Eden, at whose initiative it was instituted. One anecdote attributed the founding of the institution to a personal encounter by Sir Ashley Eden with a European afflicted by pneumonia at the Darjeeling railway station one morning. The gentleman was leaving Darjeeling because he could not afford the accommodation available at the hill-station. On enquiry later Sir Ashley was informed that the said gentleman had died on his way back to Siliguri. This brought home to him the lack of a sanatorium at in the town. Ironically, the unfortunate gentleman Sir Ashley had encountered was reputed to have died of phthisis contracted in Darjeeling![113]

The institution was for the benefit of the increasing numbers of British planter families in northern Bengal as well as 'convalescents ... who, from want of means, could not afford to take a sea-trip for the benefit of their health'.[114] The Eden Sanitarium was established with government funds and private subscriptions, including a generous one from the Maharaja of Burdwan. The total cost of the construction amounted to around two lakh rupees, of which the government of Bengal donated Rs 52,000.[115]

The chief medical officer at the sanatorium was the Civil Surgeon of Darjeeling, who was provided with a generous extra remuneration for any loss of private patients who might choose the Eden Sanitarium instead.[116] The resident medical officer was generally a Military Assistant Surgeon. It was

---

110 Dozey, *A Concise History*, p. 126.
111 Arthur Jules, *Bengal District Gazetteer: Darjeeling* (Calcutta, Bengal Government Press, 1947), p. 94.
112 O'Malley, *Bengal District Gazetteers*, p. 188.
113 Dozey, *A Concise History*, p. 88.
114 Government of Bengal Proceedings, Municipal/Medical, nos 8–17, April 1886, P/2806 (APAC), p. 37.
115 Government of Bengal, A Proceedings, Municipal/Medical Branch, 1881 (West Bengal State Archive, Calcutta, hereafter WBSA), p. 3.
116 Government of Bengal Proceedings, Municipal/Medical, nos 8–17, April 1886, P/2806 (APAC), p. 37.

instituted as a charitable trust and solicited patronage of both the government as well as that of private industries. Local private industries which included, besides the railways, several European firms based in Darjeeling and Calcutta regularly contributed to it. The government of Bengal and particularly Sir Ashley Eden as the chief benefactor had the privilege of constituting the governing body. The first governing body constituted the Senior Secretary to the Government of Bengal, present at Darjeeling (ex-officio president), the Commissioner of Rajshahi and Cooch Behar Division (ex-officio vice-president), the Secretary of Government of Bengal in the Public Works Department, the Deputy Commissioner of Darjeeling, the Agent, East Bengal Railway, the Civil Surgeon of Darjeeling, and two managers from the tea estates of Tukvar and Lebong.[117]

The Eden Sanitarium had four classes, rather like the railways in India. In a sense the sanatorium (a hospital was added in 1901) was a microcosm of British society in India. The facilities available to the residents were according to a hierarchy. The first class patients had heating in their room and a separate dining hall and brought their own servants to wait on them. The second class and inter-class patients enjoyed privacy in their wards, whereas the third class ward contained four to six free beds instituted by private charity from various sources. These included private companies catering to British Indians, such as the Darjeeling Himalayan Railways, the *Statesman* newspaper in Calcutta and various merchant firms at Calcutta and tea companies with plantations in Darjeeling. The constitutive body of the sanatorium overwhelmingly represented officialdom. An indication of the kind of patients expected at the sanatorium is to be had from the list: Europeans employed by both the tea companies at Darjeeling and the railways would comprise many of the patients at the Sanitarium.

At the time of its foundation the government sent queries to the various hospitals in Calcutta enquiring whether their European and Eurasian patients would benefit from convalescence or treatment in Darjeeling. The responses were ambivalent and modest. The principal of the Medical College at Calcutta could not 'state definitely the extent to which convalescent patients from the Medical Hospital would require a transfer to Darjeeling', and concluded that 'it would certainly benefit those suffering from functional disorders, weak digestions and other general ailments'.[118] The Superintendent of the Presidency General Hospital at Calcutta, on the other hand, would not give any estimates of the numbers of patients who would be likely to avail themselves of the sanatorium at Darjeeling, but had 'often felt the need for such a resource' and on many occasions had to 'send patients to sea whom he would have preferred to send to the Hills'.[119] Therefore trips to the sea could still be substitutes for the 'hills' in the late-nineteenth century. The superintendent at the Campbell

117 Government of Bengal, A Proceedings, Municipal/Medical, August 1881 (WBSA), p. 43.
118 Government of Bengal, B Proceedings, Municipal /Medical, Oct. 1881. File no. 11 (WBSA), p. 1.
119 Government of Bengal, B Proceedings, pp. 1–2.

Hospital was against transferring any of his patients to Darjeeling; he wrote that after many years of medical experience in various hospitals in Calcutta he would not recommend a transfer to the hospital at Darjeeling for his European patients, 'as they would not only derive no relief from the change but would most probably be infected ... by a transfer suddenly to a cold mountain climate like Darjeeling'.[120] The superintendent of the Howrah hospital was not certain as to the 'use that may be made of the Darjeeling Hospital by patients from Howrah' but thought that if the proposed hospital did succeed in sustaining itself he would probably be able to send three or four patients in a year to Darjeeling.[121] The train companies were even more hesitant to endorse the project, for they were also required to subscribe to the venture. Indeed, as the first committee to report on the proposed sanatorium pointed out, the government grant would suffice merely to level the hill-top at the site.

Therefore, the Eden Sanitarium relied on voluntary patients who suffered from medically vague conditions like 'debility' and travelled to Darjeeling to recuperate.[122] Initially, the hoteliers of Darjeeling who catered to European guests resented the institution, because it competed with them for self-referred 'patients'.[123] The institution itself was at pains to deny direct competition with the local hoteliers.[124] Notwithstanding, it is evident that the institution was mainly a convalescent centre. A report to the government of Bengal in 1898 noted, 'In no.1. of the rules of the Eden Sanitarium it is stated that the institution is intended for the accommodation and care of Europeans residing in Lower Bengal, when overtaken by sickness or accident and to provide a comfortable home for convalescents after sickness'.[125] The superintendent of the Eden Sanitarium rued that it was 'only the latter and secondary object which can be fulfilled with the present accommodation and establishment.'[126] The boarding-house aspect of the institution was exaggerated by the self-referral; moreover, relatives, friends and many servants of the patients were allowed to live with them within the sanatorium. From the beginning, the proportion of friends and relatives residing in the institution was very high. Between 1883 and 1886, the 'relatives and attendants' numbered a little more than one-third of the total inmates. By the end of the first decade of the twentieth century, friends and relatives equalled the number of patients.[127]

120 Government of Bengal, B Proceedings, pp. 1–2.
121 Government of Bengal, B Proceedings, pp. 1–2.
122 The subscribers to the sanatorium included the Darjeeling Municipality, several of the tea gardens around Darjeeling, the Darjeeling Himalayan Railway, and a not insubstantial sum of Rs 262,5,3 from the Sunday Fund of the institution itself. The idea of the 'Sunday Fund' was borrowed from the Victorian tradition of active charity-seeking hospitals in London. See Keir Waddington, *Charity and the London Hospitals: 1850–1898* (Woodbridge and Rochester, NY, Royal Historical Society, Boydell Press, 2000), p. 4.
123 Government of Bengal Proceedings, Medical, nos 1–3, Sep. 1888, IOR/ P/3184 (APAC), p. 136.
124 Government of Bengal Proceedings, Medical, nos 1–5, July 1889, IOR/P/3418 (APAC), p. 7.
125 Government of Bengal, A Proceedings, Municipal/Medical, Nov. 1899 (WBSA), p. 135.
126 Government of Bengal, A Proceedings, Municipal/Medical, Nov. 1899 (WBSA), p. 135.
127 Government of Bengal, A Proceedings, Municipal/Medical, Aug. 1909 (WBSA), p. 1.

The Sanatorium of Darjeeling

In 1901 the 'hospital' section of the Eden Sanitarium was inaugurated. Throughout the next decade the authorities of the sanatorium attempted to promote and popularize the use of the 'hospital' section of the institution with very modest success. It seems that the trajectory of the Eden Sanitarium and Hospital followed that of the town of Darjeeling itself, in its appropriation of the medicalized space towards leisure and the creation of an enclave within an enclave.

The Eden Sanitarium's chief function was that of a pleasant site for rest and comfort that was possibly sanitized and legitimized; a convalescent home rather than a hospital. What was the necessity for the institution of the Eden Sanitarium in Darjeeling at all? Darjeeling developed as a retreat for Europeans from the plains. The entire space of the Darjeeling hills was thus both a site of exclusion of Indians and the de-tropicalization of the Himalayan landscape. In the context of Darjeeling, the Sanitarium was therefore a reaffirmation of the claims of the Europeans for an exclusive space that was both social and medical. In nineteenth-century England, a convalescent home seems at first glance not so very different from the Eden Sanitarium. Florence Nightingale's instruction for a convalescent home, for instance, was that 'it should not be like a hospital at all'.[128] In England generally, the miasmatic theories dominant in the period led to convalescent homes being located in the country, as far as possible from congested urban centres, and architecture tended towards the small, cosier structures. The architecture of the Eden Sanitarium, which boasted several turrets and gables, was very different and much more grandiose.

The difference also lay in the fact that hospitals in late nineteenth-century England – with their emphasis on miasma and ventilation, on cleanliness and the separation of the sexes, which were the characteristics of the 'Nightingale wards' – were all directed towards the working classes and the poor. In the colonial context the class of Europeans who patronized the hill-station sanatoriums voluntarily were set apart by their race and wealth; the 'poorer' incumbents who were allowed beds on concessions earned Rs 300 per month or a little less – a salary beyond the reach of most Indians.

How significant was the Eden Sanitarium to the hill-station? The numbers and the flow of convalescents at Darjeeling seem to have been somewhat similar to those of the town itself. Colonel R. Macrae, the Civil Surgeon and Superintendent of Darjeeling, commented in 1907 that the Eden Sanitarium was competing with other hill-stations for patients.[129] He explained that partly the reason for the increase in the number of admissions to the sanatorium was 'general complaints in respect to diet and discomfort' and that the steward who was in charge of the meals was recently dismissed from service.[130] It seems ironic, even strange, that the Civil Surgeon of Darjeeling would find it necessary to commend improvements in the catering and waiting and regard

---

128 Jeremy Taylor, *Hospital and Asylum Architecture in England 1840–1914: Building for Health Care* (London and New York, Mansell, 1991), p. 119.
129 Government of Bengal A Proceedings, Municipal/Medical, July 1907 (WBSA), p. 15.
130 Government of Bengal A Proceedings, Municipal/Medical, July 1907 (WBSA), p. 15.

them as effective determinants of the reputation of the Sanitarium. But we may understand the function of the Eden Sanitarium in Darjeeling as a centre for Europeans to socialize among their own kind while at the same time recuperating from the fatigue induced by the heat of the tropics. Both rest and socialization were articulated in medical terms.

British Indian society at the turn of the century had a notion of leisure that was distinct and recognizable. Indeed, the world of the sahib (and the memsahib) when the official was not on tour revolved round the club of the civil station which offered him the company of other Europeans, whisky, beer and gin; and afternoon tea, bridge, tennis and the occasional cricket match. In the hill-stations these pursuits were similar, and replicated much of the Victorian pleasures of the middle and upper classes – the amateur theatre, the occasional grand ball, the daily promenades on the Mall. The region around Darjeeling also inspired sporting men as much as it did naturalists.[131] It was also in the early nineteenth century that the idea of sport was associated with leisure pursuits and a sporting world came to constitute the various outdoor pursuits of 'hunting, racing, shooting, angling, cricket, walking'.[132] One of the attractions of the Eden Sanitarium as a centre for convalescence was the fact that the town, and within it, the institution itself, had created an urban social space, critically new and demonstrably English. The older presidency towns in eighteenth-century India were colonial ports. However, their native town components were large and fairly intrusive, whereas Darjeeling was smaller in size and certainly more exclusive. But there was yet another cause for the popularity of the town and also the Eden Sanitarium that contributed both to the European population within the institution and the Englishness of Darjeeling – the tea plantations around it.[133]

From the beginning, the British planters in Darjeeling, Duars and Terai patronized the Eden Sanitarium, which remained open over the winter months to accommodate them.[134] The tea estates depended on the Sanitarium for medical help and, once it was established, dispensed with services of the doctors who

---

131 When the Darjeeling Natural History Society was founded in 1923, the articles in its short-lived journal was comprised mostly of hunting anecdotes by the planters in Darjeeling and Duars. For instance, see 'Game Birds of Sikkim Including the Darjeeling District and of the Jalpaiguri District, Bengal', *The Journal of the Darjeeling Natural History Society*, 1.1 (1926), pp. 1–3, and 'Ethics of Shooting Game with Aid of Artificial Light', p. 8; 'Tiger Stories, Leopard Stories: Two Incidents', 2.1 (June 1927), pp. 15–17.
132 Peter Burke, 'The Invention of Leisure in Early Modern Europe', *Past and Present*, 146 (1995), pp. 136–50.
133 A planter reminded potential new recruits to Darjeeling that 'English people remain essentially English, and feel that with the Suez Canal and the Mont Cenis Tunnel, home is close at hand ... there remains a country ... where Englishmen manage pretty successfully to live in a way that (with the exception of the numerous servants), fairly well resembles life in their own land'. See Samuel Baildon, *The Tea Industry: A Review of Finance and Labour, Guide for Capitalists and Assistants* (London, W.H. Allen & Co., 1882), pp. 38–39. Ironically, most of the planters were Scottish, not English.
134 Government of Bengal Proceedings, Medical/Hospitals and Dispensaries, no. 16–18, Nov. 1887, IOR/ P/2946 (APAC), p. 14.

regularly attended to British patients in the tea estates.[135] Over the years the British who sought refuge at the Eden Sanitarium were matched in numbers by the planters around Darjeeling who patronized the institution.[136] Most of the patients from the Darjeeling hill area were officials, planters, railwaymen and other non-official British who had settled in and around the Darjeeling hills. By 1916, the Eden Sanitarium emerged as the chief medical institution for Europeans of the entire area, including Terai and the Duars (the Terai Tea Planters Association began subscribing to the institution).[137] Although it emerged as the one hospital that the Europeans in the Darjeeling and even the Terai and the Duars areas depended on for medical cure, its chief role remained that of providing a medicalized space for leisure.[138] The patient lists at the Eden Sanitarium did not reflect morbidity or mortality rates in general in Darjeeling. It functioned as an enclave within Darjeeling, catering to the small section of Europeans who patronized it, which included the British planters. Although a private, charitable institution, it was funded by the Darjeeling Improvement Trust as well as by the Darjeeling Municipality on a regular basis. Its patrons included the governor of Bengal, who visited the institution every year. Finally, the symbolic significance of the Eden Sanitarium in the sustenance of a peculiarly European social space within Darjeeling was immense.

Tropical Colonies and the Practices of European Settlement

The settlement of white races in the tropics was a contentious and complex issue in every Western empire. The processes varied from the West Indies and Americas to southern Africa and from Australia to India. D.N. Livingstone has made the point that in the debates on acclimatization, particularly after the establishment of germ theory and with the optimism of men like Sambon and Manson, the focus shifted in the twentieth century from climate to the conquest of parasites and microbes.[139] Warwick Anderson has further argued that the advent of laboratory medicine in the twentieth century eclipsed the concept of acclimatization. Instead the question of the survival of the white man in the tropics came to depend on the conquest of microbes and the sanitization of the tropics – pathologizing the native population and thereby rendering the white men in the tropics, separated and sanitized, further distant from the natives.[140]

However, it is important to note that climate tenaciously remained a central trope of medical discourse in tropical colonies until the very end of colonial rule.

---

135 Government of Bengal Proceedings, Medical, Sep 1888, nos 1–3, IOR/P/3184 (APAC), p. 136.
136 Government of Bengal, A Proceedings, Finance/Medical (WBSA), 1916, p. 58.
137 Government of Bengal, A Proceedings, Finance/Medical, Sep. 1917 (WBSA), p. 157.
138 Government of Bengal, A Proceedings, Finance/Medical, Sep. 1918 (WBSA), p. 19.
139 Livingstone (1999).
140 W. Anderson, '"Where Every Prospect Pleases and Only Man Is Vile": Laboratory Medicine as Colonial Discourse', *Critical Inquiry*, 18 (1992), pp. 506–29.

'Tropicality', as expressed in climatic terms and the perpetuation of specific diseases, converged seamlessly within late colonial medical discourse in the twentieth century, generating investigation into a slew of 'tropical diseases' that encompassed everything from malaria to cholera and even diabetes.[141]

A perusal of these historians' treatment of acclimatization makes it reasonable to assume that the problem remained the same: the racial anxieties of white races in the tropics. In pursuing this question, these authors have neglected one crucial aspect of the history of acclimatization: that the actual practices of settlement by Europeans in tropical colonies took place irrespective of either the climatic trope or racial anxieties. Through a historical analysis of Darjeeling this chapter has explored, not what the white man perceived as the threat to the survival of their race in the tropics, but what were the actual practice and patterns of settlement.

A shift to such a perspective is necessary to resolve the contradiction pointed out by Harrison, that it was precisely at the time of the pessimism about acclimatization and the hardening of racial categories (after the mid-nineteenth century) that the colonization of India was at its zenith.[142] One might argue that British medical and political discourse at this time left little room for envisioning India as a settler colony. But surely all settler colonies and cultures did not have one particular historical template or a predetermined trajectory. Various kinds and practices of settlement of white peoples of European origin took place in different parts of the globe from the sixteenth century onwards. The debates on acclimatization encompassed the nineteenth and the twentieth centuries, with differing discourses: race, environment, anthropological debates on racial characteristics and 'seasoning', natural selection, the germ theory, immunization of races, degeneration and the pathologization of certain races all playing their part in the debates. In the settler colonies even in the nineteenth century enclaves remained an essential mode of European habitation. In Queensland, Australia, for instance, although workers' discourses incorporated the notion of 'white Australia', there were debates about using 'coloured labour under white leadership' to 'develop the Australian tropics' in the twentieth century.[143] These views were subsumed within the rhetoric for a white Australia. The key difference – finally resting between the 'settler colonies' of North America and Australia, and the 'enclaves' of managerial control in the Indonesian islands, Ceylon, Malaysia and the plantation areas in India – were only actualized in the late nineteenth century.[144] And even

141 See, for instance, Randall M. Packard, *The Making of a Tropical Disease: A Short History of Malaria* (Baltimore, Johns Hopkins University Press, 2007); Pratik Chakrabarti, 'Curing Cholera: Pathogens, Places and Poverty in South Asia', *International Journal of South Asian Studies*, 3 (2010), pp. 153–68. For the normalization of diabetes as a tropical disease, see D. Arnold, 'Diabetes in the Tropics: Race, Place and Class in India, 1880–1965', *Social History of Medicine*, 2 (2009), pp. 245–61.
142 Harrison, *Climates and Constitutions*, pp. 133–47.
143 Anderson, *Cultivation of Whiteness*, p. 164.
144 Livingstone, 'Tropical Climate and Moral Hygiene'. Also see Anderson, 'Immunities of Empire'.

Figure 2.3 Scenic Darjeeling

there possibilities for white enclaves persisted in (albeit marginalized) political discourse until decolonization.

The attempt to create European enclaves in the colonial tropics was a multifaceted endeavour. Once the idea of long-term acclimatization was seriously challenged in the post-1858 era, British policy in India created and encouraged enclaves in various locations, not only in the hill-stations but also in 'European-only' social and architectural sites in the civil lines, cantonments and particular residential areas in the 'white towns'. These enclaves were articulated in medical, social, sanitary and strategic terms. The layout of the hill-stations was different from the cantonments and 'civil stations' of colonial India. As Kennedy has pointed out, in the hill-stations British Indian architecture varied from small Swiss-style cottages to turreted and gabled Gothic buildings.[145] The cantonments and civil stations, in contrast, had wide, straight roads and ordered homogeneous residential bungalows and barracks. But despite dissimilarities in architecture and the layout between the civil stations and the hill-stations, in crucial aspects the hill-stations after all duplicated the civil stations – their marked architectural difference and physical distance from native towns and settlements, plenty of free, airy spaces and the availability of sewerage – all of which contributed to their perceived relative salubrity. So can we see the hill-station as a part of the continuum of the civil station, the civil lines, trips to the sea and going home to England for the British in India? It seems likely. The climate of the hill-stations provided respite from the heat of the Indian plains to European bodies, but as we have seen, their settlement and colonization had greater economic implications. It was not a coincidence that planters in Darjeeling had a strident advocate of hill sanatoriums at various forums in

---

145 Kennedy, *The Magic Mountains*, p. 3.

mid-nineteenth century London, one Hyde Clarke, who termed himself 'Agent for British settlers in Darjeeling'.[146]

One example will illustrate the processes that contributed to the colonization of Darjeeling. In 1875, one Reverend Ayerst corresponded with the government of Bengal on the subject of a European settlement near Sitong at Kurseong. His concern, he explained to the governor of Bengal, was the 'destitution' and moral corruption among the poor white Europeans in India; a subtext of concern was undoubtedly the miscegenation that invariably ensued with the lack of social status in a 'white' population.[147] He explained that 'the only way to raise them from pauperism and the influence of heathenism would be to gather them into the community of a Christian village with a quasi-English climate'.[148] The government granted him permission to look for suitable land for a European farming settlement in the lower slopes of Darjeeling, and Ayerst contemplated that the proposed grant of land would be divided into a 'Home Farm' specializing in dairy farming and small allotments of good farming land to all volunteer settlers.[149] The deputy commissioner of Darjeeling confided his misgivings about the project to the superior:

> I have very grave doubts as to whether the project could be successful under any circumstances in any part of these hills ... it is very unlikely that Europeans of any class could work ... on the hill side during the rains without serious danger to their health.[150]

The prospect of Europeans, even the indigent and the supposedly consequently immoral ones, undertaking hard manual labour in any part of the tropics was impossible. But when Ayerst was finally refused the grant of land from the government, he was informed that

> Among many other objections there is this, that almost all the available lands in the Darjeeling district have been taken up for tea plantations or cinchona plantations or Government forest reserves ... If persons with some little means were to obtain small grants of land, whereon to settle, experience in Darjeeling shows that such grants gradually become absorbed into larger properties belonging to capitalists or to companies.[151]

---

146 Hyde Clarke, 'Colonisation of British India', *Journal of the Society of Arts*, 7 (1859), p. 645. See also by the same author, 'On Hill Settlements and Sanitaria', *Journal of the Society of Arts*, 17 (1869); 'The English Stations in the Hill Regions of India: Their Value and Importance, with Some Statistics of Their Products and Trade', *Journal of the Statistical Society of London*, 44 (1881), pp. 528–73.
147 Letter from Deputy Commissioner, Darjeeling to Commissioner of Rajshahye and Cooch Behar Division, 15 April 1876, Government of Bengal, A Proceedings, General Department, June 1876 (WBSA), p. 107.
148 Letter from Deputy Commissioner, p. 107.
149 Letter from Deputy Commissioner, p. 108.
150 Letter from Deputy Commissioner, p. 109.
151 Letter from Deputy Commissioner, p. 109; letter from Officiating Secretary to Government of Bengal to the Revd W. Ayerst, 15 June 1876, p. 111.

While it is true that acclimatization theories were not in favour in the late nineteenth century and that this affected the final refusal of the grant of land, the entire area was in any case already appropriated within the larger colonial economy. Within a few decades of their annexation into British India, the Darjeeling foothills were taken over by tea plantations interspersed with stretches of 'reserved forest'. A larger European or Anglo-Indian settlement, the dream of an eccentric clergyman, could not be granted official sanction or assistance. When we remember that at the time of its establishment, Brian Hodgson contemplated that a settlement of Europeans 'of a poorer class' in Darjeeling hill areas would offer the opportunity for a fresh start to impoverished Europeans (it should, he had pointed out, be 'a perfect godsend to the peasantry of Ireland and Scotland'), we can only explain this if we take into account the capitalistic colonization of the region.[152] Several factors were relevant to the colonization of Darjeeling – large parts were 'settled' by immigrants from eastern Nepal, the cheapness of this immigrant labour and its abundant supply, although Darjeeling itself was relatively sparsely populated. Therefore, the colonization of the Darjeeling hills, the Duars and the Terai was effected in the context of the availability of labour on a large scale.

There was a paradox, therefore, in the construction of a European enclave in Darjeeling. Kennedy has addressed this duality by arguing that the nature of the colonial bureaucracy and the domestic life of the ruling class in colonial India demanded the labour and skills of Indians who by their very presence disrupted the idyll of a sanitary, European enclave in the hill-stations. My contention is that the European enclave, so far as the hill-station of Darjeeling was concerned, contended with tensions of a different order. The larger colonization and settlement of the Darjeeling hills was reflected in the urban settlement of Darjeeling. The tea plantations, with their British planters and Paharia labourers, contributed to the growth of population within the entire area, and thereby to the congestion of the idyllic spaces around and within the hill-station of Darjeeling. As demonstrated above, the settlement of Darjeeling from its very inception was based on logistics that included the presence of large numbers of natives. They served eventually not only as domestic labour for the Europeans, and as clerks for the civil administration, but also as plantation labourers in the tea estates. The expansion of Darjeeling and the discrepancies in medical discourses about its efficacy as a health resort, the establishment of the Eden Sanitarium, and its emergence as a social space rather than a strictly curative one, all can be situated in the context of one salient fact. The enclave of the Darjeeling hill-station existed in constant tension with the establishment of another institution, also of colonial origin: the plantation economy. It is in that sense that the idea of a European hill-station was an anomaly.

The hill-station of Darjeeling was an ostentatiously European social space. Its spacious bungalows, hotels, Mall and clubs, its picturesque views, and special municipal provisions, such as piped water from reservoirs, and exclu-

---

152 Hodgson, 'On the Colonization', p. 20.

sive medical institutions such as the Eden Sanitarium, marked it out as an area of special privilege in sharp contrast to the lack of sewage, drinking water and medical institutions that was prevalent in most of *moffusil* or urban sites in colonial India. Throughout the colonial period, Darjeeling would retain this air of exclusivity – of clean streets and a functional municipality – and access to well-maintained medical institutions, though its specific European composition would be challenged by the Indian elite.

The hill-station of Darjeeling was one aspect of the construction of a European sanitary enclave in colonial north Bengal. The other aspects were reserved forests and the tea plantations that appropriated the entire Darjeeling hills area, rendering the Reverend Ayerst's project of settling Europeans there impossible. The plantations, mostly managed by British planters and supervised by British doctors, but employing large numbers of tribal and low-caste labourers, were enclaves of large-scale colonial capital in northern Bengal. The tea plantations, for different reasons, emerged as exclusive sites where medical research could be pursued with relative ease, as the labourers lived in a confined area. The dynamics of following preventive health measures were also different in the sites where planters' authority was supreme and the government's bureaucratic machinery played a secondary role. In that sense they, too, were 'privileged sites' of medical practice.

CHAPTER 3

Pioneering Years in Plantation and Medicine in Darjeeling, Terai and Duars

This chapter traces the expansion of tea plantations in the three 'tea districts' of northern Bengal: the Darjeeling hills, its foothills, the Terai, and contiguously in the plains of Duars. While the enclave of Darjeeling was constructed as a European escape from tropical diseases, the plantation enclave was created through modes of heroism and adventure associated with the colonization of 'diseased' lands. The plantation system of Darjeeling and Duars marked a break from the existing agrarian policies and practices of the colonial government in India. Agrarian revenue represented the mainstay of income for the colonial government. From the mid-nineteenth century, with commercialization of agriculture and the integration of colonial India with the global economy, new models of agrarian practice were consolidated. These included the leasing of previously uncultivated (although not unoccupied) land, designated as 'wastelands' to mostly British private entrepreneurs, and the introduction of plantation crops and methods. Encouraged by government land grants, entrepreneurs introduced plantation crops such as tea and coffee, cinchona, and commercialized farming of apples and strawberries. Their cultivation benefitted from extensive research on transplantation and acclimatization of foreign species in different parts of the British Empire. Therefore, although the tea plantations were huge isolated tracts with a few resident planters and thousands of labourers, they were also part of important economic and structural changes in other parts of the country. These plantations co-existed with other modes of agrarian production; for instance, agricultural labourers in the adjacent rice fields worked as casual (*basti*) labourers within the plantations in the peak seasons.

The planters and physicians employed by the tea estates lived within the estates for their working lives. Historians of the tea plantations in Assam and Bengal writing on the labour movements in the area have validated the understanding of tea plantations as enclaves of a particular kind, isolated sites where

Contagion and Enclaves

the labourers had little freedom of mobility, and where the rule of the planter was sovereign, even in the non-contractual northern Bengal tea plantations.[1] Their remote location, difficult terrain, the characteristics of the plantation economy and the supportive but distant role of the colonial state informed medical praxis in the plantations. They were enclaves of colonial capitalism and of distinct habitation, for the management as well as the labourers, in different ways. This influenced the context of medical care in the plantations in the pioneering foundational years.

Northern Bengal as a whole was undergoing structural changes in terms of agricultural practices and demography and becoming enclaves of the colonial state. The study of these processes of change enables us to understand the permeability that existed between the enclaves and the world beyond, which was central to both the functioning of the enclave economy as well as its medical regimes.

The Formation of Plantation Enclaves in Northern Bengal

The beginnings of the colonization and settlement of Darjeeling and Terai in northern Bengal in the nineteenth century was discussed in the preceding chapter. The extension of British territories in northern Bengal by the accession of western Duars from Bhutan after 1865 led to the formation of the district of Jalpaiguri in 1869, and the emergence of a new tea industry after 1874. This newly acquired territory, Duars (later western Duars, to distinguish it from the neighbouring tract in Assam), emerged as the site of tea plantations, claimed for the most part from forests interspersed with villages where small communities of the indigenous Meches and Garos resided. At this time they practised shifting cultivation and herded buffaloes, while a few villages had a settled population of Rajbanshis and Meches who cultivated paddy.[2]

In 1864 the government appointed the first Conservator of Forests in Bengal. In the next few decades his office drew up several plans for the management and consolidation of the forests of Darjeeling and Duars for timber and other forest products. In Darjeeling the 'settlement' of the area involved the gradual displacement of the Lepchas and placement of migrants from eastern Nepal and parts of Bhutan. The parts of the districts in Darjeeling, Duars and Terai that were not reserved for forests were parcelled out as 'wasteland' to tea companies at nominal rates of revenue. Some of the land was also settled for *jotedari* (peasant-cultivator) tenure where *adhiars* (peasant-sharecroppers) cultivated jute and rice under the *jotedars*. Throughout the nineteenth century the area under the plough and the tea estates expanded; as did its population. While most of the *jotedars* were initially composed of agrarian entrepreneurs from

1 Amalendu Guha, *Planter-Raj to Swaraj: Freedom Struggle and Electoral Politics in Assam 1826–1947* (New Delhi, Indian Council for Historical Research, 1977), pp. 40–45. See Das Gupta, *Economy, Society, and Politics*, p. 69.
2 Ray, *Transformations*, pp. 21–22.

the neighbouring districts of Dinajpur and Rangpur and *adhiars* from the neighbouring Cooch Behar, over the decades much of the land was held by ex-tea-garden labourers who often worked under their *sardars* (recruiter-foremen) who owned *jotes* near the tea estates. Throughout this process the indigenous Meches and Garos migrated eastwards into the district of Goalpara in Assam, while Oraons, Santhals and Mundas migrated from the poverty-struck district of Chotanagpur to western Duars to work on the tea estates.[3]

The period when forests were being cleared and the tea bushes planted, with labourers requisitioned through *sardars* from the catchment areas, can be described as the 'pioneering' years. The tea companies borrowed the structures of the layout of the tea estates and their management ethos from previous experiences of tea planting in Assam, but were distinct in one particular feature: the recruitment of non-indentured labour.[4] The first commercial plantations were laid out in Darjeeling around 1856, but new plantations continued to mushroom in certain parts of western Duars until the first two decades of the twentieth century. I have found it analytically useful to examine medical praxis within the plantation enclaves in the 'pioneering years' across the period, because they had similar characteristics: remote, often inaccessible locations, large groups of immigrant labourers who lived in settlements under the watch of their *sardars*, and the ad hoc nature of medical care. The contexts of medical care in the pioneering years were similar in all the tea plantations, as were the principles on which the system of medical care was initially set out. Both the western Duars and Darjeeling (which district included the Terai) were Non-Regulation tracts, where the ordinary laws passed in Bengal were not applicable until a special order from the Governor of Bengal was passed. The administrative executive in charge of the district, therefore, was not the District Magistrate, as in other districts, but the Deputy Commissioner, invested with greater civil authority than the District Magistrates in the Non-Regulation districts.[5] This was a significant factor in the disease management within the plantations, for the district officer-in-charge often had a freer hand in making decisions in the Non-Regulation tracts. The tea plantations within Non-Regulation tracts were under an administration that could make immediate decisions. The British administrators here socially interacted with the European plantation management regularly and as a matter of course. On the whole, the district administration was content to let the plantation managers take responsibility for law and order and general governance within the tea estates.

3   For the commercialization of agriculture in colonial Bengal, see Bose, *Peasant Labour*, pp. 45–65. The argument of increasing differentiation in the agrarian peasantry is borrowed from Das Gupta, *Economy, Society, and Politics*, pp. 29–52, and Ray, *Transformations*, pp. 142–48.
4   Assam tea was first successfully manufactured in 1837. The Waste Land Rules of 1838 and 1854 facilitated the commercialization of large tracts of land for tea cultivation in Assam. The Workmen's Breach of Contract Act of 1859 facilitated the immigration of labourers from outside in the Assam tea plantations. See Guha, *Planter-Raj*, pp. 12–18.
5   Subba, *The Quiet Hills*, pp. 39–40; Das Gupta, *Economy, Society, and Politics*, p. 7.

Contagion and Enclaves

One instance of how the relegation of authority of the district administration to the management of the tea plantations could influence issues in health and habitation within the plantations at a basic level was the registration of vital statistics within the plantations. The Chaukidari Act was not applied within the tea estates; the managers assumed responsibility for the registration of vital statistics.[6] When the provincial government sought to extend the provisions of the Chaukidari Act to the tea plantation areas of Darjeeling, Terai, and Duars in 1893, the Darjeeling and Duars subcommittee of the Indian Tea Association protested vigorously. They represented to the Governor of Bengal that 'the intrusion of *chaukidars* appointed by the district commissioner is unnecessary and harassing'.[7] Although labourers were not under indentured contract in northern Bengal, their mobility between plantations was restricted informally by the managements. In Duars, Terai and Darjeeling, this was to limit as much as possible the migration of *sardars* with their coolies en masse to other plantations, limit the interactions of workers with potential 'political agitators' and circumscribe the role of government in the administration of the plantations as much as possible.

The district administration relied on the management to provide them with the vital statistics, and as we shall see later, some kind of inspection was introduced in the Duars in 1912 only after two reports seriously implicated the plantation management in the neglect of registration of vital statistics. In the Darjeeling and Terai, there were no such rules for allowing independent government inspections on a regular basis. Both the practicalities of administration and the social links with the British planters informed the government–plantation interactions at the district level. Interaction between European planters and British officials was frequent in everyday events, whether at social venues in Darjeeling town or polo at the Jalpaiguri club. This facilitated easy communication and trust. For instance, when the manager of Fagoo Tea Estate requested the Deputy Commissioner of Darjeeling to confirm a grant of lease even though he did not have 15 per cent planted with tea as required by law, he added a postscript about his holiday fishing in Hertfordshire.[8] John Tyson, posted at Jalpaiguri in the 1920s, made careful distinctions between shades of white among British officials and accepted hospitality from and attended *shikar* and football matches with the British planters in the Duars regularly.[9] The few

6 The village *chaukidar* (watchman) was appointed under the provisions of the Village Chaukidari Act 1870 (Bengal Act VI of 1870). The Births, Deaths, and Marriages Act (1886) extended to the whole of British India. Under the Act every birth, death and marriage had to be reported to the proper authority. 'However the reporting was voluntary not compulsory', Ray, *History of Public Health*, p. 40.
7 See Chairman's address, *Detailed Report of the General Committee of the Indian Tea Association for the End of 1893 with the Proceedings of the Annual General Meeting of April 1893* (Calcutta, W.J. Pinheiro, Cones & Co. Press, 1893, APAC), p. iv (hereafter *ITAAR*).
8 Letter from Manager, Fagoo Tea Estate, Sailihat, 6 Nov. 1899, to Deputy Commissioner Jalpaiguri, District Magistrate's Record Room, Darjeeling, General Department, Collection no. II (Settlement), file no. 2.
9 Ray, *Transformations*, p. 92.

Indian planters in the Duars and Terai (there were none in Darjeeling) resented and envied the British planters this easy source of patronage.[10]

Environmental conditions contributed to the relative freedom of the plantation management from regular government intervention. The plantation enclaves were situated in isolated areas, in terrains broken by seasonal streams and rivers, and interrupted by jungles. This made access difficult and time-consuming, to be avoided unless strictly necessary. Even more crucially, the management of the plantation enclaves were fiercely protective of their autonomous space and guarded against regulation or unsolicited advice – administrative, medical or any other. The planters established and sustained this autonomy throughout, assisted by both the remote locations of the plantation enclaves as well as by the careful construction of the trope of the manager as the paternalistic figurehead. In management discourse, the planters earned this title because the *sardars* and the labourers transferred their feudal loyalties to the manager, who earned it as a burden of his office and sustained it through the accumulation of his knowledge of the land and the labourers who lived and worked on that land.

Plantation autonomy had military dimensions. In the Duars and Terai, British planters and medical officials served in the North Bengal Mounted Rifles (NBMR), a voluntary armed force that the government created initially to defend the frontier against Bhutan. The planters used the NBMR to discipline and curb the mobility of labourers.[11] Police interference within the plantation enclaves was rare and only occurred on invitation. The management called the district police only in cases of rioting, which were very infrequent in both Duars and Darjeeling in the pioneering phase.[12]

The characteristics of plantation enclaves, of which autonomy was prominent, influenced medical infrastructure and epidemic control within, and occasionally proved a source of contention with government. As the plantations expanded their profits and output their populations rose as well, changing both their requirements for medical care and the extent of government intervention in public health in the plantations.

Expansion of Tea Cultivation in Northern Bengal

As early as 1834 a Tea Committee was appointed by the Governor General William Bentinck to 'inquire into and report on the possibility of introducing the cultivation of tea into India'.[13] After a few aborted experiments, a tea *garden*, as it was termed, was established in Sibsagar in Assam, which was later sold

10 B.C. Ghose, *The Development of Tea Industry in the District of Jalpaiguri 1869–1968* (Jalpaiguri, B.C. Ghose, 1970), p. 34.
11 Das Gupta, *Economy, Society, and Politics*, p. 68.
12 J.C. Arbuthnott, *Report on the Conditions of Tea Garden Labour in the Duars of Bengal, in Madras, and in Ceylon* (Shilling, Assam Secretariat Printing Office, 1904), p. 9.
13 W.W. Hunter, *A Statistical Account of Bengal, Vol. X., Districts of Darjiling and Jalpaiguri, & State of Kuch Behar* (London, Trubner & Co., 1876), p. 164.

to the Assam tea company in 1840.[14] Jayeeta Sharma has argued in the case of Assam that the nomenclature 'garden' implied an ordering and claiming of the land from forest, an articulation of the dichotomy between civilization and the wild, uncivilized.[15] I have found it more useful to stay with their formal nomenclature of tea estate, which reflects on the social relations of production within the plantations.

With some initiatives from the Superintendent of Darjeeling, Archibald Campbell, and with the policy of grant of lease of land for tea at nominal costs (a feature of tea industry in Assam and Duars and Terai as well), the commercial manufacture of tea in Darjeeling took off in the mid-nineteenth century. The gradual conversion of land to tea cultivation occurred through European enterprise, comprising to a great extent of retired officials – civil, medical and military personnel as well as entrepreneurs such as Johanne Wernicke.[16]

The tea industry in Darjeeling attracted diverse entrepreneurs, but they were all Europeans; that is to say, they were white, and originally from Western Europe. The government gave away land first as 'farming leases' in 1858 for a period of fifty years, at a token rent of eight annas per acre after five years.[17] Next, it formulated the first Waste Land Rules in Darjeeling district in 1859 and auctioned as freehold, large tracts designated 'wastelands', including forests and lands formerly cultivated for maize by Lepchas at the nominal price of Rs 10 per acre.[18] Between 1859 and 1861 it sold around 9000 acres of 'wasteland'. In 1861, the government introduced the 'fee-simple' which regarded wastelands in perpetuity as 'heritable and transferable' property, subject to no enhancement of land revenue; and there was no condition 'obliging the grantee to cultivate or clear any specific portion within any specific time'.[19] The Waste Land Rules permitted large-scale speculation because it legislated that only 15 per cent of the lease needed to be planted with tea. Many speculators claimed and staked out 'waste-lands' without cultivating them. In the 1860s, speculations, partially laid out tea gardens and the prospect of huge profits and quick money without going through the process of manufacturing the tea were common, and a contemporary planter remarked that 'At Darjeeling ... you will find generally that there are two utterly distinct systems carried out; one for those plantations which, like the peddler's razors, are intended for sale; and one for those which are intended, if possible, to pay'.[20]

Planters' memoirs from Darjeeling give some idea of the individuals who formed the planters' community in Darjeeling, Terai and the Duars. The Werner-

14 Hunter, *A Statistical Account*, p. 165.
15 Jayeeta Sharma, 'An European Tea "Garden" and an Indian "frontier": The Discovery of Assam', occasional paper no. 6, University of Cambridge, Centre for South Asian Studies, Cambridge, 2002.
16 Hunter, *A Statistical Account*, p. 165. See also, Dozey, *A Concise History*, pp. 196–97.
17 O'Malley, *Bengal District Gazetteers*, pp. 189–90.
18 O'Malley, *Bengal District Gazetteers*, p. 190.
19 O'Malley, *Bengal District Gazetteers*, pp. 190–91.
20 E.F. Bamber, *An Account of the Cultivation and Manufacture of Tea in India, from Personal Observation* (Calcutta, T.S. Smith, 1866), p. 1.

Table 3.1 Expansion of tea gardens in Darjeeling

Year	Gardens	Land cultivation (ac.)	Out-turn (lbs)	Labourers
1866	39	10,392	433,715	N/A
1867	40	9,214	582,640	N/A
1868	44	10,067	851,549	6,859
1869	55	10,769	1,278,869	7,445
1870	56	11,046	1,689,186	8,347
1871	N/A	N/A	N/A	N/A
1872	74	14,503	2,938,626	12,361
1873	87	15,695	2,956,710	14,019
1874	113	18,888	3,927,911	19,424

Source: Hunter, *A Statistical Account of Bengal,* vol. X, p. 165.

Stolke family, ex-missionaries and contractors in the first generation, were planters in the second generation. Both the Wernicke brothers joined as assistant managers in the Tukvar and the Makaibari tea gardens in 1865–67. Soon they leased plantations of their own at 'quite a nominal figure': they obtained 550 acres for Rs 60 (£40), claimed from 'native cultivation, chiefly of maize, and partly jungle'.[21]

In 1864 government introduced leases in Darjeeling for tea for a period of 30 years, the land being rent-free for the initial five years, and then an annual rate of 6 annas per acre on the whole area under lease.[22] Despite a slump in the tea industry in India between 1861 and 1866, the acreage in Darjeeling continued to expand and tea plantations expanded to the Terai.[23] After the initial decades of speculation in wasteland, government finally amended the rules for grants in 1898 when preliminary leases were given only after the lessee showed that he had enough capital to develop the land, and after five years a 30-year lease was granted in perpetuity on condition of cultivating tea in at least 15 per cent of the land.[24] Table 3.1 delineates the growth of the tea industry in Darjeeling.[25]

The increase in the acreage under tea, the net production of tea and the numbers of labourers to work in the tea plantations between 1866 and 1874 was spectacular. Even the genuine tea estates that did not speculate in wastelands did not use all of their land; after all, they were only required to cultivate a mere 15 per cent. The planters used the fallow and forested areas within their estates for forest products for various purposes from making tea chests to providing firewood for the labourers settled in the estates.[26] The labourers

21 'The Wernicke-Stolke Story', Mss Photo Eur 421 (APAC), p. 10.
22 O'Malley, *Bengal District Gazetteers*, p. 191.
23 Percival Griffiths, *History of the Indian Tea Industry* (London, Weidenfeld & Nicolson, 1967), p. 88.
24 O'Malley, *Bengal District Gazetteers*, pp. 192–93.
25 Hunter, *A Statistical Account*, p. 165.
26 This scheme of lease of large tracts of land of which only a portion would be used for

were generally Nepalis of various communities – Mangars, Limbus, Rais and so forth who migrated from eastern Nepal. From the outset, the relatively easy access to labour facilitated a system of free rather than indentured labour in the tea industry in northern Bengal.[27] This was extremely useful for the tea companies because immigration from Nepal was far simpler than the system of importing indentured labourers from the tribal areas of Chotanagpur and Santhal Parganas that was prevalent in Assam.

The pioneering, entrepreneurial years in Darjeeling lent opportunities to Europeans from various classes and backgrounds to find an occupation and settle in Darjeeling and in Terai. They also joined the tea companies either as assistant managers and managers in the agency houses or as owner-planters. Later many of the owner-planters turned to the large agency houses for financial support and some sold their plantations or formed joint stock companies with registered offices in Glasgow or London. They represented 'white capital' that dominated enterprise in eastern India at this time.[28] The agency houses recruited European managers to the plantations; the owners in the Darjeeling plantations, too, were all European. The British ambience of nearby Darjeeling lent a comfortable prospect to work on the tea estates in the surrounding areas.[29]

The tea planters of Darjeeling formed an association of employers, the Darjeeling Planters' Association in 1892. The Darjeeling Planters' Association affiliated itself to the principal body of tea producers in India, the Indian Tea Association, in 1910.[30] From 1892 the Indian Tea Association, a separate body, formed a Darjeeling and Dooars subcommittee which represented the Darjeeling, Terai and Duars tea planters. From the high slopes of the Darjeeling mountains, the success of the earliest tea plantations led to the expansion of the tea plantations to the lower slopes, and later on to the foothills of the notoriously unhealthy Terai.[31] At the turn of the century, the slopes and the drier tracts of the Terai were cleared for tea gardens as well as the cultivation of rice and other crops such as maize and potatoes. In 1853, in the first settlement of the Darjeeling Terai, Archibald Campbell made grants of land to cultivators for ten years.[32] In 1863 he made several grants for tea plantations under Waste Land Rules, as in Darjeeling. The tea plantations paid a very low rate of

---

tea, while the rest of the produce of the land was given to tea companies for the free use of timber, firewood, land for their labourers and grazing, had also been taken from the Assam model. In Assam the proportion was a quarter of the land to be under tea in the first five years. Guha, *Planter-Raj*, p. 13.

27 R.L. Sarkar and Mahendra P. Lama (eds), *Tea Plantation Workers in the Eastern Himalayas – A Study on Wages, Employment and Living Standards* (Delhi, Atma Ram, 1986), p. 5. See also Subba, *The Quiet Hills*, pp. 14–15.
28 Amiya Bagchi, *Private Investment in India, 1900–1939* (London, Routledge, 2000), pp. 161–62.
29 Baildon, *The Tea Industry*, pp. 35–39.
30 *The Darjeeling Branch Tea Association 1873–1973*, Mss Eur F/174/685 (APAC).
31 Griffiths, *History*, p. 88.
32 J.C. Mitra, *Final Report on the Survey and Settlement Operations in the Darjeeling Terai, 1919–25* (Calcutta, Government Secretariat Press, 1927), p. 21.

Pioneering Years in Plantation and Medicine in Darjeeling, Terai and Duars

1. Ging Tea Plantation, Darjeeling.—2. Weighing the Leaf.—3. Plucking the Leaf.—4. Rolling by Hand.—5. Withering in the Sun.—6. Rolling by Machinery.—7. Withering in the Factory.—8. Sorting by Machinery.

TEA CULTIVATION IN BRITISH INDIA

Figure 3.1 Production of Tea, Ging Tea Estate, Darjeeling

lease at Re 1–8 annas per acre of lands under tea.[33] The actual numbers of tea gardens and acreage under tea in the Darjeeling Terai is difficult to estimate because they were enumerated with the tea gardens in the Darjeeling hill area,

33 Mitra, *Final Report*, p. 29.

both being included for administrative purposes, in the district of Darjeeling. In 1925, the acreage under tea was 18,467.55 acres, and formed 22 per cent of the total area under *jotes* and grants.[34] The labourers in the Terai plantations comprised both Nepalis and those hired through contractors from the Chotanagpur and Santhal Parganas districts. The Terai Tea Planters' Association at the turn of the century, 1901–02, represented the industry to government, and facilitated recruitment of labour from the catchment area of Chotanagpur.[35]

After its annexation into British territory the western Duars was amalgamated into the new district of Jalpaiguri in 1869. A section of the Jalpaiguri district incorporated older, settled territory, which differed little in topography or cultivation from the neighbouring districts of Rangpur and Dinajpur. Here the agrarian system of revenue collection was different from the rest of Bengal; the government chose not to implement the Permanent Settlement and instead negotiated directly with the peasants.[36] In western Duars, the government became the zamindar (landlord). As *jotedars* took over large parts of the lands formerly cultivated by the local Meches (who were pushed into eastern Duars, Goalpara in Assam), the differentiation among the peasantry between the bigger *jotedar* and the *adhiar* (sharecropper) increased. Through the nineteenth century into the first decades of the twentieth, when the final settlement for the region was made, sub-infeudation of cultivable lands occurred at several levels leading to a hierarchy of peasant-landholders between the *jotedar* and the *adhiar* such as the *chukanidar* and the *dar-chukanidar*.[37] Commercialization of land occurred at a rapid pace after the annexation into the British territories. The author of the district gazetteer commented in 1911 that

> Few districts in India have developed as rapidly as the Western Duars. The northern tract along the base of the hills … is now covered by prosperous tea-gardens, separated only by rivers or occasional areas of reserved forest; east of the Torsa the chain of tea gardens continues right up to the Sankos river … South of the tea gardens as far east as the Torsha river … nearly the whole of the land is under cultivation and grows magnificent crops of rice, jute, tobacco, and mustard … even in this remote part of the district, cultivation is increasing fast, and the jungle disappearing rapidly.[38]

The tea plantation enclaves in the Duars after 1896 were under the Waste Land Rules, similar to the rules in the Darjeeling and Terai district. The lessee paid a fee of Re 1 per acre as the cost for a survey and obtained a preliminary five-year lease, which was rent-free in the first year, three annas per acre in the second

---

34 Mitra, *Final Report*, p. 13.
35 'History of the Terai Planters' Association and the Terai Branch Indian Tea Association', cyclostyled manuscript (Terai Branch of Indian Tea Association Office, Bengdubi, n.d.), p. 1.
36 Das Gupta, *Economy, Society, and Politics*, p. 27.
37 Ray, *Transformations*, pp. 161–62.
38 John F. Grunig, *Eastern Bengal and Assam District Gazetteer* (Allahabad, Pioneer Press, 1911), p. 3.

year and an additional three annas for each successive year.[39] After five years, if inspection confirmed that at least 15 per cent of the land was under tea cultivation, the lessee was entitled to a 30-year lease to be renewed in perpetuity. The rents for tea lands in the Western Duars were much lower than the agrarian revenue rates (for rice, jute etc.) in the district.[40] The plantations were charged land rent for only the portion of land that was planted with tea, the rest being classified as 'waste'. Apart from the value of forest produce, which was used both for production of tea and by the tea estate labourers, this left the plantations with the option of extending acreage under tea without paying rent for 30 years after the survey.[41]

In 1878, within four years of the first grant of lease, the European planters established the 'Dooars Planters Association' (DPA).[42] Large agency houses like Duncan Brothers and Octavius Steele controlled many tea plantations in Darjeeling, Terai and the Duars.[43] There were also a number of European-owned smaller tea companies in all the tea districts. Unlike the Darjeeling area, where the tea plantations were, 'conducted almost entirely by means of English capital and under skilled European supervision', from almost the very beginning it involved Indian entrepreneurs.[44] In 1879 a group of Bengali professionals, mostly lawyers based in Jalpaiguri, formed a joint stock company, the Jalpaiguri Tea Company, and petitioned for a lease for a tea garden.[45] They were supported by an Indian official, Bhagaban Chandras Bose, who was at that time a Deputy Magistrate at Jalpaiguri.[46] The lease of the first Indian-managed tea garden, the Mogalkata Tea Estate, was granted in 1881 and consisted of 741 acres. Several more Indian companies procured leases and established tea plantations in subsequent years, but the acreage under Indian entrepreneurship remained small in comparison

---

39 Grunig, *Eastern Bengal*, p. 85.
40 Das Gupta, *Economy, Society, and Politics*, p. 58.
41 Ray, *Transformations*, p. 76.
42 *Dooars Branch Indian Tea Association, 1878–1978, Centenary Annual General Meeting* (Binnaguri, DBITA, n.d.), p. 1.
43 At the turn of the century, the agency house of Duncan Brothers, for instance, controlled 25 tea gardens with a total acreage of 18,690 acres of tea. Griffiths, *History*, p. 117. Bagchi has noted a concentration of capital in coal, jute and tea, the principal industries in eastern India under British managing agencies, with interlocking directorships, market-sharing and control of labour supply. Bagchi (2002), pp. 170–81. After 1914 Indian entrepreneurships challenged the managing agencies' monopoly in jute and coal, but not in tea. See Omkar Goswami, 'Sahibs, Babus, and Banias: Changes in Industrial Control in Eastern India, 1918–50', *Journal of Asian Studies*, 48 (1989), pp. 289–309. At its height the Indian ownership of the plantations did not exceed one-fifth of the total acreage in Duars. In Darjeeling district, where the less lucrative Terai tea estates were located, British firms sold the less profitable tea gardens to Indian entrepreneurs. But the overwhelming majority of acreage under tea was under British ownership.
44 Quoted from the *Imperial Gazetteer of India*, Provincial Series, Bengal, vol. 2 (Calcutta, 1909), p. 201.
45 Ghose, 'Development of the Tea Industry', p. 14.
46 Kamakhya Prosad Chakraborty, *Shekaler Jalpaiguri Shohor Ebong Samajik Jibaner Kichu Katha* (Jalpaiguri, n.d.), p. 22.

to that of the British-owned plantations, never exceeding one-fifth of the total in Duars and far less in Terai. The Bengali entrepreneurs competed with the British tea companies and felt very keenly their lack of capital. They resented the comparative ease with which the British planters could access government officials and support.[47] The DPA did not include any Indian managers or companies among its members, although from around 1917 it invited a few Indian planters as guests to its annual meetings. The Indian entrepreneurs formed their own employers' organization, the Indian Tea Planters' Association (ITPA), to represent their interests as well as to spare themselves petty humiliations from the British planters.[48] As one Indian planter recounted,

> In 1918 the Jalpaiguri Tea Planters felt the need of an Association exclusively ... for the English Planters ... the DPA ... refused to give equal rights to Indian planters ... in matters of common interest. In fact an Indian Tea Planter in those days had to get down from his pony or tandem [a two-wheeled vehicle driven by a horse] if an English planter came in the same road from the opposite direction.[49]

The racial indignities suffered by the largely educated and Westernized class from which the Bengalis planters were drawn gave an edge to the rivalries between the DPA and the ITPA. The conflicts between the two employers' bodies flared especially when it was a question of the defection of labour from British tea gardens to Indian ones. Nonetheless, the two employers' bodies actively cooperated on various issues when common interests were at stake, especially in negotiations with government on medical policy and sanitation within the estates.

The tea plantations were responsible for changing the demography of the Duars permanently. The emerging public health and sanitation concerns were shaped as much by these demographic changes as by the perceived unhealthiness of the site. The tea plantations in the Duars, unlike those in Assam, did not employ indentured labour. As in Darjeeling and Terai, the Duars tea plantations also at first recruited Nepali labourers, but with rapid expansion soon had to recruit from the same areas as the Assam planters: the Chotanagpur and Santhal Parganas.[50] The recruitment from specific regions is significant because colonial discourse constructed and sustained racial typologies with reference to the labourers' bodies in terms of susceptibility to diseases, work

---

47 Amiya Kumar Bagchi has argued that the agency houses which controlled British capital in colonial India set themselves as socially and culturally distinct from native entrepreneurs in the twentieth century, and was supported by sections of the administration. See Bagchi, *Private Investment*, p. 28. But not all the planters joined the ITPA initially; there was a Hindu–Muslim divide, with Nawab Mosharraff Hossain, a *jotedar* and planter, staying away from it. He joined the ITPA at a later stage. See *Indian Tea Planters' Association Golden Jubilee Souvenir* (Jalpaiguri, ITPA, 1965), p. 10.
48 *Indian Tea Planters' Association Golden Jubilee Souvenir*, pp. 25–30.
49 Ghose, 'Development of the Tea Industry', p. 80.
50 Griffiths, *History*, p. 115.

Pioneering Years in Plantation and Medicine in Darjeeling, Terai and Duars

and immunity; and these continued to inform policy and praxis in the postcolonial period.

From the very beginning, a structural permeability had been worked into the system by which the labourers and their recruiter-foreman (*sardar*) could legally move from one plantation to another; and gangs of labourers with their *sardar* could join the plantation workforce at the peak season and be dispensed with in the lean period. This helped the plantations to secure a mobile workforce that might live and work as small peasant-cultivators in *bastis* (villages) outside the plantations but provide extra labour at the peak season to the plantations. The peasant economy survived on the subsidiary cultivation of rice and jute located around the tea plantations. The element of non-contractual labour is also important in northern Bengal plantations, because since the labourers were legally free, the government eschewed intervention within the plantations. In addition this form of recruitment provided the northern Bengal tea planters with a morally elevated position in the context of the coercion practised by the neighbouring Assam planters.[51] In Darjeeling the labourers were immigrants from eastern Nepal. In the Terai region, too, labour was free, and initially Nepali immigrant labourers worked in the foothills. Only later on in the twentieth century did the Terai Planters Association recruit labourers from the Chotanagpur and Santhal Parganas areas through the Tea Districts Labour Association. In the Duars, where the local Meches and Garos were thought to be both inadequate in numbers and unwilling to work in the tea plantations, immigrant labourers were recruited. The tea plantations close to the foothills used Nepali labourers, while the rest recruited entire families from Chotanagpur and Santhal Parganas through *sardars*.[52] The absence of a legal period of contract and, consequently, the notion of free labour informed all official negotiations between the tea plantation management and the district administration. For instance, when the government instituted an enquiry into the mode of recruitment through the *sardari* system in Assam in 1895 because of reports of coercion in the recruitment process, the northern Bengal tea districts of Darjeeling, Terai and Duars were exempted from close scrutiny.[53] The Commission concluded that since labour here was free, 'very little action on the part of Government is, at present, necessary'.[54] The free labour situation ensured that for a long time there were no properly enforced vital statistics recorded within the tea plantations in Duars, Darjeeling or Terai.[55]

51 Griffiths, an agent of British tea planters, pointed out that 'the experience of the disadvantages of the penal contract which had been gained by planters in Assam' probably contributed to the system of non-contractual labour in the Duars. See Griffiths, *History*, pp. 284–85.The planters in Darjeeling petitioned for a 'limited' contractual system. Nationalist agitations on the coercion and gross abuses of the system in Assam deterred the government from legislation.
52 Grunig, *Eastern Bengal*, pp. 107–9.
53 *Report of the Labour Enquiry Commission*, Calcutta, 1896 (APAC), p. 51.
54 *Report of the Labour Enquiry Commission*, p. 51.
55 In 1911, the district gazetteer of Jalpaiguri stated the government's position: 'With free

Contagion and Enclaves

Table 3.2 Expansion of tea gardens in the Duars

Year	Gardens	Area under tea (ac.)	Approx. production (lbs)	Labourers
1874	1	–	–	–
1876	13	818	29,520	–
1881	55	6230	1,027,116	–
1892	182	38,583	18,278,628	–
1901	235	76,403	31,087,537	68,619
1907	180	81,338	45,196,814	–
1911	191	90,859	48,820,637	75,315
1921	131	112,688	43,287,187	88,564
1931	151	132,074	66,447,715	112,591

Source: Das Gupta, *Economy, Society, and Politics*, p. 57.

Although the tea plantations in northern Bengal were grouped within their respective planters' associations, they often poached labour from among themselves by providing inducements to the *sardars*. This made the calculation of labourers within individual tea plantations very difficult. Additionally, the autonomy of the plantation enclaves in keeping records of its vital statistics made records of birth, death and sickness rates within the plantations impossible to verify independently. Nor was there any pressing need to do so. Without reliable vital statistics, and in the absence of intervention from the district administration to enforce a system of accurate recording of vital statistics, preventive health and sanitation, clean water supply or vaccinations were largely absent. The lack of legislation or government interventions at the district level sustained a system that was ad hoc and in which the responsibility of individual managers of the plantations was minimized. The rapid increase in population within the tea estates (and in the villages outside, where tenant-cultivators flooded in to grow rice and jute) in the late nineteenth and early twentieth centuries changed the demography of the district drastically. The Deputy Commissioner of Jalpaiguri informed the Labour Enquiry Commission in 1895 that 'Between 1881 and 1891 the population of the western Duars of Jalpaiguri and the Darjeeling Terai increased by 124,809 people, or 50 per cent, whereas the total average of Lower Bengal showed 7.3 per cent of increase'.[56]

---

labour it is unnecessary for Government to reserve the right of inspection, or in interference in the matter of wages, tasks, or the general management of estates'. Grunig, *Eastern Bengal*, p. 9.

56 Grunig, *Eastern Bengal*, p. 9.

Pioneering Years in Plantation and Medicine in Darjeeling, Terai and Duars

Enclaves, Paternalism and Plantation Medicine

In the pioneering phase, the colonial state intervened little within the structures of the plantation enclave system. Most early tea plantation records have not survived, and there is often little mention in government records. The government in the form of the local administration intervened only at times of crisis. Surviving management sources, however, allow us to examine this world. With a few minor differences, conditions in the pioneering years remained similar in all the tea plantations.

Initially, all the plantations had a frontier-settlement feel to them. This lasted, in the case of the Duars, until the 1920s because new tea estates continued to be established in the eastern parts of the district. In this phase, habitations within the plantations were non-existent or rudimentary for the labourers. The managers and assistant managers were accommodated in roughly constructed bungalows, usually at the centre of the tea estate.[57] The planters romanticized the pioneering phase. One anecdote is worth presenting here. Published in the *Indian Planters' Gazette*, it recounted the experience of establishing a plantation 'in the heart of the forest', building a bungalow from scratch (with the help of 'jungly aboriginals') and celebrated the idea of that bungalow being transplanted at a fresh site for another planter later.[58]

The living spaces in all plantations were segregated along racial lines. The manager and his assistants lived in bungalows at the centre, the Indian staff (clerks and the resident doctor, who were generally Bengalis) in smaller houses set apart from the bungalows, and finally the labourers in the *coolie lines*. The labourers were further separated into clusters according to their tribe and community. The coolie lines were usually located at the margins of the tea estate boundaries and comprised of huts built by the labourers themselves with bamboo and grass from the estate lands.[59]

The coolie lines were segregated to facilitate control over the labourers

---

57 Fraser, *Recollections*, pp. 45–46.
58 'It was about six years ago that a certain planter was ordered to go and open out a garden in a wild region of forest, jungle and hill torrents. He went, and pitched a small tent in the very heart of the forest, and there lived for two months under canvas, amidst the wildest scenery and jungly aborigines. He got together a lot of coolies, and commenced the planting of the tea bush. When he had matters in fair train, after a couple of months of hard toil, he bethought himself of building a bungalow. He thereupon cut up the forest trees he had felled, and laid the foundation of his house by putting into the ground the piles upon which it stands. This done, he had to cut the grass for the roof. After which he stripped jute ribbons from the canes and made himself ropes for the purpose of binding the bamboo framework, for, be it noted, that irons and nails were not to be had … this bungalow is still in existence, but it has been removed bodily from its original locality, and now adorns another garden.' Quoted from *The Indian Planters' Gazette and Sporting News*, January 1924 (APAC), p. 17.
59 G.G. Webb, who served in several tea estates in the Duars between 1908 and 1948, remembered that the only cost of building coolie lines was that of jute, 'to be converted into string, [which] could be obtained from the smallest smallholders who all grew the crop'. Mss Eur C474 (APAC).

during crises such as epidemics or riots. This liminal existence of the labourers vis-à-vis the plantations played an important role in the control of epidemics and labour unrest as well as conducting medical research. Claude Bald, whose manual of instruction for tea planters in India went through several reprints, recommended that

> If possible, coolies should be located in villages at various points on the estate, rather than congregated on one or two points only. There are various reasons for this. It is much easier to control and restrict the scope of any epidemic which may break out at any time if an affected village can be immediately segregated from the rest ... It is also an easier matter to deal with any insubordination or disaffection, if the labour force is divided up variously.[60]

Initially medical care for the management was probably not available immediately in the plantations. When Ashley Eden proposed the establishment of a hospital for Europeans in Darjeeling in 1881 he had in mind the fact that it would be very useful to the planters not only in Darjeeling but also 'tea planters from the unhealthy Dooars and Terai'.[61] In 1888 S.O. Bishop pointed out that planters were 'often situated away from European medical advice' in all the planting districts in northern Bengal and, with an eye to increasing his own practice, Bishop recommended that each planter should ensure a 'monthly visit from the doctor', that is, from the British physicians in private practice stationed in Darjeeling and Kurseong.[62]

As to medical care for the labourers, an anonymous manual written by a Darjeeling planter is instructive, for it reported that planters took care of the medical needs of the 'coolies' themselves, provided a list of likely ailments and recommended home remedies. It advised that a 'few simple home remedies' and 'strong medicine' were all that the labourers required.[63] The planters' emphasis was on 'heroic medicine' and advice tended towards administering purges and emetics.[64] The influence of 'heroic medicine' in the use of calomel is evident in the manual for estate owners.[65] It was part of planters' folklore that

60 Claud Bald, *Indian Tea: Its Culture and Manufacture, Being a Text Book on the Cultivation and Manufacture of Tea* (3rd edn, Calcutta, Thacker, Spink and Co., 1917), p. 302.
61 Memorandum by Ashley Eden, 11 June 1881, Government of Bengal, A Proceedings, Municipal Department Medical Branch, 1881 (WBSA), p. 5.
62 Bishop, *Medical Hints*, p. 113.
63 Anonymous, *Notes on Tea In Darjeeling by a Planter* (Darjeeling, Scotch Mission Orphanage Press), 1888, pp. 77–78. Such manuals and 'homemade remedy books' were in common use in the slave plantations of Southern USA in the antebellum period. But while white and black herbalism borrowed from each other in the American South, there is little evidence of British tea planters or doctors borrowing cures from indigenous practitioners of medicine. See Sharla M. Fett, *Working Cures; Healing, Health, and Power on Southern Slave Plantations* (Chapel Hill and London, University of North Carolina Press, 2002).
64 R.B. Sheridan, *Doctors and Slaves: A Medical and Demographic History of Slavery in the British West Indies, 1680–1834* (Cambridge, Cambridge University Press, 1985), pp. 329–32.
65 For another instance of a planters' manual which contains a list of home prescriptions, see A.F. Dowling, *Tea Notes* (Calcutta, D.M. Traill, 1885), pp. 36–40. The widespread

Table 3.3 Ailments and their cures

Medicine	Used for
bicarbonate of soda	dropsy, mosquito bites, wasp stings
carbolic acid	disinfectant, ulcers, scabies, (with oil) burns
chlorodyne	dysentery, diarrhoea
castor oil	purging
cholera mixture	cholera, dysentery
camphor	cholera, dysentery, repelling fleas, toothache
antidysenteric pills	dysentery
tincture of kino	diarrhoea, pyrosis
epsom salts	purging
jalap	dropsy, purging
alum	astringent, leech bites, emetic
friars balsam	cuts
aconite	rheumatism, neuralgia, toothache
arnica	bruises, sprains
phenyl	disinfectant, slight sores
podophyllin	sluggish liver
quinine	fever, tonic, neuralgia
santonine	worms
zinc ointment	ulcers, foul sores
ipecacuanha	emetic, cough, dysentery, insect bites
ammonia	headache, bronchitis, hornet stings, snake bites
borax	sore throats, skin diseases
cardamoms	preventing griping
glycerine	wound dressing, slight sores

Source: *Notes on Darjeeling Tea by a Planter*, pp. 77–78.

their workers were only satisfied with such therapies as were *seen* to produce an immediate physical effect, however painful and shocking they were for the patients. These therapies, such as they were, also served to inhibit all the most severely ill to seek medical help from the planters. A list of the usual home remedies advised by manuals, which were generally written by other experienced planters, are given in Table 3.3.

These and similar home remedies which the planters themselves provided to their labourers when necessary were a constituent of the construct of paternalism of the planter–coolie relationship. The instruction in such manuals was of the self-help and 'domestic' kind, featuring amateurish health-care instruction,

use of calomel for a range of non-venereal diseases, especially tropical fevers in the plantations, extended from India to the West Indies and even to Britain in the eighteenth century. See M. Harrison, *Medicine in the Age of Commerce and Empire: Britain and Its Tropical Colonies, 1660–1830* (Oxford, Oxford University Press, 2010), pp. 146–57.

and these reinforced the paternalism of the relationship between the planters and their labourers. Doubtless the planters could also assess if the concerned labourer was able to perform a day's work at the same time as dispensing the medicines. Most self-help remedies were directed at the labourers; the planters themselves had access to British physicians who were either on their company's payroll or could be summoned from nearby when necessary. Most planters also used the facilities at the Eden Sanitarium and the private practices of British physicians at Darjeeling and the nearby hill-station at Kurseong, particularly for the birth of their children and for any long-term illnesses.

The correspondence of Arthur Story, a young medical graduate from Edinburgh who was invited to join a tea company practice in the Duars, gives us a few rare glimpses to the workers' response to therapeutic care from the physicians. As a 'European' doctor, he was medically consulted by the planters and their families.[66] In rare instances he referred to having treated individual workers. His gardener had 'a slight dose of fever and like all these natives thought he was going to die at once – he refused to take any medicine and ran away'.[67] On another occasion a worker needed a surgery on a gangrenous leg, although it is not clear who was to perform the surgery. In any case, the afflicted man preferred not to be treated: 'the old fool refuses to have it done – so there is nothing for it but to let him die'.[68]

Some tea estates employed 'doctor babus' – so called to distinguish them from the British-qualified 'European' doctors. The doctor babus were Indian medical practitioners employed to look after the medical care of the labourers. Their qualifications and expertise were limited, if not obscure. After the Bengal Medical Registration Act of 1914, the government found that all but three had not acquired their medical degree from a recognized institute.[69] They were, in fact, like many of the medical practitioners in the rural areas of the province of Bengal, not practitioners of any of the indigenous systems of medicine but went by the title of daktar (a Bengali transliteration of 'doctor'), signifying practitioners of Western medicine.[70] In the early twentieth century, the pioneering

66 Arthur Story's letters are available in typescript form at the APAC. See Mss Photo Eur 275 (APAC). The term 'European doctor' was used for white doctors who were all British and who shared the same social spaces with the planters.
67 Mss Photo Eur 275, letter of Arthur Story to his mother from Bhogotpore Tea Estate, Bengal, 20 Oct. 1891, p. 305 of typescript.
68 Letter of Arthur Story to his mother from Bhogotpore Tea Estate, Bengal, 9 May 9, p. 296 of typescript.
69 *Annual Report on the Working of the Jalpaiguri Labour Act for 1914–15* (Calcutta, Government Press, 1915, APAC), p. 5 (hereafter *ARWJLA*).
70 In 1913 when the provincial government sought the district officers' opinion on the Bengal Medical Registration Bill (passed in 1914), the District Magistrate of Dinajpur, neighbouring Jalpaiguri, suggested that it should be applicable to municipalities, not rural Bengal, and pointed out that 'an exception will have to be made in respect of the word "Doctor". The word has been universally adopted in the vernacular as meaning any man who professes to treat his patients according to European methods ... [and] is used more as designating a profession than as a title, and it would, I think, be hardly possible to penalise its use by any class of medical professionals.' See letter of offici-

doctor babus who risked the disease, wilderness and the insecurities of life in the plantation enclaves were not qualified medical men. An Indian planter whose family was one of the first Indians to own tea estates admitted that 'In the early days no university educated men were available to work in tea gardens ... Doctors were manufactured in situ by training intelligent officers in the rudiments of medicine. So afterwards a doctor could become a garden manager.'[71] He referred possibly only to the Indian plantations, but the non-recruitment of qualified doctors was universal. In British-owned plantations, Indian doctor babus were not promoted to managerial positions.

The plantations were sites of amateurs, who were supposed to pick up skills in the course of the discharge of their duties. The gazetteer of Darjeeling emphasized in 1907 that the planter had to 'combine, as far as possible, the knowledge and skill of an agriculturist, engineer, and architect, and even, to some extent, of a doctor'.[72] The fresh recruits in the tea plantations had little knowledge or training. Probably for that reason a number of manuals for instructions to planters proliferated at the end of the nineteenth century. The author of one manual of instructions in India reinforced the amateur status of new recruits:

> the Indian tea districts have come to the notice of people in England, satisfactorily in a two-fold measure – as a field for capitalists, and as a working sphere for many young fellows who could not get into the right thing at home ... They have not felt good enough for the Church, not studious enough for the Bar, and although they might have managed to pull through the years necessary to the practice of medicine, and eventually pass, they would ... find ... lacking the capital ... for a fair professional beginning ... For many such, the [tea] districts have solved the problem of what to do.[73]

When the planters were not dispensing medicines themselves the doctor babus were expected to look after the Indian staff and the workers, while a British physician was either resident or under contract to visit on demand. In case of a serious epidemic, he intervened to supervise the doctor babu in the care of the labourers.[74] In general, between a few overworked doctor babus and a distant British doctor who merely intervened in cases of epidemics, many labourers probably resorted to their spirit-ousters and medicine men for their daily medical care.

---

ating commissioner, Rajshahi Division, to Secretary to Government of Bengal, Municipal Department, 16 August 1913, Government of Bengal, A Proceedings, Finance/Medical, November 1913 (WBSA), p. 119.
71 Ghose, 'Development of the Tea Industry', p. 292.
72 O'Malley, *Bengal District Gazetteers*, p. 109.
73 Baildon, *The Tea Industry*, pp. 35–6.
74 Arbuthnott, *Report*, p. 8.

Medicine and Entrepreneurism in the Plantation Enclaves

The letters of Arthur Story provide many insights into the daily life of a British doctor who practised in the tea estates of Duars. The principal duties of the British physicians employed by the tea companies were of a supervisory nature, except in the case of the illness of Europeans. As Story wrote to his mother on arrival at Duars,

> My duties are to go to each garden once a week if possible to see that things are all right and that they have a proper supply of Medicines and call up the Baboo doctor and if he has any special cases among the Coolies make him show them to me.[75]

Initially, the British-owned companies collaborated to recruit one doctor to serve the European population and, when necessary, supervise the doctor babus over several tea plantations. Conditions differed from one plantation to another, and unsurprisingly, workers suffered more than the managerial staff. In 1890, for instance, the Dooars Tea Company, which at that time owned the Bamandanga, Tondoo, Ghatia, Nagrakata and Indong tea estates (neighbours of the tea gardens owned by Octavius Steele, where Arthur Story was employed), noted that

> Our native staff suffered from influenza somewhat heavily. But the European escaped entirely. The year has been described as a very unhealthy one because of the prevalence of fever and fifteen Europeans dying. But as far as our company is concerned, it has been a healthy year for us.[76]

In the pioneering phase, not all the British companies subscribed to pay a 'European' doctor. Arthur Story recounted that when called to an emergency to a plantation which did not regularly subscribe to pay him, he would charge a great deal extra for his services; for instance, he charged a patient who broke a collar bone at polo Rs100, a princely sum for setting it, and Rs 50 for every subsequent visit.[77]

From his letters it appears that it took several years to establish a system of payment or indeed of dispensation of other necessities for the newly arrived physicians. Like the owner-planters in the pioneering years in northern Bengal, the European medical officers (as they were called to distinguish them from the resident Indian doctor babus) were medical entrepreneurs, similarly entrepreneurial and imbued with the self-image of heroism. The entrepreneurial aspect of their practice is illustrated by Story himself, as well as his mentor, one Dr Hawkins. In 1890, Hawkins looked after 32 tea plantations, a huge number. The task of overseeing several tea estates at the same time had especially lucrative returns, and 'he [wa]s occasionally called in to other Gardens which he

---

75 Letter from Arthur Story, to his mother at Clifton, 9 May 1891, Mss Photo Eur 275 (APAC).
76 'Annual Garden Report, Dooars Tea Company, 1890', Mss Eur E 279 (APAC).
77 Arthur Story to his mother in England from Bhogotpore Tea Estate, 9 May 1891, Mss Photo Eur 275 (APAC).

does not get a monthly retaining fee from and for such visits of course he can charge what he likes, I know he gets over Rs1,000 a month from the Gardens he attends regularly, about £700 a year.'[78] Hawkins was evidently an entrepreneur himself, much like the planter class. He owned shares in tea estates and a soda-making factory, a profitable enterprise in a planting district where whiskey and soda was a favourite among the hard-drinking planters. His protégé admired Hawkins's multiple sources of income:

> I know he has got shares in more tea gardens which must have cost him a pretty penny – he draws at the rate of Rs 1,035 a month for retaining fees alone, besides outside fees and in addition they are talking of starting a dispensary at Dam Dim and he was offered that as well – and this year he started a soda water machine ... of which he makes a good profit.[79]

The system of private practice for medical officials serving the tea gardens on contract continued throughout the 'pioneering' period. In 1920 there was a total of nine European medical officers for the hundred-odd European tea plantations. John Symington, who served at this time as the medical officer to a group of nine tea plantations pointed out that he worked on contract to the plantations where his duties were clearly defined and limited; he also engaged in a large 'private' practice.[80]

Meanwhile, in the 1890s, prospects for an enterprising doctor stretched to positions in Assam, or partnerships in private practices in the hill-stations around. Story pronounced himself satisfied for the present: 'I am drawing more pay than an assistant does in England to start with, and I expect I shall be able to save nearly £100 a year.'[81] His own contract stipulated that his practice would become his own, without payment to Hawkins or anyone else, after three years. After ten years in the plantation district, when Hawkins felt that he had saved enough to return to Britain, he offered to sell his practice to Story. His protégé also received offers of employment in the tea plantations of Assam as well as from an English physician at Kurseong to join his practice.[82] Eventually, he decided to stay where he was, for his total earnings were not inconsiderable and he considered his prospects bright. Like most tea planters in northern Bengal in the nineteenth century whose prosperity increased with the growth of the tea industry, a 'European' medical officer in a plantation had rosier prospects there than at home in Britain. According to one estimate an assistant in an English practice (which was roughly Arthur Story's position) would earn a net income of £300 per annum after five years.[83]

78 Letter from Arthur Story, Bhogotpore Tea Estate, 20 October 1891.
79 Letter from Arthur Story, Bhogotpore Tea Estate, 20 October 1891.
80 John Symington, *In a Bengal Jungle: Stories of Life on the Tea Gardens of Northern India* (Chapel Hill, University of North Carolina Press, 1935), p. 11.
81 Arthur Story to his mother from Bhogotpore Tea Estate, 20 Oct 1891.
82 Arthur Story to his mother from Nagrakata, 4 Sep. 1894, Mss Eur 275 (APAC).
83 Anne Digby, *Making a Medical Living: Doctors and Patients in the English Market for Medicine 1720–1911* (Cambridge, Cambridge University Press, 1994), p. 143.

The long-term prospects within the profession in India where a British medical officer could, like Hawkins, with medical and non-medical entrepreneurship earn a thousand pounds a year and contemplate retirement in ten years, would have been lucrative. As Douglas Haynes has pointed out, the Colonial Office could recruit and dictate terms to medical graduates at the turn of the century because the profession was getting overcrowded at this time in Britain.[84] An appointment to the Indian Medical Service was more secure, prestigious and lucrative than the offer of an appointment in a private company at a 'tea district' in India.[85] But there were only so many positions available in the IMS; meanwhile, the plantations offered good prospects to an adventurous and entrepreneurial medical man than he could obtain in England. Arthur Story received several offers, but declined to move out of northern Bengal to the tea plantations further east in Assam.[86] A British physician in private practice in Darjeeling offered him a position as well, which he declined with some regret; it would have afforded a more congenial life, but he earned more in the plantations.[87] He suffered periodically from fevers, and took two long trips: once by river to Goalunda, (Assam) and once to the sea at Ceylon to recover from his fevers. He considered himself, and fellow Europeans at some risk of death from fevers, but not enough to abandon Duars altogether.[88] He died in November 1894 of heart disease and kidney failure, exacerbated by fever.[89]

The Doctor Babus: Health Care and Indigenous Medical Practice in the Plantation Enclaves

When it was not administered ad hoc by the planters, the everyday medical care of the labourers was supposed to be undertaken by the resident medical doctors known as 'doctor babus'. These resident medical 'doctors' were usually unqualified former medical students from the 'unofficial' medical colleges that sprang up in the metropolises of Calcutta and Dhaka in the late nineteenth century, much to the frustration of British medical men who taught and practised at the prestigious and established government medical colleges. The doctor babus, or *daktars* in the vernacular, practised 'Western medicine' in the sense that they received their training, however inadequate, in Western medical institutions.[90] They were a *daktar* by default, if they did not practise Ayurveda or Unani (in which case they were designated *kavirajes* and *hakims* respectively). They abounded in

---

84 Haynes, *Imperial Medicine*, pp. 126–38.
85 A recruit to the Indian Medical Service around this time was paid Rs 420 per month, 'nearly double his market value at home'. See Harrison, *Public Health*, p. 11.
86 Arthur Story to his mother from Looksan Tea Estate, 6 Nov. 1892, Mss Photo Eur 275 (APAC).
87 Arthur Story to his mother, from Nagrakata, 4 Sept. 1894.
88 Arthur Story to his mother, from Looksan Tea Estate, 6 Nov. 1892.
89 D.P. Thompson to Mrs Story, from Looksan Tea Estate 20 Jan. 1895.
90 Projit Mukharji, *Nationalizing the Body: The Medical Market, Print and Daktari Medicine* (London, Anthem Press, 2009), pp. 7–8.

Bengal in the late nineteenth century. The British medical establishment as well as Indian graduates from the government medical schools were both suspicious of them as well as resented them for their 'substandard' qualifications and their ability to lure away patients from the legalized independent profession. The provincial Medical Registration Acts (in Bengal, in 1914) disqualified the graduates of private medical schools from government jobs. But they abounded in private practice. Their skills in medicine are debated by contemporary commentators and historians alike, but it is indisputable that *daktars*, a motley group of medical men, were plentiful in colonial Bengal.[91]

The resident medical practitioners within the plantations were doctor babus who lived on the plantation estates as one of the clerical staff, received a modest income and were generally Bengalis. A report by medical experts on malaria and blackwater fever in the plantations at the turn of the century stringently criticized the doctor babus, their incompetence and general lack of qualifications. The experts met six of the doctor babus from different plantations in Duars and were appalled by the levels of their skills. They claimed the doctor babus were ignorant and harmful. In one instance one of them prepared a gargle for a woman who 'was dying of tetanus'.[92]

To S.R. Christophers and C.A. Bentley, the medical experts who were commissioned by the government of India to investigate malaria and blackwater fever in 1906, the problem was in the system of recruitment at the plantations; as part of the Indian medical establishment, they argued for the recruitment of 'qualified' medical practitioners specifically and more generally, for the regulation and registration of local medical professionals. To that extent this was a concern about professionalization, although their commentary condemned the lack of daily medical cure for most labourers within the plantations:

> Apparently anyone who cares to call himself a 'doctor *babu*' may be engaged ... Their medical knowledge in our experience is extremely limited and their treatment of the sick as it affects the general coolie population is in our opinion in the great majority of cases of no value whatsoever. The making up and the administration of coolie medicines is generally done in a most casual and unprofessional way. Fever, if treated at all is, as a rule, ignorantly and inadequately treated. In a case of fever lasting several days we have seen a single five-grain tabloid of quinine given. Ulcer cases are almost completely neglected, except when a manager interests himself specially in some case, a little powder or carbolic oil is given to the coolie, who is left almost entirely to his own resources for dressing the sore.[93]

---

91 Sanitary Commissioner to Secretary, Government of Bengal Proceedings, Municipal/Sanitation, March 1920, no. 6 (WBSA), pp. 4–5.
92 Sanitary Commissioner to Secretary, Government of Bengal Proceedings, Municipal/Sanitation, March 1920, pp. 68–69. They were also alarmed at seeing a labourer being given nitric acid for persistent ulcers in the leg (p. 69).
93 S.R. Christophers and C.A. Bentley, *Malaria in the Duars: Being the Second Report to the Advisory Committee Appointed by the Government of India to Conduct an Enquiry regarding Blackwater and Other Fevers Prevalent in the Duars* (Simla, 1911), p. 68.

Inherent in this criticism of the doctor babus was a larger critique of the medical establishment of the tea plantations. They also suggested that, apart from the lack of qualifications, the social status of the doctor babus and their insecurities about their jobs contributed to some of their indifference. Christophers and Bentley remarked that the doctor babus frequently did not register the deaths in a tea garden because 'Too often ... these men ... are convinced that it is against their own interests to report the occurrence of more deaths than they can possibly avoid reporting.'[94] Moreover, often it was impossible for a single doctor babu to visit all the coolie lines, especially in the larger tea estates.

The status of the doctor babu appears to have been marginal and he performed other services in the tea garden if required: 'he may for part of his time be employed on clerk's duty ... taken for granted that his medical duties are insufficient to require his whole-time service'.[95] If he went on leave, even long leave, it was not considered necessary to appoint someone in his place. The numbers of resident doctor babus were too few in proportion to the population of the workers in the tea estates, therefore most labourers (unlike the management) had little direct access to everyday medical care – it was provided by the planter or the doctor babu only sporadically. In 1910, there was one doctor babu for roughly 1500 labourers in the Duars plantations.

Part of the reason for this, another medical report argued, was that the pay was meagre (between 40 to 60 rupees per month), but the planters' response was that on one occasion a tea garden could not appoint a doctor even with the payment of a hundred rupees because the 'itinerary work' of a plantation was not favoured by them.[96] The issue of the pay and the qualifications of the doctor babus was a persistent one, to be argued between the state government and the tea plantations for the next two decades. Duars being a notoriously unhealthy and inhospitable area and the medical work at the tea estates extremely arduous and ill-paid, very few of the graduates from Calcutta were willing to work there. Moreover, the medical practice was among tribal labourers, and the high caste Bengali doctors were probably reluctant to work with labourers who in the colonial framework were primitives, a fact that was internalized by the Westernized Bengali *bhadralok* and reinforced by Brahmanical notions of ritual purity. For instance, in 1868 the Bengali traveller Jankinath Basak could write a verse on Darjeeling:

> I have been to see Darjeeling
> Sonada Sukna , jhoras at Tindhura
> Mountains at Miling
> Of the Lepchas of the mountains, you can sing many praises!
> Their speech is indecipherable; [nonsensical] *kiring miring*,
> There is nothing they do not eat,
> [As if] they have just come off the trees;

---

94 Christophers and Bentley, *Malaria in the Duars*, p. 45.
95 Christophers and Bentley, *Malaria in the Duars*, p. 70.
96 Christophers and Bentley, *Malaria in the Duars*, p. 29.

Their songs and dances
Are similarly [nonsensical] *dhating dhating!*[97]

Most tea garden workers in the hill areas of Darjeeling were not Lepchas. They were Nepalis of various castes, who were all termed Paharias (hill people). The labourers called Madesias – the aboriginal people of the plains (comprising of Oraons, who were in the majority, and Mundas and Santhals) who predominated in the Duars – were of a similar social status, beyond the pale of the Hindu caste system.[98]

In the Duars, the inhospitability of the terrain and the remoteness of the tea plantations also contributed to the small numbers of Bengali bhadralok class willing to work there. The 'babus' – a class of staff, mostly Bengali, who made their living from clerical or medical work in the Duars tea gardens – were few in numbers.[99] A typical babu in a tea plantation, most probably a high caste Bengali with a basic knowledge of English, burdened with a large family, often in debt and always whining for a raise in pay, personified the figure of a class equally subject to the contempt shown the sahibs and alienated from the *sardars* and labourers, who belonged to different social worlds. A satirical verse written by an Assam planter thus represents the low status of the babus in the tea plantations and the ridiculous, often comic figures they were to the British planters:

THE BABU'S PETITION
Most Honoured Sir, I humbly beg
To send this letter by the leg
Of one poor menial from my house,
And hope, kind Sir, you will not grouse.
Its purport, how may I explain,
For I am put to greatest pain …
Kind Sir, in brief, my debts are many
And cash, alas! I haven't any
And family much increasing now,
So I must feed them anyhow.
First twins arrived, in damn great state
At howling fits they both are great
Disturbing peace of wretched mind

---

97 Quoted by Ratan Biswas, 'Bangla Sahitye Darjeeling Jela', in idem, *Madhuparni: Bishesh Darjeeling Sankhya, 1996* (Calcutta, 1996), p. 371 (my translation).
98 H.H. Risley noted in 1891 that 'In the eyes of the average Hindu the Oraons have no social status all, and are deemed to be entirely outside the regular caste system', H.H. Risley, *The Tribes and Castes of Bengal*, vol. 2 (Calcutta, Firma KLM, 1998, repr.), p. 148.
99 Dr D.N. Chatterjee, who had served in the erstwhile European-dominated coal mines in Bihar as well as supervised a UNDP-sponsored programme on birth control in the tea plantations in the Duars in the 1980s, pointed out a consistent semantic and categorical distinction between a 'doctor babu' and the 'sahib'. He stated that the terminology of the 'doctor babu' was to represent the inferior status of the doctor, however highly qualified or Westernized, vis-à-vis the plantation management (interview with Dr D.N. Chatterjee, Siliguri, North Bengal, 5 April 2005).

> Till I am almost mad, I find ...
> And so, kind Sir, I humbly pray
> Your honour to increase my pay;
> For which help I'll daily say
> A prayer to heaven that you may
> Long life, prosperity enjoy,
> And all your childs [sic] be blessed boy.[100]

Plantation society was segregated. Over the decades the babus of the various plantations built their own social worlds, with their own small 'clubs' which, much like the sahibs, organized football matches and had their own 'club' and social events.[101] Several contemporary accounts of clerical work in early twentieth century Duars mention the lack of qualifications of the clerical and medical staff who worked in the tea plantations.[102] One anecdote reveals that once recruited, the babu (a synonym for clerk) was given a small hut and often the services of a labourer who would cook for him. The sahib showed him the dispensary and explained the medicines to him, and then he was ready to make diagnoses and dispense medicines to the labourers as the doctor babu. Given the prevalence of chapters on home remedies in a contemporary planters' manual, with instructions that the planter was expected to deal with the health of the labourer directly as best he could, the anecdotes recounted above do not seem too far-fetched.[103] All of the above combined to make employment in the Duars an exceedingly unattractive prospect for qualified Indian doctors. In the Duars tea plantations the remoteness of the tea estates, the nastiness of the climate and the insecurities of life in the area are always remembered in Bengali accounts.[104]

In the tea plantations the doctor babu was generally a figure of scorn and was at best tolerated by the medical professionals of the district administration and by qualified men from outside the tea estates. The Indian tea estates, which had smaller acreage and capital, economized on medical personnel even more than the European ones.[105]

---

100 Maurice P. Hanley, *Tales and Songs from an Assam Tea Garden* (Calcutta and Simla, Thacker Spink & Co., 1928), pp. 96–97. For an analysis of the alienation of the lower middle-class Bengali men who served as ill-paid clerks in contemporary civil services and British mercantile houses in nineteenth-century Bengal, see Sumit Sarkar, 'Kaliyuga, Chakri and Bhakti: Ramakrishna and His Times', in idem, *Writing Social History* (Delhi, Oxford University Press, 1997), pp. 282–357. Located not in the urban centres, but in the remote tea districts, the babu (a category which included the doctor babus) of the tea plantations belonged to the margins of this Bengali class.
101 Kamakhya Prasad Chakrabarti, 'Cha-Shilper Goda Pottone Bangali Uddogider Bhumika', in idem, *Kirat Bhumi: Jalpaiguri Jela Sankalan* (Jalpaiguri, 1998), pp. 233–40. The sahibs played football, but preferred not to play matches against the babus. See Subhajyoti Ray, *Transformations*, p. 92.
102 Arnab Sen and Brajagopal Ghosh, *Jalpai-Duarser Jalchhabi* (Alipurduar, 2004), pp. 72–73.
103 Anonymous, *Notes on Tea*, p. 77.
104 For instance, see Shankar Rai Chaudhary, 'Cha-Baganer Babuder Sanskriti', in Gautam Rai (ed.), *Uttar Banger Janajati O Luptapray Lok Sanskriti* (Siliguri, 2004), pp. 179–87.
105 ARWJLA, 1925–26, p. 3.

The very small number of qualified doctors within the tea estates reflected, to some extent, the scarcity of qualified doctors in rural Bengal at the time. The Bengal Medical Registration Act, 1914, made it illegal for anyone to use the title of 'doctor', or for bodies like the district or union boards or railways to appoint anyone of the rank of sub-assistant surgeons, unless they had passed through a government-endorsed medical college. This made candidates from the several independent medical colleges in Calcutta or elsewhere ineligible to apply for positions in government or semi-government institutions. This was avowedly to standardize the medical education in Bengal in the Western model, which was distinct from the indigenous practitioners who were either kabirajes or hakims. As the *Indian Medical Record*, a Calcutta-based journal, pointed out, this legislation was not directed against unqualified medical practitioners as such, but was intended to curb independent medical schools, for the graduates of such unrecognized independent medical schools could practise anywhere except in the government institutions.[106]

By the end of the first decade of the twentieth century, there were many such practitioners who had probably attended a year or two of medical college, or in some cases passed through the independent colleges. Such practitioners, who called themselves daktars, often practised in rural Bengal, probably in competition with the local kabirajes and hakims.[107] The deputy commissioner of Jalpaiguri wrote to the government that the chief distinction in the district was between those appointed as sub-assistant surgeons in government institutions, and the others, whom he called the 'local native doctors'. He argued against the Bengal Medical Registration Act because he felt that the 'independent medical school man is at any rate better than a kabiraj', and that 'until medical men are a good deal more common than they are at present the moffussil public will, in my opinion, be glad to pay for what they can get without enquiring too closely into its quality'. At the same time, when he further stated that to the 'uninitiated' there was little difference between those from government-approved schools or independent schools, and that 'They are all "Native Doctors" and legislation is hardly necessary as far as this District is concerned', he was articulating the opinion of the mofussil (district) official who would have to temper government directives to the realities of his district.[108]

---

106 'The Bengal Medical Bill', *Indian Medical Record*, 34 (1914), p. 14.
107 In 1918 the Sanitary Commissioner of Bengal wrote to the government on medical practice in Bengal, 'It is a mistake to think that the people of Bengal do without medical attendance; almost all of them employ some kind of medical practitioner (hakims, baids or kabirajes), when ill. Recently I ascertained that among certain village communities in one district aggregating 20,000 people, several hundred (700 and 800) persons made their living by one or other forms of medical practice.' Letter from Dr C.A. Bentley, to Secretary, to Government of Bengal, Municipal Department, May 1918, Proceedings of Government of Bengal, Municipal/Sanitation, March 1920, no. 6, IOR/P/10765 (APAC), p. 5. Also see 'Unqualified Medical Men in Bengal', *The Lancet*, 1395 (1932).
108 Letter of officiating Deputy Commissioner, Jalpaiguri, to the commissioner of Rajshahi, 4 August 1913, Government of Bengal, A Proceedings, Finance/Medical, November 1913, no. 42 (WBSA), pp. 119–20.

The European (British) planters, probably through their experience with precisely such legislation in Assam, had a more sophisticated argument; they argued, as we have seen, that their doctor babus, though untrained, had valuable local experience. After the Bengal Medical Registration Act, 1914, the plantation management argued for an exception for the tea plantations as they were a unique case where the native doctors were familiar with the local working conditions, and they should be allowed to employ unqualified doctor babus. They negotiated with the government and were allowed to keep the doctor babus in service on the condition that they were gradually to be replaced with qualified practitioners.[109]

Bentley, at that time the Special Deputy Sanitary Commissioner, wrote to the government about the preference for untrained local men to holders of Indian diplomas among the planters:

> until recently a strong prejudice existed among both tea garden managers and European medical officers against the employment of diplomaed [sic] Indian medical men. I have frequently heard it stated that an untrained man who had gained local experience as a compounder in a tea garden ... [was] to be preferred to the doctor babu possessed of a parchment diploma ... There are many hundreds of 'doctor babus' employed in the tea gardens of Bengal and Assam ... As a result the present position of a very large number of diplomates [sic] from recognised medical schools, is deplorable ... It is not an easy thing for such men to establish themselves in private practice, on account of the strenuous competition they encounter.[110]

The question was therefore not one of the unavailability of qualified doctor babus, but of their unavailability at low cost. The lack of duly qualified Indian doctors and the value of the experience of the local untrained doctor in the planters' discourses must be situated in the context of the fact that the tea industry in colonial India depended on cheap labour, and the cheapness of the labour of the untrained 'coolie doctors' was the reason for their employment within the plantations. The long and gradual process of the rationalization of the system of medical care in the tea estates in colonial Duars did not obliterate their presence. In 1938, for a total of 155 tea gardens, there were 87 qualified resident doctors.[111] In 1944 there were still 44 tea gardens in the Duars that had no qualified resident doctor.[112]

---

109 The employment of medical practitioners who had attended a few years of medical school but not completed their education appears to have been a standard practice in the tea gardens of Assam in the nineteenth century. The government legislated against the appointment of such so-called 'coolie doctors' in 1865. Anil Kumar states that the practice continued covertly, although he provides no evidence for his argument. See Anil Kumar, *Medicine and the Raj: British Medical Policy in India 1835–1911* (New Delhi and London, Sage Publishers, 1998), p. 34.
110 Kumar, *Medicine and the Raj*, p. 34 (emphasis mine); also see IOR/P/9145 (APAC), pp. 123–24.
111 *Detailed Report of the General Committee of the Dooars Planters Association for 1938, with Proceedings of Annual General Meeting in 1939, 1938* (Calcutta, 1939, APAC), p. 143 (hereafter *DPAAR*).
112 D.V. Rege, *Labour Investigation Committee: Report on an Enquiry into Conditions of Labour in Plantations in India* (Simla, Government of India Press, 1946), p. 90.

In Darjeeling and Terai, as well, tea estates employed few qualified men. No estimates of the numbers of qualified medical practitioners in the Darjeeling and Terai plantations are available. In 1920, prior to proposing a legislation for the surveillance and standardisation of medical and sanitary provisions for workers in all the tea districts of Bengal, the under-secretary to the Government of Bengal announced 'In Darjeeling there are tea garden doctors but the number of qualified men both among them and the compounders is not at present adequate.'[113]

Given the circumstances, a substantial proportion of medical care in the tea plantations was probably undertaken by the *ojhas* – faith-healers who were probably herbalists from the tribal communities themselves, although there are no references to their role as dispensers of medicine distinct from their role as 'spirit-ousters'. Their existence was rarely recorded, except when religious fervour fomented political dissent, and their contribution to therapeutic care has never been acknowledged by official or medical sources and must remain a matter of conjecture. The planters themselves held the *ojhas* and *bhagats* in a mix of tolerance and contempt, except when they detected the practice of 'witchcraft' which threatened to destabilize working relations within the plantations, when they intervened decisively to stamp it out.[114] Any conclusion about the exact status and place of the *ojhas* in medical practice in the plantations therefore requires a contemporary approach, and is beyond the scope of this work. We can surmise that, given the limited availability of both doctor babus and dispensary medicine, they comprised an important part of daily medical care.[115] Interestingly, medical missionaries might have filled the vacuum that existed in medical care in the plantations, but there is no evidence of medical missions except in Kalimpong, which catered more to the population in and around the town than to the tea plantations. It was only at the latter end of the colonial period, in 1937, that a Catholic mission established a small dispensary with the grant of government land at Bhogibhita and Gayaganga in the Terai, which catered to the villages as well as the plantations around the region.[116]

Disease and Pioneering Plantation in the 'Unhealthy' Terrain

The pioneering years were the time of opportunity and entrepreneurship for the British physicians. They were also the years of high death rates and fatalities. At this point, the relative lack of communication and the remote location

113 Extract from proceedings of the Bengal Legislative Council held on Tuesday, 3 February 1920, Government of Bengal Proceedings, Municipal/ Sanitation, May 1920, nos 27–28, IOR/P/10765 (APAC), p. 64.
114 For instance, see typescript titled 'TEA', Mss Eur C474 (APAC), pp. 3–4.
115 See Samrat Chaudhury and Nitin Varma, 'Between Gods/Goddesses/Demons and "Science": Perceptions of Health and Medicine among Plantation Labourers in Jalpaiguri District, Bengal', *Social Scientist*, 30 (2002), pp. 18–38.
116 'Navjeevan Hospital – God's Gift to Gayaganga', *Navjeevan Hospital and Rural Health Care Centre* (Darjeeling, 2003).

of the tea estates meant that therapeutic facilities were rudimentary and ad hoc when available for the planters and the physicians themselves. In the planters' records, the pioneering years come across as one of difficult conquest of a wild country – in both the 'healthy' hills and the 'unhealthy' foothills in the Terai and the Duars. Eventually, to the amateur ornithologist and planter of Darjeeling L. Mandelli, the hardships of a planters' life, the vagaries of climate, an epidemic among his coolies and his wife's illness all seemed equally fortuitous:

> I can assure you, the life of a Tea Planter is by far from being a pleasant one ... drought at first, incessant rain afterwards, and to crown all, cholera amongst coolies ... .all these combined, are enough to drive anyone mad ... Beside I was very nearly losing my wife: she had an attack of cholera ... [117]

G.G. Webb, who referred to the Duars as the 'Planters' Grave', remembered other frequent medical emergencies when trained medical men and medicine were required and not immediately available – injuries caused by wild animals which often strayed within the plantations. His description of a planter who carried out the treatment of a neighbour after an attack by a leopard throws into graphic relief the desperate and rough-and-ready efforts planters often made on such occasions: 'The doctor lived miles away, so a near neighbour was informed by a runner. He came and poured crystals of permanganate of potash into each wound and where the deeper cuts were concerned poked them in as far as he could with his fingers.'[118]

In British experience, sickness and fatalities were accepted by the planters and their doctors as an unhappy but integral part of life; an inevitable part of entrepreneurship and settlement. When they were mentioned in the documents at all, their sicknesses seem to have been subsumed in the topos of the diseased land. 'Last week the rain began again and brought a lot of sickness with it though it was much wanted.'[119] And again, 'There have been a good many cholera cases on this garden amongst the Coolies and a good many have died but it is dying out now.'[120]

In planters' accounts the representation of Duars and Terai as unhealthy regions persisted, as did the heroic story of the conquest of unwelcoming terrain. Official discourse replicated the motif of an unhealthy land. The Terai was not only inscribed with unhealthiness but also was invariably posited against the healthiness of the high mountains. In 1843 Frederick Corbyn, a surgeon in the British Indian army, wrote about fever in the Nepal Terai, which he named 'Tarai fever'.[121] The Darjeeling Terai acquired a similar reputation. As the Darjeeling district gazetteer demarcated in 1907, 'The district is composed of two portions, the Terai, a low malarious belt skirting the base of the Himalayas,

117 Letter no. 40, 25 June 1876, Mss Eur B 411 (APAC).
118 Typescript titled 'Leopards', Mss Eur C474 (APAC).
119 Arthur Story to his mother, from Bhogotpore Tea Estate, 20 August 1891, Mss Photo Eur 275 (APAC).
120 Arthur Story to his mother, from Bhogotpore Tea Estate, 9 May 1891.
121 *India Review and Journal of Foreign Science Arts*, 8 (1843), pp. 201–10.

which is notoriously unhealthy, and the hills, where the climate is wonderfully bracing'.[122] Duars also had a reputation for being an extremely unhealthy land. When David Rennie was on the march in the area in 1865 he found it as febrile and its miasma as harmful as that in the 'more dreaded' Terai.[123] Three-and-a-half decades after the tea plantation industry in the Duars, the district gazetteer pointed out that the region 'has an evil reputation for malaria and blackwater fever comparable only to the deadliest regions of Central Africa'.[124] Story wrote, 'Talk about Africa, darkest Hindoostan is just as bad.'[125] Not just the British, Indian planters, too, romanticized the terrain. The otherwise phlegmatic autobiographical account of a Bengali planter in the Duars boasted, 'This was a land only for the saints or the satans.'[126] Climate, miasmas and the terrain appeared to be responsible for illness among the burgeoning labouring population of the plantations of the Duars and the Darjeeling foothills.

Disease was linked to the land, a familiar trend in Anglo-Indian medical traditions in the nineteenth century.[127] The formidable reputation of the Terai and Duars for malaria made it a destination for the Royal Society's Malaria Committee in 1902. Ironically, it was a report requested by the planters themselves that explicitly challenged both the 'diseased land' theory and eventually the prevalent system of medical care in the Duars. This caused a disruption of the consensus of the 'diseased land' as well as the construction of the planters' paternalistic benevolence that was supposed to have been articulated in their health care, as in all other aspects. Chapter 5 will discuss what happened when the two different consensi of the plantation enclave, that of the diseased land as well as of the paternalistic claims of the planters, were challenged.

---

122 O'Malley, *Bengal District Gazetteers*, p. 67.
123 Rennie, *Bhotan*, p. 352.
124 Grunig, *Eastern Bengal*, p. 46.
125 Arthur Story from Looksan Tea Estate, 14 August 1892, Mss Photo Eur 275 (APAC), p. 321 of typescript.
126 Ghose, 'Development of the Tea Industry', p. 12.
127 M. Harrison, 'Tropical Medicine in Nineteenth Century India', *British Journal for the History of Science*, 25 (1992), pp. 299–318.

CHAPTER 4

The Sanatorium Enclave: Climate and Class in Colonial Darjeeling

As we have seen in Chapter 2, Darjeeling was incorporated into the wider colonial polity and economy of north Bengal over the nineteenth century. Meanwhile, it also sustained its role as a resort for exclusive European medicalized leisure in the late Victorian period. As its popularity became wider, the town stretched to accommodate various demands on its multiple identities – as a European social enclave and seasonal administrative centre, as the social and medical hub for the planters of the Darjeeling, Duars and Terai. As they did over many other institutions of British privilege, the Indian elite, especially the Bengalis, staked a claim on Darjeeling. With these multiple claims over its privileges and facilities, there was also a sense of loss of Darjeeling's essential character. After the turn of the century, both British and Indian complaints echoed official discourse in an attempt to keep Darjeeling socially exclusive. Most of the other principal hill-stations felt the pressures of over-crowding and the consequent spread of diseases within the town. Kennedy argues that the incursions of Indians, 'the Intrusion of the Other', at various levels strained the resources of the hill-stations and changed their essential character.[1] I will contend here that this sense of 'intrusion' was a matter of perception both by the British and the Indian elites. Despite a real growth in its population at the turn of the century, Darjeeling remained an exclusive social and cultural space. In official reports and elite perception, it was the poorer sections within the town which acquired visibility as the undesirable 'crowd' in the late colonial period. From the turn of the century, the municipal government and the elite in Darjeeling sought to limit the short-term visits by middle-class Bengalis as well as economic migration by casual labourers to the town through various means. It was also because of this perception of loss that the administration and municipality of Darjeeling strove to retain the privileged and exclusive urban space

1 See Kennedy, *The Magic Mountains*, pp. 175–201.

that replicated the structural municipal benefits enjoyed by civil stations, such as well-maintained roads, sewerage, electric lighting and generous government grants to maintain the facilities. This was facilitated by its particular privileged position in municipal governance and grants-in-aid from provincial government in the interwar years. This municipal privilege that Darjeeling enjoyed was a reflection of the attempts to keep the town a European enclave.

Race, Class and Society in Darjeeling

At the turn of the nineteenth century, there was a large Westernized landed gentry as well as a professional class in Bengal, Madras and Bombay presidencies. In Bengal particularly, British policy had fostered a new class of educated elite, the *bhadralok*, who accepted Western education (including medical education) and Enlightenment values at the same time as critiquing British rule and colonial exploitation. The *bhadralok* therefore had a deeply conflicting relationship with the British, and eventually they claimed a place for themselves in colonial institutions such as universities, civil services and judiciary. Along with these, there were the *zamindars*, the landed aristocracy who were the 'natural allies' of the British Raj, who also often adopted Western values and social norms. Hill-stations like Simla, Mussoorie and Darjeeling became important social spaces for these Indian elite. In 1880, a prominent landlord, the Maharajah of Burdwan possessed a fine summer palace in Darjeeling.[2] Other men from professional classes such as civil servants and barristers also owned property in Darjeeling. Many others visited briefly during the summer, residing in one of the several boarding houses that sprang up to cater to Indian visitors, usually below the Mall, at the edge of the railway station.[3] The population of Darjeeling continued to expand. It was not isolated in this respect; Simla also burgeoned and accommodated Indian elite, most contentiously native princes from the neighbouring Punjab.[4]

The hill-stations, like many other sites of British privilege, thus came to be contested by the Indian elite. In doing so in Darjeeling, this predominantly Bengali elite class expanded the racial understanding of acclimatization in the mountains to include healing Indian bodies. For instance, in 1909, a scion of a *zamindar* family in Dhaka, Kumar Ramendra Narayan, who was suffering from syphilis at an advanced stage, when ulcers were breaking on to his arms and legs was advised to go to Darjeeling in the summer by his physician.[5] They simultaneously appropriated many aspects of the social space of Darjeeling. This

2 Harimohana Sānyāla, *Dārājiliṅgera itihāsa* (Calcutta, Mitram, 2005, first pub. 1880), p. 25.
3 K.C. Bhanja, *Darjeeling at a Glance: A Handbook Descriptive and Historical of Darjeeling, Sikkim and Tibet with Thrilling Accounts of Everest and Kanchenjunga Expeditions by Land and Air* (2nd edn, Darjeeling, Oxford Book & Stationery Co., 1942), p. 77.
4 Kanwar, *Imperial Simla*, pp. 95–104.
5 See Partha Chatterjee, *A Princely Imposter? The Kumar of Bhawal & the Secret History of Indian Nationalism* (Delhi, Permanent Black, 2002), p. 38.

newly acquired social space managed to accommodate Western medical values while also subverting the racial component of the sanatorium. Needless to say, this was a long drawn-out process. One example will illustrate the negotiations that formed a part of this process of the construction of *shailashahar* (mountain-town) Darjeeling.

In November 1906, the Lowis Jubilee Sanatorium, the replica of the Eden Sanitarium that catered to wealthy Indians, invited the Governor of Bengal to visit the newly built 'pthisis ward'. As we have seen in Chapter 1, at this time medical authorities condemned the climate of Darjeeling for causing various respiratory and intestinal diseases. A visit from the Governor Sir Andrew Fraser and the Civil Surgeon of Darjeeling Colonel Crofts produced a note from the latter objecting to a pthisis ward for the institution. Crofts pointed out that 'Darjeeling is not suitable for the Pthisical Ward. For the ordinary native it is too cold; it is certainly too wet ... with very little sun, and it is very much crowded ... the ground space and the cubic air space allowed ... are altogether inadequate.'[6] The governor agreed with Crofts and proposed to reject the proposal for the pthisis ward.[7] A special committee which included the Civil Surgeon and Mr Bompas, Chairman of the Darjeeling Municipality, who was also the president of the managing committee of the Lowis Jubilee sanatorium, was present at the meeting. *The Bengalee* reported that 'Colonel Crofts read a lengthy note and stated that Ranchi would be best suited to pthisical patients. Mr Bompas ... pointed out that the Pthisical ward was constructed with the consent of Government.'[8] The grant of Rs 15,000 provided by a philanthropist, Dinamoni Choudhurani of Santosh, was previously endorsed by the provincial government.[9] The Commissioner of Bhagalpur, while recommending sanction for the ward, assured the government of the suitability of the designs for the proposed ward, pointing out that 'the Executive Engineer is a member of the Committee'.[10] Next week *The Bengalee* published a scathing editorial attacking the governor himself: 'Sir Andrew Fraser is nothing if not a man of *zid* [stubbornness] ... perhaps it is in his opposition to the proposed pthisical ward in connection with the Lowis Jubilee Sanatorium in Darjeeling, that this distinguishing trait ... has most persistently thrust itself upon the public view.'[11] The editorial then detailed the three years and various medical opinions (some by Bengali doctors) that had reviewed the proposed ward and pronounced that they were satisfied. It next pointed out, 'Are we to understand that what is good for the Eden Sanitarium, to which only Europeans are admitted, is not good for the Lowis Jubilee Sanatorium which is resorted to by "natives" only?'[12]

6   *The Bengalee*, 17 November 1906 (reel no. 41, National Library, Calcutta), p. 6.
7   *The Bengalee*, 17 November 1906, p. 6.
8   *The Bengalee*, 17 November 1906, p. 6.
9   Government of Bengal Proceedings, Municipal/Medical (WBSA), p. xii of B Proceedings Index.
10 Government of Bengal, B Proceedings, Municipal/Medical, Feb. 1906, nos 139–40 (WBSA), p. 1.
11 *The Bengalee*, 27 November 1906 (reel no. 42, National Library Calcutta), p. 3.
12 *The Bengalee*, 27 November 1906, p. 3.

The editorial ended with an appeal to the government of India to intervene. The issue was next taken up at the Bengal Legislative Council. One Babu Radha Charan Pal enquired, 'Is it not a fact that three eminent medical authorities and two experienced Divisional Commissioners consulted by Government, were in favour of the construction of this ward?', and further pointed out that the 'abandonment of the design at the present juncture will mean the throwing away of so much money and labour'.[13] In the face of staunch opposition, the government assured the council that 'An endeavour is being made, in consultation with the Committee of the Sanitarium and with Medical Officers, to arrive at a decision which will be in the interests of the patients and of the public.'[14] Ultimately the government gave in and the pthisis ward stayed in place. However, it set out its view of the kind of native cases who could benefit from a stay at the sanatorium in Darjeeling:

> There can be no doubt that the climate of Darjeeling, is too damp to be a suitable one for consumptives who are in an advanced state of the disease. But the Lieutenant Governor is advised that during the dry months cases in the incipient stages, free from pyrexia, with limited lesions, or not breaking down, would be benefited by a stay in Darjeeling ... under proper supervision and treatment ... The Sanitarium however, plays a very important part from the educational point of view as regards patients and the community; for the patients learn how to treat themselves, to disinfect sputum, to eat suitable food, and they subsequently spread the knowledge.[15]

The pthisis ward was to stay; there would be some limitations on the admissions to the ward, depending on the seriousness of the patients' condition. The managing committee of the Lowis Jubilee Sanatorium agreed to certain conditions laid down by government; including the stricture that only patients in the early stages of pthisis would be allowed in the sanatorium.[16]

The episode highlighted that the social aspirations of the Bengali elites in the replication of British medical institutions altered the debate over race and acclimatization. In this sense, racial and social equality were understood to be

13 Government of Bengal, A Proceedings, Municipal/Medical, 1907, no. 86 (WBSA), p. 69.
14 Government of Bengal, A Proceedings, Municipal/Medical, 1907, no. 86 (WBSA), p. 69.
15 Government of Bengal, A Proceedings, Municipal/Medical, 1907, no. 86 (WBSA), p. 71. Letter of Secretary to Govt of Bengal to the Commissioner, Bhagalpur Division, 15 January 1907.
16 Government of Bengal, A Proceedings, Municipal/Medical, May 1907, nos 159–60 (WBSA), p. 8. As we have seen in Chapter 1, the dampness of Darjeeling was not seen as suitable for European patients with pthisis. But the perspective was not entirely unanimous. In 1886 the annual report of the Eden Sanitarium claimed that 'several especially of pthisis, derived very great benefit, the climate of Darjeeling being particularly favourable for this complaint'. Government of Bengal Proceedings, Municipal/Medical, nos 8–17, April 1886, IOR/ P/2806 (APAC), p. 37. The next year, the superintendent and civil surgeon commented on the treatment of pthisis in the Eden Sanitarium: 'This disease seems to be benefited by the change in climate in its earlier stages. When once softening commences ... the change to Darjeeling is attended with little benefit.' Government of Bengal Proceedings, Medical, Nov. 1887, nos 16–18, IOR/P/2946 (APAC), p. 14.

inextricable; what was good (medically efficacious) for the Europeans should be good for the natives as well.

The racial etiquette that excluded sometimes even the highest-placed Indians (and the Anglo-Indians) from key social spheres in British India formed the basis of support among the upper echelons of Indian society for the nationalist movement. This contest for social space also translated to an appreciation of mountain sanatoriums for the health of Bengalis.

In the twentieth century, mention of Darjeeling was found frequently among prominent Bengalis. Rabindranath Tagore, littérateur and poet, visited Darjeeling often. In November 1931 he wrote to his friend William Rothenstein, 'I have come to Darjeeling in search of health and peace of mind, but the latter has run out of stock in the present day world and I must not complain'.[17] Swami Vivekananda, resting at Darjeeling in 1897 in the palace of the Maharaja of Burdwan, wrote to a friend, 'After a great deal of hard work ... my health had broken down; necessitating a rest for my mind in the town of Darjeeling.'[18] This took many forms. For the Hindus, the Himalayas were also sacred space. Although the Hindu pilgrimage sites were located in the western Himalayas, the Garhwal district of the then United Provinces, Darjeeling was reputed to be the site of an old Buddhist monastery, the mountains themselves evoked a romantic spirituality for many nationalist Indians.[19]

As the quotes above represent, in contemporary Bengali literature by the turn of the century Darjeeling was represented as a site for regaining peace and calm away from the crowded plains, a retreat for healing tired bodies and minds away from the rigours of life in the plains; in a tone similar to British representations. For the Indian elite, the controversy over the pthisical ward of the Lowis Jubilee Sanatorium was a contest for the separateness of Darjeeling that they articulated in medical terms. When the upper- and middle-class Bengalis retreated to Darjeeling for rest and recuperation, they were in effect replicating European habits.[20] It is interesting that within a decade of the episode of the pthisis ward the Civil Surgeon of Darjeeling did not think it advisable to recommend Darjeeling to European pthisis patients, or to the poorer class of Europeans, for Darjeeling was now both crowded and expensive. A sojourn at Darjeeling could be so expensive that he claimed that 'It would be cheaper to take a trip home than to Darjeeling for people of moderate means.'[21] In 1917, Darjeeling had 351 houses (there were only 70 in 1870), and these included

17   Biswas, 'Bangla Sahitye', p. 373.
18   Biswas, 'Bangla Sahitye', p. 369.
19   Jahar Sen, *Darjeeling: A Favoured Retreat* (New Delhi, Indus Publishing Co., 1989).
20   P.J. Marshall has pointed out, in a different but similar situation, that the Indian elites replicated European styles of life in nineteenth-century Calcutta: 'By a mechanism which remains unexplained, architectural styles moved from the white town to the black town.' See P.J. Marshall, 'The White Town of Calcutta under the Rule of the East India Company', *Modern Asian Studies*, 34 (2000), pp. 307–31.
21   J.T. Calvert, 'Note on Darjeeling Climate in the Treatment of Pthisis', repr. from the *Indian Medical Gazette*, 44 (1909), p. 2.

Figure 4.1 View of bazaar, Darjeeling

the summer retreats of the Maharajas of Cooch Behar, Burdwan, Darbhanga and Digapatia; several Bengali attorneys; retired British judges, civil servants and physicians; and a few wealthy planting families.[22] While the Bengali lower middle-class clerks and merchants lived at Chandmari, near the bazaar below the Mall, the Indian aristocrats and wealthy professionals lived in the upper reaches in the British part of Darjeeling.

The Quest for Exclusivity and the Growth of Smaller Hill-stations

Several alternative health resorts for Indians of different classes were developed in this period. In 1903 the Municipal Commissioners of Kurseong, a small town at a lower height in the Darjeeling hill area, and occupied mostly by planters, appealed to the provincial government for funds to develop it as a hill resort. In their address to the governor, they pointed out the 'already overcrowded condition of Darjeeling'.[23] The governor agreed that Darjeeling was 'greatly in need of relief from over-crowding', and added that the climate of Kurseong 'is better adapted than that of Darjeeling to many constitutions, *especially those of Indian gentlemen*'.[24] Therefore, smaller hill-stations located at lower elevations needed to be encouraged to accommodate 'Indian gentlemen', taking the pressure of Indian presence off Darjeeling. At the same time, 'Indian gentlemen'

---

22 Dozey, *A Concise History*, pp. 52–59.
23 Address presented to the Lt. Governor by the Municipal Commissioners of Kurseong and reply, 23 June 1903, Government of Bengal Proceedings, Municipal/Municipal, Nov. 1903, nos 28–29, IOR/P/6565 (APAC), pp. 47–48.
24 Address presented to the Lt. Governor by the Municipal Commissioners of Kurseong and reply, 23 June 1903 (emphasis mine).

well ensconced in Darjeeling also sought to keep out countrymen of a different class. Indeed, the Maharaja of Burdwan contributed Rs 20,000 for development of the hill-cart road to Kurseong and offered further assistance.[25] A few years previously, Indian entrepreneurs had made a beginning with a proposal for a sanatorium in Kurseong, which effort was validated by the *Indian Medical Record*: 'It is strongly recommended by leading medical men.'[26]

More was to follow. Two years after the controversy over the pthisis ward, a few eminent Bengalis met government officials unofficially to discuss the establishment of sanatoria for the benefit of the 'poorer classes'.[27] They included the Maharaja of Burdwan B.C. Mahtab, Kailash Chandra Bose (lawyer and philanthropist) and Dr Nil Ratan Sarkar (a prominent physician and the founder of the Indian Medical Association). The Maharaja of Burdwan was particularly involved here. He was a noted philanthropist who had contributed to the Lowis Jubilee Sanatorium. An ardent Anglophile (he visited Britain after a Continental tour in 1908), he not only spent many summers in his palace at Darjeeling, but also possessed considerable property in the area, including in Kurseong.[28] As one of the landed elite he counted many ICS officers as friends and British aristocrats as his acquaintances, and was greatly suspicious of Indian nationalists, but even he was not immune to the prospect of racial humiliation that was always present in the minds of the Indians who interacted with the British at any level.[29] As one of the richest landlords in Bengal, Mahtab's influence was considerable; he and like-minded Indians attempted to resist the influx of middle-class Bengalis into Darjeeling itself. The philanthropists requested Colonel Pardey Lukis, the Sanitary Commissioner of Bengal, to draw up a project for a sanatorium for lower middle-class Indians somewhere in the plains of Bihar, away from the insalubrious climate of Bengal, but not located in the mountains at all. Mahtab suggested that the proposed sanatorium should be 'an institution purely for people of the poorer classes, such as the low paid clerical staff employed under Government or elsewhere'.[30] He specified that 'it should not be of the same type as the sanitarium at Darjeeling, which ... largely seemed as a hotel for visitors to that station'.[31] The concern for the development of an alternative sanatorium was to avoid Darjeeling being overrun with cheap boarding houses to accommodate the lower middle classes who had begun to throng the hill town at its edges. The Maharaja of Burdwan pointed out that he did not think

---

25 Address presented to the Lt. Governor by the Municipal Commissioners of Kurseong and reply, 23 June 1903.
26 'The Kurseong Sanitarium', *Indian Medical Record* (1894), p. 57.
27 Government of Bengal, A Proceedings, Municipal/Medical, May 1909, nos 36–37 (WBSA), p. 39.
28 B.C. Mahtab, *Impressions: The Diary of a European Tour* (London, St Catherine Press Ltd, 1908), p. 171.
29 See Mahtab, *Impressions*, esp. p. 110.
30 Government of Bengal, A Proceedings, Municipal/Medical, May 1909, nos 36–37 (WBSA), p. 39.
31 Government of Bengal, A Proceedings, Municipal/Medical, May 1909, nos 36–37 (WBSA), p. 39.

it advisable that the institution should be started at that place, 'In view of the overcrowding of Darjeeling'.[32] The alternative locations for the sanatorium they proposed were Madhupur, Deoghur and Simultola, all in the forested and hilly plateaus of the adjacent province of Bihar.[33] Ten years later, he also offered the gift of two plots of land that he possessed to the Kurseong Municipality in aid of developing the town's conservancy system, possibly again in the hope that a few civic facilities for lower middle-class visitors at the small hill town would divert them from Darjeeling itself.[34]

It is evident that at this time Darjeeling was a coveted site for medicalized leisure for affluent Indians, which effectively excluded seasonal visitors of relatively modest means. In 1915 Jadunath Ganguli, a Bengali doctor in Benares, recommended his town's value as an alternative health resort for Bengalis of modest means, pointing out that hill sanatoriums in general were too expensive 'for the average Bengali'.[35] He also noted that 'Very few of the Indian health resorts have received that stamp of efficacy for curing particular diseases, which alone enables the physician to recommend them for those diseases. So that as in Waltaire or Darjeeling, all sorts of patients rush in pell-mell.'[36] Therefore, in the new century, Darjeeling emerged as a site of contested medical discourses and of medicalized leisure for Indian bodies as well; and the resources of the town strained to accommodate them in the high season. At the same time, alternative spatial and medical discourses were suggested to develop alternative sites of rest and regeneration for Indian bodies in the tropics.

An interesting aspect of Darjeeling's supposed efficacy for Bengali physiques is that while they were a growing presence in Darjeeling, Bengali clerks were perceived to be too weak to acclimatize in Simla: 'The ill-paid and ill-fed clerks are quite unable to stand the trying cold of Simla.'[37] Instead, their positions were gradually filled by educated men from the neighbouring Punjab.

The perception of overcrowded Darjeeling was enhanced when a major landslip occurred, causing fatalities among the British as well as the Indians, and was attributed to deforestation within the town. As a result, the 'native' settlements within Darjeeling were pushed to new areas not previously considered suitable for building houses. Not only within the town itself, the immigrant population spread to the surrounding areas. In 1903, a report by a military official on the water supply at the cantonment at Jalapahar predicted the contamination of the springs that supplied water due to extending habitations above the cantonment:

32 Government of Bengal, A Proceedings, Municipal/Medical, May 1909, nos 36–37 (WBSA), p. 39.
33 Government of Bengal, A Proceedings, Municipal/Medical, May 1909, nos 36–37 (WBSA), p. 40.
34 Government of Bengal Proceedings, Municipal/Municipal, Dec. 1919, IOR/P/10520 (APAC), pp. 6–7.
35 Jadunath Ganguly, 'Benares as a Health Resort for Bengali Invalids', *Indian Medical Record*, 35 (1915), p. 43.
36 Ganguly, 'Benares as a Health Resort', p. 43.
37 Kanwar, *Imperial Simla*, p. 165.

Contagion and Enclaves

> None of these ... can be considered safe or satisfactory; they are surface springs deriving their water from the inhabited area that lies above them. It is merely a question of time, when this inhabited area shall have sufficiently polluted the derived water, so as to make it unfit for drinking: the introduction of one case of waterborne disease, such as enteric fever or cholera, might conceivably cause an epidemic even now; but it is certain that no hill population can continue with impunity, for an indefinite period, to draw its drinking water from the hill on which it lives, if the habitations are at a higher level than the springs.[38]

In 1906, the Commissioner of Bhagalpur appealed to the provincial government to allow construction at the Toong Soong Basti at Darjeeling, condemned as an unsafe area by the Landslip Committee of 1906.[39] The government refused to relax building restrictions at that site.[40] Nevertheless, the town continued to grow at the edges. In 1919 the Secretary of the Darjeeling Municipality pointed out to the government that the Sanitary Commissioner of Bengal had made a survey of the town and 'traced all sanitary defects to the want of expert supervision', recommending the appointment of a health officer for Darjeeling.[41] A meeting of the municipal commissioners of Darjeeling discussed the report:

> the defects ... brought to notice in connection with vital statistics, conservancy arrangements, food supply, and the sanitary arrangements and cubic space, etc. in hotels, boarding-houses and schools, and the want of proper arrangements in places in which mosquitoes are likely to breed ...[42]

The report recommended the appointment of a special health officer, which was only made in large cities.[43] But the difficulties of an expanding hill-station, originally intended for fewer residents than it had to host in the early twentieth century, were not to be resolved with the simple appointment of a health officer. The upper-class Bengalis felt it as keenly as the British. In 1917 some prominent Darjeeling Bengalis who belonged to the Brahmo Samaj (a socio-religious order predominantly comprising of upper-caste and affluent Bengalis) made a petition for the removal of a fish market from its vicinity.[44] The legal wrangle reached the provincial council, where the government replied that it had no knowledge

38 'Report on Water Supply at Jalapahar and Lebong', IOR/L/MIL/7/3063 (APAC), p. 1.
39 Government of Bengal, A Proceedings, Municipal/Municipal, nos 156–58, 1906 (WBSA), p. 9.
40 Government of Bengal, A Proceedings, Municipal/Municipal, nos 156–58, 1906 (WBSA), p. 9.
41 Government of Bengal Proceedings, Municipal/Sanitation, Dec. 1919, nos 61–62, IOR/P/10521 (APAC), p. 49.
42 Government of Bengal Proceedings, Municipal/Sanitation, Dec. 1919, nos 61–62, IOR/P/10521 (APAC), p. 50.
43 Hugh Tinker, *The Foundations of Local Self-Government in India, Pakistan and Burma* (New York, Praeger and London, Pall Mall Press, 1968), p. 93.
44 Government of Bengal Proceedings, Municipal/Municipal, Feb. 1918, no. 16, IOR/P/10306 (APAC), p. 27.

of the market.[45] Evidently the fish market had sprung up to meet the demands of the growing population. The increase in both the residential and seasonal populations within the town in the summer led to regular shortages of meat and milk. Most foodstuffs were expensive in hill-stations, because they had to be imported from the plains; poultry, beef, milk and other animal products continued to remain expensive. In 1916, the *Darjeeling Advertiser* demanded that the government release nearby forest land for grazing to prevent the migration of cattle farmers to nearby Sikkim in order to ensure supplies of milk and meat to the hill-station.[46] The government renewed existing leased lands leased to a British dairy farmers, but there was little other land available.[47] The perceptions of the 'overcrowding' of Darjeeling also brought about comparisons to the typical urban problems of the cities in the plains of India. For instance, in 1918 the Municipal Commissioners of Darjeeling thought it necessary to raise the fine for begging in the town 'for discouraging professional beggary' from Rs 10 to Rs 50, a huge sum, for the second offence.[48]

Municipality, Political Exclusivity and the Darjeeling Hill-station

One reason the hill-station of Darjeeling, as that of Simla and Ootacamund, retained its social exclusivity was that the British government's gradual process of 'decentralization' of power through the incremental abdication of local governance was firmly kept out of the hill-stations as well as 'backward areas', such as most regions where there was a substantial tribal population. The provincial government formed the municipality of Darjeeling in 1851, and the hill-station was one of the first to boast of a municipality in British India.[49] Its chairman was the district officer, and its members constituted entirely officials and members nominated by government, all of whom were British. After the Local Self-Government Bill in Bengal (1885), government encouraged the formation of municipalities, districts and local boards, but it was a slow process and a limited franchise based on ownership ensured that even elected members remained under the influence of the district officials. The British government's long-term vision was avowedly to encourage Indians to prove themselves capable of self-governance through their slow introduction to local government. This constitutional process was heightened after the Morley–Minto Reforms (1909), and led to a greater proportion of elected members in local bodies in all provinces, including Bengal. But officials argued for keeping the Darjeeling municipality out of the electoral process, arguing that it needed to be governed by officials directly nominated by government:

45 Government of Bengal Proceedings, Municipal/Municipal, Feb. 1918, no. 16, IOR/ P/10306 (APAC), p. 27.
46 Dozey, *A Concise History*, pp. 61–67.
47 Government of Bengal Proceedings, Municipal, Sep. 1919, IOR/P/10520 (APAC).
48 Government of Bengal Proceedings, Municipal/Municipal, Sep. 1919, nos 37–38, IOR/P/10520 (APAC), p. 49.
49 Tinker, *Foundations*, p. 30.

> The circumstances of the municipality are peculiar. There is an enormous difference between its cold-weather population and its population during the season when the place is crowded with visitors ... The present system of nomination works very well, and all interests in the town are very well represented on the body of the Commissioners, far better than they would be by a system of election.[50]

Special funds from government enabled the Deputy Commissioner of Darjeeling, R.T. Greer, to undertake the widening of the Chowrasta that led to the main promenade, as well as install electricity within the municipal limits of the hill-station in 1896–97. A few years later, the municipality widened all roads in the main town, protecting them with railings.[51] Official control over the municipality and its special status as a primarily European (British) residential town helped it obtain grants-in-aid directly from the provincial government for the hill-station and many of its institutions, including the Eden Sanitarium. In 1907, when most other municipalities in Bengal struggled due to a lack of income, the provincial government granted the sum of Rs 1, 80,000 for sewerage and septic tank improvements in Darjeeling.[52]

Historians differ in their analyses of the lack of sanitary infrastructure and public health measures in colonial India. While Ramasubban, Ray and others have argued that the colonial government did little to actively promote public health infrastructure except in cities, others such as Hugh Tinker and Mark Harrison have argued for a more sympathetic approach to British policies on public health and local self-government.[53] Harrison has argued that the indigenous elites' resistance to public health, fuelled by suspicion of Western sanitary models, as well as their reluctance to pay higher municipal taxes formed the principal bottleneck to the development of a functional public health system, especially in Calcutta, Bombay and Madras. Tinker has argued as well that, with the partial exception of Bengal, there was little enthusiasm for public health and sanitary reforms from the Indian elite. By 1920, when the Montague–Chelmsford Reforms transferred control over education and health to elected provincial governments, nationalist politics had outpaced municipal reform in colonial India. In the 1920s, therefore, Indian participation in local government was controlled by a few 'moderate' nationalists. In Bengal, municipal governance under the new system was beset with many problems, including factionalism, resistance to taxes and a very slow rate of progress in building infrastructure.[54]

---

50 Government of Bengal Proceedings, Municipal/Municipal, July 1910, IOR/P/8419 (APAC), p. 77.
51 Dozey, *A Concise History*, p. 58.
52 *Resolution Reviewing the Reports on the Working of Municipalities in Bengal, 1906–1907* (Calcutta, Bengal Secretariat Book Depot, 1908), p. 6. IOR/V/24/2855, APAC.
53 See Ramasubban, 'Imperial Health'; Ray, *History*, pp. 342–48; Tinker, *Foundations*; Harrison, *Public Health*.
54 Tinker, *Foundations*, pp. 279–80; Harrison, *Public Health*, pp. 166–201; Ray, *History*, pp. 221–53, especially for government lacunae in providing clean drinking-water supplies.

Throughout the interwar years, therefore, municipal governance and public health infrastructure in urban India remained fragmented and patchy at best; while in rural areas their development was virtually non-existent. In Bengal particularly, the functioning of local self-government after the provincialization of health services was fractious and the municipalities were often impecunious, with low rates of assessment, inefficient collections of revenue and, as the colonial officials often pointed out, an overdependence on loans or grants from provincial government. But the hill-stations, particularly Darjeeling and to a lesser extent Kurseong, remained enclaves of privilege, with their water supply and sanitation facilities provided for through provincial grants. In 1919, for instance, the provincial government offered a grant of Rs 50,000 and a long-term loan of Rs 30,000 to the Kurseong Municipality for its drainage and sewerage system.[55] And while Darjeeling continued to attract more people, the municipality provided improved facilities for 'the water supply, drainage, electric lighting' as well as a plan for a 'housing scheme to meet the growing demand for the provision of houses of a cheap and sanitary type' at a suitable location away from the main town.[56]

Not only concerned with municipal infrastructure, the municipal board, which after the elections of 1923 included Indian and European (generally British) non-officials, continued the special efforts towards preserving the greenery of Darjeeling town itself:

> arboriculture, as carried out in the town of Darjeeling, differs from that work as done elsewhere in Bengal ... the Darjeeling Improvement Fund (Town) Committee devoted their attention to planting up the slips and other bare areas, with a view to ensuring the safety of the hillsides ... ensuring the safety of the hillsides has added to the beauty of the town.[57]

The prosperous settlement of Europeans and Indians within the town, and the high municipal rates augmented with generous government grants to the Darjeeling Improvement Fund, ensured that Darjeeling remained cleaner and better provided with municipal amenities than most towns in Bengal despite overcrowding, encroachments and problems in supplies of drinking water and sewage disposal. In 1923, the annual report on the municipalities of Bengal noted the lacklustre functioning of civic municipalities in Bengal and pointed out that Darjeeling was the only exception and attributed this to the high taxes:

---

55 Reply to question by Babu Brojendra Kishore Ray in the Legislative Council, 18 Feb. 1919, Government of Bengal Proceedings, Municipal/Sanitation, Feb. 1919, P/10521, no. 4 (APAC), p. 7.
56 *Resolution Reviewing the Reports*; Govt of Bengal Proceedings, Local Self Government/Municipalities Branch, July 1923, no. 50, IOR/P/11304 (APAC), p. 48.
57 Government of Bengal Proceedings, Local Self Government/Local Self-Government, March 1921, nos 12–13, IOR/P/10980 (APAC), p. 22.

> Progress is impossible in these municipalities without an increase in income, whether by raising the rates or by more stringent assessment. The Darjeeling Municipality fully maintained its reputation as a progressive municipality ... so long as the fear of increased taxation continues to be the common meeting ground for the progressive and reactionary, municipal administration must be dreary, uneventful and barren.[58]

When this report was written nationalist movements on a mass scale were predominant, and, particularly in Bengal, local self-government was the object of nationalist political protest and boycott. But hill-stations were largely exempt from the messiness and realpolitik of urban politics in twentieth-century colonial India. It continued to be dominated by European (British) non-officials, and although in the 1920s the proportion of Indians in the municipal council increased, the chairman was still a government official. Its municipal rates continued to be higher than all other parts of Bengal.[59] Harrison and Tinker have both argued that the low rates of local taxation, forced down by the vested interests of the indigenous local elite, were responsible for the lack of long-term infrastructure in colonial India (although Tinker's argument is more tempered, blaming the essential conservatism of the central government of India as much as lack of local leadership for the lack of the development of a public health infrastructure).[60] One might equally argue that the site of Indian nationalism itself had moved decisively from contestations over local governance to national autonomy, particularly because the devolution of power at the local level was inadequate. At any rate, the hill-stations in colonial India remained enclaves where municipal administration was still controlled by officials and by a small majority of the resident population. Its average rate of taxation per head was above Rs 10 (Rs 9 in the case of Kurseong), whereas in the average district municipality in Bengal the average annual rate was Rs 3 per person.[61]

In the interwar years in Darjeeling, 30 per cent of the elected municipal commissioners continued to be British, and with another 18 per cent of officials nominated by the government, there was little agency in the hands of the Indians in local governance.[62] The rates of taxation stayed at around Rs 10 per head, at least three times higher than in the rest of Bengal. The provincial government also provided generous funding, when required, to maintain and make improvements to the sanitation, water-supply and electricity in

---

58 *Resolution on Working of Municipalities in Bengal*, Local Self-Government/Municipalities, July 1923, IOR/P/11304 (APAC), p. 48. Harrison has pointed out that in the case of Calcutta, the Indian elite who controlled the municipality of Calcutta in the late nineteenth century refused increased rates needed to implement sanitary provisions. See Harrison, *Public Health*, pp. 202–26.
59 For instance, Government of Bengal Proceedings, Local Self-Government/Municipal, May 1931, no. 1, IOR/P11942 (APAC), p. 3.
60 Tinker, *Foundations*, pp. 279–80, 287–90; Harrison, *Public Health*, pp. 202–26.
61 Bengal Local Self-Government/Municipal, May 1928, IOR/P/11705, pp. 163–64.
62 *The Annual Administration Report of the Darjeeling Municipality 1932–33*, MSS Eur D 911/1 (APAC), ff. 1.

the hill-station.[63] Although officials constantly noted the strain on municipal resources in the town, such as drinking water and proper drainage, they were always able to find the funds to augment the resources. In 1932, for instance, the deputy commissioner of Darjeeling was able to report both an increase in the catchment area in the reservoir at Senchal that supplied the town as well as extension to the pipes to deliver the water. He also effected improvements to the municipal slaughter house, made extensive repairs to the drainage in the main town and sanctioned a new generating station for providing electricity.[64]

Nor was this an anomaly so far as hill-stations went. Whereas the municipal infrastructure and facilities in north India and Punjab continued to be rudimentary, the hill-station of Simla remained relatively sheltered from experiments in elected local governments, unlike in the plains.[65]

In this period, despite complaints of overcrowding, Darjeeling remained a relatively pristine town. A Himalayan tourism route to Sikkim and Bhutan developed, and this too attracted tourists. Many seasonal visitors to Darjeeling who sought to experience the beauty of the Himalayas now preferred to go for treks to the Sikkim after a halt in the town.[66] Darjeeling was also the first stop for mountaineering expeditions.[67] The first of the Everest expeditions took place in 1921.[68] In 1928, one appreciative British visitor returned after a five-year absence to find that 'although several new buildings have sprung up ... the place is little changed'.[69]

Even for many ordinary British travellers, Darjeeling represented a base for the exploration of the quieter and more scenic routes to neighbouring Bhutan and Sikkim. Major Somerset, a doctor then serving in the IMS, went to Darjeeling in November 1944 by invitation of his patient, the secretary of the Planters' Club. There he met one Major Kidd, who was an 'old retired journalist' living in Darjeeling and who 'used to make arrangements for people to go on trek.'[70] Apart from remaining a tourist destination, Darjeeling continued to be administratively crucial because, in spite of growing nationalist criticism, the central and provincial governments continued their policy of moving the capital to hill-stations for eight months in the year.[71] During the Second World War

63 See, for instance, *Resolution Reviewing the Reports*, pp. 115–19.
64 Mss Eur C 379 (APAC), p. 255.
65 Kanwar, *Imperial Simla*, pp. 104–20, 123–29.
66 A traveller remarked in 1920, 'The journey to Darjeeling is to most people an every day event ... its comparative ease in accessibility by rail has made it a week-end affair with husbands anxious to pay a fleeting visit to their winter wives.' See R.J. Minney, *Midst Himalayan Mists* (Calcutta, Butterworth & Co., 1920), p. 4.
67 For instance, see Percy Brown, *Tours in Sikhim and the Darjeeling District* (4th edn, Calcutta, W. Newman & Co., 1944), and Bhanja, *Darjeeling at a Glance*, pp. 113–41.
68 T.S. Blakeney, 'A.R. Hinks and the First Everest Expedition, 1921', *The Geographical Journal*, 136 (1970), pp. 333–43.
69 Letter to Dorothy, 23 Oct. 1928, Mss Eur D939/17.
70 Mss Eur D 1023 (APAC), ff. 179 of typescript.
71 Kanwar, *Imperial Simla*, pp. 46–70.

Darjeeling was also a military and air base for British troops on the Eastern Front.[72]

The expansion of the hill-station and its transformation into a summer capital and administrative and strategic hub occurred despite the fact that medical discourses questioned its status as a health-giving sanatorium. The enclave of Darjeeling was sustained by a discourse of its 'healthiness', which embodied not necessarily medical insights and experiences in the tropics, but the very logic of colonial enclaves, which initiated in the first place the establishment of the hill-stations and sought, and largely succeeded in sustaining, their municipal exclusivity and privileges.

Conclusion

In the interwar period the enclave of Darjeeling changed to accommodate affluent and middle-class Indians. Indian medical discourse and popular culture both promoted 'hill climates' as healing for Indian bodies. In the process, Indians modified the racial component of not only Darjeeling as a hill-station, but the medical discourses of climate in the tropics. Darjeeling re-invented itself as a tropical enclave and promoted social exclusivity, which was also articulated in medical terms. This process was aided by the political distance of the hill-station from the intensely contested local politics of mainland Bengal. The regular improvements in sewerage, water supply and the facilities provided by the hospitals and the microbiological laboratory in Darjeeling ensured that epidemics in the hill-station were few and easily contained, unlike in the cities in the plains. Officials claimed to even contain 'hill-diarrhoea', the disease peculiar to tropical hill-stations, through improved filtration of the water supply in the town.[73] Therefore, although Darjeeling expanded to include the 'Other' in this period, it remained an enclave.

---

72 AIR 29/493 (National Archives, Kew).
73 Mss Eur C379 (APAC), p. 255.

CHAPTER 5

Contending Visions of Health Care in the Plantation Enclaves

In nineteenth-century medical, management and official discourse, the foothills of the Darjeeling (and the plains beyond), Terai and Duars were represented as sites of disease, fevers and fatalities. Malaria and blackwater fever, a particularly vicious form of fever, were widely prevalent among the planters as well as the labourers, although the indigenous *Meches* were supposed to have been immune from them. This chapter studies a particular historical moment in the formation of the plantation enclave, when its modes of functioning were challenged by a team of malariologists who were commissioned by the government of India to find out why malaria and blackwater fever were endemic to the plantations and to advise how to control the diseases. The medical experts' recommendations challenged the recruitment system, wage structure, and finally, the planters' autonomy within the plantations. In the time of interventionist external medical surveys and malaria research in the twentieth century, the modes of functioning of the plantation enclave were challenged. These surveys identified that diseases in the plantation system were due to the systems of recruitment, wage structure, and the autonomous paternalism of the planter class. In response, the planters provided an alternative vision of the 'moral economy' of the plantation system within which disease medical infrastructure and the livelihood of labourers could be managed by the paternalistic planter. The government's response was to compromise and impose a legislation that broadly confirmed the planters' vision of their enclaves.

In 1906, the government of India appointed a survey by expert medical authorities to look into the causes of and suggest methods for controlling fevers, particularly blackwater fever, which had recently caused several fatalities among the planters in the region, the consequence of a petition by the Dooars Planters Association (DPA) to the government of east Bengal and Assam. The resulting Christophers–Bentley report challenged the very foundations of the political economy of the plantations in the Duars and, by extension, all of northern Bengal. It dismissed the miasmatic theories of local disease and instead recommended that the plantations initiate a system of recruiting indentured labour that would enable the government to inspect their labourers for disease and intervene in the case of epidemics. It claimed that the remuneration to the workers was inadequate and the system of disbursing it through the recruiter-foremen (*sardars*) was responsible for keeping the workers vulnerable, malnourished and indebted. It argued for greater direct intervention by the state to control disease within the plantations. Effectively it challenged the ideological framework of the plantation enclave in northern Bengal and aimed for a dilution of the planters' autonomy through increased government intervention.

The planters and the district administration (which supported the planters' autonomy, although the government of India took a different view) lobbied the provincial government against the controversial report, and commissioned a committee to counter the recommendations of the Christophers–Bentley report and asserted the paternalistic rights of the plantation management (instead of the colonial state) over the labourers and within the plantation enclaves in their entirety. Eventually there was a compromise, with the provincial government on the recommendation of the district administration agreeing to limited legislation to increase the scope of intervention within Duars. But the Terai and Darjeeling plantations remained exempt. The implications of the two contending perspectives on the management of disease within the plantation enclaves were to resound for a long time in government policies as well as public debates.

The provincial government and the managements of the plantation enclaves reached a consensus that allowed for a limited government medical inspection within the plantations and agreed on occasional interventions by medical experts on invitation. These were negotiated through the political minefields of government policy, fear of nationalist (and later communist) politics, and the powerful tea lobby in Calcutta and London. From this point onwards, due to the limits of government influence, however partial, and medical intervention, the plantation enclaves no longer remained insulated from international medical curiosity and attention. This was not unique to northern Bengal. In contemporary Ceylon, Malay Straits and British Guyana, international medical experts and private health agencies pursued parasites and vectors that carried disease which affected the productivity of the labour force.[1] These were best achieved

---

1 The Rockefeller International Health Board initiated anti-hookworm campaigns in plantations in Ceylon and Darjeeling. It was not successful, but the initiatives underlined the plantations as the chosen sites for the implementation of Tropical Medicine. It also initiated campaigns against yellow fever and malaria in the Panama Canal, and in Egypt along the Suez Canal, sites where disease was seen to lead to 'unproductive' labour. See John H. Farley, *To Cast Out Disease: A History of the International Health Division of the Rockefeller Foundation (1913–1951)* (Oxford, Oxford University Press, 2004). The Liverpool and Calcutta Schools of Tropical Medicine trained British plantation doctors in anti-malaria techniques and sought their sponsorship for malaria research. See H.J.

within plantations, the quintessential enclaves where Tropical Medicine found its richest research sources and fields of experiment.[2] This chapter will discuss this moment of confrontation between medical experts and the colonial state and plantation management in order to analyse how this affected the insularity of the plantation enclaves and disease management within.

The Christophers–Bentley Report

In 1906, a number of planters in the Duars died of blackwater fever, which was associated with malaria in some form. One estimate put casualties in 1906 at ten per cent of the 'resident European planting population'.[3] J.A. Milligan, the settlement officer then engaged in the revenue settlement and survey of the district, noted that one of his first duties on arriving in Jalpaiguri in 1906 was to attend the funeral of a planter, and that 'this experience was repeated at short intervals during the fall of that dreadful year 1906'.[4] According to him this was the turning point when the planters realized that they needed expert medical advice to counter malaria and other fevers in the plantations instead of resigning themselves to disease and death as a matter of course.[5] By 1906 Ross's discovery of the mosquito as the malaria vector was widely disseminated, and in fact the Royal Society sent a Malaria Committee to endemic sites of the disease in Africa and India at the turn of the century. Tropical Medicine encouraged optimism for a long-term solution to morbidity and mortality in febrile but productive areas in the tropics. The planters now petitioned the government for a thorough assessment of malaria and blackwater fever in the Duars.[6] Appointed by the government of India, the committee consisted of two members: Christophers and Bentley. Christophers, IMS, was a prominent malariologist who had been a member of the Royal Society's Malaria Commission in India in 1901. He later supervised the infamous experiment on malaria control at Mian Mir in the IMS. Bentley, also of the IMS, had served in Assam

---

Power, *Tropical Medicine in the 20th Century: A History of the Liverpool School* (London and New York, Kegan Paul International, 1998).

2 For Rockefeller health campaigns in Ceylon, see Soma Hewa, *Colonialism, Tropical Disease and Imperial Medicine: Rockefeller Philanthropy in Sri Lanka* (Lanham, University Press of America, 1995).

3 Mss Eur C474, typescript titled, 'Leopards' (APAC), p. 2.

4 J.A. Milligan, *Final Report on the Survey and Settlement Reports in the Jalpaiguri District, 1906–1916* (Calcutta, 1919, APAC), p. 16.

5 Milligan, *Final Report*, p. 15.

6 Government of Bengal, Municipal/Sanitation Proceedings, March 1907 (WBSA), p. 1 of B Proceedings Index. See also Grunig, *Eastern Bengal*, p. 47. For the agreement on the part of the government of India that the matter may be 'entrusted to the Central Research Institute assisted by an Advisory Commission of selected officers', see Government of Bengal, Municipal/Sanitation Proceedings, May 1907, p. 1 of B Proceeding Index (WBSA). For the expectations of the DPA that the report would lead to solutions for the prevention of malaria and blackwater fever in the region, see Address of Chairman, DPA, at the Annual General Meeting, 8 Feb. 1909, *DPAAR*, 1911 (Calcutta, 1912, APAC), p. ii.

and acquired experience of medical practice in the tea plantations there. He later went on to become the Sanitary Commissioner of the undivided province of Bengal and, after the provincialization of the health service, the Director of Public Health in Bengal, an influential position he held for several years.

Christophers and Bentley produced two reports after their visit to the Duars: one on malaria and the other on blackwater fever in the area. Although their brief was to study two specific diseases, their reports took a broader view of disease in the plantations. These were the first comprehensive surveys of disease among the workers as well as the managerial staff in the tea plantations in northern Bengal. Their reports, particularly the one on malaria, challenged the climatic and the miasmatic concepts of disease and instead laid the responsibility for disease and malnutrition among the workers solely on the structure of the plantation economy of the region itself.[7] In the process they indicted the management of the plantations for the neglect of the labourers' health. While they made several suggestions for the prevention of malaria and blackwater fever among the managerial staff, their report linked disease among the workers directly to poverty and destitution; to the system of wages and labour control within the plantations.[8]

This approach created a point of crisis in the system of labour management, particularly for the Duars planters, but also, by implication, for the entire tea plantation area of northern Bengal. In response, the government of eastern Bengal and Assam instituted the Duars (Monahan) Committee whose report provided a point of resolution for this crisis in the plantation system.[9] This chapter explores the negotiation between the two contending interpretations of the plantation system. Both the Christophers–Bentley and the Monahan reports attempted to understand the nature of disease and workers' welfare in the Duars plantations but they differed in their understanding of where the responsibility and agency for that management should remain – with the state or the planters. Both reports ultimately claimed paternal jurisdiction over the workers' welfare – that of the government or of the planters. The differing visions of the two contending reports, concerning the economic and social structures, directly impacted on medical practices and policies within the plantations.

Free versus Indentured Labour: The Medical Dimensions

The first characteristic of the plantation system that Christophers and Bentley observed was that in the Duars (as well as in Darjeeling and Terai), labour was free; that is, they were not under a contractual agreement. There were several reasons for this. In Darjeeling, recruitment was done through *sardars* (contractors) from eastern Nepal and a similar system prevailed in Terai.[10] Apart

7 Christophers and Bentley, *Malaria in the Duars*, pp. 42–64.
8 Christophers and Bentley, *Malaria in the Duars*, pp. 67–71.
9 *Report of the Duars Committee* (Shillong, Eastern Bengal and Assam Govt Press, 1910).
10 In the Darjeeling and Terai plantations, too, the management recruited through the

from some numerically insignificant Nepali (Paharia) labour, the Duars plantations recruited from the same areas as Assam: their labourers comprised indigenous peoples from the Chotanagpur and Santhal Pargana areas of Bihar, and were mostly Oraons, Mundas and Santhals. They were collectively known as Madesias. By the time of the expansion of tea gardens in northern Bengal, the indentured system of labour in Assam had acquired great notoriety. The penal clauses for breach of control led to many abuses on the part of the planters. It also initiated nationalist criticism for the first time.[11] The contractual system in Assam was designed to provide the planter with wide-ranging powers of detention and resulted in a power equation quite hopelessly in favour of the planters. Simultaneously it provided, at least on paper, through legislation, certain safeguards for the workers while they were travelling to Assam, as well as during the period of their contract. This included a system of registration of vital statistics as well as provision for regular inspections by the government. These were generally carried out by the civil surgeons of the respective districts through the medical department of government.[12]

The system of 'free' labour was indeed important to the planters in northern Bengal as it forestalled government intervention within the plantation enclaves. In the absence of a penal contract the colonial state would not intervene in the recruitment process or enquire into the labourers' condition once they reached the plantations. For instance, the Assam Labour Enquiry (1895) reported that since labour in Duars, Darjeeling and Terai was free, it was not necessary to legislate for their health or well-being.[13] This system facilitated, moreover, the flow of Madesia workers to northern Bengal, especially because it was located nearer to the catchment areas of the Santhal Parganas and Chotanagpur than Assam. Recruiters found it easier to transport them in large numbers. In 1895 the Settlement Officer of the Western Duars noted that workers with their *sardars* who were bound for the Duars and Terai were sometimes intercepted and coerced into agreements (contracts) by the *arkatis*, commissioning agents for the less popular tea gardens in Assam.[14] In 1904, an investigation into the recruitment of labourers in India and Ceylon emphasized that the planters in

---

sardars, who worked within the plantations as well. The *sardars* also appointed intermediaries, *duffadars*, to recruit workers on their behalf. *Notes on Tea in Darjeeling*, p. 74. The Nepali *sardars* could provide large and steady numbers of workers. A planters' manual reminded one that 'Bootea Sirdars can't get Coolies so easily or in such large numbers as Pahariahs.' Bamber, *An Account*, p. 9. See also *Report of Royal Commission on Labour in India* (London, 1931), pp. 356–57 (hereafter *RCLI*).

11 After several allegations of ill-treatment of Assam tea labourers, the nationalist Indian Association sent their representative Dvarkanath Gangopadhyaya to tour a few tea estates in Assam in 1886. He published his findings of violation of contract and abuse of labourers over 13 articles in two periodicals, *The Sanjibani* and *The Bengalee*, in 1886–87. See Dvarkanatha Gangopadhyaya, *Slavery in British Dominion* (Calcutta, Jijnasa, 1972).
12 *RCLI*, p. 417.
13 *Report of the Labour Enquiry Commission* (Calcutta, 1896, APAC).
14 D.H.E. Sunder, *Final Report on the Land Revenue Settlement of the Western Duars, Bengal* (Calcutta, Bengal Secretariat Press, 1895), p. 106.

northern Bengal preferred to function outside a contractual system of recruitment.[15]

The crucial point the Christophers–Bentley report made was that there were no reliable statistics for the numbers of immigrant labourers in the plantations, creating an 'example of the working of the special system of labour peculiar to itself'.[16] Government therefore had no means of ascertaining the numbers or the vital statistics of the people working and residing within the plantation enclaves in Darjeeling, Duars and Terai. Although some plantations maintained records of births and deaths, Christophers and Bentley concluded that they were inadequate and incomplete, and even ridiculous because occasionally they 'compared favourably on paper with some of the healthiest communities in England'.[17]

Christophers and Bentley sought to 'standardize' labour management into the indentured format, and were the first government representatives to emphasize the need for a system of registration of vital statistics within the plantations, with the government inspecting the results. Why was the registration of vital statistics considered so crucial? The system of free labour that had developed uniquely in the Darjeeling foothills posed difficulties for existing international medical expertise and state policies within the more commonplace nineteenth-century institution of indentured labour in colonial plantations in Ceylon, Assam, the Malay Straits, Mauritius, South Africa and the West Indies.[18]

Christopher and Bentley, were concerned that 'since the labour force forms only a fraction of the total coolie population on a garden, a large number of the latter are not registered in any way and their sickness or death entails no responsibility upon anyone'.[19] Moreover, any worker who due to sickness or for any other reason would remain absent from the rolls of a tea estate would be struck off after one month. Such workers might still be resident within the tea estates, suffering from long illnesses, but they were 'to a large extent lost to sight'.[20] The lack of indentured labour entailed, they insisted, a floating population of migrant workers who were not only afflicted with disease themselves, but who also formed a mobile reservoir of disease which could spread to the entire district and even the entire province.[21] A few years previously, a report commissioned by the Assam government had noted the large number of temporary workers in Duars – in 1902 the number (provided by the

---

15 Arbuthnott, *Report*, p. 5.
16 Christophers and Bentley, *Malaria in the Duars*, p. 42.
17 Christophers and Bentley, *Malaria in the Duars*, p. 109.
18 H. Tinker, *A New System of Slavery: The Export of Indian Labour Overseas, 1830–1920* (London, New York and Bombay, Oxford University Press, 1974), pp. 20–115.
19 Christophers and Bentley, *Malaria in the Duars*, p. 43.
20 Christophers and Bentley, *Malaria in the Duars*, p. 45
21 Christophers and Bentley were, however, not the first to observe that newly immigrant labourers and children suffered more than the old immigrants in the tea districts. The point had been made two decades earlier in the context of immigrant indentured labour in Assam. See *Special Report on the Working of Act I of 1882 in The Province of Assam during the Years 1886–1889* (Calcutta, Superintendent of Government Printing, 1890, APAC), p. 253.

plantation managements) was estimated at 38,218 out of a total workforce of 61,784.[22] 'Floating' workers represented the danger of transmission of diseases on an epidemic scale. Therefore, Christophers and Bentley were not arguing for dismantling the plantation enclave; rather, they argued that the plantations must reinforce their boundaries, keep an account of the numbers of workers and furthermore record their vital statistics. The planters felt challenged because 'free', non-contractual labour absolved them of responsibility for the workers resident within the plantations. Moreover, any compulsory record-keeping would also render them open to government inspection.

Planter as the Provider: The Moral Economy of the Plantation Enclave

The Christophers–Bentley report raised another point: that the system of recruitment, pay and work in the plantations led directly to a cycle of impoverishment and disease. In northern Bengal unlike in Assam, the *sardars* were also the foremen who distributed work and pay among the labourers. This sustained the hierarchy between the *sardar* and 'his' workers within the plantation enclaves. After a few years, some labourers were able to save money and settle outside the tea plantations as cultivators; yet others supplemented their incomes by buying and then hiring out their bullocks for carting. They argued that such signs of prosperity among the workers were limited to a few only, mostly *sardars*, or their assistants.[23] Meanwhile newly immigrant workers were the most vulnerable to disease, partly due to lack of adequate food and nutrition. The medical experts attributed inadequate nutrition (inadequate in the sense that they perpetuated unproductive capacity) to the *sardari* system of labour in the Duars. This *sardari* system was the common method of recruitment in India's manufacturing centres particularly in the jute industry as well as in the tea plantations. It relied on clan networks to draw in dispossessed or landless peasants who would migrate on a temporary or permanent basis.[24] In northern Bengal, the plantations paid the *sardars* a certain sum for every worker that they recruited; anything between two and five rupees.[25] They were also paid a small amount, a *pice* for every day's work (*haziri*) done by each of the

---

22 Arbuthnott, *Report*, p. 1.
23 Christophers and Bentley, *Malaria in the Duars*, pp. 61–62. The *RCLI* pointed out in 1931 that not all workers had access to land for cultivation.
24 The dependence on the *sardari* system both for recruitment of labourers and for their supervision in the daily work regimes in the plantations continued even after 1924, when a separate branch of the Tea Districts Labour Association (TDLA) was formed in order to recruit for the planters in the Duars. See *ITAAR, 1921* (Calcutta, 1922, APAC), pp. 32–33. The TDLA was originally formed by planters in Assam to facilitate centralized recruitment. The Duars branch of the TDLA used garden *sardars* for recruitment in the Chota Nagpur and Santhal Parganas areas, which were its 'traditional recruiting districts'. It used paid recruiters for new recruiting areas such as the Madras Presidency. Griffiths, *History*, pp. 284–86.
25 Arbuthnott, *Report*, p. 2.

workers they had recruited. In some plantations (possibly the newly opened ones which did not already have a substantial settled community of labourers) the *sardar*'s commission was two *pice*.[26] The plantation management also gave the *sardars* a sum of money to advance as a loan to newly recruited workers, who used it to pay for their journey to the tea district and for subsistence in the initial weeks. The entire system relied on the *sardars* providing, through the planter, for the various requirements of every worker that he recruited and supervised in the plantations. This system enabled the planters to transfer the responsibility for the labourers to the *sardars*, while retaining their status as the ultimate providers and arbiters of justice. The dependence on clan networks carried an implicit notion of a moral economy sustaining a hierarchical, quasi-feudal relationship between the *sardar* and his gang, in this case, emulating the colonial system of the manager (*burra sahib*) at the top of the hierarchy. This particular moral economy was a construct, and a new one. The coexistence of the feudal and colonial capitalist system was as new as the system of work and recruitment in the tea estates, a social and economic relationship created out of the plantation economy system.[27]

Christophers and Bentley argued that the system depended too heavily on the assumed benevolence of the *sardars*: 'the real conditions are unrecognised. The relation between the *sardar* and his coolies are on a much less philanthropic footing'.[28] From a medical point of view, they found little to recommend it. This intervention by Christophers and Bentley was on the principle that the supervisory position of the state would help to rationalize the wages in the plantation system. Nutrition for the workers was important for their productivity; 'Perhaps there is nothing of more vital importance to the members of a community than that they shall obtain a physiologically adequate dietary ... proportionate to the amount of physical work expected of them'.[29] The process of government intervention to ensure fair wages was one which substituted the paternalism of the planter with that of the state. It is another matter that the example of Assam was not necessarily the most pertinent demonstration of the paternalism of the state, because the neutrality and accuracy of the government inspections had been in doubt from the time the Indian Association sent its first delegate to the tea plantations in 1886.[30]

Christophers and Bentley recognized that the economy of the plantation system left the *sardars* with little alternative but to coerce the labourers to work even when they were too ill to work, because in the case of illness or death, the

---

26 Arbuthnott, *Report*, p. 2.
27 The Royal Commission on Labour found the system unchanged in 1931, *RCLI*, p. 415. Das Gupta has argued that such a system enabled the planters to pay low wages and encourage subsistence cultivation by the tea plantation workers, thereby creating a system of 'twin dependency'. R. Das Gupta, 'Plantation Labour in Colonial India', in E. Valentine Daniel, Henry Bernstein and Tom Brass (eds), *Plantations, Proletarians, and Peasants in Colonial Asia* (special issue, *Journal of Peasant Studies*, 1992), pp. 172–91.
28 Christophers and Bentley, *Malaria in the Duars*, p. 44.
29 Christophers and Bentley, *Malaria in the Duars*, p. 5.
30 Gangopadhyaya, *Slavery*, pp. 33–35.

advances made to the *sardars* were called in by the management: workers' debts were to be accounted for by the *sardars*.[31] Nor was this unique to the Duars. In Darjeeling, the advances to workers were dispensed through and recovered from the *sardars*: 'The cooly looks to the sardar for an advance, and the sardar to the manager.'[32] In Terai as well, a similar system of organizing labour prevailed. W.M. Fraser, a planter who initially worked in Sylhet and in 1895 moved to a tea plantation in Terai, pointed out the role of the *sardar* in Terai:

> It was all very different from Sylhet, where every coolie was a unit. Here the unit was the sirdar. He it was who got the advance in money that brought the coolies in, and the whole of the pay earned by his people was handed to him. The coolies were in debt to the sirdar and the sirdar to the garden, and the only security the latter had was the presence at work of the coolies.[33]

Even before the Christophers–Bentley report, the Arbuthnott report had noted that in the Duars, the *sardars* had no security for the money loaned out to workers, and that the tea gardens considered them liable for any loss.[34] It was in the *sardar*'s interest to see that 'his' labourers worked every day and that there existed a system of intelligence through which a *sardar* could locate an absconding labourer in any tea plantation.[35] The *sardars* and the workers, the Christophers–Bentley report emphasized, were trapped within a relentless system of debts and coerced labour, because the final responsibility for the workers did not rest with the tea plantation management, but with the *sardars*. Christophers and Bentley had pointed out an essential contradiction in the paternalism of the plantation system. The planter, although symbolically the mai-baap (feudal lord), was ultimately not directly responsible for the labourers' welfare. The system ensured that the planter remained at a distance, while the *sardar*, who had limited resources, had the burden of the labourers' welfare. This misplaced responsibility was of course a direct contradiction of the claim of paternal benevolence that the management of the tea plantations assumed with respect to the workers; a claim that gained in certitude and legitimacy throughout the colonial period. The system evidently continued long after the Christophers–Bentley's report was published, and the Royal Commission recognized that the system was 'fraught with danger to the labourer, who is frequently in debt to his sardar'.[36]

The third intervention by Christophers and Bentley was on the inadequacy of the labourers' wages. The working day in each tea estate was divided into two daily tasks – the *hazira* and the *ticca*. The *hazira* was the first work of the day, and *ticca* (or *doubly*) was the second, theoretically optional task.[37] The

---

31 Arbuthnott, *Report*, p. 3.
32 O'Malley, *Bengal District Gazetteers*, p. 84.
33 Fraser, *Recollections*, p. 51.
34 Arbuthnott, *Report*, p. 3.
35 Arbuthnott, *Report*, p. 3.
36 *RCLI*, p. 399.
37 Ray has shown that the *ticca* or the *doubly* was not really optional. It comprised the essential task of the day for most workers. See Ray, *Transformations*, pp. 104–6.

first tasks varied according to the season, being the heaviest during the peak monsoon months. The men were generally given the heavier tasks of hoeing and digging, and the women and children did the plucking. Women were also allocated lighter hoeing and pruning tasks. In the winter, between November and February, work was easier and consisted of digging and clearing the trenches and drains, and some pruning.

According to Christophers and Bentley, the workers' wages were below the level of subsistence. Their perspective on subsistence was clinical: food available to the working population, they believed, should be proportionate to the amount of labour they were to expend. The average monthly pay of a coolie that the managers claimed to pay was Rs 6 for a man, Rs 4–8 for a woman, and Rs 2–8 for a working child, and these would not be sufficient to supply adequate nutrition, even compared to a famine code recommendation. After an inspection and a survey of local prices, they discovered that the real purchasing power of the wages they earned was much less than what the planters had suggested.[38] This contradicted all assertions by planters, who generally claimed that their workers were prosperous, able to save when they were thrifty, and thereby either move out and settle outside the tea estate as tenant-cultivators or buy bullocks, goats and even cultivable land with their savings. The planters argued, too, that the workers who were not able to save were either indolent or wasted their money on drink.

It is difficult to estimate the real wages of the labourers throughout the colonial period because the workers survived not only from their wages but also by cultivating rice and vegetables in small plots of land, known as *khet* land. Most plantations possessed several acres of land that were not under tea cultivation, as government required only 15 per cent of the leased land to be under tea. The plantations used the excess land for timber as well as rented some of it to their labourers as *khet*. Many workers also provided for themselves through occasional hunting game, fishing and gathering edible roots in the forests.[39] Their report argued that the low wages affected particularly the new immigrants who did not immediately have access to *khet* land.[40]

38 Christophers and Bentley, *Malaria in the Duars*, p. 51.
39 The Royal Commission on Labour in India pointed out that an evaluation of the concession to cultivate lands should be made, because there was a discrepancy (both in the tea estates and among labourers within the estates) in the distribution of land for cultivation: 'some managers charge an uneconomic rent, others charge no rent and yet others have no such land at their disposal'. See *RCLI*, p. 397. The planters usually resorted to the argument that their subsistence was provided for in kind through their subsidiary occupations. This was accepted as fact. Griffiths, *History*, p. 297. Das Gupta has pointed out that the land given for cultivation was used as a means of disciplining the labourers by taking it away. See Das Gupta, 'Exploitation of Plantation Workers, Reproduction of Labour Power and Nature of Proletarianization in North-East India', in idem, *Labour and Working Class in Eastern India: Studies in Colonial History* (Calcutta, KP Bagchi, 1994), pp. 141–74. The plantation management admitted to the Royal Commission that they had an 'understanding' among their members not to raise their wages. See *RCLI*, p. 399.
40 Not all the workers had *khet/bari* lands for their own cultivation. They were given to some labourers on condition of work in the plantations. See *RCLI*, pp. 384–85.

Christophers and Bentley also pointed out that the workers were housed in 'insanitary and inadequate shacks': 'the majority are housed in a manner at once primitive and temporary'.[41] For them, the protection of the labourer under the *sardar*, based on paternalistic terms, was not a foregone conclusion.

Their living conditions, Christophers and Bentley argued, led not only to a state of endemic malaria among the residents within the plantations, but also to other diseases including cholera, dysentery and ulcerated legs and feet.[42] They also suffered from pthisis, which was particularly prevalent among the Paharia (Nepali) labourers. Small-pox epidemics also occurred, and infective conjunctivitis was common. At this time, small-pox vaccination was available to them but they had to pay for it themselves, which they therefore ignored.[43] Christophers and Bentley emphasized the inadequacy of medical provisions, the 'incompetence' of the doctor babus and argued strongly for the appointment of 'qualified' resident doctors.[44]

The Formation of the Duars Committee

The Christophers–Bentley report laid down the framework within which health in the tea plantations of northern Bengal would be analysed and reformed. The report was also strongly contested by the medical authorities, the administration and the planters themselves. Their understanding of malaria, its causation and cures apart, the authors located disease in the Duars *not* in the land itself, but within the economic structures of their daily lives. In identifying sanitation, proper water facilities, good housing, adequate nutrition and an effective

41 Christophers and Bentley, *Malaria in the Duars*, p. 60.
42 Christophers and Bentley noted that ulcers occurred in the rainy season and could incapacitate a worker, and speculated on its bacterial origins. Like some other diseases suffered by the labours, ulcers on the legs and feet remained a constant problem, rarely addressed. In 1914, in the first annual report on the working of the Jalpaiguri Labour Act, the Civil Surgeon of Jalpaiguri remarked that the ulcers caused more sickness than malaria in the tea estates and recommended a 'scientific enquiry' into the ulcers and in the next annual general meeting of the DPA the chairman heartily endorsed it. See *DPAAR, 1915* (Calcutta, 1916, APAC), pp. 76 and x. Also see *ARWJLA, 1913–14* (APAC), p. 3. It was commented upon by the Civil Surgeon again in 1918–19. See *ARWJLA, 1918–19* (Calcutta, 1920, APAC), p. 4. In 1920 the newly established Calcutta School of Tropical Medicine asked the Indian Tea Association for patronage and in that context enquired into whether there were any specific diseases pertaining to the workers that needed to be studied. The DPA, after consultation with its British medical officers, who were organized in the northern Bengal branch of the British Medical Association, suggested an enquiry into the causes and cures of ulcers on the legs and feet. See *DPAAR, 1920* (Calcutta, 1921, APAC), p. 134. Ultimately, however, the DPA contributed a sum towards the study of malaria instead. See Chapter 5 for a study of malaria control in the tea estates. In 1947 the workers were still reported to suffer from ulcers and sores in their legs and feet, which had decreased from a high level of occurrence during the war years. See *DPAAR, 1946* (Kalimpong, 1947), p. x.
43 Christophers and Bentley, *Malaria in the Duars*, pp. 63–68.
44 Christophers and Bentley, *Malaria in the Duars*, pp. 68–71.

system of medical care as the factors that would improve the labourers' health, they emphasized human agency rather than environmental causes as the essential causal factor of disease in the plantations.[45]

The sense of a crisis created by the Christophers–Bentley report resonated in both official and management circles. For the plantation management, the crisis was in the severe indictment of their labour system. They feared that when published, the report was likely to draw unwanted nationalist criticism. Even more crucially for them, the report recommended a system of governmental agency through inspection of their plantations, which had previously been non-existent. For the local and provincial governments the report was highly embarrassing as well, because it indirectly held the government responsible for the sorry state of affairs within the plantations. It also led to a situation where the government would have to confront the planters, thereby destabilizing a status quo more or less maintained between British industry and the colonial government. The managing agencies which owned most of the larger plantations in the Duars also controlled most of the British capital in eastern India in the jute and mining industries. The tea lobby exercised a strong influence on government policy. Finally, and for the government probably the most awkward consequence of the report, it contradicted the stated policy of the government in which indentured labour was to be gradually phased out in Assam and a system of free labour installed in its place. This was to be the pattern, too, in all other plantation areas in South Asia.

Almost inevitably, therefore, the government did not publish the Christophers–Bentley report immediately. The government of India asked the Sanitary Commissioner of India if it ought to be published at all, and he replied that the government could not possibly avoid publishing the report, but since 'the report if published is likely to lead to a good deal of agitation' the government should take action to counter it before it reached the public domain.[46] The Secretary to the Home Department of the government of India also thought that the 'planters won't like the remarks on the arrangements in the Duars, but the inquiries were started at their instance and they will have to be supplied with the report'.[47] Everyone in government agreed that the report put the govern-

---

45   In that respect they valued the Assam labour system, in which every labourer under the Act of 1901 in the plantation was accounted for, and a system of regular inspections in place. The *Special Report on the Working of Act I of 1882 in the Province of Assam during the Years 1886–1889* (Calcutta, 1890, APAC), pp. 247–53. A system of inspection by government did not prevent the exploitation and high mortality and morbidity rates among tea labourers in Assam. See Rana P. Behal, 'Wage Structure and Labour: Assam Valley Tea Plantations, 1900–1947', www.indialabourarchives.org/publications. Moreover, the accuracy of much of the vital statistics collected in the Assam plantations was doubtful. See Ralph Shlomowltz and Lance Brennan, 'Mortality and Migrant Labour in Assam, 1865–1921', *Indian Economic & Social History Review* 27 (1990), pp. 85–110.
46   Memorandum of Sanitary Commissioner to the Government of India, 2 Aug. 1909, Government of India Home Proceedings (Sanitary), A (Confidential), Oct. 1909, nos 24–26 (NAI, N. Delhi), p. 1.
47   Memo of Secretary, Home Department, 18 Aug. 1909.

ment 'in a very embarrassing position', especially because it had committed itself to a system of non-contractual labour in the plantation for the future.[48] In private, government officials in Delhi conceded that the wages of the plantation workers were insufficient in both northern Bengal and Assam.[49]

Meanwhile the provincial government, confronted with the report, summoned a meeting of senior officials to discuss its strategy.[50] The Deputy Commissioner of Jalpaiguri showed a copy of the preliminary report to the chairman of the DPA, and a copy was sent on to the ITA in Calcutta. After deliberations the provincial government sent a strongly worded letter to the government of India, particularly defending the planters' benevolence and the *sardari* system of labour:

> The Lt. Governor is of the opinion that authors of the report ... have outstated the facts ... the amount of sickness and mortality among the new coolies was perhaps due to their low physical condition on arrival and not to the *sardari* system of labour, *and that in the absence of more convincing arguments the Lt. Governor cannot abandon the opinion hitherto held that the sub-Himalayan tracts are intrinsically unhealthy*.[51]

Once it came under pressure from the tea lobby and the provincial government, the government of India agreed to commission another enquiry committee to review the Christophers–Bentley report, and this time left its membership to the provincial government. It also agreed not to publish the Christophers–Bentley report until the report of the new committee was published.[52] The only dissenting note in condemning the Christophers–Bentley report and in formulating these crucial decisions was from the Sanitary Commissioner of India. He qualified his critique of the report (in the interest of medical specialization, presumably) by remarking that miasmatic causes of disease were not compatible with 'modern preventive medicine'.[53] Nevertheless he too recommended that the report be withheld until a new committee had examined its claims. The government of India next sanctioned a new committee to investigate medical and sanitary conditions of the tea labourers in the Duars.[54] As it happened, the new committee – the Monahan Committee (or Duars Committee as it came to be referred to later) – submitted its report within a few months as instructed. It

48 Memo of Secretary, Home Department, 18 Aug. 1909, p. 2.
49 Memo of Secretary, Home Department, 18 Aug. 1909, p. 4.
50 Government of India, Home Proceedings (Sanitary), A (Confidential), Oct. 1909, no.27, telegram from Government of East Bengal and Assam to Home Department, Government of India, 4 Oct. 1909.
51 Government of India Home Proceedings (Sanitary), A (Confidential), no. 47, letter from Government of East Bengal and Assam to Government of India, Home Department, 24 Dec. 1909 (NAI, N. Delhi), p. 1 (emphasis mine).
52 Memorandum of P.W. Monier, Secretary to Government of India, Home Department, 3 Jan. 1910, p. 2.
53 Memorandum of the Sanitary Commissioner to the Government of India, 13 Aug. 1910, p. 3.
54 Memorandum of H.A. Adamson, 23 Feb. 1910, and H.A. Start, 23 Feb. 1910, p. 6.

was published immediately by the provincial government.[55] The Christophers–Bentley report on malaria was published a year later by the imperial government.

The new committee had a more local composition, being chaired by the deputy commissioner of Jalpaiguri, F.J. Monahan, and including medical officials and planters from Assam. Its brief was limited; not to challenge the causes of malaria as detailed by Christophers and Bentley, but simply to examine the standards of living among the workers.[56] Its constitution differed from the Christophers–Bentley report, positing even before the enquiry began a difference between the perspectives of the local administration and medical practitioners with knowledge of local practice and those of experts from outside. The inaccuracy of this assumption (Bentley had served in Assam) did not detract from the duality posited between outside experts and those with local knowledge. The Duars Committee emphasized two principal points in their report: first, that planters' records and testimonies were more reliable than that of the workers, and second, that only those experts who had experience of working within the plantations could legitimately understand and report on its mode of functioning, whether they were medical men, planters or government experts.

The Duars Committee collected information from managements within the tea plantations rather than from the labourers because, 'Any coolies brought ... before a number of strange Europeans would inevitably become frightened and confused, and no information of value was likely to be obtained in that way.'[57] This approach is generally representative of the managerial discourse about labour within the plantations. Infantilizing the workers and rendering their utterances irrelevant remained an enduring constant in management discourse in colonial plantations. The infantilizing of the Madesia tribes who worked in the plantations, and indeed the managerial understanding of their 'primordial' social relationships, religious sentiments and ways of life are reflected in almost every report on the plantations. This served to legitimize only managerial or medical discourses on their standards of life. It also justified the resistance to the introduction of any changes in their lifestyles, on the part of the management and to an extent the local administration, the justification being that it would destabilize their natural social lives, which were 'primitive and simple'.

The other aspect was that the Committee, composed of individuals 'in the field' (and in contrast to the outsiders, the medical experts Christophers and Bentley), were the ones who, through an intimate knowledge of the workers, their daily lives and the cultural frameworks of their worlds, would be better equipped to translate their meanings to the wider audience of the state and central government. As we shall see, changes did occur in the system of medical care in the plantations in the colonial period. But these changes were always effected in the context of managerial assertions that no drastic changes in their

---

55 *Report of the Duars Committee.*
56 *Report of the Duars Committee*, p. 28.
57 *Report of the Duars Committee*, p. 2.

lifestyles, including changes to their habitations, sanitary facilities and medical dispensaries, would be acceptable to the workers.

Paternalism and Local Knowledge: The Duars Committee

Unsurprisingly, the Duars Committee report contradicted most of the findings of the Christophers–Bentley report. It recognized the lack of statistics on the plantations as had Christophers and Bentley. Unlike them, it interpreted the extent of immigration far more conservatively.[58] The report stated that the residents of the tea plantations often included relatives of the workers who were cultivators, having taken up sharecropping in the areas outside of the tea gardens, but who nevertheless lived in the tea gardens. These might include both Madesias (the Oraons, Santhals and Mundas from Chotanagpur and Santhal Parganas) as well as the Paharias (the hill-men). Therefore the tea plantations countenanced large families with ties outside the tea estate boundaries. In northern Bengal, they pointed out,

> It is to the advantage of a garden to have a large number of people who keep up a connection with it, and who, if they do not work regularly on the garden, may do so occasionally, or may attract others. In this way a large number of persons may be found living in coolie lines, who are not on the garden books and are not dependants of persons working in the garden.[59]

The Committee acknowledged that tea estates encouraged labourers to live in the coolie lines within the boundaries of the plantations so that they would have enough people to provide the requisite labour seasonally, but accepted the managerial position that the tea estates could not be responsible for their health and well-being, because many of the residents within the coolie lines were part of a floating labour population.[60] They justified the lack of vital statistics because it was an inevitable part of a system of free labour, a system, moreover, towards which the government had pledged its future policies. Next, the report emphasized the irreplaceable nature of the free-labour system, which hinged on the status and role of the *sardar*:

---

58 *Report of the Duars Committee*, p. 3. They stated that the figures of the labouring population supplied by some of the plantations (several did not supply figures because they did not keep records at all) were not useful because they did not accurately reflect the numbers of residents in the tea gardens' coolie lines, because the 'permanently employed represent not the total number of persons employed but the average daily muster of labourers turning out to work, which is a very different thing'.
59 *Report of the Duars Committee*, p. 3.
60 G.G. Webb had remarked on the easy mobility between the coolies within the plantations with their friends and neighbours outside in the *bastis*: 'garden coolies when they had accumulated sufficient money used to become farmers and small holders on Government waste land. There was much coming and going between these people and their relations and friends on the Estates'. Typescript 'Leopards', Mss Eur C474 (APAC), p. 11.

a sardar is the leader of coolies recruited from a certain local area ... His tribesmen live around him in the garden lines, and he holds a social position similar to that of a village headman ... He and his followers are bound together by ties of country ... and although he can usually count upon the support of the manager of the garden, his position mainly depends upon the maintenance of his popularity among the members of his own patti [gang] ... strong prima facie reasons exist why a sardar should deal justly with his coolies.[61]

The Duars Committee explained the charge of oppression by the *sardars* in terms of clan and village networks; and stressed the feudal relationship and the moral economy of the relationship, rather than the numerous instances of oppression within the plantations. They also situated any disputes between the *sardar* and his workers in terms of disputes between the 'coolies'. Therefore, the position and the status of the manager retained its pristine quality, reflecting management understanding of the social relations in the plantations; the position of the manager as the fair and ultimate arbiter of justice was not compromised. It re-endorsed the role of the *sardar* as the first point of authority for the worker and situated the *sardar* as the dispenser of patronage among the workforce.[62]

The system of free labour, the Duars Committee argued, made necessary both the existence of a floating population, unaccounted for and beyond the responsibility of the tea gardens, as well as the crucial role of the *sardar* in the entire system of labour within the plantations. In effect, the system transferred the moral responsibility for the welfare of the workers to the middlemen, the *sardars*. It led to a situation where the reservoir of infection, any infection, within the tea gardens was finally the floating population of the *bastis*.

The lack of figures makes it difficult to estimate the actual number of floating workers. In fact Grunig noted in 1911 that not more than ten per cent of the working population was on the move, settled as they were in several tea gardens with their own plots of land to cultivate and also often in a state of indebtedness. He quoted from the district commissioner's report in 1900:

a coolie has taken advances from the garden and has not repaid the money or the garden has lent him money to buy a pair of bullocks, taking the animals themselves as security. This is a very common practice. As long as the coolie remains on the garden the Manager is not likely to be hard on him, but if he attempts to leave for another garden, he could not hope for any consideration. He, therefore, is practically bound to stop where he is.[63]

Once it re-established the legitimacy of the system of non-contractual labour, the Duars Committee report ascribed the lack of hospitals in the Duars to cultural dispositions among the labourers: 'caste prejudices are a great difficulty'.[64] An

61 *Report of the Duars Committee*, p. 7.
62 *Report of the Duars Committee*, p. 7.
63 Grunig, *Eastern Bengal*, p. 109.
64 *Report of the Duars Committee*, p. 28. The Christophers–Bentley report on the other hand emphasized that 'In our experience coolies are by no means averse to accept treatment

argument for a cultural understanding of the ways of life of the people led to conclusions about their responses to provisions for sanitary measures such as toilets and pipe wells as well as to hospitals and doctors.[65] The report rejected the system considered in the Arbuthnott report of 1904, which commended the system then prevalent in the plantations of Ceylon where labour also was free. In Ceylon there was legislation in place to compel management to contribute towards group hospitals and medical facilities for all workers. Instead, the Duars Committee stressed that the nature of investment in medical facilities for the workers should be voluntary.[66] Meanwhile, so far as the medical facilities were concerned, the Duars Committee agreed with the Christophers–Bentley Committee that they needed improvement; they identified the training of the resident doctor babus and the establishment of 'branch dispensaries' to take the load off individual doctor babus who were supposed to tour coolie lines spread over eight to ten miles each day.[67] As for housing conditions, the Duars Committee report sympathized with the unwillingness of most plantation managements to undertake improvements in the *coolie lines*, attributing this to the labourers' reluctance to live in more comfortable houses: 'Coolies prefer to lead their own life in the lines, and strongly object to interference with their domestic arrangements.'[68] The Duars report borrowed from H.H. Risley's *Tribes and Castes of Bengal*, a massive colonial ethnographic project, where the Oraons were described as a 'slovenly race' and their dwellings as 'badly built mud huts'.[69] Nicholas Dirks has argued that the colonial state was an 'ethnographic state' in the late nineteenth century, when the anthropological and official understanding of Indian social formation was reified within the caste system and, through Risley, racialized as well.[70] Risley's ethnographic project was to instil caste as the primary civil institution in colonial India; one that was also closely related to physical anthropology and the racial distinctions within the

---

    if they realise that it is likely to be of any use.' See Christophers and Bentley, *Malaria in the Duars*, p. 69. They pointed out besides that 'hospitals do not exist in the Duars, and there are no facilities for the treatment of surgical or other in-patients. Dispensaries also, in the ordinary acceptance of the word, are almost entirely absent. We know of three or four only to which the term might be applied with any accuracy', Christophers and Bentley, *Malaria in the Duars*, p. 69.

65 This was most explicitly stated at the time of a campaign against hookworm started by the government of Bengal, which singled out the coal mine areas and the tea estates as the sites of examination. See speech of Chairman, DPA, in *DPAAR, 1918* (Calcutta, 1919, APAC), p. x. For a discussion on the hookworm survey, see Chapter 6. When government officials recommended well-stocked dispensaries or provisions for a few hospital beds, or even piped water for the workers to prevent bowel diseases, the stock response of the planting industry was similar. For an analysis of the slow growth of medical infrastructure in the region see Chapter 6.

66 *Report of the Duars Committee*, pp. 29–30.

67 *Report of the Duars Committee*, p. 30.

68 *Report of the Duars Committee*, p. 33.

69 *Report of the Duars Committee*, p. 33.

70 Nicholas B. Dirks, 'Castes of Mind', *Representations*, 37, special issue: *Imperial Fantasies and Postcolonial Histories* (1992), pp. 56–78.

caste system, in which framework the tribal populations of the Oraons, Mundas and Santhals were racially condemned to the lowest status, beyond civilization. The wide acceptance of this ethnographic formulation set indigenous tribes such as the Oraons and Mundas as uncivilized, unchanged tribal groups at the very edge of civilized Hindu society. At the same time that it recognized that adequate housing and piped water was expensive and therefore as yet unavailable, recommending provisions for 'more comfortable housing', sanitary facilities and piped water, the Duars Committee posited sanitary provisions as culturally repugnant and somehow alien to their labourers, and themselves as the custodians of a gradualist programme of sanitary reform.[71]

The Contingent Solution: Disease Control and the Enclave System

In this chapter I have highlighted the different and conflictual ideals of health care in the plantation enclaves, that of the planters versus experts in Tropical Medicine. Within the plantation enclaves, and especially in the Duars and the Terai, where the land was colonized from grasslands or forests and cultivated for the first time, disease and often death were accepted as an unpleasant but inevitable part of the process of colonization of the area. The planters dealt with disease among their labourers and themselves in the same way that they managed other necessities of life in the area. A rough-and-ready system of medical care had evolved, its chief characteristic being a great dependence on the competence and the kindness of the individual planters.

After a couple of decades, when some plantations had settled into regular production of tea with a relatively settled labouring population within the plantations, an enquiry from medical experts into the causes of fevers, the most common disease, turned unexpectedly for the planters into a critique of the entire plantation economy. Pressure from the planters and the local government led to another enquiry that was to counter the claims of the first.

I have highlighted the differences between the two reports to project the divergent discourses within the colonial order so far as plantation health was concerned. On the one hand there was a committee of experts who spent four months in the area, focusing intensely on two specific diseases and intent on their resolution. The resolution they proposed was one of more active government agency within the plantations. Their recommendations were for a set of policies that combined a system of registration of immigration, and adequate legislation that would enable periodic government inspections, keep count of immigration into the district and attempt to impose the rule of law by the substitution of the paternalism of the state for paternalism of the planter.[72] On the

71 *Report of the Duars Committee*, pp. 34–36.
72 Das Gupta has shown that in the coal mining area of Asansol where such government supervision was in existence, the sanitary and medical provisions for the workers were 'absent or inadequate'. See R. Das Gupta, 'Migrants in Coal Mines: Peasants or Proletarians, 1850s–1947', *Social Scientist*, 13 (1985), pp. 18–43.

other hand, the Duars Committee Report represented a closer alliance between the local administration and the planters. Imbued with the topos of the men on the spot, they professed an intimate knowledge both of the area and the peoples who worked in the plantations. In effect their report distanced itself from what they perceived as a clinical, impersonal understanding of health in the plantations. Instead, they posited an alternative view. It was one, they argued, that was enriched by cultural understanding of their labourers and at the same time cognizant of the logistic and economic limitations on the management. Their report delved deep into colonial structures of knowledge and borrowed extensively from colonial ethnography of tribal peoples to reinforce the notion of the workers in Assam. This committee conferred with the managers and assistant managers for informed knowledge about the culture and ways of life of the labourers.[73] The outcome was a much more contingent solution.

Yet the Duars Committee report was no mere refutation of the Christophers–Bentley critique: the two reports had a great deal in common in their advocacy of sanitary facilities and living space within the plantations. Thus the conflict in the divergent discourses of the two reports were between two interpretations of the responsibility of the planters; one, that of the experts from outside who thought of the planters as capitalists who had ultimately to retain and sustain productive labour, the role of state being to oversee the welfare of the labourers. The alternative view was articulated by the plantation doctors and the local administration that saw labour welfare in terms of paternalistic benevolence and the occurrence of diseases a problem of the peculiarities of location. In the process, they categorically denied that the workers were ill-paid, attributing some of the obvious malnourishment either to their state of impoverishment prior to arrival or to the uniquely high price of foodstuffs in the particular year of Christophers–Bentley's survey.

Both the reports contained certain sites of consensus; one was the general incompetence of the resident doctor babus; another was the need to invest in

---

[73] The inspiration for this view of the reification and of the essentialization of the customs and culture of Indian communities in the British period is Edward Said, *Orientalism* (London and Henley, Routledge and Keagan Paul, 1978), and Nicholas B. Dirks, *Castes of Mind: Colonialisma and the Making of Modern India* (Princeton, NJ, Princeton University Press, 2001). Almost every planter's memoir resonates with many instances of the reification of the labourers' culture as well as their infantilization. For one such instance, see the interview with William Webb, Mss Eur R 187 (APAC). In 1911, in response to a government resolution on compulsory education, the DPA announced that 'the Association does not approve of the principle of compulsory education ... and considers that any attempt at compulsory education of coolie children is unlikely to be successful or to produce beneficial results commensurate with the disturbance of ancient customs involved'. *DPAAR, 1911* (Calcutta, 1912, APAC), p. iv. Nor was this infantilization and primitivization limited to the European planters. The Indian planters generally made similar arguments. When the first labour seat was proposed by the GOI in 1933 for the 1935 Provincial Assembly elections, the Dooars Planters' Association, the Darjeeling Planters' Association and the Indian Tea Planters' Association protested on the grounds that the labourers were simple and ignorant people incapable of comprehending or appreciating democratic representation. See *DPAAR, 1932* (Calcutta, 1933, APAC), pp. 112–15.

long-term medical infrastructure, including dispensaries and qualified doctors, safe sources of water supply to prevent cholera and the gradual introduction of quinine for the workers. The planting industry was quick to formally endorse and publicize the distinction that the Duars Committee made between the economic status of the workers and the sanitary state of their living conditions. While they were willing to admit deficiencies in the latter, they unwaveringly defended the adequacy of the former.[74] The Duars Committee strongly argued against legislation of the kind in effect in Assam, which would bind the labourer in a penal contract and simultaneously make the management responsible for the health care of its labourers.[75]

In response to the reports, the provincial government proposed legislation where the tea estates would submit vital statistics of their labourers. These would be checked by the Civil Surgeon of the district, who would also conduct a minimum of 60 annual inspections among the tea estates and make recommendations for the improvement of the sanitary and medical conditions. But his recommendations would be classed as 'suggestions' and therefore would not be compulsory. It did not provide for government control over the recruitment process, or lay down regulations for the establishment of dispensaries, hospitals or sanitary facilities. It proposed to implement this initially in Western Duars for a term of five years, and then to extend provisions to the plantations in Darjeeling and Terai. The government of Bengal passed the Jalpaiguri Labour Act in 1912.

The conflict between the divergent visions of health care within the plantation enclave resulted in an uneasy, contingent resolution. But from this time, the plantation enclaves were firmly within the remit of international medical attention from specialists of Tropical Medicine. They provided the sites for the study, prevention and cure of various 'tropical' diseases including malaria, hookworm, kala-azar and leprosy in a relatively controlled environment and on supposedly quiescent residents. Government intervention increased as well, although the supervision of the district administration over the plantation enclaves was cautious and sporadic. Nevertheless, in the next 40 years, the plantations oversaw, with government encouragement and resources, researches and preventive and curative projects on malaria, hookworm, leprosy and dysentery by medical experts from London, Liverpool and Calcutta. They also carried out, with varying degrees of tenacity and success, measures to prevent infant mortality, encourage reproductive health and provide basic sanitary facilities for the labourers within the plantation enclaves. The plantation enclave was now firmly on the horizons of the colonial state as well as of Tropical Medicine, and was set as one of the sites of the circulation of scientific and medical knowledge creation and diffusion.

---

74 See speech of the Chairman, DPA, at the annual general meeting of 20 Jan. 1912, *DPAAR, 1911* (Calcutta, 1912, APAC), p. ix. See also *IPTAAR, 1911* (Calcutta, 1912, APAC), p. 9.
75 *Report of the Duars Committee*, p. 29.

CHAPTER 6

The Plantation Enclave, the Colonial State and Labour Health Care

In this chapter, I will examine public health and medical infrastructure in the tea plantations in the context of their physical location and economic position as enclaves of specialized medical attention. An analysis of disease, medicine and health in a plantation economy can be made from an understanding of public health in a privileged area of colonial economy. Were the public health measures, which were not undertaken in rural India due to lack of financial resources, carried out in the tea plantations? Official discourse and planters' perspectives emphasize the view that the plantations were a privileged, segregated sector so far as the availability of medical care was concerned. This was attributed to the economist logic, articulated in various government reports as well as by planters associations, that planters invested in medical care to ensure high productivity. I intend to argue here that although the tea plantations were often constituted as areas of focus for government policies in public health, as well as sites for the study of diseases prevalent in the plantations, the provisions for health care did not follow the pattern of 'privilege' for the purpose of better health care for the labourers. The management of disease in the tea plantations was dictated by a range of imperatives: some economic, others political, and each such contingency was related to the nature of the plantation system as it developed in northern Bengal in the colonial period. The logic of 'economic imperatives' that were supposed to impel sanitary policies within a controlled population is a functionalist notion. Such logic was often articulated in the discursive practices of the planters and even more particularly of those of the medical officials who worked in the plantations. A closer examination of the sanitary policies and aspects of disease management in the plantations, however, reveals a world that was enmeshed politically, socially and economically in many ways to form a system which had several inherent contradictions.

In this chapter I will demonstrate that several factors disrupted the economist logic that planters invested in medical and sanitary infrastructure within the plantations because it was commercially important for them to keep their labour healthy. There was a difference between the rhetoric and practice of the functionality of productive labour. The northern Bengal plantations did not have to spend too much money or effort to recruit labour. In colonial Duars and Darjeeling labour was relatively abundant (more so than in Assam, for instance). This was the specific nature of the colonial enclave of the plantations of northern Bengal. The absence of a system of indentured labour furthered a plantation economy that borrowed extensively from pre-colonial socio-economic relations, but had features that were uniquely colonial. While the pursuit of profit and a monopoly over cheap labour informed most of the approaches taken by the tea plantation managements, both British and Indian, the managements claimed that it was a mode of production that sustained a paternalistic relationship between the manager and the workers. Such managerial perspectives informed the pace and nature of the establishment of medical infrastructure within the plantations.

The system of health care in the plantations of northern Bengal therefore involved periodic attempts at government intervention, the characteristics of the plantation system itself and the extension of the study of Tropical Medicine in colonial India in the twentieth century. The relationship between the plantation system and the colonial state worked out in the years subsequent to the controversial Duars Committee report. This relationship shaped the three most important developments in the region's health care system: the professionalization of the medical practitioners, the collection of vital statistics of birth and death rates of the workers and the development of the medical infrastructure of the plantations.

The Jalpaiguri Labour Act and the Enclave in Western Duars

In this section I will highlight the three areas that the annual reports of the Jalpaiguri Labour Act (JLA) focused on: registration of the labour force, maintenance of vital statistics within the plantations and the drawing of boundaries of the plantation estates from the villages. I will argue that the attempts to enumerate the labour force, which engaged the attention of government officials and necessitated the intrusion of inspections, paradoxically endorsed the viability of the plantations as enclaves in government policies. This was often at odds with the interests of the tea plantations themselves because the system depended at critical moments on labour supplies from outside the estates.

The system of free labour in the Duars, Terai and Darjeeling areas ensured that there was no documentary evidence of the actual numbers of workers or their dependents within the tea estates. There were two ways in which the number of labourers in the tea estates could be ascertained. The first was the estate accounts. The tea estates kept records of the daily tasks (*hazira* and *ticca*) done by the workers. A *dafadar* kept a note of the number of tasks performed by each worker on behalf of the *sardar*, for purposes of payment.[1] This did not, of course, include the numbers of dependents within the estates. Besides, seasonal workers came down from the mountains to work on clearing the jungles in the winter, whose names were not recorded, and their numbers were unknown.[2] Christophers and Bentley estimated that about 25 per cent of the labourers settled on the tea estates were dependents who were not recorded in the garden books.[3] Other temporary workers settled in the *bastis* outside the boundaries of the tea estates and came to work in the peak seasons. Moreover, all workers absent for longer than a month were removed from the records.[4]

The Bengal government had introduced a system of recording the vital statistics of the labourers, through gradual registration, but it was voluntary and generally of little consequence. In 1873 the Bengal Births and Deaths Registration Act made records compulsory in some towns.[5] The Bengal Local Self Government Act, 1885, provided for registration of births and deaths by the union committees (at the village level). The agency for collecting the statistics was the village *chaukidar* (watchman), under the Village Chaukidari Act, 1870.[6] As we have seen in the previous chapter, the planters protested strongly against the intrusion of village *chaukidars* within the tea estates. The government gave in and the Act was not extended to the tea plantations of northern Bengal. Vital statistics within the plantations were provided by the managers to the local police *thana*.

In Assam, the system of indentured labour had ensured such recording, which made it possible for government to keep an eye on the demographic changes within the area and possibly to take steps to locate epidemics in time to take preventive measures in the rest of the district. The Jalpaiguri Labour Act (JLA), 1912, stipulated for a census of the tea gardens, and for the recording of the vital statistics of each tea garden to be inspected by a state government nominee, the Civil Surgeon of Jalpaiguri. The information on vital statistics was compiled monthly by the doctor babus and countersigned by the managers of the respective tea estates.

In 1912, the year that the JLA was passed, the Bengal provincial government allotted one representative from the planting districts of Darjeeling, Terai and northern Bengal to sit on the Bengal Legislative Council. Mr A.W. Chaplin was enthusiastic about the Act at the Council. It would, he said, be welcomed by the planters:

> for the reason that it will ensure the accurate registration of vital statistics and thus protect them against exaggerated and irresponsible statements regarding the health of their coolies. The ... coolies on the tea gardens are, as a whole, well cared for and looked after by their employers, and I believe

1 Arbuthnott, *Report*, p. 5.
2 Arbuthnott, *Report*, p. 2, and Christophers and Bentley, *Malaria in the Duars*, p. 36.
3 Christophers and Bentley, *Malaria in the Duars*, p. 36.
4 Christophers and Bentley, *Malaria in the Duars*, p. 45.
5 Ray, *History*, p. 21.
6 Ray, *History*, p. 40.

that the working of the Act will tend to show that the death rate is not now abnormal or even as high as is presumed in some quarters.[7]

In the very first report the Civil Surgeon, Major D. Munro, reported that the census of the population of the tea gardens had been taken but was not reliable and the problem of the dependents who lived in the coolie lines but were invisible in the garden records persisted:

> All these figures ... refer to the working population which is different from the actual population in the coolie lines, including a number of children, aged people and outsiders, who are non-workers. For them no figures are available and for that reason I gave up that attempt.[8]

He next observed that the birth rate per thousand in the tea gardens (37.97) was higher than in the Jalpaiguri district (35) and that the average death rate per thousand (32.77) on the other hand was lower than the average in the district (33.81), although the death rate in Bengal as a whole was 29.77.[9] Two other observations were significant: he placed little reliance on the monthly sickness statistics provided by most of the doctor babus in the tea gardens, and at the same time contended that there was no direct connection between the numbers of entries under cholera and the supply of piped water to the tea gardens. Instead, he attributed cholera and the deaths, under an ailment he diagnosed as 'choleraic diarrhoea', to food that was consumed by the workers in the *hats* (markets) located outside the tea gardens.[10]

In fact the first report on the working of the JLA set the precedent for a pattern that would be replicated in both official and managerial discourses in colonial Duars – that the birth and death rates were invariably better within the tea estates than outside; and often the Civil Surgeon would confirm the managerial assertions that diseases, when they occurred, were invariably due to external influences. The number of tea estates actually inspected was far from the 60 recommended annually by government.

During the years when the British Civil Surgeon was away on war duty and was replaced by an officiating Indian, the statistics provided by the managers were more closely analysed. In 1914, the acting Civil Surgeon, R.B. Khambata, pointed out that yet again the figures were favourable in the tea estates. The death rates per thousand within the Duars plantations (29.12) – as shown in Table 6.1 – were lower than those in the Jalpaiguri district (34.57) and those in Bengal (31.57).[11] He insisted that the lower death rates did not signify that tea garden workers were not dying in fewer numbers, but simply that they were not at the time resident in the tea plantations:

---

7 DPAAR, *1912* (Calcutta 1913, APAC), p. 59.
8 ARWJLA, *1912* (Calcutta, 1913, APAC), p. 1.
9 ARWJLA, *1912*, p. 3.
10 ARWJLA, *1912*, p. 4.
11 ARWJLA, *1914* (Calcutta, 1915, APAC), p. 2.

Table 6.1 Vital statistics in the tea estates of Duars, Jalpaiguri district and Bengal

Year	BR* in Duars	BR in Jalpaiguri	BR in Bengal	DR in Duars	DR in Jalpaiguri	DR in Bengal
1913–14	37.97	35.00	35.30	32.77	33.81	29.77
1914–15	36.98	36.60	33.86	29.12	34.57	31.57
1915–16	35.76	37.03	31.80	27.92	34.18	32.83
1916–17	36.59	33.82	31.89	28.07	33.96	27.37
1917–18	39.48	37.40	35.91	28.07	34.59	26.19.
1918–19	29.51	–	–	47.86	–	–
1919–20	34.1	–	–	31.75	–	–
1920–21	38.87	–	–	29.15	–	–
1921–22	39.78	–	–	24.93	–	–

* All rates are expressed *per thousand*. BR=birth rate; DR=death rate.
Source: *Annual Report on the Working of the JLA* for the respective years. From 1918 the reports ceased making comparisons between the Duars tea estates and the district figures.

> this death-rate of 29.12 per mille is after all a *crude* death rate ... [it] does not take into account all deaths which might have occurred in hospital in Jalpaiguri town or in districts outside the boundary of [the] tea garden area, although the disease contracted might have been actually on the tea garden. It is by no means an unfrequent [sic] occurrence that as soon as cholera or any epidemic disease breaks out the tea garden coolies ... leave the garden or the district entirely and die somewhere else ... probably in their own district ... The correct thing of course would be to add the deaths of those garden coolies and of their relations who have died outside the garden boundaries, although during life they must have lived actually on the garden. If this important fact is taken into consideration, then the death rate would certainly be higher than what is recorded.[12]

This statement is even more significant given that in 1914 cholera was prevalent in epidemic form in the district. Typically, the managers and British plantation physicians attributed dysentery and cholera to 'outside influences' while the Indian (temporary) Civil Surgeon insisted that many workers fled the plantations and went sometimes to the Jalpaiguri town or even to their villages when afflicted with diseases in epidemic form.

The JLA specified that each employer 'keep registers of all persons employed on the estate ... and of their dependents'.[13] In the first few years, whatever the inadequacies and inaccuracies of collection of the vital statistics were, the report purported to provide an annual census of the total population of the tea

12 *ARWJLA, 1914*, pp. 2–3.
13 Government of India Proceedings, Education/Sanitation, October 1912, nos 12–13, Appendix U (NAI), p. 13.

estates. No formal negotiations appear to have taken place with the government on the issue, but from 1918 to 1919 the JLA annual report enumerated only the *working* population of each tea estate.[14] Nor did the reports provide any explanation for the change in the system of enumeration.

The JLA also provided for a provision for inspection by the government of the plantation records because these records excluded the workers who lived within the tea estates and who were probably employed during the peak season but not otherwise, or were ill for longer than a month and were no longer enumerated in the daily work parades. The enumeration of the working population excluded also the *basti* population outside, which provided seasonal labourers for the tea estates. The actual total number of such seasonal workers in all the tea estates in Jalpaiguri cannot be ascertained.

In 1920, the ITA published statistics that showed the total number of 'outside' temporary labour within tea estates (the figures refer only to the tea estates that were members of the ITA) to be 876 permanent outside labourers and 2863 temporary outside labourers. This, compared to the 97,937 labourers who worked within the tea estates, shows very small ratio of *basti* (outside) labourers.[15] There being no independent inspection of the numbers of labourers in the above tea estates, the figures are impossible to verify. Moreover, there was never any definition of what constituted the 'working population'. All tea estates claimed to settle more labourers than they would need if every one of them worked the entire month, because they pointed out that 'absenteeism' and alcoholism prevented the labourers from working more than an average of 18 days within the plantations.[16]

I have stressed the inadequacies of the system of registration of vital statistics within the tea plantations and the complicity of the inspectors of the JLA with the management of the tea plantations. It has been argued by Dipesh Chakrabarty, in the case of the jute mills of Calcutta, that the development of a system of information collection and the imposition of 'industrial discipline' as in industrialized nations was irrelevant because of the unskilled nature of work in the mills.[17] This is equally true of work within the tea plantations, including in

---

14 *ARWJLA, 1918–19* (Calcutta, 1919, APAC), p. 2.
15 *IPTAAR, 1920* (Calcutta 1921), pp. 390–91.
16 In 1946 the labour enquiry report reported an 'absenteeism rate' of 31.8, 27.7 and 27.6 per cent for the tea estate workers surveyed in Duars, Terai and Darjeeling respectively and noted that, 'The cause of the high rate of absenteeism has often been explained by saying that the labourer has his own cultivation to attend to. This explanation does not appear to be valid for it is seen that even during the months when a cultivator has little to do on his own land, absenteeism in tea gardens is high. Many managers put it down to laziness on the part of the workers and to their belief that they earn sufficient for their needs by working about 4 days in a week. The workers, on the other hand, ascribe it to the need for rest after the tiresome and arduous work in the tea gardens. Sickness, chiefly, malaria, is also an important cause of absenteeism.' Rege, *Labour Investigation Committee*, p. 79.
17 Dipesh Chakrabarty, *Rethinking Working Class History, Bengal 1890 to 1940* (Princeton, and Guildford, Princeton University Press, 1989), pp. 65–115.

the factories, where despite partial mechanization, most of the labour involved manual work. For this reason, the tea plantations employed women and children as well in plucking leaves; heavy work such as digging was done by the men. In this situation, productivity was linked not so much to industrial discipline and surveillance as to the availability of plenty of cheap, unskilled labour that could be replaced easily. Therefore, diseases and malnourishment among individual workers posed little threat to overall production within the plantations.

Subhajyoti Ray has added to this insight in his study of tea garden labourers in colonial Duars. He concludes that instead of a system of surveillance and information-gathering, in a system of free labour the planters devised other strategies for eliciting the loyalty of the labour force. This included supporting some of their activities, such as the illegal brewing and sale of *pachwai* (an alcoholic home-brew also known as *hanria*) and opposing restrictions on grazing in the forest lands, which contested the government's attempts to increase its excise and forest revenues.[18]

I agree with Ray that the planters' strategy of identifying with the labourers' interests against encroachments from the state (so long as it did not interfere with their own interests) was a substitute for the strict discipline of the daily muster in the Assam plantations. My contention is that the lack of a systematic collection of vital statistics had less to do with information-collecting for the planters' managerial regime than with the legal interventions of the colonial state within the plantations. The system of vital statistics was initiated to facilitate a minimum of government intervention within the tea estates. This was an attempt, on the part of the government, to put some sort of legal and formalized qualification to the planters' informal but absolute sovereignty within the plantations. The planters' agreement to it was occasioned by their aim to demonstrate that the tea estates were sanitary enclaves, thereby situating the diseases in the *bastis* outside. As its functioning demonstrated, the annual working of the JLA served to emphasize the tea estates' territories as distinct from those of the *bastis* beyond and to re-endorse the managerial discourse of contamination from without.

The influenza epidemic of 1918–19 reinforced this perception through the testimonies of the medical officers within the plantations. The plantations which sent accounts of the epidemic to the Civil Surgeon claimed that the disease came from neighbouring gardens or from the *bastis*, or even, more generally, from the 'outside'. The Civil Surgeon reproduced verbatim the reports from the tea estates without qualification: 'At Chulsa Tea Estate, the disease first appeared in July at Metelli bazaar (situated just near the western boundary) having been introduced by some Marwari shopkeepers on their return from Calcutta. It then spread to the tea garden.'[19] Meanwhile the New Dooars Tea

---

18 Ray, *Transformations*, pp. 92–93.
19 Government of India, A Proceedings, Education/Sanitation, March 1919 nos 17–39 (NAI, New Delhi), pp. 94–95. Also see Government of Bengal Proceedings Municipal/Sanitation, April 1919, APAC/P/10521 (APAC), p. 7.

Contagion and Enclaves

Company reported that 'during the first week of December new coolies came from Nagpur and infected others'.[20] All the reports follow the same trend: reports from the Tondoo Tea Estate recorded that 'The disease was introduced … early in December by an infected woman from Tandoo Basti'; and authorities at Meenglas reported that 'At Meenglas Tea Estate the infection was introduced from the bazaar'.[21] Similar reports came in from Chengmari: 'A Kaya (Marwari shopkeeper) … brought the disease from a neighbouring bazaar'; and the Civil Surgeon of Jalpaiguri noted that the 'The Manager of the Baradighi Tea Estate reports that the disease travelled up the railway lines, whence it spread to large bazars and the gardens.'[22]

Having been validated during the influenza epidemic of 1918–19, the official discourse reinforced the supposition that the bazaars and *bastis* outside the tea plantation enclaves were the cause of the spread of disease within. The cholera epidemic of 1919, too, therefore continued to emphasize the idea of contamination from 'outside'. That year the Chairman of the DPA in his annual address blamed 'outside coolies' for the spread of epidemics.[23] It was not only influenza but all diseases that were supposed to have originated outside of the tea estates. This belief persisted in managerial discourse and was often repeated without qualifications in official discourse. While the bazaars, the *basti* labourers and the *bastis* themselves emerged as the reservoirs of disease and contamination, the formal and informal *faltu* (temporary) and *basti* labourers remained crucial to the functioning of the plantation economy. In the post-First World War years the tea industry announced that the plantations in Duars and Terai faced a labour shortage because the influenza epidemic had caused high mortality rates among the estate as well as depleted the 'surplus labour' from the *bastis*.[24]

The emphasis of the inspections under the JLA was on the containment of epidemics, preferably within the tea estates. The British Civil Surgeons generally agreed with the management of the tea estates that

> The management were doing their best to check the disease [cholera] by disinfection, vaccination and segregation. The water-supply, which was from pipes, was above suspicion. It was probable that the disease was being spread by contamination of food and milk by flies.[25]

While some tea plantations provided for piped water, the majority depended on the seasonal springs. The vexed issue of the extent of the responsibility of the tea gardens towards everyone who lived within them, and the *bastis* immediately outside, persisted. The Chairman of the DPA declared in 1919 that cholera epidemics could be localized due to provision of piped water in some tea gardens, and blamed the *basti* population for the spread of the cholera

20 Government of India, A Proceedings, Education/Sanitation, March 1919 nos 17–39, p. 95.
21 Government of India, A Proceedings, Education/Sanitation, March 1919 nos 17–39, p. 95.
22 Government of India, A Proceedings, Education/Sanitation, March 1919 nos 17–39, p. 96.
23 *DPAAR, 1918* (Calcutta, 1919, APAC), p. x.
24 *DPAAR, 1921* (Calcutta, 1922, APAC), p. xi.
25 *ARWJLA, 1918–1919* (Calcutta, 1919, APAC), p. 3.

(whereas the Civil Surgeon, also British, blamed the contaminated food and milk), and stated that the responsibility for these should rest on the government rather than the tea estates themselves:

> your Committee would appeal to Government ... to improve the water-supply and sanitation of the bustee and Government bazaars in the neighbourhood of the tea garden area ... [It] is disheartening when cholera and such like are brought in from the bustees ... [It] is impossible to keep the people on the garden separate from their friends and relations who live outside.[26]

There was a consensus between the planters and the district officials who were responsible for the functioning of the JLA that although sanitation within the plantations could be improved, it was the area outside the plantations that was responsible for many of the diseases within them, particularly cholera and dysentery. These, enumerated as 'diseases of the bowels', were second only to fevers in terms of mortality rates in the Duars, and officials attributed this not to lack of piped water within the plantations but to the workers' propensity to consume contaminated or rotten food procured outside the plantations.

The issue of the extension of the authority of the plantations to the *bastis* and markets outside their boundaries came to the fore in 1913 when the manager of one tea estate wrote to the secretary of the Indian Tea Association to request special powers for the British physicians employed by the tea estates that would enable them to ban the sale of impure or stale foodstuffs in the hats around the tea plantations under their supervision.[27] But other British medical men employed by the plantations refused to extend their jurisdictions outside the boundaries of the tea estates even if it was permitted by the government. One claimed that it would be 'pointless' because the final authority to ban any foodstuff would rest with the local administration. He argued instead for independent powers to ban foodstuffs without reference to government officials, just as planters took autonomous decisions within the plantations:

> If any such scheme were at all to be introduced the opinion and decision of the Medical Officer concerned would have to be absolute ... The loss of 'izzat' in a country like India in the event of the Medical Officer's opinion being overruled would be fatal to his influence over the coolies in his ordinary work.[28]

26 *DPAAR, 1919* (Calcutta, 1920, APAC) p. xi.
27 *DPAAR, 1913* (Calcutta, 1914, APAC), pp. 175–76. The inspection of the bazaars had deeper implications than the effective elimination of inedible foodstuffs. The weekly *hats* (markets) were the one place where the workers could go out of the tea plantations and mingle with workers from other plantations, and to the management this raised the possibility of collective action by the labourers in case of grievances. All tea plantations in the Duars attempted to limit the *hats* to one day, Sunday (thus circumscribing the mobility of the workers) instead of having *hats* on different days for separate plantations. See Ray, *Transformations*, p. 95. The *hats* were also sites of contestation between the planters and the local *jotedars* on whose lands they were often located. In times of scarcity the planters sometimes forced the *jotedars* to reduce the prices in the *hats*.
28 *DPAAR, 1913* (Calcutta, 1914, APAC), letter from Dr James Conway, Central Duars, to the Secretary DPA, 1 May 1913, p. 177.

There was a discrepancy between the medical discourse of the plantation doctors and the extension of the influence of medical men from the plantations to the areas outside of the tea estates. The British medical officers asked for an extension of their influence over the tea estates outside their boundaries, into the bazaars and the *bastis*. But besides the speeches at the annual dinners, there were no attempts by the tea estates to lobby the government for such control. This discrepancy existed because the plantation management preferred whenever possible to transfer the pecuniary responsibility for sanitary and medical provisions to the government. In this case, the DPA decided that it was the responsibility of the government to appoint inspectors to examine the foods sold in the *hats* near the tea gardens and made a petition to the same effect.[29]

In the first five years of the enactment of the JLA, certain trends emerged. The first was that the registration of vital statistics resulted in information that both the birth and death rates within the plantations were more favourable than those outside the plantations, within the district. The reports pointed out that moreover there was the problem of the *bastis* situated outside the tea plantations, which were linked to the tea estates through economic and social networks and exchanges. The planters ignored this link when it came to preventing disease by sustaining the jurisdictional divide between the plantation enclave and the 'outside', including the *bastis* and the bazaars. While the management within the tea plantations insisted that almost every disease apart from malarial fevers was brought about by 'outside' coolies, the responsibility for the sanitation and medical facilities in the *bastis* outside the tea gardens (and sometimes for populations residing inside the tea plantations who, the management or the doctors insisted, did not contribute to the tea garden) was not assumed by the management. The government, either the state government or the district boards, was expected to be responsible for them.

Rhetoric and Practice: Legislative Proposals and Sanitary Enclaves

The JLA only applied to the tea estates in Duars, which were under the jurisdiction of the Jalpaiguri district board. At the time of its enactment it was intended that it would be extended eventually to Darjeeling and Terai. But the provisions of the Act could not be extended beyond Jalpaiguri. Even in the Duars tea plantations the Act had limited application and impact.

Its provisions were initially for five years, possibly in order to have a certain infrastructure of sanitation and provisions of government inspection in place. After five years the Deputy Commissioner suggested that the Act needed to be extended ('the health of the labour force employed, as a whole, is distinctly better than that of the cultivators in the adjoining villages') and claimed that the district Civil Surgeon performed all the inspections.[30]

29 *DPAAR, 1913*, letter from Secretary, DPA, to Deputy Commissioner of Jalpaiguri, 5 May 1913, pp. 178–79.
30 Memorandum by Commissioner, Rajshahi, 2 March 1918, Government of Bengal Proceed-

The number of inspections by the Civil Surgeon within the tea estates was far less than stipulated. These were as follows:[31]

1913–14: 46	1917–18: 23	1921–22: 19
1914–15: 2	1918–19: 5	1922–23: 0
1915–16: 2	1919–20: 2	1923–24: 0
1916–17: 9	1920–21: 2	1924–25: 4

The government of Bengal proposed that the European (British-owned) tea estates should assume the responsibility for their own sanitation, a responsibility provided to the Civil Surgeon under the JLA. Consequent to the delegation, the Civil Surgeon's responsibility under the Act was to be limited to inspecting the Indian tea estates.[32] Of course this proposal demonstrates yet again the implicit faith of the Bengal government in the British tea estates' management. It also follows another familiar pattern of negotiations between the state government and the DPA, that of allocating resources for sanitary improvements. Despite their insistence on the necessity for the control of the *bastis* and the bazaars, the DPA was not willing to stretch its own resources so far as sanitary measures were concerned. It refused to allow the British medical officers to assume responsibility for the inspections and instead suggested that the government should nominate the Deputy Sanitary Commissioner posted in the district to take over the inspections.[33]

Eventually the provincial government reconfirmed the appointment of, in addition to the Civil Surgeon, the Deputy Sanitary Commissioner, Rajshahi Circle, and the Sanitary Commissioner, Bengal, as ex-officio inspectors under the Act. They also appointed R.G. Griffin, Deputy Sanitary Commissioner and the Special Officer in charge of the ongoing hookworm campaign in the district as the inspector under the Act.[34] Griffin sent in a report in which he pointed out several deficiencies in medical and sanitary provisions in the tea estates.[35] Although briefer, the substance of his report read much like that of Christophers and Bentley. More than a decade after that fateful document was published the conditions of existence appeared almost unchanged. Griffin noted that though there were some pipes, most labourers relied on kutcha wells for water: 'Water-supply, in most cases ... is badly controlled ... Many of the cholera epidemics are traceable to uncontrolled water-supply being infected.'[36] Similarly, the

---

ings, Municipal/Sanitation, May 1920, nos 7–8, P/10765 (APAC), p. 11. Griffin sent in a report where he pointed out the several deficiencies in medical and sanitary provisions.
31 Source: the *Annual Report on the Working of the JLA* for the respective years.
32 Letter of Secretary, Municipal Department, Government of Bengal, to Commissioner, Rajshahi, 19 June 1919, Government of Bengal Proceedings, Municipal/Sanitation, May 1920, no. 13, IOR/P/10765 (APAC), pp. 14–15.
33 Letter from Chairman, DPA, to the Deputy Commissioner, Jalpaiguri, 5 Sept. 1919, p. 17.
34 Notification by Government of Bengal, Municipal Department, 3 July 1919, p. 15.
35 Letter from Sanitary Commissioner, Bengal to Secretary of Government of Bengal, 16 Feb. 1920, pp. 18–19.
36 Letter from Sanitary Commissioner, Bengal to Secretary of Government of Bengal, 16 Feb. 1920, p. 18.

Contagion and Enclaves

workers' food mostly consisted of 'common coarse rice', the supply of which was 'left principally to a band of profiteers, living in each garden, who charge a high rate without regard to the quality'.[37] He pointed out that sanitation was non-existent, and registration of vital statistics was 'far from satisfactory', yet again referring to the temporary or *faltu* (casual) workers, and commented that 'proper and systematic inoculation for cholera and small-pox is badly wanted'. There were some exceptions. A few plantations vaccinated their workers and provided for cheap rice and essential foodstuffs 'owing to the abnormal rise in the price of food-grains' (this was not a regular facility).[38] Unsurprisingly the DPA and its employees, the British Medical Officers, protested strongly about his remarks on the sanitary and medical provisions in the Duars.[39] An interesting feature at this time is that in both medical and official discourses, in addition to the bazaars and the *bastis*, the Indian tea estates emerged as the focal points of the management of disease.

The issue of sanitary enclaves also highlights the role of the colonial government, including both the local officials and the provincial government, which accorded the tea estates a great measure of independence within their boundaries. Such autonomy was facilitated by the acquiescence of government to the managements' perceptions of the nature, characteristics and working culture of the tea plantations themselves. When some interventions or recommendations on policy did take place they were pressured through the government of India, as with the Royal Commission for Labour in 1931.

We have seen an example of how the government of Bengal was complicit in sustaining managerial discourse on the unchanging and pristine nature of tribal populations in the events preceding the JLA when it accepted the planters' testimonies on the *sardars*' role of 'village headman' within the tea estates. In 1911, the Factories Act excluded the tea estate factories from its provisions, which included sanitation for its workforce. The logic for the exclusion was that the tea estates were seasonal factories, not permanent ones, and therefore could not be expected to provide the same sanitary provisions as permanent factories. After the results of the investigations into hookworm (mostly funded by a Rockefeller grant) showed the shocking incidence of hookworm within the tea industry, especially in the plantations in Darjeeling, there were appeals from individuals within the tea plantations for legislation to ensure

---

37 Letter from Sanitary Commissioner, Bengal to Secretary of Government of Bengal, 16 Feb. 1920, p. 18.

38 Letter from Sanitary Commissioner, Bengal to Secretary of Government of Bengal, 16 Feb. 1920, p. 18.

39 Letter from Commissioner Rajshahi to Secretary to Government of Bengal, Municipal Department, 5 May 1920. The Chairman of the DPA protested that 'the report presents a very exaggerated view of the present state of affairs, and it conveys a false impression of the sanitation and medical arrangements, speaking generally'. The Chairman's letter enclosed a note from the honorary secretary of Northern Bengal Branch of the British Medical Association, E.M. Marjoribanks, in which he agreed that Griffin's report was a 'gross exaggeration'. Government of Bengal Proceedings Municipal/Sanitation, Oct. 1920, nos 6–7, IOR/P/10765 (APAC), pp. 10–11.

conservancy by employers engaging more than 50 labourers.[40] The Bengal government however, was reluctant to legislate for conservancy within the tea plantations. The secretary in charge, L.S.S. O'Malley, chose to refer instead to the Factories Act of 1911, which had provisions for sanitation and conservancy, and commented that Mr Irwin 'was a day too late for the fair'.[41] Since the tea and coffee estates (along with some others) were specifically exempt from the provisions of the Factories Act, the comment served no more than to record the government's displeasure towards any initiatives for such legislation.

I have stressed the general sympathy with which the district administration regarded the views of the tea estate management as well as their 'European medical officers'. The district officers believed that the workers within the tea estates, barring a few stray instances (usually from the Indian estates), were generally well-off and needed no intervention from the government. In 1918, the year when the JLA reported exceptional mortality rates within the tea estates, due to the global influenza pandemic as well as a cholera epidemic, the Deputy Commissioner of Jalpaiguri F.W. Strong wrote to the government that

> The coolies in the Duars live under more natural conditions than they do in Assam, are kindly treated, and by no means overworked. They live under more sanitary conditions and enjoy a better water-supply and better medical attendance than the surrounding villagers and are, on the whole, happy and contented.[42]

It is evident from the annual reports on the working of the JLA that the Civil Surgeon and the district officials trusted implicitly managerial assertions about the conditions of work and disease among the labourers in the plantations. The statistics in the reports were provided by the management, and they were never independently verified and indeed there was no mechanism through which they could be verified. Nor did the local administration wish to interfere in disease management and health administration within the tea plantations. As I discussed earlier, the focus was firstly on the control of epidemic diseases in the immediate vicinity of the plantations, and secondly on concluding, on the basis of unsupervised collection of statistics within the plantations, that the vital statistics within the tea plantations were more favourable, and therefore life in the coolie lines was more comfortable than in the *bastis* outside them.

---

40 In particular, one Mr Irwin put forth a resolution to this effect in the Bengal Legislative Council. After a sharp rebuke from O'Malley, the Secretary to Government of Bengal in charge of local self-government, he withdrew the resolution. Extract from proceedings of Bengal Legislative Council held on Tuesday, 3 Feb. 1920, Government of Bengal Proceedings, Municipal/Sanitation, May 1920, nos 27–28, IOR/P/10765 (APAC), p. 59.
41 Extract from proceedings of Bengal Legislative Council held on Tuesday, 3 Feb. 1920, p. 59.
42 Letter from F.W. Strong, Deputy Commissioner, Jalpaiguri to Commissioner Rajshahi, 27 May 1918, Government of Proceedings, Municipal/Sanitation , May 1920, nos 10–11, IOR/P/10765 (APAC), p. 12.

Sanitary Enclaves and Local Politics

Political events in the province and the wider context of the nationalist movement in India played a part in the local politics of the Darjeeling and Jalpaiguri districts after the First World War, and influenced the course of government intervention and medical policies within the plantations. In 1919, the Montagu–Chelmsford reforms initiated the period of Dyarchy, where certain subjects, such as education, local self-government and health, were managed by ministers who were elected to the provincial councils through an 'electoral college' of representatives elected to the municipal and district boards on a wider franchise than ever before. At the municipal level, the franchise after the Montague–Chelmsford reforms extended from 6 to 15 per cent of the population (except the Presidency towns of Bombay, Calcutta and Madras where the franchise was restricted to house owners who possessed a property of a certain value) and in rural areas from 0.6 to 3.2 per cent of the population.[43] The reforms also aimed to accelerate the process of substituting official chairmanship of municipalities and district boards with non-officials, a measure encouraged by the Decentralisation Report of 1909 and initiated from 1916 onwards.[44] As Hugh Tinker has pointed out, although the aim of the government of India in producing the Montagu–Chelmsford Report was to encourage a graduated policy towards self-government, paradoxically it resulted in the rejection of power by the nationalists, particularly Gandhi and a large section of the Congress, at the local level and an intensification of the nationalist struggle for a change of power in the national political arena.[45] The first ministry in Bengal was therefore formed by a minority, a politically moderate section led by S.N. Banerjea. After an initial boycott, in 1923 a section of the Congress, the Swarajists, opted to participate in the local elections in order to subvert them from within. By 1924, it was evident that the Dyarchy had failed because, as Tinker noted, 'the "transferred" departments were managed by the Members of the "reserved" departments throughout the term of second legislature: and so there was no popular control whatsoever over local government policy from 1924 to 1927'.[46]

It was in this period of Dyarchy that the Government of Bengal sought to implement the abortive Tea Gardens Public Health Bill. The divergent interests within the district board in Jalpaiguri, and more significantly, the ambivalence of the tea industry about legislation for sanitation and medical facilities, prevented the enactment of a separate Board of Health for all tea plantations in the Darjeeling and Jalpaiguri districts.

The proposal was to form a separate Board of Health in the tea districts, which would provide for the registration of vital statistics as well as standardization of provisions for the prevention of epidemics and for medical care within

---

43 Tinker, *Foundations*, p. 148.
44 Tinker, *Foundations*, p. 148.
45 Tinker, *Foundations*, pp. 105–7.
46 Tinker, *Foundations*, p. 136.

all the tea plantations of Bengal, including Darjeeling, Terai and the Duars. The draft of the bill was circulated and reminders were sent to the district officials and the tea associations for discussion of the proposals.[47]

The DPA was initially lukewarm about the suggestion that its arrangements needed any improvement, particularly through government legislation and inspections, however cursory they had been in the past. Their chairman reiterated the point of contamination from without instead: 'A large part of the disease which has to be fought upon the Duars tea gardens comes from the "bustee" area which adjoins the tea district. My committee most certainly consider that, if legislation is to be applied it must be applied to the bustee area also.'[48]

In the Duars, the debates over the Bengal Tea Gardens Public Health Bill were informed by the struggle for control over the district board of Jalpaiguri between the landed *jotedars*, the planters' representatives, and affluent professionals of the district. As the proposals were abandoned in the Duars, the Dyarchy government did not have the political will to formulate the bill in Darjeeling and Terai either.

As we have seen previously, the tea plantation areas of Darjeeling and Duars were non-regulation tracts, where district officials held greater power than in regulation districts. In 1919 the devolution of power at the local levels led to the formation of several local boards in Bengal.[49] In the Jalpaiguri and Darjeeling districts no village (union) boards were formed. In Jalpaiguri district a local (sub-district level) board was created in only one subdivision (Alipur Duars). In response to a letter from the provincial government with enquiries regarding the establishment of local boards in Jalpaiguri, the deputy commissioner and the district board argued to the government for three local boards in Jalpaiguri, including one for Duars.[50] The provincial government would have to legislate separately for the local boards, and this did not materialize.

There were precedents in the nature of administrative solutions in favour of industrial areas situated within a larger district. In Asansol, where predominantly British capital was invested in coal mining, for instance, a Board of Health had been formed within the mining area in 1912. But the Board of Health in Asansol was one of the special local government institutions created for the coal industry. In 1914, after representations from the Indian Mining Association, the provincial government granted the rights to build roads to the local board of Asansol, redistributing the power to make that decision from the Burdwan

---

47 Letter from A.H.C. Jackson, Under-Secretary to Government of Bengal, Municipal Department, to Commissioner, Rajshahi, 14 May 1920, Government of Bengal Proceedings, Municipal/Sanitation, May 1920, no. 26, IOR/P/10765 (APAC), p. 57.
48 Letter from W.L. Travers, Chairman, DPA, to Commissioner, Rajshahi, 5 May 1920, Government of Bengal Proceedings, Municipal/Sanitation, Oct. 1920, nos 6–7, IOR/P/10765 (APAC), p. 11.
49 Tinker, *Foundations*, pp. 106–25.
50 Letter from Secretary Government of Bengal Municipal Department to Commissioner of Rajshahi, 4 Aug. 1919 and letter from Commissioner of Rajshahi to the Secretary, Municipal Department, 31 March 1920, Government of Bengal Proceedings, Municipal/Local Self Government, May 1920, IOR/P/10761 (APAC), pp. 121–22.

Contagion and Enclaves

district.[51] In the jute industrial areas, where British capital also dominated, a similar case was made for the separation of Bhatpara (where the jute mills were situated) from its larger hinterland, Naihati.[52] These adjustments were the special concessions to the industries dominated by British capital, some of which were later taken over by Marwari traders.[53] These areas, with the slow devolution of power at the level of local administration after 1885, retained a great deal of autonomy vis-à-vis the local elites who assumed control over the allocation of such funds as existed within the district boards.[54] The control of funds of the district board was important for expenditure on infrastructure required for the industry, such as roads and bridges.

In the tea plantation areas, that is, districts of Darjeeling, Terai and Duars, the situation was different because district officers had special powers and the regulations of the Bengal government were not applicable there unless by special ordinance. The devolution of power at the district and local board levels, therefore, did not occur in Darjeeling district (which included Terai) or Duars, which was a part of the Jalpaiguri district. In both the districts, therefore, the deputy commissioners in charge of the district administration had greater civil and police powers than any other district officer within the province. In

---

51 Government of Bengal Proceedings, General/Local Self -Government, March 1914, OR/P/9375 (APAC), p. 456.

52 In 1899 the government of Bengal separated the municipality of Bhatpara from that of Naihaiti, which was dominated by the local landed Indian elite. In Bhatpara itself the jute mill owners were frequently in conflict with the Indian *zamindars* who owned the *bastis* outside the mills where the workers resided. At the same time the jute mill owners depended on an alliance with the local propertied elite especially in times of worker 'unrest'. See Subho Basu, *Does Class Matter? Colonial Capital and Workers' Resistance in Bengal 1890–1937* (New Delhi and Oxford, Oxford University Press, 2004), pp. 74–112.

53 Omkar Goswami has argued that beginning from the postwar years, and particularly after 1930, the managing agencies which controlled jute and coal in eastern India were compelled to sell their shares to Marwari traders and accommodate some of them as directors in their companies. A few of them were bought outright by Marwari traders. The Marwari traders could not, however, buy shares in the tea industry because the British tea companies were registered in the London Exchange, which the Marwari traders could not reach. See Omkar Goswami, '*Sahibs, Babus,* and *Banias*: Changes in Industrial Control in Eastern India, 1918–50', *Journal of Asian Studies*, 48.2 (1989), pp. 289–309. The Bengali-owned tea companies were taken over by Marwari traders from the 1940s. See also, Sibsankar Mukherjee, 'Changing Control in Some Selected Tea Producing Companies of Jalpaiguri Town', *Social Scientist*, 6 (1978), pp. 57–69.

54 Such autonomy was contested by the local elite, usually ineffectually. The provincial government and the district officer in question usually ruled in favour of the industrial enclaves. In 1919, for instance, the Burdwan district board protested the allocation of a large part of the district's collection to the Asansol local board, arguing that it interfered with the administration of the district board of Burdwan as well as deprived the other subdivisions of a fair share of resources for constructing roads. The government overruled the objection on the basis of a letter from the district magistrate. Letter from Secretary Government of Bengal Municipal Department to Commissioner Burdwan District, 26 Feb. 1919, Government of Bengal Proceedings, Municipal/Local Self Government, June 1919, IOR/P/10519 (APAC), p. 71.

The Plantation Enclave, the Colonial State and Labour Health Care

Darjeeling a local board was established in Kurseong, but there were no union boards at the village level even after the Montagu–Chelmsford reforms. The elected portion within the Darjeeling district board remained nominal, and its chairmanship remained in official hands due to 'local reasons'.[55] Evidently it was because the government did not wish to relinquish official control over an important hill-station where Europeans resided in large numbers.[56]

After the Decentralisation Commission report, the district officer in Jalpaiguri argued that legislation for local self-government at the village level was not feasible because it was a 'backward' district and the experiment of such local governance should first be made in the more advanced districts.[57] Once the government announced the resolution on local self-government in 1918, the deputy commissioner of Jalpaiguri initially made a case for his retaining the chairmanship of the district board and, moreover, looked upon himself (and his office) as the arbiter of conflicts between the various elite factions within the district – the Indians and the Europeans (who were usually British) and the *jotedars* and the planters:

> asking my opinion as to whether the system of allowing District Boards to elect their own Chairmen should not be introduced in this district ... to introduce such a system in Jalpaiguri would ... be a mistake ... Owing to the fact that Jalpaiguri is a planting district the European element on the District Board is exceptionally strong ... [If] there were any question of electing either a non-official European or a non-official Indian to the Chairmanship, a certain amount of jealousy and racial feeling would inevitably be aroused and the existing harmony would be interrupted.[58]

Immediately after the War, the Jalpaiguri board continued to be mostly filled by officials nominated by the government, including representatives from the tea and rail industries and Indian professionals and landed men. In 1921 the government admitted that out of the 16 members of the Jalpaiguri district board, 14 were nominated and two elected by the Alipur Duars local board. Of the nominated members, five were officials and of the non-officials, 'three represent[ed] the European tea industry, three represent[ed] partly the Indian tea industry and partly other interests extending over the whole district and the remaining three may be regarded as respectively the interests of the Bengal

---

55 Resolution no 290 L.S.G., Government of Bengal Proceedings, 19 Jan. 1931, Local Self Government/Local Boards, Dec. 1931, P/11942 (APAC), p. 5.
56 Tinker has noted that 'In most provinces officials only retained control in a few backward areas, or in towns with some special character, such as the frontier trading post of Bhamo in Burma, or some of the hill-stations with their hot-weather invasions.' Tinker, *Foundations*, p. 120.
57 Letter from Commissioner, Bhagalpur Division to the Secretary to Government of Bengal, General Department, 7 Aug. 1916, Government of Bengal Proceedings, Municipal/Local Self-Government, Aug. 1917, IOR/P/10114 (APAC), p. 81.
58 Letter from Deputy Commissioner of Jalpaiguri to the Commissioner of Rajshahi, 19 March 1919, Government of Bengal Proceedings, Municipal/Local Self- Government, Dec. 1919, IOR/P/10589 (APAC), p. 171.

Duars Railway, the Cooch Behar State and the Baikunthapur Estate'.[59] In 1923, the deputy commissioner of Jalpaiguri relinquished the chairmanship of the district board, and the first non-official chairman was the government pleader, Rai Kalipada Banerjee. The tea industry continued to have representation at the district board. In the 1920s, provincial 'augmentation' grants and local collections from revenue cesses increased district boards' revenues, and they were 'encouraged to expand'.[60] Government augmentation grants to all the districts in Bengal comprised a total of Rs 3.84 lakhs in 1926–27, which rose to Rs 13.85 lakhs in 1932–33.[61] But as Tinker has pointed out, most of the funds were spent under the heading 'education': sanitation and health were a very low priority for the elected local bodies.[62] In 1926–27, for instance, the districts boards in Bengal spent only a total of Rs 22 lakhs under the heading 'health and sanitation', which rose to Rs 3,466,000 in 1932–33.[63]

Simultaneously, as we have seen in the episode of the Christophers–Bentley report, the influence of British tea plantations extended beyond the tangible benefits of representation within the district board. The largely British DPA contested the rapid growth of Indian-owned tea gardens through the purchase of *jote* lands for tea cultivation in the 1920s.[64] Despite conflicts and competition, the ITPA and the DPA had moments of agreement, particularly as to restrictions on the raising of workers' wages after the First World War, and later, in the resistance to government when it proposed a labour seat in the Legislative Council in 1937.[65]

The disparity in the tea industry between the Indian and the British planters was reflected in the varied sanitary and medical facilities that they provided respectively. The Indian estates, with a smaller acreage under tea and small-capital margins, probably cut down costs severely in the provision for medical facilities. Most of the JLA reports noted that while some of the 'European' (British-owned) tea estates were attempting to provide piped drinking water to the workers and appointing qualified doctor babus, the Indian-owned estates made little attempt to do so.[66] In the perspective of both the DPA and deputy commissioner, the improvement of sanitary facilities within the tea estates became the problem of greater supervision over the Indian tea estates. Simultaneously, most of the

---

59 Question asked by Kishori Mohan Chaudhuri, at the meeting of 14 March 1921, Government of Bengal Proceedings, Local Self Government/Local Self Government, IOR/P/10980 (APAC), p. 35.
60 Tinker, *Foundations*, p. 164.
61 Naresh Chandra Roy, *Rural Self-Government in Bengal* (Calcutta, University of Calcutta, 1936), pp. 94–95.
62 Tinker, *Foundations*, p. 164.
63 Roy, *Rural Self-Government*, pp. 94–95. The average annual income of a district board in Bengal in 1931–32 was Rs 600,000, derived mainly from local land revenue cesses, ferries, motor vehicles etc. (p. 80).
64 *DPAAR, 1926* (Jalpaiguri, 1927, APAC), pp. 56–59.
65 See Chairman's speech, *DPAAR, 1922* (Jalpaiguri, 1923, APAC), p. viii. See also, letter from Secretary, Indian Tea Planters' Association to Chairman, DPA, 26 Aug. 1932, *DPAAR, 1932* (Jalpaiguri, 1933, APAC), p. 120.
66 *JLAAR, 1921–22* (Calcutta, 1922, APAC), p. 4.

JLA reports generally agreed with the DPA in situating the problem of sanitation outside the plantation areas. Therefore, the question of control came to rest also on the areas outside of the boundaries of the tea estates.

The third element in this complex relationship was the local *jotedars* who were suspicious of the tea estates' control of spreading beyond their boundaries into the *hats* and the *jote* areas. They were also reluctant to concede to the extension of government supervision over their own labourers in the agricultural areas. When the JLA was put through the legislative council in 1912, an Indian member, Dulal Chandra Deb, asked for an amendment by which the word 'labourers' would be substituted for 'persons' and the words 'for the purpose of carrying on the tea industry or tea cultivation' be added after 'labour'.[67] The government refused the amendment on the grounds that the local administration was entitled, through the provisions of the Act, to make exceptions for employers of temporary labour (for digging a ditch or building a house, for instance), and that it had the right to intervene and ask employers of labourers numbering above 50 to provide medical and sanitary benefits to its employees.[68] Interestingly, the representative of the planters, A.W. Chaplain, supported the government and claimed that tea garden coolies were not labourers in the sense that the word could be employed in the tea estates of Assam, reinforcing their claim that their labourers were free.[69] This incident illustrates the nature of tensions that existed between the local *jotedars* and the planters, with suspicions about the extension of supervision and control by the government on both parts. Given the representation and the influence of the tea estates within the district administration, the *jotedars* tended to equate district administration with the tea planters.

One recurring grievance that the local elites (both the Bengali professionals and *jotedars*) had was that a large portion of the funds of the district board was allocated to the tea estate areas. In April 1921 one Babu Kishori Mohan reminded the Bengal Legislative Council that despite a petition placed before the Jalpaiguri board, the district administration spent most of the public works cess (from which a major component of the district board's income came) in the tea garden areas. The government replied that

> In the tea garden portion of the *khas mahal* area sanitary and medical arrangements were made at the expense of the tea gardens and not of the Board. A portion of the Board's income, which otherwise would have had to be spent on medical and sanitation work, was consequently set free and devoted to extra road making in that area.[70]

67 Government of India Proceedings, Education/Sanitation, Oct. 1912, nos 12–13, Appendix W (NAI), pp. 17–19.
68 Government of India Proceedings, Education/Sanitation, Oct. 1912, nos 12–13, Appendix W, pp. 17–19.
69 Government of India Proceedings, Education/Sanitation, Oct. 1912, nos 12–13, Appendix W, pp. 17–19.
70 Government of Bengal Proceedings, Local Self-Government, June 1921 no. 9, IOR/P/10980 (APAC), pp. 9–11. The provincial government made a special further grant of rupees 1.5 lakhs for road construction in the tea garden areas.

Contagion and Enclaves

The reality was that the district board spent very little of its income on medical and sanitary facilities in the entire district, which included the areas outside of the plantations. In 1921 a government statement tabled at the council meeting revealed that between 1916–17 and 1919–20, the district board's expenditure on medical relief had been 3.9, 3.1 and 4.7 per cent of its total income respectively.[71]

Grants from the provincial government to the district tended to focus on the tea industry despite regular opposition from the Indians in the district board. This was illustrated in an instance of providing for deep wells which could supply clean drinking water.[72] If deep wells were to be bored, the planters' view was that the government should bear the expense. The chairman of the DPA noted, in a special address to the Governor who had stopped at Duars in 1913 on his way to Darjeeling,

> We still maintain that so long as the question remains in the experimental state and while the ultimate results are as yet doubtful, it is the duty of Government as our landlord, to aid us in a matter of such great importance to the welfare of the industry and the health of the population.[73]

The provincial government subsequently sent an engineer to investigate the possibilities of boring deep wells, especially at the foothills where shortages occurred every summer.[74] Following the survey, the government offered to pay half the estimated cost of one lakh rupees for 25 borings if the district board consented to pay the other half of the total costs.[75] The *jotedars* and the other Indian members forced a resolution refusing to pay.[76]

When the government proposed the Bengal Tea Gardens Public Health Bill, the local *jotedars* were discomfited by the prospect of a separate sanitary enclave because of the anticipated split in the public works cess, the main source of income for the district board.[77] The government replied that although

---

[71] Government of Bengal Proceedings, Local Self Government, July 1921, no. 50, P/10980 (APAC), p. 29.

[72] The tea estates in the foothills often drew piped water from the *jhoras* for the tea bushes, which were possibly used by the labourers for their domestic purposes as well. In some places water was scarce. Fraser gives an account of laying a pipeline for a newly planted tea estate. *Recollections*, pp. 47–51.

[73] DPAAR, 1912 (Calcutta, 1913, APAC), p. xiii. See also *Tour[s] of H.E. the Right Hon Baron Carmichael of Skirling, Jalpaiguri, Oct 31st to Nov. 2nd, 1912* (Calcutta, 1912, APAC), p. 15.

[74] Government of Bengal Proceedings, Municipal/Local Self Government, Sep. 1916, nos 13–16, IOR/P/9889 (APAC), pp. 15–17.

[75] Government of Bengal Proceedings, Municipal/Local Self Government, Sep. 1916, pp. 15–17.

[76] Government of Bengal Proceedings, Municipal/Local Self Government, Sep. 1916, pp. 15–17.

[77] Question asked by Panchanan Barma, 17 Jan. 1922, Government of Bengal Proceedings, Local Self Government/Public Health, Jan. 1922, no. 7, P/11163 (APAC), p. 9. He also enquired if any members of the district board would be nominated to the Tea Gardens Board of Health.

the district roads cess was not to be allocated to the proposed health board, the district board 'might make a contribution'.[78] The Indian members at the board included *jotedars* and professional men, only five of the 15 members. Five British planters and five British officials were also members of the board.

The issue of legislative intervention to secure a 'sanitary enclave' within the tea estates was therefore complex. On the one hand, the British medical officers within the tea estates sought to externalize the problem and posited the issue of the bazaars and the *bastis* as centres of disease. The British planters, too, contributed to the discourse of contamination from outside, but they externalized the problem and demanded government intervention. As influential members of the district board, they succeeded in investing the district board's funds in the appointment of one Sanitary Inspector for the bazaar areas outside the tea estates in 1928.[79] The district officials – the Civil Surgeon and the Deputy Commissioner – as shown earlier, generally concurred with the plantation management in identifying the bazaars and the *bastis* as the source of the disease and opted for accepting managerial assertions regarding the health of the labourers.

The local elite formed a complex grid of interests as their representation within the district board exemplifies. Overall, the Indian planters opposed any measures for sanitary reforms within their plantations; the ITPA stated categorically that there was no need for such a bill, nor was there any public demand for it. It argued instead that

> It is likely to cause a great deal of harassment to the coolie population in and about the tea-gardens and is likely to scare away *bustee* coolies from the neighbourhood of tea-gardens, the economical effect of which on the garden coolies as well as on the management would be severe. Moreover, the isolation of the tea-garden area uncontaminated by touch with the rest of the dist[rict] is an impossibility.[80]

The local *jotedars*, on the other hand, were opposed to a separate board because it would diminish the area under the district board and its influence, and moreover they would be taxed for the funds of a board in which they would not have significant representation (the proposed board was to have 15 members of whom one would be nominated by the district board). They voiced their disquiet to the government:

---

78 Government of Bengal Proceedings, Local Self Government/Public Health, Jan. 1922, p. 9. In the statement the government provided the names of the members of the district board at this time. It demonstrates the heavy representation of the official and non-official British element in the district board. The official and the European planting members were clearly dominant numerically.

79 Government of Bengal Proceedings, Municipal/Sanitation, Nov. 1918, no. 3, P/10307 (APAC), p. 9. See also address of Chairman, DPA in *DPAAR, 1918* (Calcutta, 1919, APAC), p. x.

80 Government of Bengal Proceedings, Local Self Government/Public Health, Oct 1930, no. 61, IOR/P/11872 (APAC), pp. 67–68.

> No separate Board of Health is necessary for the area in question and that the matters dealt with in the Bill may be as well dealt with the district board whose jurisdiction should not be taken away ... A special committee may be constituted consisting of district board members as well as outsiders to deal with the matters.[81]

The issue was complicated by intersecting vested interests; some *jotedars* such as Nawab Mosharruff Hossain, for instance, also owned large plantations. Hossain was the vice-chairman of the district board for several years, and a regular invitee to the annual general meetings of the DPA after 1920. In 1927 he became a minister in the provincial government.[82]

The Bengal government itself lacked the will to extend interventions within the plantations, either through legislation or inspections within the tea plantations. In the event of contemporary nationalist and labour movements in the interwar years, the government sought to effect sanitary measures within the tea estates through the creation of a separate local board where the planters' influence would predominate. This was in line with its policy in industrial sites elsewhere in Bengal. However, its proposals were met not only with opposition from the Indian planters but also, subtly, from the British-dominated DPA. It is here that the difference between the rhetoric and practice of sanitary enclaves becomes important, since the DPA insisted that it was willing to cooperate with a separate board provided the plantations were not made financially responsible for the *basti* lands:

> In order to control an outbreak of epidemic disease it is essential that the area which would come under the jurisdiction of the Board of Health should include all the Government Jote and Khas land within a well defined area in the neighbourhood of the gardens. Your Committee has persistently impressed upon Government the desirability of definitely describing the boundaries in the scope of the Bill, but at the same time it should be clearly understood that the Dooars Tea Industry would look to Government to pay an equitable proportionate amount for all parts of the prescribed area not situated on land leased to Tea Companies.[83]

---

81 Government of Bengal Proceedings, Local Self Government/Public Health, Oct 1930, no. 61, p. 73. So far as the Asansol Board of Mines was concerned, the district board had protested that the Asansol board received special treatment and provincial grants were not made to the rest of the subdivisions in the district. As in the Duars, additional provincial grants to the Assam board were spent on building roads for better communications.

82 *DPAAR, 1927* (Jalpaiguri, 1928, APAC), p. vi. The MLA from the European planters' constituency claimed to the Royal Commission in 1929 that the district board would have been 'persuaded' by the DPA if the provincial government had pushed through the legislation. See *DPAAR, 1929* (Jalpaiguri, 1930, APAC), p. xi.

83 Address of Chairman, DPA, at the annual general meeting of the DPA, *DPAAR, 1923* (Jalpaiguri, 1924, APAC), p. vii. It is significant that in the same speech the Chairman of the DPA referred to the special concession made by government to exempt the tea industry from the Factories Act. Therefore, the agreement to a board of health could also possibly have been perceived by both the planters and the government as a compensatory concession to legislation for labour health.

The lands that would be under the control of the proposed board were demarcated specifically by the DPA – it asked for an extensive sphere of influence for the proposed Board including the *bastis*.[84] The *jotedars* of the *basti* lands, on the other hand, were evidently reluctant to pay an extra cess for the creation of a board of health which would be controlled by the planters. The Indian tea planters, some of whom were also *jotedars*, rejected the plan for the Board.

The Bengal Tea Gardens Public Health Board Bill was introduced in 1923, but later withdrawn. Under the system of Dyarchy, the elected representative controlled the local self-government department but had little power to extend revenues. The finances for all sanitary schemes were localized; they had to depend on the district revenues with a few 'augmentation grants' from the provincial government. All in all, there was very little will on the part of the government to carry through the legislation. Faced with the task of placating the planters on the one hand and the Indian *jotedars* on the other, it chose to withdraw the bill.

A few years later, W.L. Travers, the DPA representative, informed the Royal Commission on Labour in India when it visited the Duars that

> If the Calcutta Agency Houses and Home Companies agree I shall be ready and willing to negotiate with the Government for a Bill under which not only the tea producing area of Jalpaiguri, but also a certain area of adjoining bustee land would come under the control of a Board of Health. I understand that the District Board was opposed to the Bill, but I would appeal to the Board to withdraw their opposition and to aid, not to hinder our efforts.[85]

A proposal to reintroduce the bill in the provincial legislature was revived in 1930, but it was dropped as well.[86] Therefore, in the Jalpaiguri district the DPA alleged that the Indian *jotedari* interests sabotaged a separate health board for the tea plantation areas in the Western Duars, and it is undeniably true that the Indian planters and *jotedars* were opposed to such a scheme. But in the Terai, and particularly in Darjeeling, where there were no powerful *jotedars* in the district board, neither the Darjeeling Planters Association nor the Terai Planters Association wanted legislation to enforce uniform sanitary measures and medical policies. The Darjeeling and Terai subcommittees of the ITA discussed the proposals when they were first made and a committee including the district deputy commissioner even drew up an ambitious plan in which the proposed board would absorb the revenues from the Darjeeling Improvement Board. But the general sentiments among the planters were not in favour of the Board: 'Particulars of the proposals were circulated to those concerned, and it was found that the view was very strongly held that in the present condition

---

84 'Collection of Opinions on the Bengal Tea Gardens Public Health Bill, 1923', Government of Bengal Proceedings, Local Self Government/Public Health, Oct. 1930, no. 58, IOR/P/118972 (APAC), pp. 67–70.
85 *DPAAR, 1929* (Jalpaiguri, 1930, APAC), p. xi.
86 Government of Bengal Proceedings, Local Self-Government/Public Health, Oct. 1930 nos 58–64, IOR/P/11872 (APAC), pp. 60–119.

of the industry the whole scheme was much more elaborate than could be undertaken.'[87]

When the government suggested that formalized sanitary enclaves, with the plantation estates responsible for public health within the legislated enclaves, be implemented in the mining industry in Bengal, the ITA pointed out to the government that the Asansol case was different. They claimed that in Darjeeling and Terai the tea estates were leased directly from the government and therefore it was the government's responsibility to pay for the costs of the proposed board.[88] In this they echoed the sentiments of the Planters' Association in the Duars. The government did not press for legislation for Darjeeling and Terai separately. In 1931 the Royal Commission for Labour in India recommended a board where the planters' representatives would predominate and make decisions and implement policies with regard to all sanitary and medical matters within their individual jurisdictions.[89] Neither the planters nor the government took any active steps towards it, and the plans for such sanitary boards remained on paper.

The episode of the abortive Tea Gardens Public Health Bill highlights a paradox of the plantation enclaves in colonial India. While the government acknowledged the plantations as special zones that might have local institutions to sustain a distinct sanitary and medical enclave, the planters themselves either partially (in the case of British planters) or wholly (so far as the Indian planters were concerned) rejected the plan. Why was this rejected, particularly when, as we have seen above, the planters and their medical officials made clear distinctions between the unsanitary bazaars and *bastis* and the relatively sanitized tea estates? The answer, unsurprisingly, was in the economic logic. The bazaars and the *bastis* were needed to sustain the plantation economy. At the same time, as we have seen, both in the Darjeeling and Duars districts, the planters' associations demanded that the government as the tenant should pay for the cost of sanitary measures in the *bastis* and the bazaars.

The Medical Economy of the Plantations

The dynamics of the system of health care within the plantations were determined in the context of profits and parsimony. The relations of production were peculiar to colonial capitalism; with workers as subsistence farmers, the use of intermediaries such as the *sardars* and the particular context of racial authority that was such an integral aspect of the relationship between the planters and the workers. In such a situation the provisions for health care retained the element of arbitrariness that had been their characteristic in the pioneering years. The authority of the planters in their respective tea estates over the health care system (as in everything else) prevented the rationalization of medical services

---

87 *IPTAAR, 1920* (Calcutta, 1921, APAC), p. 38.
88 *IPTAAR, 1920*, p. 38.
89 *RCLI*, p. 418.

in the tea plantations. In 1947, when the first ever comprehensive survey of medical facilities in the tea estates of India was conducted by the government of India, E. Lloyd Jones explained that

> The great drawback is that the health policy still remains in the hands of the individual managers to a very great extent, and this is of great importance when matters involving capital expenditure are at issue. The majority of managers are still paid on a basis of a fixed salary plus percentage of profits ... [T]here is a very natural tendency to cut down on expenditure which, although it might be profitable as a long term policy, is not going to show any dividends during the existing manager's term of office. This affects the amount a manager is likely to spend on any long term health policy very adversely.[90]

The system of pay linked to percentage of profits and the short-term vision it induced determined the overall strategy of the tea companies in northern Bengal. Therefore, investments in infrastructure such as piped water and proper plinths for the workers' houses were limited to a few of the larger tea estates, and there too they were not maintained regularly. This reinforced the paternalistic system where care for the labourers was incorporated within a system of supervisory benevolence. The availability of health care during illness was a gift which a loyal worker might or might not receive; it depended on the benevolence of the planter. Jones noted a striking instance of this system:

> In one particular case a company had spent over 1,000 rupees on expensive treatment for one of their coolies who was suffering from an obscure medical complaint, but refused a water point inside their garden hospital, although this would probably have been repaid a thousand fold in a few years.[91]

In such a circumstance a great deal of the health care available to the workers was in the form of charity provided by kindly planters, usually as rewards to loyal and hard-working workers. Such a system represented the very basis of the structural economy of the plantations. The above quote has resonances with the instructions provided to planters in the handbook of the Tea Districts Labour Association:

> The great majority of the Tea Estates situated in the Dooars and Terai have ... adopted 'sirdari' recruitment, which, in view of their birthright of recruiting free from legal restrictions ... the onus of making the Estate attractive to labour is thrown on the Management. The ordinary Indian labourer is unable to appreciate and, in fact, cares very little for the conveniences of modern hospitals and medical treatment ... [F]ifty percent of the 'attractions' of an Estate may be summed up in the personality of the Manager ... the sahib ... to whom it is possible to go when in trouble and who will trust you if need

---

90 *Standards of Medical Care for Tea Plantations in India: A Report by E. Lloyd Jones, M.D. Deputy Director General of Health Services* (Delhi, Government of India, Ministry of Labour, 1947), p. 14.
91 Jones, *Standards of Medical Care*, p. 14.

be with an advance of money; such a sahib is the epitome of attractiveness of an Estate where it is possible to live and work in comfort and without peril to the soul.[92]

Managerial discourse emphasized the structure of the tea plantation economy which constructed the role of the manager as provider and protector of the labourers. The managers meanwhile practised financial stringency mitigated by occasional acts of generosity to a few selected labourers. This arbitrariness was replicated downward in the hierarchy. We are reminded here of the *sardar* so reviled in the Christophers–Bentley report, who occasionally threw feasts for his workers but accepted no responsibility for their basic care in times of sickness.

The tea companies, particularly those controlled by the Agency Houses, themselves attempted to cut down the costs of health care for the labourer, and to keep costs similarly low for the managerial staff. One instance of the latter was in financing a branch of the Lady Minto Indian Nursing Association (LMINA) in Jalpaiguri, to make available two nurses who would provide services to the planter families in the district. The DPA subscribed to the LMINA, two of whose nurses were stationed in Jalpaiguri from 1907 onwards. They supplemented the efforts of the British medical officials and stayed over at the plantations at the request of concerned patients, at a fee. The planters used their services at the time of childbirth as well as for general nursing. The arrangement was that each tea garden would contribute Rs 2500 to pay for the annual salaries of the two nurses stationed at Jalpaiguri, and each tea estate initially paid a rate of half an anna per acre of tea under cultivation. In 1908 itself, however, the tea companies dithered about the expense, and the managing agents and proprietors based in Calcutta expressed doubts if it was necessary at all. The British medical officers had to appeal to the ITA through the DPA for greater generosity for funds to finance the Minto nurses.[93]

While the proprietors quibbled over the expense of maintaining nurses, the British planters and the doctors in the Duars considered it a necessary insurance. The agents at Calcutta finally conceded to a guaranteed amount based on the acreage of tea planted in each garden, subject to the regular submission of accounts by the Jalpaiguri branch of the LMINA. Apart from the regular 'guarantee fund', the Jalpaiguri establishment of the Minto nurses was further supplemented by subscriptions from the residents of the stations, the Bengal–Dooars Railway and the 'planters generally'.[94] The 'guarantee subscriptions' by the managing agents and the proprietors were inadequate, and most planters contributed personally to the maintenance of the Jalpaiguri branch. They perceived it as both a personal insurance and an act for the common good of

---

92 *Tea Districts Labour Association, Handbook of Castes and Tribes Employed on Tea Estates in North East India* (Calcutta, Catholic Orphan Press, 1924), p. 5.
93 *DPAAR, 1909* (Calcutta, 1909, APAC), pp. v–vi.
94 *DPAAR, 1909* (Calcutta, 1910, APAC), pp. ii–iv.

the 'planting community'.[95] Although there were occasional disagreements with the Minto establishment in Jalpaiguri, over the years it provided for the steady supply of reliable British nurses to attend to the planters and their families.[96] Of course most planters sent their children to the 'hills' for the greater part of the year.[97] This instance highlights the reluctance of the Agency Houses, which took decisions in distant Calcutta and even further away Glasgow, to spend on medical facilities in general, even for the planters.

The stringency practised by the managing agencies, therefore, occasionally extended to its managerial staff as well. In such cases the local management depended on themselves and private subscriptions from the local British official and non-official population. Another form of gratuitous financial assistance available to planters was through the Tea Planters' Benevolent Institution, a charitable trust set up by the ITA. The ITA formed and managed the trust to utilize the estate of William Jackson of Glasgow, who in 1921 bequeathed half of his wealth 'for the purpose of establishing a trust fund for the benefit of tea planters and their wives and families in sickness'.[98]

So far as the labourers were concerned, the medical economy and structure of production within the plantations created a system where the nature and availability of care was capricious and dependent on the will of the individual managers. In areas where more generalized attempts were made to provide medical relief, the issue was connected more to the labourers' daily survival than medical care or sanitary provisions. As we have seen, after the price rise during the War, some tea estates procured rice and sold it at a discount to their workers. This method of foodstuff distribution was more widely followed during the Second World War, when food was in short supply, especially in Bengal.[99] In the face of the enormous rise in prices the planters attempted to control speculation and high prices in the local *hats*, without a great degree of success. The DPA officially decided to buy rice and distribute a food ration to all workers regularly.[100] This was in the context of a shortage of labour due to war (Ray has noted that during the war years the DPA's labour rules broke down and the tea estates often competed for *basti* labour and provided them food as enticement).[101]

95 *DPAAR, 1912* (Calcutta, 1913, APAC), p. xii.
96 The LMINA nurses were recruited from Britain and usually served two years at each post. See Interview with Dorothy Thomas, who served as a LMINA nurse in Jalpaiguri between 1930–32. Mss Eur/R 136 (APAC).
97 Interview with Father W.K.L. Webb, Mss Eur/R 187/2 (APAC).
98 *IPTAAR, 1922* (Calcutta, 1923, APAC), pp. 23–24.
99 For a survey of the Bengal administration during famine, see Rakesh Batabyal, *Communalism in Bengal: From Famine to Noakhali, 1943–47* (New Delhi and London, Sage, 2005), pp. 71–164.
100 Griffiths, *History*, pp. 312–19. The *Labour Investigation Committee* noted in 1946 that 'The cost of living has gone up by at least 200 per cent in Dooars since 1939. Similar figures are not available for the Darjeeling district. But it may be assumed that the cost of living has gone up similarly there also … the labourers' earnings including … concessions has only doubled since 1939'. Rege, *Labour Investigation Committee*, p. 86.
101 Ray, *Transformations*, p. 160.

In other respects as well, the planter raj faced unprecedented changes during the last year of the war. In 1946–47, the Communist Party of India organized railway unions at the Bengal Dooars Railway, and also attempted to organize the tea plantation workers. The tea workers participated with tenant-sharecroppers in the Tebhaga movement of 1946–47.[102] The participation of some of the workers in the Tebhaga movement prompted fears about a more general Communist uprising within the tea estates, and it was at this time that the planters conceded a raise in daily wages.[103] However, it was not until after the Indian Independence that trade unions could effectively organize themselves within the tea estates.[104] Even then, the planters allowed only the non-Communist unions to organize legally within the plantations, and watched their progress carefully.

Another concession in lieu of increased wages, first started by some tea estates in the 1920s, was the payment of money to women workers a little before and immediately after childbirth, and if the infant survived its first year. This was evidently in the context of the labour shortage immediately after the First World War and the influenza epidemic that followed it. In 1922, Curjel noted the practice in her survey.[105] One of the British medical officers of the DPA, Dr McCutcheon, told the Royal Commission on Labour in 1929 that 'as a general rule, we give maternity allowances'.[106] The planters informed the Commission that legislation on maternity benefits was unnecessary because the 'maternity allowances now given voluntarily were sufficient'.[107] The Commission pointed out that there were inequalities in the distribution: 'in certain cases allowances are considerably below the average and in some are non-existent'.[108] In 1937, in an attempt to standardize and fix a ceiling on all benefits received by the workers, the DPA fixed a rate of Rs 15 as the maximum 'to be distributed according to the manager's discretion', with another ten rupees for the infant in the first year.[109] When the government of Bengal enforced a minimum maternity allowance of Rs 12 per birth, G.P. Macpherson, the planters' representative in the Council, recommended those tea estates which paid more than that sum to continue to pay the extra amount as a long-term investment.[110] The implementation of the maternity allowance was ad hoc and varied from one tea estate to another.[111] In periods of labour shortage, the reproduction of labour

---

102 For an analysis of the Tebhaga movement see Das Gupta, *Labour*, pp. 223–37. See also Ray, *Transformations*, pp. 173–82.
103 Sharit Bhowmik, *Class Formation in the Plantation System* (New Delhi, Peoples' Publishing House, 1981), p. 148.
104 Bhowmik, *Class Formation*, pp. 149–50.
105 *DPAAR, 1923* (Jalpaiguri, 1924, APAC), pp. 97–98.
106 *DPAAR, 1929* (Jalpaiguri, 1930, APAC), p. 165.
107 *RCLI* (London, 1931), p. 412.
108 *RCLI*, p. 412.
109 *DPAAR, 1937* (Calcutta, 1938, APAC), p. 391.
110 *DPAAR, 1941* (Calcutta, 1942, APAC), p. xix.
111 The 'maternity allowance' was possibly perceived as *baksheesh* (a tip) by the management as well as the labourers. See Chatterjee, *A Time for Tea*, p. 83.

assumed greater significance. Immediately after the First World War, when labour shortage affected tea production in all the plantations, a government report found that 'Though the [maternity] benefit is paid by most of the sampled gardens in the Dooars, there is no uniformity in the matter ... In the Terai and Darjeeling also, there is no uniformity about payment of the benefit.'[112] Therefore, in the interests of the reproduction of its workforce, where the plantations did invest to facilitate the daily survival and the reproduction of their labourers, the investments were ad hoc, as in other health matters.

Conclusion: Paternalism, Colonial Enclaves and Health Care

Medical care on tea plantations in India has grown with the industry.
– Major E. Lloyd Jones, IMS[113]

The first report on the standards of medical care by a medically qualified professional after the one by Christophers and Bentley was commissioned by the government of India and conducted by E. Lloyd Jones in 1947. Both his report, specifically on the standards of medical care in the plantations, and that of R.V. Rege, the chairman of the Labour Board of India, who conducted a study on the living conditions of tea garden workers in 1946, testify to the widespread availability to selected tea plantation labourers of sanitation, water supplies, access to a dispensaries and hospital care.[114] The reports, commissioned by the Labour Ministry of the Government of India, used managerial records, which despite their flaws revealed great improvement in the availability of medical care for the labourers over the years between 1890 and 1947. These included a rise in birth rates, decrease in death rates, decline in infant mortality rates and an increase in the availability of qualified doctors and medical infrastructure such as hospitals and dispensaries from the time of the establishment of the tea plantations in the late nineteenth century.

Their recommendations encompassed a range of measures for preventive and curative medicine within the plantations. Rege's report also strongly recommended a better wage structure and other benefits for the workers, stating that the existing system was very inadequate. To an extent, these reports anticipated the reformism and optimism of the incipient nation-state. But partly the reports also revealed a duality that reflected a deeper problem of health care and disease management in the northern Bengal plantations: where large-scale production for tea was pursued, but within a system that looked to short-term profit. In all aspects, the economic aims and social relations of production did not change fundamentally from the days of the pioneering planters.

112 Rege, *Labour Investigation Committee*, p. 92. The amount of the lump sum paid on the birth of a child and if it survived the first year of infancy varied between ten to eighteen rupees and eight *anna* in the Duars, and as widely as between Rs 2–8–0 to 19–8–0 in the Terai and Darjeeling.
113 Jones, *Standards of Medical Care*, p. 13.
114 Rege, *Labour Investigation Committee*, pp. 87–94.

To some extent, the story of the system of medical care in the plantation economy of northern Bengal reflects the greater history of colonization itself. Just as the jungles were cleared at the frontiers of northern Bengal, where cultivation was commercialized gradually but inexorably, and immigrant populations were brought and settled both in the plantations and outside in the *bastis* as sharecroppers, so the administration of health care in the tea plantations too was streamlined and attempts made to fit the labourers into the production of work and their bodies into productive agents of their labour. Therefore, it was evident that on the whole there would be more doctors, midwives, dispensaries and occasionally even piped water available to the labourers in the plantations in 1947 than there had been in, say, 1890.

However, the process was disjointed, not because it was not a reasonable course for planters to invest in workers' health as the tea plantations became more established (as they did). Not even because there were conflicts between the plantation management and the local government over jurisdiction and responsibility for the preventive aspect of health care in the region. Such conflicts did of course inhibit the development of a vigorous public health system within the tea plantations. But more than any of these was the nature of the tea plantations as they developed, the territorial sovereignty that the managers claimed and the social relationship of production in the plantation structure they enjoyed – a system where the long-term economic rationale was often obfuscated and a more diffused paternalism prevailed. It was a system that could condone a manager lending a labourer money in advance for a wedding or a funeral – a personal and intimate gesture at an individual level. But it would not be considered economically viable for that very same plantation manager to invest in infrastructure for health in the long term.

This apparent contradiction in the story of health care in the plantations was replicated in the nature of the plantation system itself. The nature of the plantation system appeared contradictory because its objectives were those of capitalist production on a mass scale, but the production relations in the colonial plantation society were framed in terms that enabled management to be erratic and self-willed. This was no accident. It comprised the very core of the plantation structure, in which the economic and social relations were mediated through the paternalistic notions of the tea plantation management. The district or the provincial governments rarely interfered, except in moments of threatened overspill outside the tea gardens, either of diseases or of labour 'unrest'.

CHAPTER 7

Tropical Medicine in Its 'Field': Malaria, Hookworm and the Rhetoric of the 'Local'

This chapter studies the dynamics between colonial enclaves and Tropical Medicine in the twentieth century. Despite the acceptance of germ theory, British Indian medical discourse and practice never abandoned miasmatic and climatic theories of disease. In colonial India, Tropical Medicine continued to connect diseases with specific 'zones' and 'localities'. Research in Tropical Medicine reiterated the importance of 'local factors' constructed through ecological, climatic or cultural modes. From their contribution to Tropical Medicine, through the 'experiments' and verification of disease theories in their localities, to the contribution to the control of archetypical 'tropical' disease in Bengal and India generally, the tea plantations were an important site for the exploration of new ideas and experimentation. In the case of research in anti-malarial sanitation, a focus on the local ecological conditions of the tea plantations in Darjeeling foothills merged seamlessly with factors such as the cultural behaviour of plantation labourers – all framed in a set of conditions termed the 'local'. Simultaneously the political economy of the tea plantations inhibited both anti-malarial sanitation as well as systematic and full use of quinine prophylaxis within these 'local' sites. Similarly, when the Indian Research Fund Association (IRFA) proposed a hookworm project to assess the feasibility of its eradication, the medical experts chose the Darjeeling hill plantations as their first, experimental site. The results of the hookworm survey showed a very high incidence among the plantation labourers. The planters, while providing the plantation space for the surveys, were not persuaded to install sanitary facilities for the workers, nor did the government initiate legislation to facilitate it. Therefore, following the survey in Darjeeling and subsequent ones in Duars and Terai, the problem of hookworm eradication in the plantations remained unresolved.

This chapter argues that Tropical Medicine was enriched by studies in colonial enclaves which facilitated wide-ranging studies on preventive and therapeutic aspects of the internationally competitive specialism. These studies validated the value or significance of 'local factors' in epidemiology as they did in governance itself. There were no structural therapeutic or public health benefits to the enclaves in the process.

Malaria in the Darjeeling Foothills

Most of the sicknesses in the Duars and the Terai were related to malaria and blackwater fever. Tea plantations were established in the Darjeeling foothills and the Duars a few decades before Tropical Medicine was institutionalized and Patrick Manson assigned to malaria the role of the paradigmatic disease of the tropics, 'the greatest scourge of mankind ... eminently a tropical disease'.[1] Historians have pointed out that the institutionalizing of Tropical Medicine was effected in the context of professional interests and imperialist visions.[2] Institutional bases for research in India were set up gradually in the first decades of the twentieth century, but various malarial theories jostled for recognition and the sanitarian principles of miasmatic changes persisted for a long time.[3]

Malaria research in the Darjeeling foothills was enmeshed in debates over malaria-control policies in India and in international malaria research. In the early twentieth century, scientific medical research in India focused urgently on cholera and plague, but particularly after 1911 when the Indian Research Fund Association (IRFA) was formed, which invested in malaria research as well.[4] The story of international malaria research and India in the twentieth century is one of incremental increase in specialized knowledge about malaria, the identification of various anophelines, formation of malaria 'brigades', mapping of malaria through malaria surveys and various 'controlled experiments' to eliminate infected anophelines.

Tea chests from the Darjeeling foothills were familiar commodities in the auction houses of Mincing Lane in London at the turn of the nineteenth century.[5] It was at the turn of the century that the anopheline of the same region would become the subject of study by a scientific institution in London. In 1902, the Indian government invited the Malaria Committee of the Royal Society, which

---

1 Patrick Manson, 'On the Necessity for Special Education in Tropical Medicine', in a speech delivered at St George's Hospital at the opening of the Winter Session, 1 Oct. 1897, PRO/CO/885/7/9 (APAC), p. 7.
2 M. Worboys, 'Germs, Malaria and the Invention of Mansonian Tropical Medicine', in D. Arnold (ed.), *Warm Climates, Western Medicine: The Emergence of Tropical Medicine, 1500–1900* (Amsterdam and Atlanta, GA, Rodopi, 1996), pp. 181–207. Also see Haynes, *Imperial Medicine*, pp. 126–72.
3 Worboys, 'Manson, Ross, and Colonial Medical Policy'.
4 Harrison, *Public Health*, pp. 158–65.
5 The first samples of tea from India were sent to Mincing Lane in 1838, these being tea made from indigenous wild Assam tea plants. See 'The Story of Indian Tea', in *The Tea and Coffee Trade Journal*, 56 (March 1929), pp. 372–97.

had been to Africa in 1901, to visit India.[6] Their Indian tour included the city of Calcutta and the Duars, as well as the Jeypore Hill tracts in southern Bihar and the British Punjab. Christophers pointed out later that the visit 'quite apart from its direct scientific results, had a great effect upon the future course of malaria work in that country'.[7] It was one of the numerous studies on malaria in India; the first three decades of the twentieth century saw a deluge of malaria research in colonial India.[8] The Royal Society committee found the phenomenon of 'anophelism without malaria', which suggested that the degree of infection in a place need not be directly proportional to the number of anopheles in the locality. Therefore, in the very first scientific report on malaria in the Darjeeling foothills, the importance of its location was established. The report emphasized also that anophelines were of various kinds; on this trip, the Commission discovered two new species of anopheles in the Duars, which they had not encountered elsewhere in India. Malaria could no longer unambiguously be linked to sanitary conditions or climatic fluctuations: 'From Calcutta to Duars the places were under practically identical conditions ... In Calcutta, however, we had abundant *A.Rossii* and no malaria, and in the Duars a relatively small number of *A.Fluviatilis* and a large amount of malaria.'[9]

This linked specific localities with the breeding sites of particular species of anopheline carriers.[10] The report remained within official and scientific circles. The planters, and even the doctors practising in the tea estates, do not appear to have engaged with the details of this first scientific research on malaria in the region. The planters petitioned later, in 1906, for a detailed scientific study of the causation of blackwater fever and malaria in the region.[11] The government acceded to their request, and the reports of the consequent Christophers–Bentley report threw a long shadow on both the discourse of malaria in India and locally on the management of disease in the tea plantations.

---

6   See Power, *Tropical Medicine*, p. 22.
7   Christophers, 'John William Watson Stephens, 1865–1946 ', *Obituary Notices of Fellows of the Royal Society*, 5 (1947), pp. 524–40 (528).
8   W.F. Bynum has pointed out that in 1929 when J.A. Sinton compiled a bibliography of malaria in India, it filled 200 pages and included in addition 2200 items from scientific and medical journals, government publications and reports. W.F. Bynum, 'Reasons for Contentment: Malaria in India, 1900–1920, '*Parassitologia*, 40 (1998), pp. 19–27 (21).
9   S.P. James, 'Malaria In India', *Scientific Memoirs by Officers of the Medical and Sanitary Department of the Govt Of India*, NS 2 (Calcutta, Periodical Publications, 1902), p. 76.
10 Ross, who was in the neighbouring Terai while he was in the IMS, also noticed the great paucity of anophelines there. He wrote to Manson on 6 September 1898 from Kurseong, 'I don't believe fresh malaria was about at all at Naxalbari at this season.' Ronald Ross and L.J. Bruce-Chwatt, *The Great Malaria Problem and Its Solution: From the Memoirs of Ronald Ross with an Introduction by L J Bruce-Chwatt* (London, Keynes, 1988), p. 194. See also, *Obituary Notices of Fellows of the Royal Society*, 1 (1933), p. 111.
11 See Chapter 5.

From Locality to Demography: The Tropical Aggregation of Labour

The circumstances in which Christophers and Bentley compiled the report on malaria in the Duars have been highlighted in previous chapters. Here I will re-examine their report in the context of malarial research and the impact of the research on the northern Bengal region. The report linked the malarious Duars to several other parts of India, and indeed, of the world. By referring to research on immunity conducted by Robert Koch, and by the Italian researcher Angelo Celli (in the Roman Campagna), they associated malaria with congregations of a labouring population in any region:

> We may say that in our researches on malaria we have for some time recognised the almost constant association of labour camps with severe malaria ... [It] lies the explanation of the association of outbreaks of malaria with soil disturbance, opening up of new country and so on. It is not the soil disturbance, we believe, but the occurrence of labour camp conditions, or what we shall call for convenience of description THE TROPICAL AGGREGATION OF LABOUR, in association with these enterprises which has given them their evil reputation.[12]

Along with earlier works by Koch and Celli, the report also referred to Stephens and Christophers, and connected their research to malaria in the Duars and posited that

> A condition of continual immigration similar to that described by Koch is conspicuously present in the Duars, Assam and elsewhere in India, where the constant introduction of non-immune immigrants may be likened to the continual heaping of fresh fuel upon an already glowing fire ... This factor, which when it acts temporarily, is capable of producing epidemic malaria and when long continued must give rise to an increased endemicity, we shall term for descriptive purposes the FACTOR OF NON-IMMUNE IMMIGRATION.[13]

Their report concluded that the congregation of newcomers at any industrial sites, harbours, jute mills, tea plantations and railway lines was linked to the persistence of malaria in endemic form. They argued that the centres of endemic malaria were located in centres of 'industrial activity', which were constantly in a state of 'exalted malaria'. When sick workers moved out of the area they carried the malarial infection with them, acting as mobile reservoirs of malaria.[14] The thesis of the tropical aggregation of labour, or the human factor in malaria, gained in credence and attained legitimacy through its reiteration at national and international fora. By 1927 the human factor in malarial infection was an accepted scientific theory through reiteration in published work on malaria in India.[15] In 1929 the League of Nations Malaria Committee carried out

12 Christophers and Bentley, *Malaria in the Duars*, p. 2.
13 Christophers and Bentley, *Malaria in the Duars*, pp. 3–4.
14 Christophers and Bentley, *Malaria in the Duars*, p. 14.
15 For instance, see Patrick Hehir, *Malaria in India* (London and Oxford, Oxford University Press, 1927), pp. 45–49.

an inspection tour of India at the invitation of the Government of India. Christophers wrote the preface to their report and cited the factor of non-immune immigration at industrial sites as a major cause of the spread of malarial fever in India, particularly mines, plantations and harbours.[16] The theory became the fulcrum of a discourse on malaria that emerged with great clarity in later years.

Several years after their controversial study on Duars, Christophers, at that time the Director of the Malaria Bureau of India, wrote a report on the prevalence of malaria, blackwater fever and anchylostomiasis in the coal mines at Singhbhum.[17] Some of his recommendations were similar to those made in the Duars some 20 years previously, such as the screening of existing European bungalows, their location outside the sites of infection and the encouragement of the use of quinine.[18] Christophers argued that the aggregation of labour contributed to great malarial infection among new immigrant workers in an industrial site. He claimed that permanent workers at any site acquired an immunity to malaria through repeated infections suffered by the newly immigrant labourers and by newborn children and infants. Therefore, even if the spleen rate (the principal indicator of high endemicity) of a given area showed a high endemicity of malaria, the adult population who comprised the main productive element would not be affected. This realization, he emphasized, would avert the need for expensive sanitary measures and also reduce the expenditure on quinine by discouraging its use as prophylaxis.

Acquired Immunity, Race and Acclimatization

There was one other aspect to the issue of acquired immunity to malarial fever: immunity through racial acclimatization. The question asked by medical experts was, Were some races more liable to acquire immunity through repeated attacks of malaria than others?

16 Christophers and Bentley presented the argument at the Indian Medical Congress in Bombay in 1909. See Arabinda Samanta, *Malarial Fever in Colonial Bengal: Social History of an Epidemic, 1820–1939* (Calcutta, Firma KLM, 2002), p. 36. In his preface to the report of the League of Nations Malaria Commission to India, Christophers emphasized again this aspect of malaria in industrial locations. The League of Nations Malaria Committee endorsed the theory of non-immune immigration into industrial locations as a principal cause of malaria: 'From the results of ... investigations and from our own few observations made on the spot, we have come to the conclusion that the hyper endemic areas although sparsely inhabited are very often the areas where large plantations and large industrial undertakings are situated and which are therefore often the site of a considerable immigrant population coming from other districts. It is in these hilly districts covered with forest or jungle, with a sparse population that the immigrants are quickly mown down. Infant mortality in these districts is extremely high.' *Report of the Malaria Commission on Its Study Tour in India Aug 23rd to Dec 28, 1929* (Geneva, League of Nations Publications, 1930), p. 31.

17 S.R. Christophers, *Enquiry on Malaria, Blackwater Fever and Anchylostomiasis in Singhbhum; Report no 1. Preliminary Investigation into the Conditions on the Bengal Iron Company's Mines at Manharpur, January* (Patna, Superintendent, Government Printing, Bihar and Orissa, 1923).

18 Christophers, *Enquiry on Malaria*, p. 29.

When Christophers and Bentley wrote their report on malaria in the Duars they referred to the issue and specifically denied that the racial factor was of importance:

> Race appears to play but little part in influencing the prevalence of infection, though some races appear to be more profoundly affected by the disease than others. In several instances where we have examined the children of hill and plains people living on the same garden under similar conditions, but with the two races widely separated, we have found the rate of infection and of enlarged spleen to be practically the same.[19]

However, Christophers referred to certain 'susceptible races' when he wrote his report on Singhbhum in 1923. The European staff and the skilled labour (mostly Hindus and Muslims) were categorized as the 'susceptible' races. He stated on the other hand that the unskilled mine workers were 'indigenous, largely aboriginal' and as adults were 'fairly immune to malaria'. This immunity, he noted, came after a period of 'acute infestation' of malaria for a period of around two years – a process he compared to the 'salting of animals in trypanosomiasis'.[20]

In 1926, when the Public Health department of the government of Bengal reported its findings on anti-malarial measures in a tea estate in Duars, it echoed these sentiments. In an area of malarial hyper-endemicity like the Duars, it sketched out the possibilities of infection very similar to the conclusions reached in the mining areas of Bihar:

> If a mixed population of men, women and children who were susceptible to malaria were introduced into such an area, there would in the first instance be an explosive outbreak of malaria amongst the new comers ... In a vigorous race, there would be a 'rally' in the individual against the parasite and gradually a tolerance or relative immunity would be developed ... A time would come when the only persons not possessing a relative immunity would be newly born children. These would all be intensely affected and would suffer from continuous fever until they either died or gradually acquired a relative tolerance.[21]

Such a conception of immunity from malarial infection that posited distinctions between 'vigorous' races and others not so vigorous led almost inevitably to the conclusion that certain communities were more likely to acquire immunity than others: 'Coolies from the Jeypur Hill Tracts will, therefore, be less likely to suffer on arrival than Chota Nagpuris ... [T]here are certainly racial differences.

---

19 Christophers and Bentley, *Malaria in the Duars*, p. 23.
20 Christophers, *Enquiry on Malaria*, p. 30. See also idem, 'The Mechanism of Immunity against Malaria in Communities Living under Hyper-endemic Conditions', *Indian Journal of Medical Research*, 12 (1924), pp. 273–94. This view of acquired immunity in hyper-endemic regions confirmed similar findings by Schaffer in Sumatra.
21 Government of Bengal, Public Health Department, *Report of the Malaria Survey of the Jalpaiguri Duars* (Calcutta, Bengal Government Press, 1926), p. vii.

Santhals, for instance, seem to get immune more quickly than Nepalese, who would appear to possess small powers of immunity production.'[22]

This concept of immunity to malaria through repeated attacks of fever was a little different from the older, nineteenth-century ideas of racial immunity to fever. In the mid-nineteenth century Rennie, in his account of the Bhutan campaign of 1865, mentioned that the Meches, the pre-colonial inhabitants of the region, were peculiarly immune to fevers: '[The Meches] are a singular tribe, enjoying excellent health where other races, dark and fair, sicken and die – while again they contract malignant fevers when removed from their own locality into districts considered by us comparatively salubrious.'[23]

Rennie conceived of racial immunity to fevers as an immunity that was both racial and locational. He linked racial immunity to acclimatization in a specific locality, outside of which the entire race would perish. This notion was current among both medical practitioners and colonial ethnologists. In 1872 E.T. Dalton had thus remarked about the Meches in his *Descriptive Ethnology of Bengal*:

> Their constitutions have become so much accustomed to the malarious influences of the Terai, that apparently they cannot live without the poisonous gases that they imbibe there, and in the purer atmosphere of the plains, or in breathing the more invigorating air of the higher ranges, they pine and die.[24]

This particular link between racial immunity, location and fever had become irrelevant in the twentieth century, for by the time Christophers and Bentley wrote their report on malaria in the Duars, the Meches had migrated already towards the eastern parts of the district, where tea plantations had not yet been claimed from the forest. The Meches were gradually pushed out of the district towards Goalpara in Assam throughout the colonial period.[25]

In the twentieth century, the issue of immunity in India remained important, and was linked to both racial and locational categories. A textbook on tropical health written by a Bengali physician, B.N. Ghosh, which was first published in 1912 and went through seven editions, understood immunity to malaria in racial terms:

> The question whether immunity is possible may be answered in the words of Manson as 'yes/no' ... Some races and certain individuals are, however,

---

22 Government of Bengal, Public Health Department, *Report of the Malaria Survey*, p. vii.
23 Rennie, *Bhotan*, pp. 347–48.
24 See A. Mitra, *The Tribes and Castes of West Bengal* (Alipore, West Bengal Government Press, 1953), p. 224. Dalton's *Descriptive Ethnology* was compiled in 1872, under the aegis of the Asiatic Society of Bengal. His ethnography was later used by the decennial census survey that was initiated in 1871–72.
25 Ray, *Transformations*, p. 79. The Meches's demographic insignificance and unwillingness to work in the newly established tea plantations resulted in their marginalization. However, the theory that they were immune to malaria persisted in twentieth-century ethnographic accounts of the Meches. For instance, see Charu Chandra Sanyal, *The Meches and the Totos: Two Sub-Himalayan Tribes of North Bengal* (Darjeeling, University of North Bengal, 1973), p. 7.

less susceptible of malarial influence than others, but very few are absolutely immune. The Chinese, the Malays and some other dark skinned races also appear to enjoy a comparative immunity – an immunity considerably less pronounced, however, than that enjoyed by the African and West Indian negro.[26]

The Malay and Chinese labourers, like those in the West Indies and Africa, were recruited as labourers in the various plantations of the Malay archipelago and the Caribbean islands. Such a notion of acquired immunity contributed to the discourse of body typologies of productive labourers and to a certain extent informed recruitment policies. In the seventh edition of his textbook Ghosh echoed the exact words used by Christophers when he referred to the partial immunization of adults in a hyper-endemic area: 'There is thus a definite acquired immunity to malaria, comparable to the "salting" of animals in trypanosomiasis.'[27]

When Patrick Hehir wrote *Malaria in India* in 1927, although he emphasized that 'Against malarial infection there is no absolute immunity, hereditary or acquired', he also reiterated that 'dark-skinned races, living in malarious regions, possess a relative immunity to malarial infection. This is explicable as an acquired immunity'.[28] He further quoted Koch to argue that the 'acquired immunity' occurred relatively rapidly in cases where quinine was not used. Hehir presented complex arguments on the factors that led to acquired immunity in certain groups of people, particularly in adults in hyper-endemic areas.[29] This emphasis on acquired immunity from malaria also reinforced arguments against the adoption of more expensive quinine prophylaxis as well as anti-malarial sanitation in the plantations. As we shall see later in this chapter, the focus on immunity studies encouraged some planters to promote research to hasten 'acquired immunity' among the labourers.

Prevention versus Prophylaxis: Mian Mir and the Malaria Debate in India

The Malaria Committee of the Royal Society, facilitated by the government of India and supervised by Stephens and Christophers, also conducted an early experiment on anti-malarial sanitation between 1902 and 1909 at Mian Mir, a military cantonment near Lahore in the Punjab. The experiment, according to W.F. Bynum, 'attracted a passion rivalled in the history of malariology only by the decades long bickering between Ross and Grassi'.[30] The reports, in brief,

---

26 B.N. Ghosh, *A Treatise on Hygiene and Public Health, with Special Reference to the Tropics* (6th edn, Calcutta, Scientific Publishing Company, 1927), p. 482.
27 B.N. Ghosh, *A Treatise on Hygiene and Public Health, with Special Reference to the Tropics* (7th edn, Calcutta, Scientific Publishing Company, 1930), p. 511.
28 Hehir, *Malaria*, p. 39.
29 Hehir, *Malaria*, pp. 38–45.
30 For a narrative of the controlled experiments at Mian Mir and the controversy between Ross and Christophers, S.P. James and indeed almost all of the Indian medical establishment,

concluded that anopheline control was not feasible in a controlled area. The Indian medical establishment at Mian Mir was responsible for the eclipse of anti-malarial sanitation in India through government initiatives for some time. It led to the preference for the large-scale use of quinine as prophylaxis.

Sheldon Watts has pointed out that Christophers, as the chief malariologist of India until the mid-1930s, in his official capacity as Director of the King Institute and later at the Central Research Institute, kept the focus of malarial interest in India away from the canals and irrigated rice fields and instead concentrated on a quinine policy.[31] Watts has argued that this was also motivated towards preserving the irrigation policy of the government in British India, particularly the canals in the Punjab, from which private investors in England earned rich dividends and the government of India reaped the benefits of substantial agricultural revenue.

Watts's thesis requires certain qualifications. The irrigation canals of the Punjab were important, but not merely as a source for generating revenue for the gentlemen capitalists in England. The canals were the basis of the agrarian economy of British Punjab, which was commercialized and expanded greatly under British rule. Two-fifths of the army in colonial India were recruited from the rural peasantry of the Punjab; the loyalty of this army, so crucial after 1857, was tied to the prosperity of the agrarian economy of British Punjab.[32] And as Ira Klein has pointed out, Watts ignored the various studies especially, by Bentley in Bengal, that drew links between ecological degradation and the incidence of malarial fever in colonial Bengal.[33]

Moreover, there was more to the evolving discourse of malaria and practices of anti-malarial sanitation in India than a simple dichotomy between the 'sanitarian' approach and the 'scientific one' of malarial prophylaxis through the use of quinine. Most malariologists in India emphasized quinization, led as they were by Christophers at the Malaria Bureau of India. But even Ross, who battled the IMS establishment to focus more on anti-malarial sanitation, argued that

> We do not yet know all the dangerous species of mosquito, nor do we even possess an exhaustive knowledge of the haunts and habits of any one variety ... Before practical results can be reasonably looked for, however, we must find precisely (a) what species of Indian mosquito do and do not carry malaria? (b) What are the habits of dangerous varieties?[34]

---

see Bynum, 'An Experiment That Failed: Malaria Control at Mian Mir', *Parassitologia*, 36 (1994), pp. 107–21.
31 Sheldon Watts, 'British Development Policies and Malaria in India 1897–c.1929', *Past and Present*, 165 (1999), pp. 141–81.
32 Rajit K. Mazumdar, *The Indian Army and the Making of Punjab* (Delhi, Permanent Black, 2003), pp. 47–63.
33 Ira Klein, 'Development and Death: Reinterpreting Malaria, Economics and Ecology in British India', *Indian Economic and Social History Review*, 38 (2001), pp. 147–79.
34 See Malcolm Watson, 'Malaria and Mosquitoes: Forty Years On' *Journal of the Royal Society of Arts*, 87 (1939), p. 485.

Therefore there was no question of indiscriminate implementation of anti-malarial sanitation even by its strongest advocate. It entailed detailed research into the habits and breeding places of anopheline mosquitoes. It is here that the question of 'locality' became important in the research into specific anopheles and their habitations. In the next three decades, malarial research all over the world as well as in India would demonstrate the enormous variety of types as well as habits and breeding of anopheles, which were found to differ from one terrain to another, thereby making the question of locality a crucial one. In 1913, still convinced that the destruction of parasite-carrying anopheles was possible, Ross presented the success of the campaigns towards total extermination of malaria in the Panama Canal, in Ismailia in Egypt (near the Suez Canal) and in rubber plantations of the Malay Straits – these were all colonial enclaves, where controlled extermination of anopheline carriers was possible. Despite the rhetoric of European settlements in the tropics, Ross did not contemplate large-scale prevention in rural areas in either Africa or India.[35] Many years later Malcolm Watson would point out that Ross had insisted that he was 'much misrepresented' and that he had 'never thought and certainly never stated that it would "be possible to exterminate mosquitoes throughout Africa, for instance. I have always referred especially to large *towns*."'[36] Therefore it is essential not to posit Ross's anti-malarial sanitation in direct opposition to the quinization policy of Christophers and the Indian medical establishment.

In India, Ross's advocacy of anti-malarial sanitation had little impact. The experiments at Mian Mir cantonment by the government of India were said to hinder the possibilities of sanitation in the entire country in the first two decades of the twentieth century. Significantly, as Bynum has pointed out, the Mian Mir experiment involved not only the destruction of anophelines through various means but also attempted control through quinization of the troops at the cantonment. Segregation of the European troops through the removal of native habitations, which were close to the European barracks, 'first, a syce line, and then a whole bazaar', was also undertaken.[37] Christophers and some of his colleagues, such as S.P. James and J.A. Sinton, were undoubtedly the most vocal and outspoken partisans of the employment of quinine prophylaxis as the best mode to control malaria. But the quinization approach was combined with sporadic implementation of anti-malarial sanitation as well as segregation, which were all attempted, in various degrees, in the tea plantations.

Anti-malarial Sanitation and the Importance of Location

As research in Tropical Medicine translated into the field, it reiterated the significance of the 'local' conditions, using the plantation enclaves as their

---

35 R. Ross, 'Medical Science and the Tropics', *Bulletin of the American Geographical Society*, 45 (1913), pp. 435–38.
36 See Watson, 'Malaria and Mosquitoes', p. 483.
37 Bynum, 'An Experiment', p. 112.

Tropical Medicine in Its 'Field'

experimental 'fields'. This was especially applicable in anti-malarial sanitation programmes. At the turn of the century medical research in India was conducted mostly by individual IMS officials, with very little institutional support from the government. Ross's own experiences in this regard when he was posted in India was typical of the IMS's attitudes towards research in the field.[38] The establishment of the Royal Society's Malaria Committee, and the two institutes of Tropical Medicine at Liverpool and at London, contributed to the gathering of momentum of research on Tropical Medicine. In India, malaria research was initially conducted at the Central Research Institute and carried on by the Indian Research Fund Association, which was set up in 1911 and subsidized partly by the government of India. It was funded in part through private subscriptions and published the *Indian Journal of Medical Research*, which was edited by the Sanitary Commissioner of India and the Director General of the IMS.[39] It also appointed the Scientific Advisory Board, of which both Christophers and Ross were members. Besides the army cantonments, other sites where they attempted anti-malarial sanitation were at the industrial enclaves of mining towns and tea plantations (Mian Mir, for example, was a cantonment).

The Imperial Conference on Malaria in Simla, 1909, led to the formation of a Central Malaria Committee, to direct the course of anti-malaria operations in the different provinces through their supervision of the special provincial malaria committees.[40] At the 1909 conference in Simla J.T.W. Leslie, the Sanitary Commissioner, pointed out that the Drainage Committee of Bengal had found that the success or the failure of any anti-mosquito campaign depended on the study of the local ecological conditions in a targeted area.[41] Therefore the occasional sanitarian approach to the prevention of malaria in Bengal, as in the rest of India, emphasized a close knowledge of local ecology and disease patterns. The assumption was that preventive work on malaria in any region could only be successful if it were both selective and circumscribed.[42] The logic of location, so pervasive in British Indian medical discourse, outlasted the sanitarian epidemiological models and became a significant factor in malaria research:

> Although our knowledge of the etiology of malaria and its treatment is fairly extensive ... the scientific study of its epidemiology is only beginning ... we cannot devise the simplest and best preventive measures until the epidemiology is thoroughly understood ... we have little exact knowledge of the distribution of malaria in the country, of the local conditions which favour it, and of the best means to render these causes inoperative.[43]

38 Ross, *Memoirs: With A Full Account of the Great Malaria Problem and Its Solution* (London, John Murray, 1923), pp. 203, 239–47, 314–15.
39 Harrison, *Public Health*, p. 164.
40 Harrison, *Public Health*, p. 297.
41 Sanitary Commissioner to the Secretary, Municipal Department, Government of Bengal Proceedings, Municipal/Sanitation, nos 1–2, March 1911, IOR/P/8686 (APAC), p. 3.
42 Sanitary Commissioner to the Secretary, Municipal Department, Government of Bengal Proceedings, Municipal/Sanitation, nos 1–2, March 1911, p. 3.
43 Extract from proceedings of the Malaria Conference in Simla held 12–18 Oct. 1919,

This was in accordance with the general views of the government of India on sanitation programmes of any kind in India; the failures of which, it stated, were due to the short-sightedness of the local sanitary boards and the 'apathy, fatalism, and resentment of interference' of the 'uneducated masses'.[44] Medical officials believed that the success of any sanitary reform for the civilian population in India depended on the knowledge of the local conditions: the people as well as the land. Any move for sanitary reform

> must recognise the diversity of local conditions in a country which includes numerous communities, castes and creeds and which exhibits almost every variety of climate, temperature, humidity and level of sub-soil water, from the Deltas of Bengal with their steamy atmosphere and dense lush vegetation to the burnt brown hills of the north-west frontier.[45]

The emphasis on locality and local knowledge that formed such a strong element in colonial administration in India informed medical research and practice at various levels. British Indian epidemiological theories emphasized the agency of local factors in the causation of disease. The debate on the aetiology of cholera in the late nineteenth century, and D.D. Cunningham's rejection of Koch's theories and then his modified acceptance of the idea of the cholera germ, demonstrated the ecological aspect of the emphasis on the local. The tenacity of the Indian medical establishment's perception of India's disease terrain as both unique and as a territory that needed experience and familiarity to be medically understood demonstrates the persistence of the rhetoric of the 'local'.[46] The insect-vector theory and the subsequent research on malaria reinforced the idea of the crucial importance of local disease factors. This notion was compatible with the British administration in India, where local knowledge was both a condition and a validation of rule. The diversity in the anopheline species, and the variables in their breeding patterns revealed by research, highlighted the local to the degree that, except for the assumption that anopheline mosquitoes caused malarial fever, very little else could be taken as given. This emphasized the point that no steps could be taken regarding the prevention of malaria in any area without exhaustive malarial surveys taken beforehand. Or else, as likely as not, they would prove to be a waste of resources. The link between ecology and epidemics was made by medical men in Britain as well in the interwar years. As Mendelsohn has pointed out, in the interwar years medical scientists

---

Government of Bengal Proceedings, Municipal/Sanitation, July 1910, nos 14–15, IOR/P/8419 (APAC), p. 30.

44 Resolution nos 888–908, Government of India, Education/Sanitation, *Indian Journal of Medical Research*, 1 (1914), p. 590.
45 Resolution nos 888–908, pp. 591–92.
46 Jeremy D. Isaacs, 'D.D. Cunningham and the Aetiology of Cholera in British India, 1869–1897', *Medical History*, 42 (1998), pp. 279–305. Also see M. Harrison, 'A Question of Locality: The Identification of Cholera in British India, 1860–1890', in D. Arnold (ed.), *Warm Climates, Western Medicine: The Emergence of Tropical Medicine, 1500–1900* (Amsterdam and Atlanta, GA, Rodopi, 1996), pp. 133–59.

working on 'bacteriological epidemiology' in Germany and Britain borrowed increasingly from older traditions of epidemiology as well as new mathematical models to formulate what he described as 'holistic' and 'non-reductionist' explanations of epidemics. This culminated in the concept of 'equilibrium', which included ecological explanations and mathematical models to analyse the state of 'natural equilibrium' between host and pathogen.[47] But although IMS officials working on malaria in the interwar years probably borrowed their epidemiological ideas from contemporary British medicine, or at least were aware of the trends, in India this trend long preceded that in Britain, particularly in the activities of the anti-contagionists in the nineteenth century. Moreover, the concept of the 'holistic' medical approach differed between Britain and its colonies. While in Britain it was about combining complementary medical approaches, in the colony this holism really represented locating causation in the wider cultural practices of the disease-stricken, as well as economic factors relating to the inclusion of many parts of India into the network of the colonial economy.

Between 1906 and 1927 sustained malaria research by the IRFA and the Malaria Bureau of India resulted in a 'malaria map' of India. Medical experts surveyed specific areas, some of which they selected for malaria research. The identification of these selected areas depended on the links between malaria control and economic productivity or political strategy. For instance, when the plans for a new capital at Delhi were being finalized, a malaria survey recommended locating the imperial capital at the southern site rather than the northern, which was found to be more susceptible to malaria.[48] When a new port was urgently needed on the east coast of India, the safe harbour of Vizag was found to be ideal except for the problem of malaria. In this project, the port authorities took advice from the experts at the Malaria Bureau and funded the necessary measures for anti-malaria works.[49] The metropolitan cities of Bombay, Calcutta and Madras all had certain anti-malarial surveys conducted. The malaria map and the surveys described the conditions of areas that were of particular importance either politically or strategically, or from a commercial point of view.

---

47 J. Andrew Mendelsohn, 'From Eradication to Equilibrium: How Epidemics Became Complex after World War I', in Christopher Lawrence and George Weisz (eds), *Greater Than the Parts: Holism in Biomedicine 1920–1950* (New York and Oxford, Oxford University Press, 1998), pp. 303–31.

48 The 'malaria map', funded mostly by the IRFA in urban, commercial and industrial sites in India, was highlighted by the League of Nations' Health Committee, which visited India and compiled a report on malaria at the invitation of its government in 1926–27. *Report of the Malaria Commission*, p. 17. This followed the widespread malaria surveys of the League's Health Committee after the First World War.

49 *Report of the Malaria Commission*, p. 19.

The *Anophelines* of the Plantation Enclaves: The Experiment at Meenglas Tea Estate

The recurrent epidemics in rural lower Bengal had devastated many areas in the nineteenth century and contemporary British medical discourse relegated the disease in Bengal to a civilizational degeneracy, beyond even the reforming momentum of British rule.[50] The Bengal government conducted some anti-malarial operations in the highly endemic lower Bengal, particularly Burdwan, between 1906 and 1911, but these were largely unsuccessful.[51] The anti-malarial operation at the Meenglas Tea Estate in the Duars was different, because the area of operation was a tea plantation with boundaries and under the control of its management. The Meenglas estate was owned by the managing agency of Duncan Brothers Limited. The funds for the Meenglas experiment were paid entirely by the Bengal government. The operations lasted about eight years, and in many ways set the precedent for the course of anti-malarial work in the tea plantations for the next 25 years. The issues that emerged from Meenglas were thus of crucial importance.

The work at the Meenglas Tea Estate commenced in 1917.[52] C.A. Bentley made the initial proposal for the project in 1914 and achieved it by diverting funds from the IRFA for jungle-clearing in the Murshidabad district, reinforcing the privileged status of the plantation enclaves. The government simultaneously proposed a second site for a similar project in Asansol, at the site of British-owned mines, but this did not materialize. The aim of the Meenglas 'experiment' was to prevent the breeding of carrier-anophelines where the land was cut up by several seasonal *jhoras* (streams). In the Darjeeling foothills, the seasonality of the streams depended on the terrain; those on the slopes remained dry for most of the year, while those closer to the plains flowed continuously except in the summer.[53] Other ecological characteristics of the area were the proximity of jungles, rice fields and three fast-flowing rivers. The aim of the 'experiment', apart from the usual examination of anophelines to determine the carriers, was to attempt subsoil drainage to control the breeding of carrier-anophelines in a small, targeted area. The controlled targeted area was initially three-quarters of a mile, following the view of Malcolm Watson, whose successful policies in Malaya had shown that the flight of anophelines did not exceed half of a mile.[54] Although the Meenglas experiment was not as controversial as that of Mian Mir, medical opinion about its success was still qualified.

50   Mark Harrison, '"Hot Beds of Disease": Malaria and Civilization in Nineteenth-century British India', *Parassitologia*, 40 (1988), pp. 11–18. See also D. Arnold, '"An Ancient Race Outworn": Malaria and Race in Colonial India, 1860–1930', in Waltraud Ernst and Bernard Harris (eds), *Race, Science and Medicine* (London, Routledge, 1999), pp. 123–43.
51   A.B. Fry, *First Report on Malaria in Bengal* (Calcutta, Bengal Secretariat Book Depot, 1912), pp. 10–26; IOR/P/8686, p.3.
52   See Government of Bengal Proceedings, General/Sanitation, Sept. 1914, nos 1–2, IOR/P/9375 (APAC), pp. 4–9.
53   *Report of the Malaria Survey of the Jalpaiguri Duars*, p. vi.
54   *Report of the Malaria Survey of the Jalpaiguri Duars*, p. viii.

Tropical Medicine in Its 'Field'

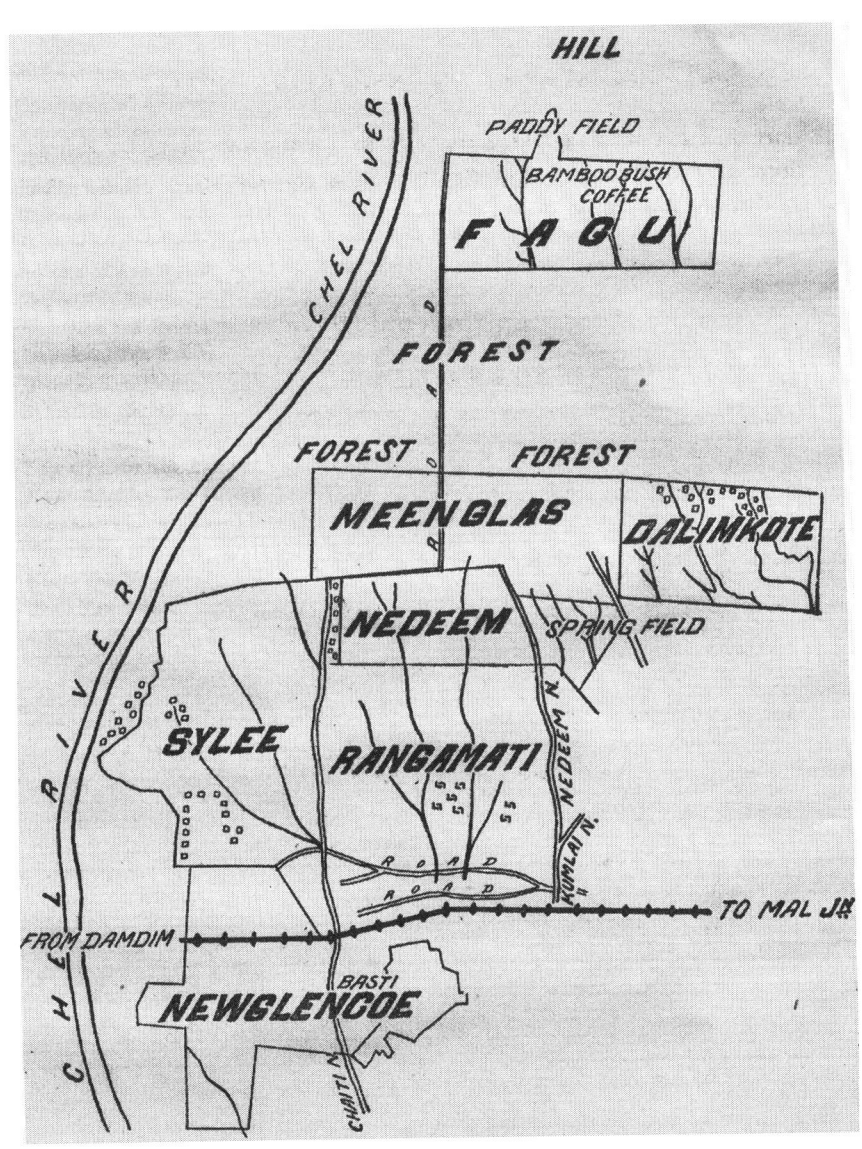

Figure 7.1 Malaria Experiments at Meenglas Estate

At Meenglas, the local characteristics of the anophelines were further emphasized by the identification there of the three most dangerous carriers: *A.maculatus*, *A.listoni* and *A.culcifacies*. These bred in clear, running streams.[55] But the medical experts found that the anopheline which inhabited the jungle near the Meenglas estate, the *A.aitkeni*, was utterly harmless, unlike the *A.umbrosus*

---

55 *Report of the Malaria Survey of the Jalpaiguri Duars*, p. ix.

163

Contagion and Enclaves

of the Malayan jungles which was a proven carrier.[56] The Meenglas experiment verified that underground drainage of streams could control the breeding of anophelines. Where they could not implement subsoil drainage researchers used the method of oiling stagnant pools with kerosene to prevent breeding. The experiment demonstrated that the spleen index of the children and malarial fever could be reduced for a limited period within the controlled area.[57]

There were fluctuations in the reports of malaria in the controlled area. In 1924, there was 'an increase in the crude spleen index, the malaria death-rate, and malaria sickness rate with a decline in the birth rate, and no change in the total death rate'.[58] But in 1925, the Director of Public Health's department reported that the spleen index in the previous year had declined from 53.2 to 51.8, and therefore the effect of the operations was satisfactory.[59] In the next two years the spleen index at Meenglas was recorded at 56.5 in 1925 (this contradicted the figures given in the report for the year 1925) and 56.6 in 1926, the average of the previous quinquennium being 59.2. The death rate from malaria was 1.5 per mile in 1926, against 4.6 in 1925, and the average of the previous quinquennium was 5.09.[60] The death rate from all causes was 39.2 in 1926, against 33.2 in 1925 and 39.4 the previous quinquennium. These numbers were moreover qualified, because the 'number of malaria deaths might be more than actually returned', since the number of deaths under 'other fevers' rose in the same period.[61]

One fact stood out from the results of the Meenglas 'experiment': the average overall death rate in the Meenglas tea estate did not decline. The labourers continued to die from causes other than malarial fever such as diarrhoea and dysentery, chest complaints and other afflictions. This proved that anti-malarial measures in themselves would not reduce the overall death rates of the workers drastically. Admittedly, the effects of malaria included sickness and debility more than a quick death. The reports stated that the spleen index first decreased and then stabilized, and remained 'almost static' from 1923 to 1927.[62]

The Meenglas operation aimed not just to reduce malarial fevers within that particular tea plantation estate, but also to retest Watson's theses regarding subsoil drainage that had proved expensive but useful when applied in the rubber estates of Malaya. In effect, Meenglas was to demonstrate the feasibility of subsoil drainage operations for larvae control for the tea estates all over the Terai and the Duars. The report concluded,

56 *Report of the Malaria Survey of the Jalpaiguri Duars*, p. ix.
57 *Annual Report for the Director of Public Health, Bengal, 1920* (Calcutta, Bengal Secretariat Book Depot, 1922), p. 14.
58 *Annual Report for the Director of Public Health, Bengal, 1925* (Calcutta, Bengal Secretariat Book Depot, 1927), p. 60.
59 *Annual Report for the Director of Public Health, Bengal, 1925*, pp. 43–44.
60 *Annual Report for the Director of Public Health, Bengal 1926* (Calcutta, Bengal Secretariat Book Depot, 1928), p. 50.
61 *Annual Report for the Director of Public Health, Bengal 1926*, p. 50.
62 *Annual Report for the Director of Public Health, Bengal, 1927* (Calcutta, Bengal Secretariat Book Depot, 1929).

> The measures put into operation at Meenglas for the reduction of anopheles have been entirely successful ... *As regards the actual reduction of malaria, this is a point on which it is very difficult to form an exact opinion, mostly owing to the factor of shifting population. Only a small population of the labour is permanent, others come and go.* Judged by the spleen index in the whole community, there would appear to have been little achieved ...[63]

That there was little evidence either way that malaria could be reduced within the plantation enclaves through subsoil drainage in a controlled area reiterates a public health problem quite familiar to any preventive project in the tea gardens – that of the mobility of the free labour. We know that the *basti* labour flanking the tea gardens were used in peak times but the management did not assume responsibility for them. The system of tea production relied on the seasonal labour from the *bastis*; yet every epidemic disease in any plantation was rumoured to have originated first from the *bastis*. Yet the logic of the production of tea demanded a labour force that would work in the peak periods and preferably be settled outside the plantations, so the management was relieved of year-round responsibility towards them. This paradox, referred to in the last chapter, was starkly in relief after the Meenglas scheme.

There was one more, crucial conclusion from the Meenglas experiment. The survey noted that 'in such a hyper-endemic district as the Duars, anti-mosquito measures in a restricted area are apt to give benefits apparently hardly commensurate with the trouble taken'.[64] The problem was stated in clear terms: *all* the tea plantations in the area had to invest in anti-larval schemes for the reduction of malarial sickness to be effective. The cost of the entire project was Rs 16,000 (initial cost) and an annual expenditure of Rs 800 for the maintenance of the drainage and oiling.[65] If all the plantations in the area agreed to cooperate and conduct anti-malarial operations simultaneously, the incidence of infection would decrease; otherwise, as an isolated experiment the Meenglas would not be particularly successful. This had, indeed, been the conclusion of the Assistant Director of Public Health, Malaria Research, R.B. Khambatta, who had visited Meenglas in July 1923 accompanied by the Director of Public Health. Khambatta had also served as acting Civil Surgeon for Jalpaiguri and was therefore familiar with the health issues of the tea plantations.[66] The project was jeopardized also by the migration of anopheles from outside the drained areas.[67] When researchers deemed insufficient the quarter of a mile radius for effective control, they coaxed the neighbouring tea plantations into investing a little on spraying kerosene in their streams.[68] This was inadequate, for in the

63 *Report of the Malaria Survey of the Jalpaiguri Duars*, pp. ix–x (emphasis mine).
64 *Report of the Malaria Survey of the Jalpaiguri Duars*, pp. ix–x.
65 *Report of the Malaria Commission*, p. 17.
66 *DPAAR, 1923* (Jalpaiguri, 1924, APAC), p. 105.
67 *DPAAR, 1923*, p. 105.
68 *Report of the Malaria Survey of the Jalpaiguri Duars*, p. 5. The adjustment from the three-quarter mile to the entire Meenglas tea estate was based on Ross's calculation of $M = 1-40/a$, M representing the infection rate and 'a' the anopheline mosquito per head,

Contagion and Enclaves

Table 7.1 Spleen index of tea estates in Mal tea district of Duars in 1926

Tea estate	Number examined	Spleen index
Meenglas	394	53.5
Lower Fagoo	134	60.4
Nedeem	99	77.7
Sylee	294	75.8
Dalinkote	194	86.1
Rangamati	410	89.2
New Glencoe	255	89.4
Neora Nuddee	123	86.2
Total and average	1903	76.6

Source: Government of Bengal, Public Health Department, *Report of the Malaria Survey of the Jalpaiguri Duars*, Calcutta 1926, pp. 7–8.

Table 7.2 Spleen index of tea estates in Nagrakata tea district of Duars in 1926

Tea estate	Number examined	Spleen index
Kurti	232	64.2
Hope	276	82.6
Jiti	335	84.5
Hille	208	85.6
Total and average	2954	77.7

Source: Government of Bengal, Public Health Department, *Report of the Malaria Survey of the Jalpaiguri Duars*, Calcutta 1926, pp. 7–8.

final report the problem was highlighted yet again: 'the infected mosquitoes are still migrating from the neighbouring gardens. If this influx could be stopped (and this can be done only when the surrounding gardens would adopt similar measures) the effect would be immensely greater.'[69]

The final report on the project, a survey, demonstrated that the spleen index in Meenglas itself improved, but the scheme seemed not to have any effect in lowering the endemicity in the area.

---

whereby, it was found at the end of 1920, 'that to keep up the spleen rate of 93.58 percent ... a minimum number of 667 carrier mosquitoes per head of population was required, that is by the scheme as it stood then, not more than five-sixths of the original rate of mosquitoes per head could be reduced'. The Public Health department in Bengal under Bentley was thus experimenting with the findings of Ross and also Watson, who first implemented subsoil drainage in Malaya. The application of mathematical calculations to determine the extent of infection in a locality was begun by Ross in 1904 and used by the Ross Institute in Ceylon in 1930. See Gordon Harrison, *Mosquitoes, Malaria and Man: A History of the Hostilities Since 1880* (London, John Murray, 1978), p. 206.

69 *Report of the Malaria Survey of the Jalpaiguri Duars*, p. 49.

There was a final crucial point in anopheline control in Meenglas, and that was the existence of paddy fields close to the plantations and often within them. As we have seen, many plantations in the region allotted a part of their vast estates (staked out as 'wastelands') to the labourers where they grew vegetables and some rice. This served both as an inducement to retain labour in the tea plantations, for the allotments were made on the condition of work, and also to keep the wages low. Moreover the allotments served as instruments of control, for the workers had no tenants' rights to their allotments and the Royal Commission on Labour (1931) recorded that such *bari* allotments to workers could be cancelled and the worker dismissed without notice.[70] The cultivation of rice required a great deal of stagnant water in the fields and bred carrier-anophelines. For the Meenglas experiment, the cultivation of rice was stopped once the problem was identified, but that was *within* the Meenglas tea estate. Neighbouring estates did not follow up with like measures, therefore the migration of anopheline mosquitoes continued to subvert anopheline control within the experimental area. The final recommendations for the report unambiguously insisted, 'Paddy cultivation should not be allowed.'[71]

The factor of the cultivation of rice in the increase of malarial fever was acknowledged by C.A. Bentley who was the Director of Public Health in Bengal in 1925.[72] Arabinda Samanta reads Bentley's report uncritically as a condemnation of British policies of creating railways and embankments, which contributed to the lack of inundation, leading to stagnant anopheline breeding water in many parts of lower Bengal. The contribution of roads and railways to malaria in Bengal was the source of great debate in colonial India, and there was nationalist criticism of the destruction of traditional embankments and new construction sites. However, Bentley's contribution to the debate was significant because his solution was to implement the Italian concept of *bonificazione*, which concept, he said, 'embodies measures designed for a double purpose, viz. to improve agriculture and improve health'.[73] In the context of (Western) Bengal he advocated anti-malarial sanitation not through the drainage of rice fields, but through further inundation, preferably through irrigation on the model of Punjab and Sindh. Therefore he did not offer a criticism of the development policies of the government, but rather sought to clearly probe the problem and suggested solutions that would lead to more, rather than less, investment in irrigation.[74] Bentley first read a summary of his thesis in 1913, in a paper titled 'Some Problems Presented by Malaria in Bengal' at the sanitary conference in Madras. His conclusions did not find favour with the British and Indian medical establishment. In an editorial the *Indian Medical Gazette* declared

70 *RCLI*, pp. 384–85.
71 *Report of the Malaria Survey of the Jalpaiguri Duars*, p. 48.
72 C.A. Bentley, *Malaria and Agriculture in Bengal: How to Reduce Malaria in Bengal by Irrigation* (Government of Bengal, 1925). Also see Samanta, *Malarial Fever*, esp. pp. 33–73.
73 See Bentley, *Malaria and Agriculture*, p. 125.
74 For a criticism of his thesis that flooding, not drainage, would solve the problem of malaria in the Bengal plains, see C.A. Bentley, 'Malaria and Agriculture in Bengal', *The Lancet*, 206 (31 Oct. 1925), pp. 926–27.

that Bentley's assessment could be 'misinterpreted' (doubtless as a critique of colonial modernizing strategy) and stressed that his views were those of an economist, not a scientist. It claimed that depopulation in parts of Bengal had occurred due to the natural silting up of rivers, and 'Drainage and engineering schemes can effect but little against nature.' The *IMG* went on to conclude that natural devastations had always occurred over time everywhere in the world, and that 'During all great natural changes people who cannot adapt themselves to the changing environment must necessarily suffer.'[75] The contradictions of the logistics of malaria control within the plantation economy were fundamental and could not be resolved, it appeared, from within it.

There was one further aspect to this contradiction. Anophelines of all varieties caught at the Meenglas Tea Estate and its environs were diligently examined. Some were sent to the Central Malaria Bureau at Kasauli for examination. The investigations revealed that there were, in total, 14 varieties of anophelines in the area.[76] However, the dangerous carriers were fewer in number, such as the *A.maculatus*, *A.minimus* and *A.culcifacies*. A survey of the ecology of malaria in the jungle areas of Bengal revealed that jungles did not breed anopheline carriers. Rather, the clearing of jungles and the substitution of tea bushes (or rice fields) did away with the harmless anophelines such as *A.aitkeni* and *A.barbirostris*. Once the jungles were cleared, they were replaced by the carriers:

> The coolie lines nearest the jungle are the least malarious, those situated in the middle of the open area have breeding of carrier species going on all sides of them. Madarihat, in the Duars, situated in a clearing in the jungle area, is notorious for its malaria. Here within the jungle itself only *A.barbirostris* and *A.leucosphyrus* were found, where in the cleared area *A.maculatus*, *A.minimus*, *A.culcifacies*, *A.fuliginosus*, *A.maculipalpis*, and *A.philppinensis* are found. Wherever deforestation is carried out, the harmless jungle species of Anopheles disappear and are replaced by the dangerous carrier species.[77]

It seemed the carriers of malaria were to be found in the rice fields and in the cleared areas of the tea estates, breeding in small *jhoras* or seepage areas. Sustained investigations revealed that malaria was, in effect, compatible with habitation and human livelihood itself. As to whether that led government policymakers to think of malaria as a consequence of modern agrarian development, distressing yet somehow inevitable, is not certain. But these conclusions, and simultaneous studies like those of Bentley on the links between embankments and malaria, led to the conceptual linking of malaria to modernity and development.[78] It also contributed to the nationalist critique of British policies

75 'Some Malarial Problems in Bengal', *Indian Medical Gazette*, 48 (1913), pp. 112–13.
76 Bhupendra Mohan Khan, 'Records of Anophelines from the Bengal Dooars', *Indian Medical Gazette*, 64 (1929), p. 496.
77 'Jungle and Malaria in Bengal', *Indian Medical Gazette*, 65 (1930), p. 639.
78 Bentley, *Malaria and Agriculture in Bengal*, esp. pp. 21–37, 48–64. For the links between nationalist discourse on malaria and the construction of roads, railways or embank-

in India. In the case of the rice fields of Bengal, Bentley had provided a solution: more agrarian development through irrigation. Bentley added another twist to the *bonificazione* scheme – he coined the term 'human bonification', by which he meant the encouragement of voluntary anti-malaria cooperative societies in the villages that would carry out anti-malaria sanitation (without cost to the respective district boards or the provincial government) at a local level.[79] In the case of the Terai and the Duars no ecological solutions were conceptualized and local anti-malaria societies were non-existent.

So far as the provincial government was concerned, the experiment at Meenglas demonstrated that anopheline control was possible under two conditions. First, it would require the cooperation of neighbouring tea estates in any region. Coordination between neighbouring tea gardens had simultaneously to begin and sustain malarial operations and this was difficult.

Second, paddy cultivation within the tea estate lands would have to be stopped. Since the political economy of the plantations depended on the labourers' access to land to grow paddy, this was not a condition likely to be met. The situation was complicated by the fact that the planters used the results of the Meenglas experiment to situate the source of malaria in the rice fields in the *bastis* outside the tea plantations.

Not just in the Duars, but in the whole of colonial Bengal the rice fields were held to be the cause of malarial fever in the twentieth century. Just as they were impossible to obliterate in the rest of Bengal, the case for malaria control in the Duars too was laid to rest with the emphasis on paddy cultivation. Similarly, the study that revealed the direct link between deforestation, the obliteration of harmless anophelines and the rise in the breeding of dangerous anopheline carriers implied a similar condition; tea bushes had been claimed from the wild jungles and malaria seemed an inevitable by-product of the modernization and settlement of these parts. This was ironic, for it had been the call of Tropical Medicine to render the 'gift of half of the world', to make it possible for humanity to penetrate impenetrable tropical jungles and make them habitable.[80]

---

ments, see Sandeep Sinha, *Public Health Policy and the Indian Public: Bengal 1850–1920* (Calcutta, Vision Publications, 1998), pp. 104–48, and Samanta, *Malarial Fever*, pp. 33–73. Neither of the two authors, however, critically analysed the medical debates around malaria and development in colonial Bengal. Klein has studied the relationship between ecology, environmentalism and malaria in colonial India and has argued that there was a relative decrease in malaria mortality in Bengal in the mid-1920s as compared to the late nineteenth century. He attributed this to the rise in immunity in the surviving populations in the worst-affected districts of Bengal and pointed out that therefore 'death by development' was a price paid by the poorest and most ill-nourished sections of the population. Klein, 'Development and Death'.

79 Government of Bengal Proceedings, Local Self-Government/Local Boards, no. 31, IOR/P/11569 (APAC), pp. 69–70.
80 For the consequences of the commercialization of agriculture and malaria in colonial Bengal, see Rajat K. Ray, 'The Crisis of Bengal Agriculture, 1870–1927 – The Dynamics of Immobility', *Indian Economic and Social History Review*, 10 (1973), pp. 244–79.

A Tale of Two Sites: Mian Mir and Meenglas

Ronald Ross visited India in 1926–27. On this trip he attended the inauguration of the commemorative gate raised in his honour at his old laboratory in Calcutta at the invitation of the Director of the new Calcutta School of Tropical Medicine (CSTM), J.W.D. Megaw. The *Indian Medical Gazette* pointed out that his visit was 'exceedingly timely'.[81] This was in reference to the increase in the number of malariologists in the IRFA, and the appointment of qualified malariologists at some railways and at the Vizagapatam harbour. It referred too to the increase of interest on the part of some industrial and commercial concerns, such as the Bombay cotton-mill owners and the members of the ITA, which, it stated, took 'malaria in the tea gardens of the Dooars and Assam very seriously'.[82]

Therefore Ross's visit to the Duars and Terai area, his comments on the Meenglas experiment and his speech to the planters in the region can be analysed to delineate the issues crucial to the management of malaria in the Darjeeling foothills.

Ross made the trip to the plantations in India as a representative of the new Ross Institute at Putney, where research into Tropical Medicine was to be supported by industrial interests. He gave lectures at the Terai Planters Club and the Dooars Planters Club and later visited Malaya at the invitation of Malcolm Watson. He also visited the operations at Meenglas on 20 January 1927 and insisted that the project would have had assured success if the project had been extended to a wider area.[83]

Almost two decades previously, in the acrimonious debate on the failure of the anti-malarial measures at Mian Mir, Ronald Ross had alleged both the lack of adequate data and the faulty application of scientific knowledge in the Mian Mir operations. To him the fact that anophelines could be destroyed in any area had acquired perfect certainty; what remained to be done was to calculate certain variables and local factors:

> The logical basis of the great measure of mosquito reduction is absolute ... The proposition, like the multiplication table, does not require experimental proof, and is incapable of disproof ... We have still to determine (a) the radius of operations required to reduce the density of a given species of mosquito to a given percentage and (b) the percentage of mosquito reduction required in order to obtain ultimately a given percentage of malaria reduction.[84]

One of the criticisms by Ross of the Mian Mir operations was that too little money had been spent, and if a cantonment had to be made free of malaria the

---

81 'The Future of Malaria Control in India', *Indian Medical Gazette*, 62 (1927), p. 29.
82 'The Future of Malaria Control in India', p. 30.
83 Ronald Ross, *Malaria – Control in Malaya and Assam: A Visit of Inspection, 1926–7* (London, Wellcome Library, n.d.), p. 22.
84 'Seventy-second Annual Meeting of the British Medical Association Held at Oxford, July 26th–29th, 1904, Proceedings of Sections/Tropical Medicine,' *British Medical Journal*, 2 (1904), pp. 632–35 (635).

authorities would have to invest in anopheline control in the same way that they would think to invest in drains and sewerage. In Meenglas the malarial surveys were made; the entomological studies and spleen index in Meenglas and neighbouring tea estates were examined. Ross found subsoil drainage too expensive for the terrain; Rs 16,000, plus the annual expenses of drainage, had been spent by the state government in Meenglas. The Meenglas experiment mapped the anopheline infectivity of two districts in the region, and reduced the spleen index of the Meenglas tea garden to a certain extent. The problems faced by the medical experts at Meenglas were not lack of scientific knowledge or unwillingness to apply that knowledge, but the logistic impossibility of extending the area under operation. While anti-malarial operations clearly pointed out that the stream-breeding anopheles could easily migrate from neighbouring tea estates, the management of the estates would not invest in subsoil drainage. Meanwhile, the government's budget for the operation was limited and would not extend to cover the entire region.

Although Ross found many faults with the anti-malarial operations at Meenglas, it did not generate a controversy to the same extent. The experiment at the ill-fated cantonment of Mian Mir had been such an embarrassment that its very name had to be changed to Lahore Cantonment to avoid the notoriety associated with anti-malarial measures at that site.[85] By the time the Meenglas experiment took place, malarial research of the previous two decades had increased the sheer volume of information about malaria. There was now sophistication in malarial research and the many variables of 'species sanitation' prompted more detailed sanitarian measures.[86] They included methods of spraying (spray cans were first used and discarded, and a special pack was designed for the coolie sprayer) and subsoil drainage.[87] The report on Meenglas also recommended locating the coolie lines at the centre of the plantations, as far as possible from the infective *bastis* and rice fields. Since most of the land in the tea plantations was utilized already, and the coolie lines were usually situated at the borders of the estates, this recommendation was not particularly realistic. Nor was the suggestion that the cultivation of paddy be stopped, for that disrupted the logic of the plantation economy. So far as provincial government was concerned, the agency for control of malaria was now vested in the planters themselves.

The significance of the 'controlled' experiment with anti-larval measures at Meenglas lies in its consequences for anti-malarial sanitation in other malaria-endemic areas of Bengal. The Bengal government asserted that the experiment at Meenglas (and a similar experiment at the mining sites of Singaran and Topsi

85 Bynum, 'An Experiment That Failed'.
86 The term 'species sanitation' was first used by Swellengrebel-Graf in 1919, and denotes the destruction of specific anopheline mosquitoes in a particular breeding environment. It involved prior investigation within the targeted area to determine the carriers unique to the locality. See D.J. Bradley, 'Watson, Swellengrebel and Species Sanitation: Environmental and Ecological Aspects', *Parassitologia*, 36 (1994), pp. 137–47.
87 *Report of the Malaria Survey of Jalpaiguri Duars*, p. 48.

Contagion and Enclaves

in Bengal) demonstrated that eradication of malaria would not be possible in hyper-endemic areas:

> Information of the greatest value has been gained by these two experiments, which show the extraordinary difficulty of producing a reasonable reduction of malaria ... [T]he cost of effective anti-mosquito measures of the kind employed with success at Panama, and more recently in parts of America, is in the present financial condition of the country likely to prove an insuperable obstacle to success.[88]

The lessons learnt at Meenglas were used by the Public Health Department to negate the possibility of drainage operations in any of the cultivated sites of the intensely malarial lower Bengal.

Tropical Medicine and Entrepreneurial Patronage

The institutionalization of Tropical Medicine was effected at the turn of century. While the metropolitan government supported the London School of Tropical Medicine, largely private interests supported the Liverpool School. The Liverpool School sent research expeditions to many places in the tropics for malarial research – Sierra Leone, Gold Coast, Panama, Egypt and Greece (which was not in the tropics but was malarious) – between 1899 and 1914. Some of them were commissioned specially by the Suez Company, for instance.[89]

In the first decade of the twentieth century, as we have seen, the government of India under Curzon established some research institutions in India. The Board of Scientific Advice did not initially focus on medical research, but rather on botany and geology.[90] But it gave an impetus to organized scientific research 'contained well within the government', which was different from the more individualistic and dispersed scientific research of an earlier period.[91] A great deal of research on malaria took place in the first two decades of the twentieth century at various research institutes in India.[92] Most of them were funded and motivated by various government agencies.

The CSTM was instituted in 1921.[93] The CSTM, and attached with it the Institute of Hygiene and Carmichael Hospital, was funded by the governments of India and Bengal, and a large number of donations from the Indian elite. It also succeeded in attracting a few subscriptions from British-dominated industries

---

88 *Annual Report for the Director of Public Health, Bengal, 1920*, p. 15.
89 For a comprehensive list of the general details, finance and research output of the Liverpool School, see Power, *Tropical Medicine*, pp. 249–55.
90 Roy M. MacLeod, 'Scientific Advice for British India: Imperial Perceptions and Administrative Goals, 1898–1923', *Modern Asian Studies*, 9 (1975), pp. 343–84.
91 MacLeod, 'Scientific Advice', p. 383.
92 O.P. Jaggi, *Medicine in India: Modern Period* (Delhi, Oxford, Oxford University Press, 2000), pp. 161–64.
93 H. Power, 'Sir Leonard Rogers FRS (1868–1962): Tropical Medicine in the Indian Medical Service', PhD thesis, University of London, 1993, pp. 143–82.

in eastern India such as the jute, mining and tea industries.[94] After a great deal of correspondence, the ITA at Calcutta agreed to the payment of twenty thousand rupees for five years to support research on kala-azar in the Assam tea plantations. This worked out to one *anna* per acre of tea under cultivation for all members. After four years, research on kala-azar had exceeded the sum sanctioned and now the total cost of the research in Assam was Rs 27,200. The ITA suggested that the kala-azar research in any case overlapped with research conducted by the state of Assam; therefore the research funds might be now directed to malarial studies in the tea plantations. The CSTM was unwilling to abandon the research at this late stage. After negotiations, they decided that the excess of Rs 7200 would be paid by the ITA. On its part, the CSTM would depute C. Strickland, head of the entomology department, to conduct a preliminary survey of malaria in Assam and northern Bengal. The 'expert survey' could cost around Rs 13,000 per annum.[95] The ITA noted that 'The idea was that, with the results of the preliminary investigation as a guide, it would be much easier to estimate the utility of the suggested malarial research.'[96]

The CSTM'S survey was done in Assam, where the total production of tea was more than two-and-half times that of northern Bengal. The next year, at its annual meeting, the Chairman of the Dooars Planters Association floated the idea of a research institute in the Duars, perhaps as a branch of the CSTM, to investigate malaria in the Duars. The British doctors employed by the plantations were also in favour of it. However, the suggestion of the Chairman was directed not only to members of his Association but also to government:

> to the Government of India ... I maintain that the Dooars presents unique conditions for the study of malaria and other obscure tropical diseases in so much as there is a large population living under conditions which allow the history of treated cases to be followed up for years.[97]

The Chairman of the ITA, who was also present as a guest at the meeting, was more realistic about government investment, rejected the idea of spending around Rs 50,000 annually for anti-malarial sanitation and suggested instead a scaled-down 'preliminary malaria map'.[98] The DPA decided this was useful and in 1926 the CSTM sent Strickland to Duars who conducted a preliminary survey. The DPA declared that the malaria survey was 'a valuable basis for future campaigns'.[99]

94 H. Power, 'The Calcutta School of Tropical Medicine: Institutionalizing Medical Research in the Periphery', *Medical History*, 40 (1996), pp. 197–214.
95 *IPTAAR, 1923* (Calcutta, 1924, APAC), p. 27.
96 *IPTAAR, 1923*, p. 28.
97 *DPAAR, 1925* (Jalpaiguri, 1926, APAC), p. ix.
98 *DPAAR, 1925*, p. xx.
99 *DPAAR, 1926* (Jalpaiguri, 1927, APAC), p. vii. Strickland's report on Assam included recommendations for drainage and flushing, and also 'education' of the coolies. See C. Strickland, *Abridged Report on Malaria in the Assam Tea Gardens* (Calcutta, Indian Tea Association, 1929). Although the anophelines of Assam had characteristics that were

As we have seen, Ross visited the area in 1926–27. He was invited to the annual meeting of the DPA and addressed the gathering of members and guests. Also present was C.A. Bentley, the Director of Public Health in Bengal who had assumed responsibility for the overall supervision of the Meenglas project. One of Ross's objectives was to gather support for the newly formed Ross Institute at Putney, London. He began by referring to his visit to the Darjeeling Terai 28 years ago, and remarked on the prosperity of the tea industry since then: 'the majority of those present appear to have thriven on it'.[100] He then demanded,

> I now ask what does the Dooars intend to do? There have been several Commissions of investigation in the district in bygone times, including Dr Stephens and Dr Christophers about 26 years ago, and Colonel Christophers and Dr Bentley in 1908, another Commission a year or two later, and more recently you have had the work of Colonel Stewart and the comprehensive survey last year conducted by Dr Strickland.[101]

Despite Ross's attempts to persuade them, neither the DPA nor indeed the planters in Darjeeling and Terai invested in anti-malarial sanitation. Entrepreneurial patronage facilitated certain studies on malaria in the Darjeeling foothills. The arrangement between the CSTM and the DPA resulted in several malaria surveys of the region, including Darjeeling and the Terai. Strickland published several papers on malaria in the hills, in the foothills of Darjeeling, the Terai and the Duars. Most of the studies located the extent of infectivity of carrier-anophelines and the specific conditions under which they could breed, and in one case a tea estate carried out some anti-malarial drainage in Darjeeling.[102] Other malaria research in the region studied comparative causes of epidemics of malaria in hill-stations, such as Shillong (Assam) and Kurseong (Darjeeling).[103] The Terai Planters' Association also funded a survey once more through the agency of the CSTM.[104]

In this period the tea plantations were sites of malarial research in terms of the opportunities provided by the terrain, the labourers and a limited financial

---

distinct from those of Duars, for instance *A.umbrosis* was a carrier in Assam whereas the Meenglas experiment proved that *A.umbrosis* was harmless in Duars, there were some familiar problems. The chief one was of the existence of rice fields and the cultivation of rice by some of the workers. See also, Strickland, 'The Mosquito Factor in the Malaria of Assam Tea Gardens', *Indian Medical Gazette*, 60 (1925), pp. 514–23.
100 *DPAAR, 1926* (Jalpaiguri, 1927, APAC), p. xvii.
101 *DPAAR, 1926*, p. xviii.
102 C. Strickland, 'Malaria on Ambootia Tea Estate near Kurseong and the Success of Some Anti-malarial Operations', *Indian Medical Gazette*, 59 (1924), pp. 119–20. See also, C. Strickland and H.P. Chaudhuri, 'More on Hill Malaria', *Indian Medical Gazette*, 71 (1936), pp. 267–69.
103 C. Strickland, 'Notes on Malaria in the Hill-Stations in or near the Eastern Himalayas', *Indian Medical Gazette*, 59 (1924), pp. 549–50. Strickland emphasized 'engineering works' over 'personal prophylaxis'.
104 C. Strickland and K.L. Chowdhury, *Blackwater Fever and Malaria in the Darjeeling Terai* (Calcutta, 1931), p. 3. D.N. Roy and K.L. Chowdhury, 'The Parasitology of Malaria in the Darjeeling Terai', *Indian Medical Gazette*, 65 (1930), pp. 379–80.

patronage. Christophers admitted in his preface to the League of Nations Malaria Commissions report that anti-malarial initiatives rarely proceeded from surveys to preventive operations in the tea estates in India. Although he was at pains to project anti-malarial operations in favourable light in most parts of India, he conceded that

> At present, after a 'survey' and recommendations, nothing very much often follows, largely because it is then left to the manager of such estates to do what he can, whereas the proper course would be to engage a suitable man to reside on the area and see to the carrying out of whatever was possible.[105]

During the visit of the Royal Commission on Labour in 1931, the DPA promoted both the experiments at Meenglas and the survey by Strickland as evidence of the planters' sincere efforts to control malaria within the area as evidence of good intent.[106]

A crucial hindrance to the efforts on the part of the tea estates in northern Bengal and in Assam to engage in anti-malarial operations was that the managers of the estate were personally responsible for the finances of the tea estate. Any long-term investment in a tea estate would detract from immediate profits and targets, and thereby from the commission received by each manager. Strickland suggested that the managers not be made responsible for the anti-malarial sanitation work: 'the practice will act like a dead weight on all the efforts of those who are trying to do some good'.[107] But the plantation managements made no structural changes to their system of remuneration in response.

The tea industry's contribution to the CSTM was meagre and limited in scope. As we have seen, it preferred that the government make the investments in both research and implementation of anti-malarial sanitation programmes. The contributions and the resultant surveys seem to have been for rhetorical effect more than anything else.

From the perspective of managerial priorities, immunity studies presented a more attractive proposition than systematic anti-malarial sanitation or the full-scale implementation of a quinine policy. The Ross Institute at Putney, which was supported partly by the ITA in London, opened a branch in Shillong, India, in 1930, consisting of a director, G.C. Ramsay, and one assistant. When drainage measures did take place in India under the supervision of the Ross Institute, they tended to be concentrated in Assam where the large managing agencies had contiguous territories and several tea gardens under their control. In Assam, which was in more remote northeast India, moreover, the import of labour was much more expensive and difficult than in northern Bengal. When some anti-malarial operations did take place in northern India between 1935–39, they were concentrated in Assam rather than Terai or Duars, where both the acreage and the capital outlay were relatively modest. The Ross

---

105 *Report of the Malaria Commission*, p. 26.
106 *DPAAR, 1929* (Jalpaiguri, 1930, APAC), p. 11.
107 Strickland, 'The Mosquito Factor'.

Contagion and Enclaves

Institute participated in some anti-malarial operations in northern Bengal as well as Assam and further conducted some reports on anti-malarial preventive measures in northern India from the mid-1930s.[108] Medical experts observed that Duars and Terai lacked in the initiatives towards species anti-malarial prevention.

The shortage of quinine during the Second World War aggravated the problem of malaria in all the plantations, including those in northern Bengal.[109] In 1946 two studies were conducted on the living conditions of the plantation labourers and the medical facilities available there. Both the reports were commissioned by the government in the postwar context of the emergent independent state of India. The Labour Enquiry Report of 1946 and the enquiry into the medical facilities received by the workers in the plantations noted the low standards of health and the high prevalence of diseases, including malaria, among the working population of northern Bengal.[110] Deaths by 'fever' remained the single largest cause of death in the plantations. As for anti-malarial works, one of the reports commented that

> Very little anti malaria work is being done at present in the Dooars and what little is being done is confined to shading and draining of the streams … In the Terai and Darjeeling also very few gardens have done any anti malarial work, in spite of the heavy incidence of malaria. The little work that is done in a few gardens is confined to spraying wells occasionally in the lines.[111]

Enclaves and Sanitation: Research on Hookworm in the Plantations

While anti-malarial sanitation in the plantation enclaves drew the interest of medical researchers, international scientific organizations and the government, another 'tropical' disease, hookworm, also drew similar focus on the plantations. Hookworm, or anchylostomiasis, is caused by parasitic worms that attach themselves to the human gut with hook-like teeth. The parasites enter the human body through contact with human faeces, usually by boring tiny holes through bare feet or, less often, through the mouth. Hookworm infestations in human intestines can cause severe anaemia, listlessness and emaciation. Unlike malaria, the hookworm projects represented government's and international organizations' resolve to encourage sustained public health programmes through a bio-medical model. The cycle of the disease and the certainty of its cure through the use of thymol caused medical authorities to assume that it

---

108 The Ross Institute of Tropical Hygiene, London School of Hygiene and Tropical Medicine, Supplementary Report to the Indian Tea Association, 1934, Mss Eur/F174/1212 (APAC). See also Griffiths, *History*, p. 357.
109 B. Chatterjee, 'Treatment of Malaria in the Present Emergency', *Indian Medical Gazette*, 77 (1942), pp. 701–2.
110 Rege, *Labour Investigation Committee*, pp. 89–91.
111 Rege, *Labour Investigation Committee*, p. 91.

could be eradicated relatively shortly through mass public health campaigns. In contrast to the anti-malaria campaigns, the hookworm projects therefore eschewed both medical research and wider social and economic constituents of disease.

In 1913, the newly formed IRFA provided the requisite funds for equipment and laboratory staff for Clayton Lane, the Civil Surgeon of Darjeeling, to conduct a hookworm survey in Darjeeling district. The Darjeeling Planters' Association agreed to allow him to investigate the tea plantation labourers for the disease and to treat them if necessary. Major Clayton Lane found that 70 per cent of the working population of the tea plantations suffered from hookworm infestation and attributed this to the lack of latrines in the coolie lines.[112] He proceeded to medicate the labourers in selected plantations with thymol, which cured existing infections. Although the after-effects of thymol were very unpleasant, he oversaw the de-infestation of hookworm in the targeted area.

But it required a permanent sanitary infrastructure to avoid re-infestation. Clayton Lane attempted to prevail upon the planters to install latrines and borrow pits in the coolie lines to prevent the high incidence. In the hill-station of Darjeeling, human waste was either cleared through septic tanks in selected bungalows, or collected by night-soil carriers and disposed through a chute to the hillsides outside the boundaries of the municipality. But in the coolie lines in the plantations there were no sanitary or sewerage facilities. Hookworm affected the productivity of the labour force drastically, and using an economic rationale Clayton Lane urged the planters:

> obviously, putting aside entirely the humanitarian point of view, and taking no consideration of such moral obligations as the employer of labour has imposed on him by his position, firstly that infected labour is not capable of the same output of work as uninfected labour, and secondly that it is less reproductive.[113]

Clayton Lane's project enthused some planters in Darjeeling in the immediate aftermath of the study, and they promised to provide for sanitation for their labourers. He published letters from grateful planters who claimed that his hookworm project improved the productivity of their workforce 'to an almost incredible degree'.[114] But in a familiar trend, a majority of the planters in Darjeeling chose not to invest in sanitary provisions within the coolie lines – again, possibly because the plantation system relied on the availability of large numbers of cheap, unskilled labour, and sick workers were easily replaceable.

---

112 Clayton Lane, 'The Treatment of Ankylostomiasis, or Hookworm Disease', *Indian Medical Gazette*, 50 (1915), pp. 241–45.
113 Clayton Lane, 'Lecture Delivered to the Members of the Darjeeling Planters' Association on April 29, 1916 on "The Incidence, Effects, and Prevention of Hookworm Infection" as They Concern the Planter', *India Health Bulletin* 1 (repr., Simla, 1924, APAC), p. 3.
114 Clayton Lane, 'The Hookworm and the War Loan', *Indian Medical Gazette*, 52 (1917), pp. 161–64.

In 1918, the government of Bengal accepted assistance from the Rockefeller Foundation (RF) to do a survey of the prevalence of hookworm in rural Bengal. The International Health Division (IHD) of the RF actively encouraged anti-hookworm campaigns in Canada, Brazil, Chile, India, Ceylon and Malaysia. As John Farley has argued, the Sanitary Commission of the RF first conducted anti-hookworm campaigns among the impoverished black population of the American South. In 1910–17, anti-hookworm campaign in several rural counties in Virginia and North Carolina focused on identifying the extent of the disease among the population, curing the infections through mobile dispensaries. Finally, in collaboration with local governments, they provided for 'public education' campaigns through public lectures, leaflets and school essay competitions so that the concerned communities could observe hygienic practices to prevent the disease. This programme provided the model for the activities of the IHD abroad, particularly in areas where they perceived that the productivity of labour was severely affected by hookworm disease. The clear framework of IHD was public health philanthropy which they posited against charity. It involved the participation of local governments and facilitation by the RF for dispensaries and public health campaigns in the initial phase. In the long term, the local administration and the community was expected to provide for disease control on their own.[115] In this case, the IHD provided Rs 6000 for microscopes and staff training for the project. In 1918, after a survey in the Burdwan district and in several jails, the Sanitary Board of the government of Bengal proposed a hookworm campaign in the jute mills, Asansol mining district and the Duars tea plantations.[116]

The Bengal government assigned a deputy sanitary officer to conduct a survey in the Duars plantations. As we have seen previously, Griffin conducted the operation and, as his predecessors Christophers and Bentley, also showed that the sanitary facilities, provisions for piped drinking water and generally bad working conditions all contributed to rampant disease; not only hookworm, but also dysentery, malaria, phthisis, ulcers, malnutrition and low wages within the working population within the plantations. Unsurprisingly, the DPA objected that Griffin's criticisms were 'a tissue of inaccuracies'.[117] Although British physicians employed in some plantations in the Duars medicated infected workers with thymol to cure anchylostomiasis, there was no large-scale anti-hookworm public health campaign within the plantation enclaves.

In 1920, the newly established CSTM focused on hookworm, kala-azar, leprosy and diabetes. The areas they chose for research surveys were the largely British-owned jute, tea and mining industries. The CSTM identified three diseases: kala-azar in the Assam tea plantations, anchylostomiasis or hookworm among jute mill workers and epidemic respiratory diseases among the coal

115 Farley, *To Cast Out Disease*, pp. 2–41.
116 *DPAAR, 1918* (Calcutta, Catholic Orphan Press, 1919, APAC), p. 265. See also Government of Bengal Proceedings, Municipal/Sanitation, IOR/P/10737 (APAC), p. 123.
117 Chairman Dooars Planters' Association to Commissioner Rajshahi, Government of Bengal Proceedings, Municipal/Sanitation, IOR/P/10765 (APAC), pp. 10–11.

mine workers. The CSTM planned to conduct surveys of other diseases such as bacillary dysentery, blackwater fever and filariasis at a later stage in the same areas.[118]

The hookworm surveys by the CSTM extended to the tea plantations in the Darjeeling foothills as well. In 1927, Dr Maplestone from the CSTM visited the Duars and requested the DPA to allow him to conduct a small survey to gauge the extent of anchylostomiasis among the workers in the Duars tea plantations. His objective was to understand 'local conditions' that precipitated hookworm disease. And after the failure of the RF's mass public health campaigns, he wanted to see if the treatment of, and sanitary provisions for, heavily infected workers would contain the disease in a controlled area.[119] He concluded his survey and treatments in a few selected plantations in 1928–29.[120] He found the best treatment for hookworm was carbon tetracholoethylene instead of the more commonly used carbon tetrachloride, which was far more toxic. Later, he communicated his findings to the planters but unlike Clayton Lane and Griffin, he did not insist on large-scale sanitary provisions within the plantation enclaves. This was probably because the CSTM did not view its role as prescriptive at all, and was content to carry out its research for its own sake.

Hookworm infestation continued to remain prevalent in epidemic proportions among the workers in Darjeeling, Duars and the Terai. The Royal Commission on Labour in India reported in 1931 that there was 'evidence to show that a large proportion of tea garden labourers are infected with hookworm'.[121] The Commission recommended mass treatment of workers and provisions for sanitation for the workers:

> In most plantation areas ... latrines are uncommon, and although it may be impracticable to have these dotted over the plantation for working gangs, it should be possible to provide a sufficient number near the house lines and in the vicinity of the tea factory. In this connection we deprecate the wholesale exemption of the Assam and Bengal tea factories from compliance with section 13 of the Factories Act on the grounds that such factories are seasonal and built on open spaces where the workers have free access to the jungle.[122]

The government ignored the Commission's recommendation to legislate for comprehensive sanitary facilities for the labourers within the plantation enclaves. The planters themselves did not provide for sanitation facilities, regardless of the long-term economic benefits such provisions might have afforded the tea industry. In 1946, in the first survey of living conditions of labourers in the tea plantations after the Royal Commission report, D.V. Rege noted that 'dysentery, hill-diarrhoea, and hookworm are common among the workers on the

118 Hon. Secretary of CSTM to Secretary ITA, 7 Sep. 1920, *IPTAAR, 1920* (Calcutta, 1921, APAC), pp. 313–19.
119 Chairman's address, *DPAAR, 1927* (Jalpaiguri, 1928, APAC), p. xx.
120 Chairman's address, *DPAAR, 1929* (Jalpaiguri, 1930, APAC), p. viii.
121 *RCLI*, p. 409.
122 *RCLI*, p. 410.

hills'.[123] As demonstrated previously in the instance of anti-malaria sanitation, the publications of the medical reports were an end in themselves, and did not lead to action.

Tropical Medicine and the Logic of Location

So far we have seen that the Darjeeling foothills and the plains of the Duars were the subject of studies in Tropical Medicine in London and then in colonial Calcutta. The notion of the causation of malarial fever in industrial locations all over colonial India came to rest largely in the factor of non-immune immigration and the tropical aggregation of labour, confirming Schaffer's findings in Sumatra. When the Bengal government began the malaria control programme at Meenglas, the medical experts borrowed from the knowledge of anophelines and preventive work done by Ronald Ross (the anopheline count-per-head of the population factor in infectivity) and Malcolm Watson (subsoil drainage) and sought to retest their thesis in that locality. The tracts of Duars and the Darjeeling Terai were at once connected to the entire tropical world and to the world of metropolitan and colonial Tropical Medicine.

In this respect, the Darjeeling foothills were not unique. Colonial realities informed, complicated and challenged the inadequacies of current medical theories in the metropolis. In a recent publication, Helen Tilley, through an analysis of the medical, scientific, ecological and anthropological debates on the African Research Survey (1929–39), argued that Africa was a 'living laboratory' for scientists in the interwar years. She has argued that unlike the 'controlled' laboratory, the complexity and heterogeneity of African conditions informed medical theories in Britain which challenged 'reductionist' biomedicine in Britain as well as 'vertical' theories of disease control so far as species sanitation in malaria was concerned.[124]

The central problem of the 'living laboratory' is, to my mind, neither its multifarious nature nor its ability to confound medical theories conceived in diverse conditions. It is rather in the content of its location in the political economy, demonstrated most clearly in the implementation of medical theories, however complex and modified, in the said colonies. In the case of the African Research Survey, Tilley has not analysed the medical practices in rural Africa (as opposed to medical theories of species sanitation in the region), nor has she questioned its use (or experimentation), however limited, in urban spaces or areas of white settlement.

The tea plantations in the Darjeeling foothills were, as we have seen, at the forefront of the latest research on malaria in the early twentieth century. Simultaneously, the prevention of malaria was articulated in the rhetoric of the

---

123 Rege, *Labour Investigation Committee*, p. 91.
124 Helen Tilley, 'Africa as a "Living Laboratory": The African Research Survey and the Colonial Empire: Consolidating Environmental, Medical and Anthropological Debates, 1920–1940', DPhil. dissertation, University of Oxford, 2001.

uniqueness of the *local*. Contemporary research on such conditions as the hospitability of the different terrain to particular subspecies of the vector anophelines merged seamlessly with concerns over the peculiarities of labouring populations within the tea plantations and outside them, at the *bastis* – all framed in a set of conditions termed the 'local'. The objection raised by the workers to the use of quinine as prophylaxis was also an issue of their own particular customs and ways of life. The planters argued that quinine prophylaxis could not be administered to the workers for such 'primitive' peoples could not be forcibly brought under a prophylactic regime.

A similar trajectory is evident in the research and control programmes of another typically 'tropical' disease: anchylostomiasis. Identified at once with poor, ignorant communities in the USA and Latin America, it fitted the profile of a typical tropical disease. Unlike malaria, the diagnosis, cure and long-term prevention of hookworm disease seemed relatively simple and was uncontested by medical authorities of the time.

Nevertheless, the labouring population of the tea plantations provided the ideal space for anti-hookworm programmes in Darjeeling and the Duars. This 'research', or more accurately the eradication programmes, was conducted in the context of international cooperation as well as government and entrepreneurial sponsorship for Tropical Medicine. For instance, R.G. Griffin of CSTM experimented with the alternatives to thymol with chenopodium oil as well as with other 'anti-antihelminthics … for expelling hookworms', including an emulsion of liquid paraffin and milk on plantation labourers in the Duars.[125] The 'experiments' did not lead to systematic preventive measures within the plantations, and the disease survived in epidemic proportions among the working populations. The 'surveys' and 'experiments' by the IRFA as well as the CSTM provided evidence that the eradication and long-term prevention of hookworm disease would greatly increase the productivity of the labourers.

Despite the new scientific knowledge and vocabulary, Tropical Medicine in India also persistently sustained the discourse of 'local conditions' and their unique link with parasitical as well as helminthic diseases. The discourse of the local was echoed in official discourse, according to which the 'local conditions' were manifest, it claimed, in two different ways. So far as the workers were concerned, the planters generally claimed that the administration of prophylactic doses of quinine to prevent malaria or the installation of latrines to prevent hookworm disease was generally futile because the 'primitive' labourers were resistant to them. The planters insisted also that the local government should not interfere in the management of disease within the plantations. Instead, the close knowledge of the labourers and their customs that the management possessed enabled them to decide best what needed be done for the health of their labourers. The majestic announcement of the planters' spokesman, W.L. Travers, after the visit of the Royal Commission on Labour to the tea estates, is representative of managerial claims on behalf of the labourers and formed the

---

125 *DPAAR, 1920* (APAC), pp. 126–27.

justification for a non-interventionist approach to public health infrastructure within the plantations:

> Our labouring population, or the great majority of it is drawn from the races of Chota Nagpur. These races have their own religion, languages, and racial customs to which they naturally cling most persistently. Many of their racial and religious customs tend to impede the work of health improvement and welfare, and therefore it is of great importance that all measures for their uplift in any direction should be under the control and direction of persons who really know and understand the customs, traditions and habits of these aboriginal people.[126]

On the other hand, the idea of 'species sanitation' in Tropical Medicine contributed to the discourse of the local condition in the prevention of malaria everywhere in the tropics. And even in the case of hookworm disease, researchers in the CSTM found it useful to study 'local' conditions of the disease.[127]

The dual imperatives of the local and the international sustained the growth of knowledge in Tropical Medicine, and the tea plantations in the Darjeeling foothills contributed to leading research on Tropical Medicine. They were the sites of many 'unique' conditions, conditions for testing scientific theories. As noted above, the Chairman of the DPA promised similar unique local conditions when asking the government to fund malaria research in the Duars. Partly this appeal was rhetorical. The planters' associations generally sought to shift pecuniary responsibility for any research or sanitary works to the government in its role as the *zamindar* (landlord) of the district, while retaining the claim to absolute authority over their workers and their plantation. Partly, too, the distinctiveness of the region and its local conditions contributed in various aspects to the knowledge of Tropical Medicine.

At the same time, the political economy of the plantations contributed to a complex set of factors that inhibited both anti-malarial sanitation as well as systematic and full use of quinine prophylaxis within the tea plantations. Anti-malarial operations were not undertaken on a sustained basis, with both the local and provincial governments claiming with scientific authority that the management had to be responsible for the elimination of mosquito breeding in its lines. The management on its part shifted the responsibility from the plantations to the *bastis*, thereby rhetorically situating the plantations themselves within a sanitary enclave. The responsibility for the prevention and control of malaria, however, was accepted neither by the planters' associations nor by the provincial or local governments. Some British medical men who were employed by the plantations made isolated attempts to destroy anopheline breeding within a decade of the discovery of the mosquito-vector transmission by Ronald Ross.[128]

126 *DPAAR, 1929* (APAC), p. x.
127 The emphasis on 'local conditions' within Tropical Medicine research in India was sustained with reference to beriberi as well. See Arnold, 'British India and the "Beri-Beri Problem", 1798–1942', *Medical History*, 54 (2010), pp. 295–314.
128 'The Campaign against Malaria in the Duars', *The Lancet*, 172 (18 July 1908), p. 174.

Managers in several plantations also made similar efforts in a few scattered instances.[129] Similarly, while some plantations invested in a few latrines for their labourers and provided for thymol to their resident doctor babus to cure hookworm disease, these measures remained inadequate to prevent epidemic hookworm disease. The logistics and structure of the plantation economy did not have to accommodate any enduring system for long-term preventive health. In colonial India research in Tropical Medicine did not translate from the 'field' to the structures of public health.

---

129 Strickland, 'Malaria on Ambootia Tea Estate', pp. 119–20.

CHAPTER 8

Habitation and Health in Colonial Enclaves: The Hill-station and the Tea Plantations

So far we have discussed the impact of colonization and consequently medical policies in two different, contiguous enclaves: the hill-station of Darjeeling and the tea estates in its adjoining regions of northern Bengal. The town of Darjeeling, originally conceived of as a European sanitary enclave, invited from the very beginning traders, immigrant labourers and Indian civil officials and servants; and with its development came the greater colonization of the entire Terai and Duars areas. As we have seen, the town of Darjeeling was neither an indisputably healthy hill-station, nor was it a white enclave. Certain areas within Darjeeling were marked out for the exclusive use of the European population and the Eden Sanitarium was one of them. The hill-station signified an enclave because the British perceived it as a secluded site, more salubrious and scenic than the dreaded hot and dusty Indian plains. The town itself, controlled directly by the colonial administration, provided a space for medicalized leisure to the European population; and the Eden Sanitarium provided an exclusive space unavailable in the plains for the rejuvenation of white bodies. Through these various institutions the British population in India sustained a socially exclusive site for themselves in some parts of Darjeeling. As a consequence, the medical facilities within the urban space of Darjeeling were of a much higher standard in the colonial period than in the surrounding areas. These places were kept relatively free from encroachment from local Indian influences. In that sense, the town of Darjeeling was an enclave of particular, privileged medical infrastructure. This medical infrastructure was not merely about clinical medicine, doctors and hospitals, but was an enclaved privilege in a medical paradigm defined in terms of colonial ideas of tropical heat, filth and human habitation.

The tea plantations in the Darjeeling district and in the adjoining Duars that were established in the same phase of colonization as Darjeeling were enclaves of a different sort. First, their management mostly comprised of European personnel whose social world and medical requirements corresponded with those of the

Europeans in Darjeeling; therefore the provisions for their health care constituted their own doctors with British qualifications as well as the option to go to the privileged site of Darjeeling in cases of emergency. Second, the identity of the plantations as enclaves was embedded within the structure of the tea plantation economy in colonial northern Bengal. As we have seen, the system of free labour and the necessity for a working population that provided seasonal labour was achieved through the gradual settling of ex-tea garden labourers in *bastis* outside the plantations. Simultaneously, planters kept an eye on encroachment by other agencies, including the government and political parties.

Although situated in relatively remote areas, with vast tracts of land allocated to tea plantation, the isolation of the tea estates was not entirely due to geographical factors. Mines and plantations represented special sites, the habitations of the workers being placed together – very different from the chawls or hatas inhabited by the industrial workers in the mills of Kanpur or Bombay, for instance, where labourers lived in equally crowded and unsanitary habitations, which were rented to them by private landlords and were contiguous to the mills, not remote and cut off from the respective cities.[1]

In that sense, the plantations, too, had a dual identity: they were porous and yet were enclaves. The provisions of health care for the labourers in the plantations were located within the system of production of the plantation; paternalistic and individualistic. At the same time, the labourers and their bodies within the plantations provided a unique site for the testing of medical techniques and theories in the expanding specialization of Tropical Medicine in the twentieth century. The plantation management used the symbiotic relationship between the plantation and the *bastis* to engage in a continuous negotiation with the government over the responsibility for the health care of workers within the *bastis*. In this context, the *bastis* and the sites outside the plantations emerged as the sites of disease in managerial and often official discourse. Much like the healthy–unhealthy dichotomy of the hill-town of Darjeeling vis-à-vis the 'plains', such a duality was not sustainable. The discourse, however, enabled the managerial element within the plantations, much like the European population in Darjeeling, to sustain the myth of the healthy–unhealthy duality vis-à-vis the plantations and the *bastis* and more importantly to retain administrative and political control over the labourers in the hands of the planters.

After the Second World War and in the post-Independence era, the two coterminous enclaves met with different fates. The aspect of rejuvenation for

---

1 For a vivid description of working-class habitations, the overcrowded *hatas* where street life merged in many ways with the workers' lives within their homes in colonial Kanpur, see Chitra Joshi, *Lost Worlds: Indian Labour and Its Forgotten Histories* (Delhi, Permanent Black, 2005), pp. 121–26. Prashant Kidambi has argued that in early twentieth century Bombay, the Bombay Improvement Trust which was intended originally to provide sanitary and cheap accommodation for workers failed in its project, and instead of in the Trust's tenements, the working classes lived in the over-crowded private *chawls* near the mills and docks in the heart of the city. See Kidambi, 'Housing the Poor in a Colonial City: The Bombay Improvement Trust, 1898–1918', *Studies in History*, 17 (2001), pp. 57–79.

Contagion and Enclaves

white bodies in Darjeeling became irrelevant in this period. The British presence in the entire northern Bengal area was represented mostly by the planters. The exclusive and elite aspect of medical services in the Darjeeling was now represented by the Dooars and Darjeeling Home, a specialized hospital that the planters' associations of northern Bengal established within the premises of the old Planters' Club. The plantations themselves, on the other hand, by the very nature of their isolated circumstance and the labour habitations within the tea estates, remained the focus of government health policies, thereby accentuating the differences, especially at the level of government policy, from the surrounding countryside.

As we have seen in Chapter 1, Darjeeling was incorporated in the wider colonial polity and economy of northern Bengal over the nineteenth century. Simultaneously, the town of Darjeeling stretched to accommodate various demands on its multiple identities – as a European social enclave and seasonal administrative centre, as well as the hub for the planters of the hill area, and as an aspirational social site of rejuvenation for the Bengali elites.

In the early part of the twentieth century the town of Darjeeling accommodated the settlement of diverse social and economic interests within itself. After Independence, its characteristic changed at a more fundamental level. With the transfer of power in 1947, the numbers of British/European civil servants within the Indian administration dwindled to a very small minority. The European character of the hill-station was then mostly defined by the British planters. The 'Sterling companies', that is, the British-owned tea companies (the Indian-owned companies were invariably registered in India and were called 'Rupee companies') and their British recruits stayed on in India after Independence.

The question here is, what transformations occurred in Darjeeling after the Indian Independence, bereft of its special status as the summer seat of government and the chosen leisure site of the ruling classes? The tea industry in northern Bengal also accommodated large-scale changes in its structures of functioning after the Second World War and the transfer of power. The newly emergent nation-state positioned itself, too, as the arbiter between labour and industry, borrowing some of the rhetoric from its predecessor, the colonial state. However, the nature of structural changes initiated by the independent nation-state was of a more interventionist nature. In this chapter I shall examine some of these structural changes which affected the medical infrastructure of Darjeeling and the plantations in the immediate post-Independence India.

Darjeeling after Independence

Like all former colonial hill-stations, Darjeeling refashioned itself as a tourist town, famed for its scenic view of the Kanchenjunga, its charming colonial architecture and quaint ambience. The Indian nationalists including Gandhi himself had frequently criticized the transfer of government administration to the 'hills' for up to eight months in the year. In postcolonial India, the seat of the central and Bengal governments remained in Delhi and Calcutta permanently. While Simla remained a state capital of the newly formed Himachal Pradesh state, the status of Darjeeling and Ootacamund changed drastically, reduced as they were to being mere district headquarters and provincial towns. As in other hill-stations, the British gradually left, only a few remaining to the last, owing their tenacity to nostalgia, the lethargy of age, and often, an inadequate pension that would further reduce after conversion to the British pound.

The changed character of Darjeeling was reflected in the fact that there was no longer a racially exclusive town, or indeed, medical institutions. The government took over the management of the Eden Sanitarium after 1950, and amalgamated it with the main public hospital of the town, Victoria Hospital. At the time of amalgamation the Eden Hospital, 'subscribed mainly by the Planters' Associations', was the best-equipped hospital in the area, with its 'major X-ray set, Electric Diathermy, and Electric Vibrator Apparatus', and carried out X-ray work for other hospitals in the district.[2] The European planters, deprived of an exclusive medical institution, established the Dooars and Darjeeling Medical Association, a private hospital mainly for the use of the planters. For that purpose they relinquished part of the Planters' Club, a gracious building overlooking a ridge with views of the mountains.[3] Its chief medical supervisors were British, initially an ex-army man.[4] The respective Planters' Associations in Darjeeling, Terai and the Duars subscribed to it, which enabled British planters and their families to use it as their principal medical establishment.[5] The appropriation of the Eden Sanitarium and hospital by government merely led to the establishment of another exclusive medical institution in Darjeeling. The town itself maintained its own hospitals, with a few charitable dispensaries in the remote tahsils. Yet, the appropriation by the Indian elite of the climatic theories of health continued, sustaining the status of Darjeeling as a health resort. A Bengali philanthropist, S.B. Dey, donated a substantial sum of money for a TB hospital in Jadavpur near Calcutta. The TB hospital built a branch in Kurseong, the smaller hill-station near Darjeeling, to facilitate convalescence for its TB patients.[6] Therefore, long after the Germ theory of TB was established and 'phthisis' no longer remained a disease category, the presumption of well-being for a respiratory patient in a cool hilly climate survived in Indian medical discourse and practice.

---

2 A. Mitra, *West Bengal Census 1951: District Handbook: Darjeeling* (Alipore, 1954), p. 1. See also Rāhula Sāṅkṛtyāyana, *Dorjeliṅg-paricaya* (Calcutta, Ādhunika Pustaka Bhavana, 1950), p. 128.
3 *DPAAR, 1948* (Kalimpong, 1949, APAC), p. xxxiii.
4 *IPTAAR, 1950* (Calcutta, 1951, APAC), p. 107.
5 *IPTAAR, 1951* (Calcutta, 1952, APAC), p. 122.
6 Dash, *Bengal District Gazetteer*, p. 97.

The Writing on the Wall: Privilege and 'Industrial' Labour

At the moment of Indian Independence, the racial/sanitary enclave of Darjeeling and the structural enclave of the tea plantations got conflated, for a brief period. The planters, unlike the British missionaries in neighbouring Sikkim, had depended directly on their social status as 'Europeans' in British India for a number of informal advantages from government.[7] Immediately after the war and the Indian Independence, the special status of Darjeeling as a European sanatorium diminished with the exodus of the British civil and military officials. At this time, the British planters comprised mostly the European population of the region. A contemporary reminiscence by a woman who belonged to a planter family recounted Christmas in 1947, the year of Independence. In the sodden early hours of the next morning a few of the planters fantastically plotted for a separatist movement – for a 'British Sikkim' – which was to be an island of Britishness in the tea estates.[8] The planters in the Duars, Terai, as well as in Darjeeling petitioned the newly instituted office of the high commissioner of Britain in India that the British component of the entire region represented by the planters, was prominent enough to deserve a separate consul or, as the deputy high commissioner described it, 'a small outpost' in the northern Bengal region.[9] The high commission did not pursue this, because the deputy high commissioner who toured the northern Bengal tea districts reported that such an enclave of a British outpost was impossible. The tea plantations were scattered and isolated from each other, and the establishment of a consulate would be difficult. For the planters, an emotional sense of loss at the dismantling of the British Empire was overlaid with more urgent tones, following the new resolve of the emergent nation-state to act as the arbiter between the tea industry and the interests of the labourers. The reality was that it was a process that had begun from the 1940s, when the tea plantation enclaves were being threatened in various ways.

This breach was different in character from the fissures within the enclaves in the colonial period when the district officials were generally respectful of the authority of the tea estate managers, and scattered labour recalcitrance was kept a close secret except in times of overspill. Previously, we have seen that such changes occurred immediately after the Second World War, when the railway workers unionized and in turn mobilized tea workers. The Tebhaga movement, in which many tea garden workers participated with their kin among the ex-tea workers who were sharecroppers, also contributed to the sense of impending, fundamental changes among the planters.

---

7 For an account of missionary activity in education and medicine in Kalimpong see Alex Mackay, *Their Footprints Remain: Biomedical Beginnings across the Indo–Tibetan Frontier* (Amsterdam, Amsterdam University Press, 2007).
8 Jennifer Fox, *In the Shade of Kanchenjunga* (London, British Association for Cemeteries in South Asia, 1993), p. 161.
9 'Tour Notes of the Acting Deputy Commissioner for the United Kingdom, Calcutta, Dooars, Darjeeling and Kalimpong Areas', IOR/L/PJ/7/13925 (APAC), p. 1.

Other factors simultaneously contributed to the crumbling autonomy of the plantations. The mobilization of labour for the Second World War, particularly on the eastern frontier, absorbed labour from the plantations and their catchment areas. During the hard years of the Bengal famine, the tea estates procured rice, the staple food, and some other essentials such as jaggery and oil – sometimes from the local markets, often from outside, to feed their labourers, both permanent and *faltu*. The district officials as well as the provincial government assisted the planters' associations in the procurement of rice. The wages were calculated partly in kind. During the war years the tea estates, European- and Indian-owned, competed among themselves to obtain *basti* labour.

From the early 1940s, the plantations were no longer isolated, virtually sovereign estates. When the government of India instituted enquiries into the conditions of the plantation workers in 1946, they were unmoved by the planters' protests that the time was not convenient for such an enquiry. The reports, examined to some extent in Chapter 4, made wide-ranging recommendations.[10] These included the establishment of a pyramid of large 'group hospitals' and better-stocked and well-attended dispensaries at the individual tea gardens. Griffiths, an ICS officer who was later employed as adviser to the ITA during the 1950s, commented that 'In his study of the medical organization of the tea industry, Jones revealed himself as something of a theorist with a bureaucratic desire for uniformity.'[11] Jones recommended a three-tier system of hospitals within the plantations (regional hospitals/group hospitals/garden dispensaries). However, he principally emphasized the need for preventive health and health care at the level of the garden dispensaries:

> the fact remains that the vast bulk of the mortality, and even more of the morbidity of the tea gardens ... is the result of conditions arising from poor diet, inefficient sanitation, contaminated and insufficient drinking water, the ignorance of the workers, which are easy to recognise, and do not ordinarily require elaborate facilities for diagnosis, or highly specialised treatment.[12]

The focus by government on labour health was part of a larger concern for the lives of the plantation workers; this included a move for minimum wage, paid holidays and other benefits. This was the time when the tea estates were unionized, and the planters participated in the unionization by patronizing the 'moderate' Congress unions rather than the more radical Communist ones.[13] The unionization of the tea estate workers in northern Bengal was a complex phenomenon, beyond the scope of this work. For our purposes it suffices to point out that the nature of relations between labour and management changed to a great extent. For instance, after 1948, the Indian Tea Association handbooks

10 Of the two reports, one focused on the standards of living of the plantation workers (Rege, *Labour Investigation Committee*). The second concentrated specifically on medical infrastructure in the plantations (Jones, *Standards of Medical Care*).
11 Griffiths, *History*, p. 361.
12 Jones, *Standards of Medical Care*, p. 20.
13 The point has been made by Ray, *Transformations*, p. 196.

always provided statistics on the number of strikes in each tea district in India. The mai–baap (paternalistic) relationship between the planter and his workers did not disappear overnight, but had to accommodate intermediaries such as trade unionists and labour officers.[14]

The negotiations for all-India legislation began with a tripartite meeting between the government, labour representatives and the industry held on 31 March 1948. Wage increases were high on the agenda. The chairman of the DPA reported to the members of his association,

> at the outset it was made clear that an agreement would have to be made for some increase not necessarily because labour was as it was often stated underpaid, but that the standard of living of tea garden labour had to be raised and that there was ample room for improvement on both counts.

So that was the writing, quite plain on the wall.[15]

The negotiations were long and often acrimonious. Apart from the abolishing of the piece wage, the settlement for a minimum wage and other benefits, the workers also demanded medical facilities that, they insisted, should be controlled by the government rather than the plantations. The government's intent to intervene within the plantations, however, did not extend to such lengths. The chairman explained to his members that

Labour wanted the whole thing under Government including the appointing of Dr. Babus, nurses and the whole shooting match at of course our expense. This we would not agree to and Government accepted our views that control over Estate Medical arrangements should be in our own hands.[16]

The new government insisted on the 'conception of labour's partnership in industry', and the agenda for the meeting included the fixing of new wages, standards of medical care and discussion of outline of legislation covering all plantations.[17] After several rounds of negotiations, the Plantation Labour Act (PLA) of 1951 was passed by the government of India. The Act specified the numbers of hospitals and doctors, maternity benefits and crèches, as well as the abolition of piece rate (wage paid by amount of work done, namely the hazira and the ticca and the introduction of minimum wages, the construction of pucca houses and provisions for clean water and conservancy facilities for the workers. The measures were to be at the expense of the tea industry, which were to be provided with some government concessions on quotas of steel and cement, which were rationed in the post-Second World War years. The PLA represented a significant degree of state intervention within the plantations.[18]

14 Ray has pointed out that in the process of unionization the workers were left with little autonomy or agency in the actual negotiations with the government. The long-term impact of the war and the Tebhaga movement was that it 'strengthened the hand of the government vis a vis the planters'. Ray, *Transformations*, pp. 196–97.
15 *DPAAR, 1948–49* (Kalimpong, 1949, APAC), p. 24.
16 *DPAAR, 1948–49*, p. 24.
17 *Summary of Proceedings of the Second Session of the Industrial Committee on Plantations Held at New Delhi on 31st March and 1st and 2nd April, 1948*, IOR/V/26/670/73 (APAC).
18 Mss Eur F174/1022 (APAC).

The planters negotiated to a great extent, claiming, for instance, that large 'group hospitals' need not be provided by the plantations and should instead be the responsibility of the government:

> It is considered that the Plantation Industry can no longer be described as working in undeveloped areas, and that, by reason of their substantial contributions to general revenues they should not be expected to provide these facilities which are in other industries provided by the State.[19]

They pointed out also that the industry was expected to provide ten hospital beds for every thousand workers, whereas the national average of hospital beds in India was 00.24 per thousand.[20] The planters' desire to make the government responsible for the health care of its workers was, as we have seen, hardly a new phenomenon, nor was the comparison between the facilities provided by the tea industry with those enjoyed by other agricultural labourers.

However, the new government viewed the tea plantations as enclaves where, through legislation, medical facilities not available elsewhere in rural India might be enforced. In principle, this was similar to the colonial government's legislation, in the JLA. The provisions of the PLA far exceeded any recommendations made by the Royal Commission of India, 1931, many of which had not been implemented until then. In the immediate aftermath of the war and Independence, the Indian state and the newly established trade unions pushed through the PLA under the principle of the 'partnership between labour and industry' where the labourers were conceived to have a share in the profits of the companies. Although the provisions of the PLA were never implemented fully, they nevertheless demarcated a new relationship between the planter and labourer, where the planter was no longer to be the provider and the protector of the labourer.

'The Measure of a Sahib'

> A tea garden in Darjeeling hills is run on tradition; the whole structure is founded on the ideals laid down by the pioneer planters who set out the estates ... Once they are convinced ... that the new Sahib is a sound and strong character, they accept his authority without question ... Because the manufacture of tea at remunerative prices is largely dependent upon cheap, unskilled labour, the relations between garden coolies and estate managers is the single most important factor in the production of tea.[21]

In spite government legislation to systematize and streamline the availability of basic medical care for the labourers, the extent to which medical care within the plantations was dependent upon the idiosyncrasies of individual planters is

19 'Draft Model Rules for Plantation Labour Act, 1951', Mss Eur F174/1021 (APAC), pp. 2–3.
20 'Draft Model Rules for Plantation Labour Act, 1951', p. 3.
21 David Wilson Fletcher, *The Children of Kanchenjunga* (London, Constable and Co. Ltd, 1955), p. 22.

evident from David Fletcher's reminiscences. He relates an anecdote when Tuli, a woman worker in the plantation where he was an assistant, was injured. She came to his bungalow and was attended by his wife, who cleaned her wound and then asked him if Tuli would be able to stand the sting of iodine. He replied, 'To the coolie mind, a medicine that doesn't have some immediate effect is not potent enough … Iodine will at least convince this woman of its potency!'[22]

This was of course the legacy of 'heroic medicine' for the labourers in planters' folklore, unchanged from its nineteenth-century form. So little is known of workers' perceptions of their own illnesses, or indeed of their own world of ojhas and healers who existed side by side with the doctor babus (and in all probability provided a major part of the health care to the working population of the estates), that we cannot surmise what Tuli herself made of the iodine on her wound.

Change in health care, or indeed any structural changes in the tea plantations, was gradual and slow despite government legislation and intervention. The actual implementation of the PLA took several years, indeed even in the 1970s many tea companies had not complied with its various regulations.[23] The important factor in the postwar and Independence years was that the enclaves of the tea plantations was encroached upon on a more systematic scale than ever before. In the post-PLA years the planters continued to cite labourers' cultural values as justification for the lack of basic sanitary facilities in the plantations.[24] The tea plantations by their very enclaved nature were expected by the state and the trade unions to provide for health services in a way that was not available to ordinary residents of the district.

Tropicality, Postcoloniality and Enclaves

This book has studied the interaction between Tropical Medicine, colonial enclaves and the colonial state. With decolonization within the British Empire, the organic links between colonialism and Tropical Medicine and the colonized states were severed. The medical speciality of Tropical Medicine has survived through its clinical and research institutions, but through negotiations of a different order. Its practitioners in Britain are engaged more closely with

---

22 Fletcher, *The Children of Kanchenjunga*, p. 46.
23 A government inspector's report in 1972 noted that on an average there was one medical practitioner for 1750 workers and makes a comment that is familiar to us: 'the workload of the individual doctor has been heavy'. *Annual Report of the Administration of the Plantation Labour Act 1951, for the Year Ending 1972* (Alipore, n.d.), pp. 3–4. Two years later the annual report recorded 105 cases of prosecution against employers, generally for 'violation of welfare provisions'. *Annual Report of the Administration of the Plantation Labour Act 1951, for the Year Ending 1974* (Alipore, n.d.), p. 3.
24 Sharit K. Bhowmik, 'Labour Welfare in Tea Plantations: An Assessment of the Plantation Labour Act', in Sebastian Karotemprel and B. Dutta Roy (eds), *Tea Garden Labourers of North East India: A Multi-Dimensional Study* (Shillong, Vendrame Institute, 1990), pp. 187–99.

international health organizations such as the WHO, for instance, are funded by several international medical charities and have formulated strategies that continue to sustain its legitimacy as an academic discipline. But if the tropics still provide the contexts for medical research and international health programmes for myriad diseases, it is through a model of development that was distinct from the triumphant imperialism at the turn of the nineteenth century. 'Tropical disease' continues to be a medical category; presently, it comprises of diseases prevalent in exotic and under-developed parts of the world, and may include a spectrum of infectious diseases, from HIV/AIDS to trachoma, onchocerciasis, as well as the more familiar malaria and filariasis.[25]

In postcolonial India, therefore, the sites of what were formerly colonial enclaves became irrelevant. This moment of rupture between colonialism and racialized, exclusive medical and political enclaves came when the British high commission declined to establish a British consulate at Darjeeling to cater to the British planters and retired civilian and military personnel in the region. Darjeeling is now a mere district capital and one hill-station among several, and like them is trading the vestiges of its colonial past to compete for domestic and international tourists. It is also the site of a long-standing regional and ethnic separatist dispute in West Bengal because the Gurkhas, the dominant majority, as well as other indigenous people of the region, believe that they have been short-changed in the development stakes of independent India.[26] The tea plantations have survived as well; but as we have seen, with their autonomy severely curtailed. This is not to suggest, of course, that sites of privilege disappeared in postcolonial India; if anything, privilege and social space were even more entrenched at multiple sites, those of ethnicity, caste, gender, class and the urban–rural inequalities. But the era of tropical enclaves ended with colonialism.

---

25 See, for instance, Howard Wolinsky, 'Tropical Travel Medicine: A Growing Interest in Tropical Medicine Reflects the Increasing Incidence of Tropical Disease in the Western World', *European Molecular Biology Organization*, 9 (2008), pp. 714–16; Peter J. Hotez, 'Tropical Diseases Research: Thirty Years and Counting', *PLOS Neglected Tropical Diseases*, 2 (2008), pp. 1–2.

26 Snehamoy Chakladar, *Sub-regional Movement in India, with Reference to Bodoland and Gorkhaland* (Kolkata, K.P. Bagchi, 2004); Tanka Bahadur Subba, *Ethnicity, State and Development: A Case Study of the Gorkhaland Movement in Darjeeling* (New Delhi, Har Anand Publications, 1992).

Bibliography

Unpublished Official Sources

Asia, Pacific and Africa Collections, British Library, London (APAC)

Government of Bengal Proceedings and Consultations
Medical (1861–90)
Municipal (Local Self Government/Local Boards, 1888–1935, Medical, 1892–1936, Sanitation/Public Health, 1900–37)
MSS Photo Eur 421, MSS Eur E 341, MSS Eur F/174, MSS Eur C474, MSS Photo Eur 275, MSS Eur E 279, MSS Eur B 411, MSS Eur C 379 MSS Eur R 187, MSS Eur /R 136, MSS Eur D 1023, MSS Eur IOR Neg 11665
Public and Judicial Department Records (miscellaneous, as cited in text)

National Archives of India, New Delhi (NAI)

Government of India Proceedings
Sanitary, Medical, Public and Judicial (1900–24)
Education, Lands and Health
Health (1925–42)

The National Archives, Kew

War Office, Colonial Office (miscellaneous, as cited in text)

West Bengal State Archives, Kolkata (WBSA)

Government of Bengal Proceedings
Local Self Government/Local Boards (1885–1937), Medical 1880–1920, Public Health (1921–37)
Revenue: Excluded Territories (1930–36)
General: Sanitation (1869–1920)

The Wellcome Library, London

MS 6933 (scrapbook compiled by James Cantlie)

District Magistrate's Record Room, Darjeeling
Settlement (1890–96)
Terai Branch Indian Tea Association Office, Bengdubi
'History of the Terai Planters' Association and the Terai Branch Indian Tea Association', cyclostyled manuscript
Private Papers

Published Official Sources

Annual Report of the Administration of the Plantation Labour Act 1951, Government of West Bengal, 1970 to 1972.
Annual Report of the Calcutta School of Tropical Medicine Institute of Hygiene and the Carmichael Hospital for Tropical Diseases, Calcutta School of Tropical Medicine Institute of Hygiene and the Carmichael Hospital for Tropical Diseases, 1920 to 1925.
Annual Reports of the Director of Public Health for Bengal, Government of Bengal, Public Health Department, 1920 to 1940.
Annual Reports of the Sanitary Commissioner for Bengal, Government of Bengal, 1869 to 1910.
Annual Reports on the Health of the Population of West Bengal, Government of West Bengal, 1948 to 1951.
Annual Reports on the Working of Hospitals and Dispensaries under the Government of Bengal, 1930 to 1938.
Annual Reports on the Working of the Jalpaiguri Labour Act for 1914–15 (Calcutta, Government Press, 1915, APAC).
Arbuthnott, J.C., *Report on the Conditions of Tea Garden Labour in the Duars of Bengal, in Madras, and in Ceylon* (Shilling, 1904).
Bentley, C.A., *Malaria and Agriculture in Bengal: How to Reduce Malaria in Bengal by Irrigation* (Government of Bengal, 1925).
Christophers, S.R., *Enquiry on Malaria, Blackwater Fever and Anchylostomiasis in Singhbhum: Report no 1. Preliminary Investigation into the Conditions in the Bengal Iron Company's Mines at Manharpur, January 1923* (Patna, Superintendent, Government Printing, Bihar and Orissa, 1923).
Christophers, S.R., and Bentley, C.A., *Scientific Memoirs Officers of the Medical and Sanitary Departments of the GOI, Being the First Report to the Advisory Committee Appointed by the GOI to Conduct an Enquiry regarding Black-water and Other Fevers Prevalent in the Duars* (Calcutta, Superintendent, Government Printing, India, 1909).
— *Malaria in the Duars: Being the Second Report to the Advisory Committee Appointed by the Government of India to Conduct an Enquiry regarding Blackwater and Other Fevers Prevalent in the Duars* (Simla, Government Press, 1911).
Dash, Arthur Jules, *Bengal District Gazetteer: Darjeeling* (Alipore, Bengal Government Press, 1947).
Detailed Report of the General Committee of the Dooars Planters Association, Dooars Planters Association, 1908–1952 (MSS Eur F174/686–730, APAC).
Detailed Report of the General Committee of the Indian Tea Association, Calcutta, 1893–1951 (MSS Eur F/174/584–645, APAC).
Fry, A.B., *First Report on Malaria in Bengal* (Calcutta, Bengal Secretariat Book Depot, 1912).
— *Second Report on Malaria in Bengal* (Calcutta, Bengal Secretariat Book Depot, 1914).

Grunig, John F., *Eastern Bengal and Assam District Gazetteer* (Allahabad, Pioneer Press, 1911).

Hodgson, Brian H., 'On the Colonization, Commerce, Physical Geography etc. of the Himalaya Mountains and Nepal', *Selections from Records of Government of Bengal*, nos 27–32 (Calcutta, 1857).

Hunter, W.W., *A Statistical Account of Bengal, Vol. X., Districts of Darjiling and Jalpaiguri, & State of Kuch Behar* (London, Trubner, 1876).

Imperial Gazetteer of India, Provincial Series, Bengal, vol. 2 (Calcutta, Superintendent, Government Publishing, 1909).

James, S.P., 'Malaria in India', *Scientific Memoirs by Officers of the Medical and Sanitary Department of the Govt Of India*, NS 2 (Calcutta, Periodical Publications, 1902).

Jones, E. Lloyd, *Standards of Medical Care for Tea Plantations in India: A Report Government of India* (New Delhi, Ministry of Labour, 1947).

Memorandum of the Services of Dr A. Campbell, Bengal Medical Services, Supt of Darjeeling, and in Charge of Political Relations with Sikim, with Official Notices of the Same, and a List of Papers on Statistical and Other Subjects Contributed by Him, and Published in India, from 1833 to 1855 (Hastings, Osborne, 1856).

Milligan, J.A., *Final Report on the Survey and Settlement Reports in the Jalpaiguri District, 1906–1916* (Calcutta, 1919).

Mitra, A., *West Bengal Census 1951: District Handbook: Darjeeling* (Alipore, Superintendent Government Printing Press, 1954).

Mitra, J.C., *Final Report on the Survey and Settlement Operations in the Darjeeling Terai, 1919–25* (Calcutta, 1927).

O'Malley, L.S.S., *Bengal District Gazetteers: Darjeeling* (Calcutta, 1907).

Rege, D.V., *Labour Investigation Committee: Report on an Enquiry into Conditions of Labour in Plantations in India* (Simla, 1946).

Report of Royal Commission on Labour in India, London with Minutes of Evidence (London, 1931).

Report of the Duars Committee (Shillong, Eastern Bengal and Assam Govt Press, 1910).

Report of the Labour Enquiry Commission (Calcutta, Bengal Secretariat Press, 1896).

Report of the Malaria Commission on Its Study Tour in India Aug 23rd to Dec 28, 1929 (Geneva, League of Nations Publications, 1930).

Report of the Malaria Survey of the Jalpaiguri Duars (Calcutta, Government of Bengal, Public Health Department, 1926).

Report on Dargeeling: A Place In the Sikkim Mountains, Proposed as a Sanitarium, or Station of Health (Calcutta, 1830).

Special Report on the Working of Act I of 1882 in the Province of Assam during the Years 1886–1889 (Calcutta, Superintendent of Government Printing, 1890).

Strickland, C., *Abridged Report on Malaria in the Assam Tea Gardens* (Calcutta, Indian Tea Association, 1929).

Summary of Proceedings of the Second Session of the Industrial Committee on Plantations Held at New Delhi on 31st March and 1st and 2nd April, 1948 (APAC, n.d.).

Sunders, D.H.E., *Final Report on the Land Revenue Settlement of the Western Duars, Bengal* (Calcutta, Bengal Secretariat Press, 1895).

Tour[s] of H.E .the Right Hon Baron Carmichael of Skirling, Jalpaiguri, Oct 31st to Nov. 2nd, 1912 (Calcutta, Superintendent Government Printing, 1912–16).

Triennial Report of the Working of Hospitals and Dispensaries in the Presidency of Bengal for the Years 1938, 1939 and 1940 (Alipore, 1940).

Other Published Sources

Anonymous, *Notes on Tea in Darjeeling by a Planter* (Darjeeling, 1888).
Avery, Mary H., *'Up in the Clouds': or Darjeeling and Its Surroundings, Historical and Descriptive* (Calcutta, W. Newman and Co., 1878).
Baildon, Samuel, *The Tea Industry: A Review of Finance and Labour, Guide for Capitalists and Assistants* (London, 1882).
Bald, Claud, *Indian Tea: Its Culture and Manufacture, Being A Text Book on the Cultivation and Manufacture of Tea* (3rd edn, Calcutta, Thacker, Spink, and Co., 1917).
Bamber, E.F, *An Account of the Cultivation and Manufacture of Tea in India, from Personal Observation* (Calcutta, T.S. Smith, 1866).
Bentley, C.A., 'Some Malarial Problems in Bengal', *Indian Medical Gazette*, 48 (March 1913), pp. 112–13.
— 'Malaria and Agriculture in Bengal', *The Lancet*, 206 (31 Oct. 1925), pp. 926–27.
— *Malaria and Agriculture in Bengal: How to Reduce Malaria in Bengal by Irrigation* (Calcutta, Bengal Secretariat Book Depot, 1925).
Bhanja, K.C., *Darjeeling at a Glance: A Handbook Descriptive and Historical of Darjeeling, Sikkim and Tibet with Thrilling Accounts of Everest and Kanchenjunga Expeditions by Land and Air* (2nd edn, Darjeeling, Oxford Book & Stationery Co., 1942).
— *The Wonders of Darjeeling and the Sikkim Himalaya* (Darjeeling, 1943).
Bishop, S.O., *Medical Hints for the Hills* (Darjeeling, Scotch Mission Orphanage Press, 1888).
Brown, Percy, *Tours in Sikhim and the Darjeeling District* (4th edn, Calcutta, W. Newman and Co., 1944).
Campbell, A., 'Note on the Culture of the Tea Plant at Darjeeling', *Journal of the Agri-Horticultural Society of India*, 6 (1848), pp. 123–35.
— 'On the Cultivation of Cotton in the Darjeeling Morung and the Capabilities of That Tract for the Extensive Growth of Superior Cottons', *Journal of the Agri-Horticultural Society of India*, 7 (1850), pp. 287–89.
— 'On the Lepchas', *Journal of the Ethnological Society of London*, 1 (1869), pp. 143–57.
— 'On the Tribes around Darjeeling', *Transactions of the Ethnological Society of London*, 7 (1869), pp. 144–59.
Chatterjee, B., 'Treatment of Malaria in the Present Emergency', *Indian Medical Gazette*, 77 (1942), pp. 701–2.
Christophers, S.R., 'The Mechanism of Immunity against Malaria in Communities Living under Hyper-endemic Conditions', *Indian Journal of Medical Research*, 12 (1924), pp. 273–94.
Clarke, Hyde, 'Colonisation of British India', *Journal of the Society of Arts*, 7 (1859), p. 649.
— 'On Hill Settlements and Sanitaria', *Journal of the Society of Arts*, 17 (1869).
— 'The English Stations in the Hill Regions of India: Their Value and Importance, with Some Statistics of their Products and Trade, *Journal of the Statistical Society of London*, 44 (1881), pp. 528–73.
Crawford, D.G., *Roll of the Indian Medical Service 1615–1930* (London, London Stamp Exchange, 1986, first pub. 1930).
Crommelin, J.A., 'A Brief Account of the Experiments That Have Been Made with a View to the Introduction of the Tea Plant at Darjeeling', *Journal of the Agri-Horticultural Society of India*, 8 (1852), pp. 91–95.
Darjeeling and Its Mountain Railway: A Guide and Souvenir (Calcutta, Caledonian Printing Co., 1921).

The Dorjeeling Guide: Including a Description of the Country, and of Its Climate, Soil and Productions, with Travelling Directions etc. (Calcutta, Samuel Smith, 1845).

Dowling, A.F, *Tea Notes* (Calcutta, D.M. Traill, 1885).

Dozey, E.C., *A Concise History of the Darjeeling District with a Complete Itinerary of Tours in Sikkim and the District* (2nd edn, Calcutta Art Press, Calcutta, 1922).

Fletcher, David Wilson, *The Children of Kanchenjunga* (London, Constable and Co. Ltd, 1955).

Fraser, W.M., *The Recollections of a Tea Planter* (London, Tea and Rubber Mail, 1935).

Ghose, B.C., 'The Development of the Tea Industry in the District of Jalpaiguri: 1869–1968', *Jalpaiguri District Centenary Souvenir* (Jalpaiguri, B.C. Ghose, 1970).

Ghosh, Birendra Nath, *A Treatise on Hygiene and Public Health, with Special Reference to the Tropics* (6th and 7th edns, Calcutta, Scientific Publishing Company, 1927 and 1930).

Giles, G.M., *Climate and Health in Hot Countries and the Outlines of Tropical Climatology: A Popular Treatise on Personal Hygiene in the Hotter Parts of the World, and on the Climates That Will Be within Them* (London, Bale and Danielsson, 1904).

Handbook of Castes and Tribes Employed on Tea Estates in North East India (Calcutta, Tea Districts Labour Association, 1924).

Hanley, Maurice P., *Tales and Songs from an Assam Tea Garden* (Calcutta and Simla, Thacker, Spink, and Co., 1928).

Hathorn, F.G., *A Handbook of Darjeeling: With Brief Notes on the Culture and Manufacture of Tea, and Rules for the Sale of Unassessed Waste Lands* (Calcutta, 1863).

Hehir, Patrick, *Malaria in India* (London and Oxford, Oxford University Press, 1927).

Hodgson, Brian H., *Papers Relative to the Colonization, Commerce, Physical Geography etc. of the Himalaya* (Calcutta, 1857).

Hooker, Joseph Dalton, *Himalayan Journals: Notes of a Naturalist in Bengal Sikkim and Nepal Himalayas etc.*, vols 1 and 2 (New Delhi, repr. 1999, first pub. 1854).

Indian Tea Planters' Association Golden Jubilee Souvenir (Jalpaiguri, ITPA, 1965).

Khan, Bhupendra Mohan, 'Records of Anophelines from the Bengal Dooars', *Indian Medical Gazette*, 64 (1929), p. 496.

Keble, J.A., *Darjeeling Ditties and Other Poems: A Souvenir* (Calcutta, Calcutta General Printing Co., 1908).

Lane, Clayton, 'The Treatment of Ankylostomiasis, or Hookworm Disease', *Indian Medical Gazette*, 50 (1915), pp. 241–45.

— 'The Genus Ancylostoma in India and Ceylon', *Indian Journal of Medical Researches*, 6 (1916), pp. 74–92.

— 'The Hookworm and the War Loan', *Indian Medical Gazette*, 52 (1917), pp. 161–64.

— 'Lecture Delivered to the Members of the Darjeeling Planters' Association on April 29, 1916 on "The Incidence, Effects, and Prevention of Hookworm Infection" as They Concern the Planter', *India Health Bulletin* 1 (repr.), Simla, 1924 (APAC).

Louis, J.A.H., *The Gates of Thibet: A Bird's Eye View of Independent Sikkhim, British Bhootan and the Dooars as a Doorga Poojah Trip* (Calcutta, Catholic Orphan Press, 1894).

Macpherson, W.G., 'Memorandum on Hill Diarrhoea and Its Treatment by Perchloride of Mercury', *Indian Medical Gazette*, 22 (1887), pp. 193–94.

Minney, R.J., *Midst Himalayan Mists* (Calcutta, Butterworth & Co., 1920).

Mitra, A., *The Tribes and Castes of West Bengal* (Alipore, West Bengal Government Press, 1953).

— *West Bengal Census 1951: District Handbook: Darjeeling* (Alipore, West Bengal Government Press, 1954).

Newman's Guide to Darjeeling and Neighbourhood: A Historical and Descriptive Handbook etc. (8th edn, Calcutta, Newman, 1927).

Bibliography

O'Brien, R.D., *Darjeeling: The Sanitarium of Bengal and Its Surroundings* (Calcutta, W. Newman & Co, 1883).

Pearson, J.T., *Note on Darjeeling* (Darjeeling, 1839).

Pinn, Fred, *The Road of Destiny: Darjeeling Letters, 1839* (Calcutta and Oxford, Oxford University Press, 1986).

Rennie, David Field, *Bhotan and the Story of the Dooar War: Including a Three Months Residence in the Himalayas etc.* (London, John Murray, 1866).

Risley, H.H., *The Tribes and Castes of Bengal*, vol. 2 (Calcutta, Firma KLM, 1998, repr., first pub. 1892).

Ross, Ronald, 'Medical Science and the Tropics', *Bulletin of the American Geographical Society*, 45 (1913), pp. 435–38.

— *Memoirs: With A Full Account of the Great Malaria Problem and Its Solution* (London, John Murray, 1923).

— *Malaria-Control in Malaya and Assam: A Visit of Inspection, 1926–1927* (Wellcome Library, n.d.).

Ross, Ronald, and L.J Bruce-Chwatt, *The Great Malaria Problem and Its Solution: From the Memoirs of Ronald Ross with an Introduction by L.J. Bruce-Chwatt* (London, Keynes Press, British Medical Association, 1988).

Roy, D.N., and K.L. Chowdhury, 'The Parasitology of Malaria in the Darjeeling Terai', *Indian Medical Gazette*, 65 (1930), pp. 379–80.

Roy, Naresh Chandra, *Rural Self-Government in Bengal* (Calcutta, University of Calcutta, 1936).

Roy, Sarat Chandra, *The Oraons of Chota Nagpur: Their History, Economic Life, and Social Organization* (Ranchi, S.C. Roy, 1915).

Sāṅkrtyāyana, Rāhula *Dorjeliṅg-paricaya* (Calcutta, Ādhunika Pustaka Bhavana, 1950).

Śānyāla, Harimohana, *Dārajiliṅgera itihāsa* (Calcutta, Mitram 2005, first pub. 1880).

Strickland, C., 'Malaria on Ambootia Tea Estate near Kurseong and the Success of Some Anti-malarial Operations', *Indian Medical Gazette*, 59 (1924), pp. 119–20.

— 'Notes on Malaria in the Hill-Stations in or near the Eastern Himalayas', *Indian Medical Gazette*, 59 (1924), pp. 549–50.

— 'The Mosquito Factor in the Malaria of Assam Tea Gardens', *Indian Medical Gazette*, 60 (1925).

— *Abridged Report on Malaria in the Assam Tea Gardens* (Calcutta, Indian Tea Association, 1929).

Strickland, C., and H.P. Chaudhuri, 'More on Hill Malaria', *Indian Medical Gazette* (1936), pp. 267–9.

Strickland, C., and K.L. Chowdhury, *Blackwater Fever and Malaria in the Darjeeling Terai* (Calcutta, 1931).

Sunder, D.H.E., *Final Report on the Land Revenue Settlement of the Western Duars, Bengal, Calcutta* (Calcutta, Bengal Secretariat Press, 1895).

Symington, John, *In a Bengal Jungle: Stories of Life on the Tea Gardens of Northern India* (Chapel Hill, University of North Carolina Press, 1935).

Watson, Malcolm, 'Malaria and Mosquitoes: Forty Years On', *Journal of the Royal Society of Arts*, 87 (1939), p. 485.

Contemporary Journals

The Bengalee
Biographical Memoirs of Fellows of the Royal Society
British Medical Journal
Indian Journal of Medical Research
Indian Medical Gazette
Indian Medical Record
Indian Planters' Gazette and Sporting News
Journal of the Agri-Horticultural Society of India
Journal of the Anthropological Institute of Great Britain and Ireland
Journal of the Darjeeling Natural History Society
Journal of the Ethnological Society of London
Journal of the Society of Arts
Journal of the Statistical Society of London
The Lancet
Obituary Notices of Fellows of Royal Society
Tea and Coffee Trade Journal
Transactions of the Ethnological Society of London

Secondary Sources

Aiken, Robert S., 'Early Penang Hill Station', *Geographical Review*, 77 (1987), pp. 421–39.

Alatas, Syed Hussein, *The Myth of the Lazy Native: A Study of the Image of Malays, Filipinos and Javanese from the 16th to the 20th Century and Its Function in the Ideology of Colonial Capitalism* (London, Cass, 1977).

Alavi, Seema, *Islam and Healing: Loss and Recovery of an Indo-Muslim Medical Tradition, 1600–1900* (Basingstoke, Palgrave Macmillan, 2008).

Anderson, Warwick, '"Where Every Prospect Pleases and Only Man Is Vile": Laboratory Medicine as Colonial Discourse', *Critical Inquiry*, 18 (1992), pp. 506–29.

— 'Immunities of Empire: Race, Disease and the New Tropical Medicine, 1900–1920', *Bulletin of the History of Medicine*, 70 (1996), pp. 94–118.

— *Cultivation of Whiteness: Science, Health and Racial Destiny in Australia* (Carlton South, Victoria, Melbourne University Press, 2002).

— *Colonial Pathologies: American Tropical Medicine, Race and Hygiene in the Philippines* (Durham, NC and London, Duke University Press, 2006).

Arnold, David, 'Medical Priorities and Practice in Nineteenth Century British India', *South Asia Research*, 5 (1985), pp. 167–83.

— *Colonizing the Body: State Medicine and Epidemic Disease in Nineteenth-Century India* (Berkeley and London, University of California Press, 1993).

— 'The Discovery of Malnutrition and Diet in Colonial India', *Indian Economic and Social History Review*, 31 (1994), pp. 1–26.

— '"An Ancient Race Outworn": Malaria and Race in Colonial India, 1860–1930', in Waltraud Ernst and Bernard Harris (eds), *Race, Science and Medicine* (London: Routledge, 1999), pp. 123–43.

— *The Tropics and the Traveling Gaze: India, Landscape, and Science, 1800–1850* (Delhi, Permanent Black, 2005).

— 'Diabetes in the Tropics: Race, Place and Class in India, 1880–1965', *Social History of Medicine*, 2 (2009), pp. 245–61.
— 'British India and the "Beri-Beri Problem"', 1798–1942', *Medical History*, 54 (2010), pp. 295–314.
Arnold, David (ed.), *Imperial Medicine and Indigenous Societies* (Manchester and New York, Manchester University Press, 1988).
— *Warm Climates, Western Medicine: The Emergence of Tropical Medicine, 1500–1900* (Rodopi, Amsterdam, 1996).
Attewell, Guy, *Refiguring Unani Tibb: Plural Healing in Late Colonial India* (Hyderabad, India, Orient Longman, 2007).
Bagchi, Amiya K., *Private Investment in India, 1900–1939* (London, Routledge, 2000).
— 'Colonialism and the Nature of "Capitalist" Enterprise in India', in idem, *Capital and Labour Redefined: India and the Third World* (London, Anthem, 2002), pp. 91–136.
Bagchi, Amiya K., and Soman, Krishna (eds), *Maladies, Preventives and Curatives: Debates in Public Health in India* (New Delhi, Tulika, 2005).
Bala, Poonam, *Imperialism and Medicine in Bengal: A Socio-historical Perspective* (New Delhi and London, Sage, 1991).
Basu, Subho, *Does Class Matter? Colonial Capital and Workers' Resistance in Bengal 1890–1937* (New Delhi and Oxford, Oxford University Press, 2004).
Basu, Swaraj, *Dynamics of a Caste Movement: The Rajbansis of North Bengal, 1910–1947* (New Delhi, Manohar, 2003).
Batabyal, Rakesh, *Communalism in Bengal: From Famine to Noakhali, 1943–47* (New Delhi and London, Sage, 2005).
Bates, Crispin, 'Coerced and Migrant Labourers in India: The Colonial Experience', *Edinburgh Papers in South Asian Studies*, 13 (2000).
Bayly, C.A., *Indian Society and the Making of the British Empire* (Cambridge, Cambridge University Press, 1988).
— *Empire and Information: Intelligence Gathering and Social Communication in India, 1780–1870* (Cambridge, Cambridge University Press, 1996).
Behal, Rana P., 'Wage Structure and Labour: Assam Valley Tea Plantations, 1900–1947', www.indialabourarchives.org/publications.
Bhadra, Mita, *Women Workers of Tea Plantations in India* (New Delhi, Heritage, 1992).
Bhadra, Mita, and R.K. Bhadra (eds), *Plantation Labourers of North-East India* (Dibrugarh, 1997).
Bhattacharya, Sanjoy, Mark Harrison and Michael Worboys, *Fractured States: Smallpox, Public Health and Vaccination Policy in British India 1800–1947* (Hyderabad, Orient Longman, 2005).
Bhowmik, Sharit K., *Class Formation in the Plantation System* (New Delhi, People's Publishing House, 1981).
— 'Labour Welfare in Tea Plantations: An Assessment of the Plantation Labour Act', in Sebastian Karotemprel and B. Dutta Roy (eds), *Tea Garden Labourers of North East India: A Multi-dimensional Study* (Shillong, Vendrame Institute, 1990), pp. 187–99.
Biswas, Ratan, 'Bangla Sahitye Darjeeling Jela', in idem, *Madhuparni: Bishesh Darjeeling Sankhya* (Calcutta, 1996), pp. 369–75.
Blakeney, T.S., 'A.R Hinks and the First Everest Expedition, 1921', *The Geographical Journal*, 136 (1970), pp. 333–43.
Bose, Sugata, *Peasant Labour and Colonial Capital: Rural Bengal since 1770* (Cambridge, Cambridge University Press, 1993).
Bradley, D.J., 'Watson, Swellengrebel and Species Sanitation: Environmental and Ecological Aspects', *Parassitologia*, 36 (1994), pp. 137–47.

Breman, Jan, *Taming the Coolie Beast: Plantation Society and the Colonial Order in Southeast Asia* (Delhi: Oxford, Oxford University Press, 1989).

Brockway, Lucile H., *Science and Colonial Expansion: The Role of the British Royal Botanic Gardens* (New York: London, Academic Press, 1979).

Bryder, Linda, *Below the Magic Mountain: A Social History of Tuberculosis in Twentieth-Century Britain* (Oxford, Oxford University Press, 1988).

Burke, Peter, 'The Invention of Leisure in Early Modern Europe', *Past and Present*, 146 (1995), pp. 136–50.

Bynum, W.F. 'An Experiment That Failed: Malaria Control at Mian Mir', *Parassitologia*, 36 (1994), pp. 107–20.

— 'Reasons for Contentment: Malaria in India, 1900–1920', *Parassitologia*, 40 (1998), pp. 19–27.

Caplan, Lionel, 'Bravest of the Brave: Representations of the Gurkha in British Military Writings', *Modern Asian Studies*, 25 (1991) pp. 571–98.

Catanach, I.J., 'Plague and the Tensions of Empire: India 1896–1918', in D. Arnold (ed.), *Imperial Medicine and Indigenous Societies* (Manchester and New York, Manchester University Press, 1988), pp. 149–71.

Cell, John W., 'Anglo-Indian Medical Theory and the Origins of Segregation in West Africa', *The American Historical Review*, 91 (1986), pp. 307–35.

Chakladar, Snehamoy, *Sub-regional Movement in India, with Reference to Bodoland and Gorkhaland* (Kolkata, K.P. Bagchi, 2004).

Chakrabarti, Pratik, *Western Science in Modern India: Metropolitan Methods, Colonial Practices* (New Delhi, Permanent Black, 2004).

— 'Of Empire and Other Parasites: Tropical Medicine in British India', *Biblio: A Review of Books*, 12 (2007), pp. 20–21.

— '"Signs of the Times": Medicine and Nationhood in British India', *Osiris*, 24 (2009), pp. 188–211.

— 'Curing Cholera: Pathogens, Places and Poverty in South Asia', *International Journal of South Asian Studies*, 3 (2010), pp. 153–68.

Chakrabarty, Dipesh, *Rethinking Working Class History, Bengal 1890 to 1940* (Princeton, Princeton University Press, 1989).

Chakraborty, Kamakhya Prosad, 'Cha-Shilper Goda Pottone Bangali Uddogider Bhumika', *Kirat Bhumi: Jalpaiguri Jela Sankalan* (Jalpaiguri, 1998), pp. 233–40.

— *Shekaler Jalpaiguri Shohor Ebong Samajik Jibaner Kichu Katha* (Jalpaiguri, n.d.).

Chandavarkar, Rajnarayan, *The Origins of Industrial Capitalism in India: Business Strategies and the Working Classes in Bombay, 1900–1940* (Cambridge, Cambridge University Press, 1994).

Chatterjee, Aditi, *The Changing Landscapes of the Indian Hill-stations: Power, Culture and Tradition* (Calcutta, Prabasi Press, 1997).

Chatterjee, Partha, *A Princely Imposter? The Kumar of Bhawal & the Secret History of Indian Nationalism* (Delhi, Permanent Black, 2002).

Chatterjee, Piya, *A Time for Tea: Women, Labor, and Post/Colonial Politics on an Indian Plantation* (Durham and London, Duke University Press, 2001).

Chatterji, Joya, 'The Fashioning of a Frontier: The Radcliffe Line and Bengal's Border Landscape, 1947–52', *Modern Asian Studies*, 33 (1999), pp. 185–242.

Chaudhary, Shankar Rai, 'Cha-Baganer Babuder Sanskriti', in Gautam Rai (ed.), *Uttar Banger Janajati O Luptapray Lok Sanskriti* (Siliguri, 2004), pp. 179–87.

Chaudhury, Asim, *Enclaves in a Peasant Society: Political Economy of Tea in Western Dooars in Northern Bengal* (New Delhi, People's Publishing House, 1995).

Chaudhury, Samrat, and Nitin Varma, 'Between Gods/Goddesses/Demons and "Science": Perceptions of Health and Medicine among Plantation Labourers in Jalpaiguri District, Bengal', *Social Scientist*, 30 (2002), pp. 18–38.

Cohn, Bernard S., 'The British in Benares: A Nineteenth Century Colonial Society', in idem, *An Anthropologist among the Historians and Other Essays* (Delhi and Oxford, Oxford University Press, 1987), pp. 422–62.

Copland, Ian, *The British Raj and the Indian Princes: Paramountcy in Western India: 1857–1930* (London, Sangam Books, 1982).

Curtin, P.D., 'Medical Knowledge and Urban Planning in Tropical Africa', *The American Historical Review*, 90 (1985), pp. 594–613.

— *Death by Migration: Europe's Encounter with the Tropical World in the Nineteenth Century* (Cambridge, Cambridge University Press, 1989).

— 'Readjustments in the Nineteenth Century', in idem, *The Rise and Fall of the Plantation Complex: Essays in Atlantic History* (Cambridge, Cambridge University Press, 1990), pp. 173–88.

Daniel, E. Valentine, Henry Bernstein and Tom Brass, *Plantations, Proletarians, and Peasants in Colonial Asia* (London, Frank Cass, 1992).

Das Gupta, Ranajit, 'Migrants in Coal Mines: Peasants or Proletarians, 1850s–1947', *Social Scientist*, 13 (1985), pp. 18–43.

— *Economy, Society, and Politics in Bengal: Jalpaiguri 1869–1947* (Delhi, Oxford University Press, 1992).

— 'Plantation Labour in Colonial India', in E. Valentine Daniel, Henry Bernstein and Tom Brass (eds), *Plantations, Proletarians, and Peasants in Colonial Asia* (special issue, *Journal of Peasant Studies*, 1992), pp. 172–91.

— *Labour and Working Class in Eastern India: Studies in Colonial History* (Calcutta, KP Bagchi, 1994).

Dasgupta, Atis, 'Ethnic Problems and Movements for Autonomy in Darjeeling', *Social Scientist*, 27 (1999), pp. 47–68.

Digby, Anne, *Making a Medical Living: Doctors and Patients in the English Market for Medicine, 1720–1911* (Cambridge, Cambridge University Press, 1994).

Dirks, Nicholas B., 'Castes of Mind', *Representations*, 37, special issue: *Imperial Fantasies and Postcolonial Histories* (1992), pp. 56–78.

— *Castes of Mind: Colonialism and the Making of Modern India* (Princeton and Chichester, Princeton University Press, 2001).

Echenberg, Myron, *Black Death, White Medicine: Bubonic Plague and Public Health in Colonial Senegal, 1914–1945* (Portsmouth, NH, Heinemann, 2002).

Ernst, Waltraud, and Bernard Harris, *Race, Science, and Medicine, 1700–1960* (London and New York, Routledge, 1999).

Farley, John H., *Bilharzia: A History of Imperial Tropical Medicine* (Cambridge and New York, Cambridge University Press, 1991).

— *To Cast Out Disease: A History of the International Health Division of the Rockefeller Foundation (1913–1951)* (Oxford, Oxford University Press, 2004).

Fett, Sharla M., *Working Cures: Healing, Health, and Power on Southern Slave Plantations* (Chapel Hill and London, University of North Carolina Press, 2002).

Fisher, Michael H., *Indirect Rule in India: Residents and the Residency System, 1764–1857* (Delhi and New York, Oxford University Press, 1991).

Forrest, Denys Mostyn, *Tea for the British: The Social and Economic History of a Famous Trade* (London, Chatto and Windus, 1973).

Fox, Jennifer, *In the Shade of Kanchenjunga* (London, BACSA, 1993).

Gangopadhyaya, Dvarkanatha, *Slavery in British Dominion* (Calcutta, Jijnasa, 1972).
Goerg, Odile, 'From Hill-station (Freetown) to Downtown Conakry (First Ward): Comparing French and British Approaches to Segregation in Colonial Cities at the Beginning of the Twentieth Century', *Canadian Journal of African Studies/Revue canadienne des études africaines*, 32 (1998), pp. 1–31.
Goswami, Omkar, '*Sahibs, Babus,* and *Banias*: Changes in Industrial Control in Eastern India, 1918–50', *Journal of Asian Studies*, 48 (1989), pp. 289–309.
Griffiths, Percival, *History of the Indian Tea Industry* (London, Weidenfeld & Nicolson, 1967).
Grove, Richard H., *Green Imperialism: Colonial Expansion, Tropical Islands and the Origins of Environmentalism, 1600–1800* (Cambridge, Cambridge University Press, 1995).
Guha, Amalendu, *Planter-Raj to Swaraj: Freedom Struggle and Electoral Politics in Assam 1826–1947* (New Delhi, Indian Council for Historical Research, 1977).
Haan, Arjaan de, *Unsettled Settlers: Migrant Workers and Industrial Capitalism in Calcutta* (Hilversum, Verloren, 1994).
Haley, Bruce, *The Healthy Body and Victorian Culture* (Cambridge, MA, and London, Harvard University Press, 1978).
Hanley, Maurice P., *Tales and Songs from an Assam Tea Garden* (Calcutta and Simla, Thacker Spink & Co., 1928).
Hardiman, David, *Missionaries and Their Medicine: A Christian Modernity for Tribal India* (Manchester, Manchester University Press, 2008).
Harrison, Gordon, *Mosquitoes, Malaria and Man: A History of the Hostilities since 1880* (London, John Murray, 1978).
Harrison, Mark, '"Hot Beds of Disease": Malaria and Civilization in Nineteenth-century British India', *Parassitologia*, 40 (1988), pp. 11–18.
— 'Tropical Medicine in Nineteenth Century India', *British Journal for the History of Science*, 25 (1992), pp. 299–318.
— *Public Health in British India: Anglo-Indian Preventive Medicine 1859–1914* (Cambridge, Cambridge University Press, 1994).
— 'Medicine and the Culture of Command: The Case of Malaria Control in the British Army during the Two World Wars', *Medical History*, 40 (1996), pp. 437–52.
— 'A Question of Locality: The Identification of Cholera in British India, 1860–1890', in D. Arnold (ed.), *Warm Climates, Western Medicine: The Emergence of Tropical Medicine, 1500–1900* (Amsterdam and Atlanta, GA, Rodopi, 1996), pp. 133–59.
— '"The Tender Frame of Man": Disease, Climate and Racial Difference in India and the West Indies, 1760–1860', *Bulletin of the History of Medicine*, 70 (1996), pp. 68–93.
— *Climates and Constitutions: Health, Race, Environment and British Imperialism in India, 1600–1850* (New Delhi and Oxford, Oxford University Press, 1999).
— *Medicine in the Age of Commerce and Empire: Britain and Its Tropical Colonies, 1660–1830* (Oxford, Oxford University Press, 2010).
Haynes, Douglas M., *Imperial Medicine: Patrick Manson and the Conquest of Tropical Disease* (Philadelphia, University of Pennsylvania Press, 2001).
Headrick, Daniel R., *The Tools of Empire: Technology and European Imperialism in the Nineteenth Century* (New York and Oxford, Oxford University Press, 1981).
— *The Tentacles of Progress: Technology Transfer in the Age of Imperialism, 1850–1940* (New York and Oxford, Oxford University Press, 1988).
Hewa, Soma, *Colonialism, Tropical Disease, and Imperial Medicine: Rockefeller Philanthropy in Sri Lanka* (Lanham, University Press of America, 1995).
Hotez, Peter J., 'Tropical Diseases Research: Thirty Years and Counting', *PLOS Neglected Tropical Diseases*, 2 (2008), pp. 1–2.

Isaacs, Jeremy D., 'D.D. Cunningham and the Aetiology of Cholera in British India, 1869–1897', *Medical History*, 42 (1998), pp. 279–305.

Jaggi, O.P., *Medicine in India: Modern Period* (New Delhi, Oxford University Press, 2000).

Jeffery, Roger, *The Politics of Health in India* (Berkeley and London, University of California Press, 1988).

Johnson, Ryan, 'European Cloth and "Tropical" Skin: Clothing Material and British Ideas of Health and Hygiene in Tropical Climates', *Bulletin of the History of Medicine*, 83 (2009), pp. 530–60.

Jones, Margaret, *Health Policy in Britain's Model Colony: Ceylon (1900–1948)* (Hyderabad, Orient Longman, 2004).

Joshi, Chitra, *Lost Worlds: Indian Labour and Its Forgotten Histories* (Delhi, Permanent Black, 2003).

Kanwar, Pamela, 'The Changing Profile of the Summer Capital of British India: Simla 1864–1947', *Modern Asian Studies*, 18 (1984), pp. 215–36.

— *Imperial Simla: The Political Culture of the Raj* (Delhi, Oxford University Press, 1990).

Karotemprel, Sebastian, and B. Dutta Roy (eds), *Tea Garden Labourers of North East India: A Multi-dimensional Study* (Shillong, Vendrame Institute, 1990).

Kazi, Ihtesham, 'Malaria in Bengal from 1860 to 1920: A Historical Study in a Colonial Setting', PhD dissertation, University of Michigan, 1986.

Kennedy, Dane, *The Magic Mountains: Hill-stations and the British Raj* (Berkeley and London, 1996).

Kenny, Judith T., 'Climate, Race, and Imperial Authority: The Symbolic Landscape of the British Hill Station in India', *Annals of the Association of American Geographers*, 85 (1995), pp. 694–714.

Kidambi, Prashant, 'Housing the Poor in a Colonial City: The Bombay Improvement Trust, 1898–1918', *Studies in History*, 17 (2001), pp. 57–79.

King, Anthony D., *Colonial Urban Development: Culture, Social Power and Environment* (London, Henley and Boston, 1976).

Klein, Ira, 'Death in India: 1871–1921', *Journal of Asian Studies*, 32 (1973), pp. 639–59.

— 'Development and Death: Reinterpreting Malaria, Economics and Ecology in British India', *Indian Economic and Social History Review*, 38 (2001), pp. 147–79.

Kosambi, Meera, and John E. Brush, 'Three Colonial Port Cities in India', *Geographical Review*, 78 (1988), pp. 32–47.

Kumar, Anil, *Medicine and the Raj: British Medical Policy in India 1835–1911* (New Delhi: London, Sage, 1998).

Kumar, Deepak, *Science and the Raj, 1857–1905* (Delhi, Oxford University Press, 1995).

— 'Perceptions of Public Health: A Study in British India', in Amiya Kumar Bagchi and Krishna Soman (eds), *Maladies, Preventives and Curatives: Debates in Public Health in India* (New Delhi, Tulika Books, 2005), pp. 44–59.

Livingstone, David N., 'Tropical Climate and Moral Hygiene: The Anatomy of a Victorian Debate', *British Journal for the History Science*, 32 (1999), pp. 93–110.

— *Putting Science in Its Place: Geographies of Scientific Knowledge* (Chicago and London, University of Chicago Press, 2003).

Lyons, Maryinez, *The Colonial Disease: A Social History of Sleeping Sickness in Northern Zaire, 1900–1940* (Cambridge and New York, Cambridge University Press, 1992).

Mackay, Alex, *Their Footprints Remain: Biomedical Beginnings across the Indo–Tibetan Frontier* (Amsterdam, Amsterdam University Press, 2007).

Mackenzie, John M. (ed.), *Imperialism and the Natural World* (Manchester and New York, Manchester University Press, 1990).

MacLeod, Roy M., 'Scientific Advice for British India: Imperial Perceptions and Administrative Goals, 1898–1923', *Modern Asian Studies*, 9 (1975), pp. 343–84.

Mahtab, B.C., *Impressions: The Diary of a European Tour* (London, St Catherine Press Ltd, 1908).

Manderson, Lenore, *Sickness and the State: Health and Illness in Colonial Malaya, 1870–1940* (Cambridge, Cambridge University Press, 1996).

Mangan, J.A, *Athleticism in the Victorian and Edwardian Public School: The Emergence and Consolidation of an Educational Ideology* (London and Portland, OR, Frank Cass, 2000).

Marks, Shula, 'What Is Colonial about Colonial Medicine? And What Has Happened to Imperialism and Health?', *Social History of Medicine*, 10 (1997) pp. 205–19.

Marshall, P.J., 'The White Town of Calcutta under the Rule of the East India Company', *Modern Asian Studies*, 34 (2000), pp. 307–31.

Mazumdar, Rajit K., *The Indian Army and the Making of Punjab* (Delhi, Permanent Black, 2003).

Mendelsohn, J. Andrew, 'From Eradication to Equilibrium: How Epidemics Became Complex after World War I', in Christopher Lawrence, and George Weisz (eds), *Greater Than the Parts: Holism in Biomedicine 1920–1950* (New York and Oxford, Oxford University Press, 1998), pp. 303–31.

Meyer, E., '"Enclave" Plantations, "Hemmed-in" Villages and Dualistic Representations in Colonial Ceylon', *Journal of Peasant Studies*, 19 (1992), pp. 199–228.

Mintz, Sidney W., *Sweetness and Power: The Place of Sugar in Modern History* (New York, Viking, 1985).

Mitter, Partha, 'The Early British Port Cities of India: Their Planning and Architecture, Circa 1640–1757', *Journal of the Society of Architectural Historians*, 45 (1986), pp. 95–114.

Mohapatra, Prabhu Prasad, 'Coolies and Colliers: A Study of the Agrarian Context of Labour Migration from Chota Nagpur, 1880–1920', *Studies in History*, 1 (1985), pp. 247–303.

Mukharji, Projit, *Nationalizing the Body: The Medical Market, Print and Daktari Medicine* (London, Anthem Press, 2009).

Mukherjee, Abhijit, 'Natural Science in Colonial Context: The Calcutta Botanic Garden and the Agri-Horticultural Society of India, 1787–1870', PhD dissertation, Jadavpur University, Calcutta, 1996.

— 'The Peruvian Bark Revisited: A Critique of British Cinchona Policy in Colonial India', *Bengal Past and Present*, 117 (1998), pp. 81–102.

Mukherjee, Sibsankar, 'Emergence of Bengalee Entrepreneurship in Tea Plantations in a Bengal District, 1879–1933', *Indian Economic and Social History Review*, 13 (1972), pp. 487–512.

— 'Changing Control in Some Selected Tea Producing Companies of Jalpaiguri Town', *Social Scientist*, 6 (1978), pp. 57–69.

Nair, Janaki, *Miners and Millhands: Work, Culture, and Politics in Princely Mysore* (New Delhi, Sage, 1998).

Navjeevan Hospital and Rural Health Care Centre (Darjeeling, 2003).

Neilds-Basu, Susan M., 'Colonial Urbanism: The Development of Madras City in the Eighteenth and Nineteenth Centuries', *Modern Asian Studies*, 13 (1979), pp. 217–46.

Oldenburg, Veena, *The Making of Colonial Lucknow, 1856–1877* (Princeton, Princeton University Press, 1984).

Packard, Randall M., *The Making of a Tropical Disease: A Short History of Malaria* (Baltimore, Johns Hopkins University Press, 2007).

Palladino, P., and M. Worboys, 'Science and Imperialism', *Isis*, 84 (1993), pp. 91–102.

Panter-Downes, Mollie, *Ooty Preserved: A Victorian Hill-station* (London, H. Hamilton, 1967).
Pemble, John, *The Invasion of Nepal: John Company at War* (Oxford, Clarendon Press, 1971).
Pettigrew, Jane, *A Social History of Tea* (London, National Trust, 2001).
Philip, Kavita, *Civilising Natures: Race, Resources and Modernity in Colonial South India* (Hyderabad, Orient Longman, 2003).
Pinch, William R., 'Same Difference in India and Europe', *History and Theory*, 38 (1999), pp. 389–407.
Pinn, Fred, *The Road of Destiny: Darjeeling Letters, 1839* (Calcutta, Oxford, Oxford University Press, 1996).
Power, Helen J., 'Sir Leonard Rogers FRS (1868–1962): Tropical Medicine in the Indian Medical Service', PhD dissertation, University of London, 1993.
— 'The Calcutta School of Tropical Medicine: Institutionalizing Medical Research in the Periphery', *Medical History*, 40 (1996), pp. 197–214.
— *Tropical Medicine in the Twentieth Century: A History of the Liverpool School of Tropical Medicine, 1898–1990* (London: New York, Kegan Paul International, 1999).
Pradhan, Kumar, *The Gorkha Conquests: The Process and Consequences of the Unification of Nepal, with Particular Reference to Eastern Nepal* (Calcutta and Oxford, Oxford University Press, 1991).
Pradhan, Queeny, 'Empire in the Hills: The Making of Hill Stations in Colonial India', *Studies in History*, 23 (2007), pp. 33–91.
Ramanna, Mridula, *Western Medicine and Public Health in Colonial Bombay 1845–1895* (London, Orient Longman, 2002).
Ramasubban, Radhika, 'Imperial Health in British India, 1857–1900', in Roy Macleod and Milton Lewis (eds), *Disease, Medicine, and Empire: Perspectives on Western Medicine and the Experience of European Expansion* (London and New York, Routledge, 1988), pp. 38–60.
Ray, Kabita, *History of Public Health: Colonial Bengal, 1921–1947* (Calcutta, Bagchi & Co., 1998).
Ray, Rajat K., 'The Crisis of Bengal Agriculture, 1870–1927: The Dynamics of Immobility', *Indian Economic and Social History Review*, 10 (1973), pp. 244–79.
Ray, Subhajyoti, *Transformations on the Bengal Frontier: Jalpaiguri, 1765–1948* (London, Routledge, 2002).
Regmi, D.R., *Modern Nepal: Rise and Growth in the Eighteenth Century* (Calcutta, Firma KL, 1975).
Renford, Raymond K., *The Non-Official British in India to 1920* (Delhi, Oxford University Press, 1987).
Rosenberg, Charles E., and Janet Golden, *Framing Disease: Studies in Cultural History* (New Brunswick, NJ, Rutgers University Press, 1992).
Rothermund, Dietmar, and D.C. Wadhwa (eds), *Zamindars, Mines and Peasants: Studies in the History of an Indian Coalfield and Its Rural Hinterland* (Delhi, Manohar Books, 1978).
Rupke, Nicolaas (ed.), *Medical Geography in Historical Perspective* (London, Wellcome Trust, 2000).
Said, Edward, *Orientalism* (London and Henely, Routledge and Keagan Paul, 1978).
Samanta, Arabinda, *Malarial Fever in Colonial Bengal: Social History of An Epidemic, 1820–1939* (Kolkata, Firma KLM, 2002).
Sanyal, Charu Chandra, *The Meches and the Totos: Two Sub-Himalayan Tribes of North Bengal* (Darjeeling, University of North Bengal Press, 1973).
Sarkar, R.L., and Mahendra P. Lama (eds), *Tea Plantation Workers in the Eastern Himalayas: A Study on Wages, Employment and Living Standards* (Delhi, Atma Ram, 1986).

Sarkar, Sumit, *Writing Social History* (Delhi, Oxford University Press, 1997).
Schenk-Sandbergen, Loes, and Niren Choudhury, *From Heroines to Beneficiaries: From Beneficiaries to Heroines? The Impact of a Small-scale Irrigation Project on Gender in the West Bengal Terai* (Delhi, Manohar, 2003).
Sen, Arnab, and Brajagopal Ghosh, *Jalpai-Duarser Jalchhabi* (Alipurduar, 2004).
Sen, Jahar, *Darjeeling: A Favoured Retreat* (New Delhi, Indus Publishing Co., 1989).
Sen, Samita, *Women and Labour in Late Colonial India: The Bengal Jute Industry* (Cambridge, Cambridge University Press, 1999).
Sharma, Jayeeta, 'An European Tea "Garden" and an Indian "Frontier": The Discovery of Assam', occasional paper no. 6 (2002), University of Cambridge, Centre for South Asian Studies, Cambridge.
Sheridan, Richard B., *Doctors and Slaves: A Medical and Demographic History of Slavery in the British West Indies, 1680–1834* (Cambridge, Cambridge University Press, 1985).
Shlomowltz, Ralph, and Lance Brennan, 'Mortality and Migrant Labour in Assam, 1865–1921', *Indian Economic & Social History Review*, 27 (1990), pp. 85–110.
Sinha, Sandeep, *Public Health Policy and the Indian Public: Bengal, 1850–1920* (Calcutta, Vision, 1998).
Sivaramakrishnan, Kavita, *Old Potions, New Bottles: Recasting Indigenous Medicine in Colonial Punjab 1850–1945* (Hyderabad, India, Orient Longman, 2006).
Stepan, Nancy, *Picturing Tropical Nature* (Ithaca, NY, Cornell University Press, 2001).
Stokes, Eric, *The English Utilitarians and India* (Oxford, Oxford University Press, 1959).
Subba, Tanka Bahadur, *The Quiet Hills: A Study of the Agrarian Relations in Hill Darjeeling* (Delhi, ISPCK, 1985).
— *Dynamics of a Hill Society: The Nepalis in Darjeeling and Sikkim Himalayas* (Delhi, Mittal, 1989).
— *Ethnicity, Sate and Development: A Case Study of the Gorkhaland Movement in Darjeeling* (New Delhi, Har Anand, 1992).
Swanson, Maynard, 'The Sanitation Syndrome: Bubonic Plague and Urban Native Policy in the Cape Colony, 1900–1909', *Journal of African History*, 38 (1977), pp. 387–410.
Taylor, Jeremy, *Hospital and Asylum Architecture in England 1840–1914: Building for Health Care* (London: New York, Mansell, 1991).
Tilley, Helen, 'Africa as a "Living Laboratory": The African Research Survey and the Colonial Empire: Consolidating Environmental, Medical and Anthropological Debates, 1920–1940', DPhil. dissertation, Oxford University, 2001.
— *Africa as a Living Laboratory: Empire, Development, and the Problem of Scientific Knowledge, 1870–1950* (Chicago, University of Chicago Press, 2011).
Tinker, Hugh, *The Foundations of Local Self-Government in India, Pakistan and Burma* (New York: London, Praeger: Pall Mall Press, 1968).
— *A New System of Slavery: The Export of Indian Labour Overseas, 1830–1920* (London, New York and Bombay, Oxford University Press, 1974).
Vaughan, Megan, *Curing Their Ills: Colonial Power and African Illness* (Oxford, Polity Press, 1991).
Waddington, Keir, *Charity and the London Hospitals: 1850–1898* (Woodbridge and Rochester, NY, Royal Historical Society, Boydell Press, 2000).
Washbrook, D.A., 'Progress and Problems: South Asian Economic and Social History c.1720–1860', *Modern Asian Studies*, 22 (1988), pp. 57–96.
Watts, Sheldon, 'British Development Policies and Malaria in India 1897–c.1929', *Past and Present*, 165 (1999), pp. 141–81.

Wolinsky, Howard, 'Tropical Travel Medicine: A Growing Interest in Tropical Medicine Reflects the Increasing Incidence of Tropical Disease in the Western World', *European Molecular Biology Organization*, 9 (2008), pp. 714–16.

Worboys, Michael, 'The Emergence of Tropical Medicine: A Study in the Establishment of a Scientific Speciality', in G. Lemaine et. al. (eds), *Perspectives on the Emergence of Scientific Disciplines* (The Hague and Paris, Mouton, 1976), pp. 76–98.

— 'Manson, Ross, and Colonial Medical Policy: Tropical Medicine in London and Liverpool, 1899–1914', in Roy MacLeod and Milton Lewis (eds), *Disease, Medicine, and Empire: Perspectives on Western Medicine and the Experience of European Expansion* (London and New York, Routledge, 1988), pp. 21–37.

— 'Germs, Malaria and the Invention of Mansonian Tropical Medicine', in David Arnold (ed.), *Warm Climates, Western Medicine: The Emergence of Tropical Medicine, 1500–1900* (Amsterdam and Atlanta, GA, Rodopi, 1996), pp. 181–207.

Index

A.aitkeni 163, 168
A.barbirostris 168
acclimatization, concept of 47–51, 85
acquired immunity to malaria, concept of 153–156
A.culcifacies 163, 168
adhiar (sharecropper) 54–55, 62
A.Fluviatilis 151
African Research Survey (1929–39) 180
agrarian practice, models of 53
agrarian system, of revenue collection 62
Agri-Horticultural Society 26
ailments and their cures 69
A.listoni 163
A.maculatus 163, 168
A.minimus 168
anchylostomiasis. *See* hookworm
Anderson, Warwick 47
Anglo-Bhutan war (1865) 15, 25, 33
Anglo-Indian medical perception 17
Anglo-Indian settlement 51
anopheles mosquitoes 151, 158, 165, 168, 171
  of plantation enclaves 162–169
anti-hookworm campaigns 100n1, 129, 178, 181
anti-malarial sanitation in India 10, 156
  discourse of malaria and practices of 157
  and human bonification scheme 169
  implementation of 158
  and the importance of location 158–161
  at Mian Mir and Meenglas 170–172
  Ross's advocacy of 158
  tropical medicine and entrepreneurial patronage 172–176
  voluntary anti-malaria cooperative societies 169
anti-mosquito campaign 159
anti-parasite programmes. *See* parasite-control programmes
anti-vector programmes. *See* vector-control programmes
Arbuthnott report (1904) 107, 115
Arnold, David 5, 8, 16–17
A.Rossii 151
Assam Labour Enquiry (1895) 103
Assam labour system 110n45
Assam tea company 58
A.umbrosus 163
Ayerst, Reverend 50, 52
Ayurveda medicine
  kavirajes 74
  practitioners of 7

bacteriological epidemiology 161
Bald, Claude 68
Basak, Jankinath 76
basti
  labourers in 53, 126, 145, 165, 189
  outside sanitary enclaves 125

Index

seasonal labourers from 124
beggary, fines for discouraging 93
Bengal Births and Deaths Registration Act (1873) 121
Bengal Dooars Railway 144, 146
Bengal Legislative Council 87, 121, 137
Bengal Local Self Government Act (1885) 121
Bengal, northern
  plantation enclaves, formation of 54–57
  tea cultivation, expansion of 57–66
Bengal Tea Gardens Public Health Bill 133, 138, 141
Bentinck, William 57
Bentley, C. A. 75–76, 80, 101–102, 104–115, 121, 129, 147, 152, 154–155, 162, 167–169, 174, 178
bhadralok 76–77, 85
bhagats 81
biomedicine 5, 180
Bishop, S. O. 68
blackwater fever 10, 75, 83, 99, 101–102, 150–151, 153, 179
Board of Health 132–133, 140–141
Board of Scientific Advice 172
bonificazione, Italian concept of 167, 169
Bose, Bhagaban Chandras 63
Brahmo Samaj 92
branch dispensaries 115
Breman, Jan 9–10
British imperialism, effects of 2
British medical institutions 87
British-owned plantations 64
British physicians. *See* 'European' doctors
British Raj 16, 85
British tea companies 64
British troops, in tropical mountains 32–40
Bruce, David 3
Burdwan fever 41
Burdwan, Maharaja of 42, 88, 90–91

Calcutta School of Tropical Medicine (CSTM) 10, 170–175, 178–179, 181–182
  hookworm surveys by 179
calomel 68
Campbell, Archibald 22–28, 43, 58, 60

Cantlie, James 40
carbon tetrachloride 179
carbon tetracholoethylene 179
carrier mosquitoes 151, 158, 162–164, 166n68, 167, 169, 174
cash crops, cultivation of 2
Catholic mission, establishment of medical dispensary 81
Central Malaria Committee 159
Chaplin, A. W. 121, 137
charitable hospitals and dispensaries 6–7
chaukidars 56, 121
chenopodium oil 181
cholera 2, 19, 30, 38, 48, 118, 130
  aetiology of 160
  epidemic of 1919 5, 126, 129, 131
  medical policy towards control of 6
  and mountain sanatoriums 15
choleraic diarrhoea 122
Christophers–Bentley report 99–102, 144
  contradictions with Duars Committee report 113–116
  on discourse of malaria in India 151
  on disease control and the enclave system 116–118
  on formation of Duars Committee 109–113
  on medical dimensions of free *versus* indentured labour 102–105
  on moral economy of plantation enclave 105–109
Christophers, S. R. 75–76, 101–117, 121, 129, 147, 151–159, 174–175, 178
Chulsa Tea Estate 125
cinchona plantation 9, 26–27
'civil stations' of colonial India 49
Civil Surgeon of Jalpaiguri 109n42, 121, 126
colonial capitalism 10, 52, 54, 106, 142
colonial enclaves
  healthcare system in 147–148
  medicalized leisure in 42–47
  plantation and sanatoriums as 9–13
  and practices of settlement 7–9
colonialism
  and medicine in India 4–7
  and tropical medicine 2–4
colonial medicine 3, 15

211

distinction with colonizing aspects of biomedicine 5
colonial plantation society 148
colonial system of the manager (*burra sahib*) 106
Communist Party of India 146
contractual system, in recruitment process 103
coolie doctors 80. *See also* daktar; doctor babus
coolie lines 16, 67–68, 76, 113, 115, 122, 168, 171, 177
  sanitary provisions and reforms 116
Corbyn, Frederick 82
corporeal exertion 30
Crofts, Colonel 86
Curtin, Philip 3

dafadar 120–121
daktar 75
  practice of 'Western medicine' 74
  title of 70, 79
Dalton, E. T. 155
Darjeeling Advertiser 93
Darjeeling, hill station of
  after independence 186–187
  anti-hookworm programmes 181
  beggary, fines for discouraging 93
  British troops in 32–40
  and colonial economy 25–28
  colonization of 50–51
  diseases contracted in 37
  Eden Sanitarium and hospital 42–47, 52
  establishment of 13
  European enclave, construction of 51
  European's life in 30, 35
  expansion of 21–25
  and growth of smaller hill-stations 89–93
  healthiness of the climate of 30–31
  hill-diarrhoea, susceptibility of European visitors to 40–42
  hookworm survey 177
  introduction of tea 26
  Lowis Jubilee Sanatorium 86
  migration of labourers 25
  municipality and political exclusivity 93–98
  overcrowding, perception of 91, 93, 94, 95, 97
  plantation system of 53
  privilege and 'industrial' labour 188–191
  race, class and society in 85–89
  railway connectivity 27
  sanatorium 28–31
  during Second World War 98
  as site for rejuvenation of health 38
  special health officer, appointment of 92
  street map of 28
  tea gardens, expansion of 59
  tea industry in 58–59
  tea plantations 13, 25, 51
  Titalya, treaty of (1817) 21
  Toong Soong Basti 92
  Waste Land Rules (1859) 58, 60, 62
Darjeeling Himalayan Railway 27, 43
Darjeeling Improvement Fund 95
Darjeeling Improvement Trust 47
Darjeeling Municipality 47, 86, 92, 94, 96
Darjeeling Natural History Society 46n131
Darjeeling Planters' Association 60, 141, 177
Deb, Dulal Chandra 137
Decentralisation Commission 135
deforestation 91, 168–169
Descriptive Ethnology of Bengal (Dalton) 155
Dirks, Nicholas 115
disease control, 'vertical' theories of 180
'diseased land' theory 83
diseases
  ailments and their cures 69
  of bowels 127
  contracted in Darjeeling 37
  and pioneering plantation in 'unhealthy' terrain 81–83
  specific to the hills 40–42
dispensary medicine 81
doctor babus 70–72, 74–81, 109, 115, 117, 121–122, 183, 192
  availability of 81
  pay and the qualifications of 76
  social status of 76
Dooars and Darjeeling Medical Association 187

Index

Dooars Planters Association (DPA) 63, 64, 99, 129, 173, 175
Dooars Planters Club 170
Dooars Tea Company 72
drainage and sewerage system 95
Drainage Committee of Bengal 159
Duars 15, 33
  as Planters' Grave 82
  representation as an unhealthy region 82–83
  system of medical care in 83
Duars (Monahan) Committee 102
  contradictions with Christophers–Bentley report 113–116
  formation of 109–113
  paternalism and local knowledge 113–116
Duncan Brothers Limited 63, 162
Dyarchy, period of 132–133, 141
dysentery 2, 10, 19, 33, 109, 118, 123, 127, 164, 178–179
  prevalence in hill-stations 31

East Indian Railway 27
economic migration, by casual labourers 84
Eden, Ashley 42–43
  proposal for establishment of hospital for Europeans 68
Eden Sanitarium and hospital 42–47, 52, 70, 86, 94, 187
English East India Company (EEIC) 19, 23
  Sagauli, treaty of (1816) 21
  Sikkim Terai, annexation of 24–25
  war with Gorkha Kingdom of Nepal 21
Enlightenment values 85
epidemic diseases 123, 131, 140, 165
  control of 3, 5
  management of 5
  respiratory 178
Ethnological Society of London 27
'European' doctors 70
  opportunity and entrepreneurship for 81
  principal duties of 72
  private practice 72–74
European medical officers 72–73, 80, 131
  See also, 'European doctors'
European settlement 36, 158

colonial enclaves and practices of 7–9
medicine and the tea economy 15–17
tropical colonies and practices of 47–52
Everest expeditions 97

Factories Act (1911) 130, 131, 179
faltu (temporary) workers/labourers 126, 130, 189
Farley, John 178
farming leases 58
filaria parasite, transmission of 3
Fletcher, David 192
forest management 26
Fraser, Andrew 86
Fraser, W. M. 40, 107
free labour, notion of 65, 103, 113–114
free *versus* indentured labour, medical dimensions of 102–105
frontier settlement zones 10

Ganguli, Jadunath 91
Germ theory of TB 187
Gorkha Kingdom of Nepal 21
government-aided hospitals 7
Greer, R. T. 94
Griffin, R. G. 129, 178–179, 181

hakims 74, 79
Harrison, Mark 6, 28, 48, 94, 96
Haynes, Douglas 74
hazira 107, 120, 190
health care system
  colonial enclaves and 147–148
  for planting community 120, 142–147, 185
Hehir, Patrick 156
Herbert, J. D. 21–22, 29, 33
heroic medicine 68–69, 192
hill-diarrhoea 40–42
  causes of 42
  consequence of 41
  nomenclature and diagnosis of 40–41
hill-plains dichotomy, in colonial India 19–21, 34
hill-stations of colonial India 10–12
  acclimatization theories 16
  development of 18
  governance of 20

213

layout of 49
medical discourses and institutions 16
municipal administration in 96
practices of settlement, medicine and the tea economy 15–17
quest for exclusivity and growth of 89–93
rate of taxation per head in 96–97
Himalayan tourism 97
Hindu pilgrimage sites 88
Hodgson, Brian 22, 30, 51
'holistic' medical approach, concept of 161
Home Farm 50
home remedies 68–69, 78
Hooker, Joseph Dalton 14–15, 24, 30–31, 38
hookworm 10, 16 See also, Rockefeller Foundation
　carbon tetracholoethylene for treatment of 179
　infestation 176–177, 179
　'public education' campaigns 178
　research on 176–180
　survey in Darjeeling district for 177
hookworm project 149, 176–177
housing scheme, plan for 95
human bonification 169

immunity to malaria, concept of 153–156
Imperial Conference on Malaria (1909), Simla 159
indentured labour 25, 64, 110
　free labour versus 102–105
　system of 60, 120–121
Indian Civil Service 6
Indian Journal of Medical Research 159
Indian Medical Gazette 167, 170
Indian Medical Service (IMS) 6, 7, 74
Indian Mining Association 133
Indian Research Fund Association (IRFA) 149–150, 161–162, 170, 177, 181
Indian Tea Planters' Association (ITPA) 60, 64, 127, 136, 139, 189
　charitable trust set up by 145
indigenous medicine
　epistemologies of 7
　practice in plantation enclaves 74–81
　practitioners of 70

See also Ayurveda medicine; Unani medicine; Western medicine
influenza epidemic (1918–19) 125–126, 131, 146
insect-vector theories 2, 160
IRFA. See Indian Research Fund Association (IRFA)

Jalapahar 22–23, 27, 32–34, 39, 91
Jalpaiguri Labour Act (1912) 118
　amendments 137
　Civil Surgeon's responsibility under 129
　enactment of 128
　and enclave in western duars 120–128
　legislative proposals and sanitary enclaves 128–131
Jalpaiguri Tea Company 63
jhum (shifting) cultivation 25
JLA. See Jalpaiguri Labour Act (1912)
joint stock company 60, 63
Jones, E. Lloyd 143, 147, 189
jotedars (peasant-cultivators) 54, 62, 133, 135, 137–141
Journal of Society of Arts 27
jute industrial areas 134

kala-azar 16, 118, 178
　funds to support research on 173
kavirajes 74, 79
Keble, J. A. 35, 39
Kennedy, Dane 11–12, 19, 35, 49, 84
Khambata, R. B. 122, 165
khet land 108 s
King, Anthony D. 11
Kurseong hill resort 89–90, 95

Labour Enquiry Commission 66
Labour Enquiry Report (1946) 176
labourers for tea plantations
　free labour, notion of 65
　non-contractual 65
　recruitment of 64–65, 75
　sardari system for 65
labourers' wages 107–108, 111, 189–190
　payment of money to women workers 146
labour management system 102, 104
labour welfare 117

Index

Lady Minto Indian Nursing Association (LMINA) 144
    guarantee fund 144
land lease
    to British dairy farmers 93
    for tea plantations 58–59, 63
Landslip Committee (1906) 92
Lane, Clayton 177
League of Nations Malaria Committee 152, 175
Lepchas community 22, 25–26, 28, 54, 58, 77
Liverpool School 10, 172
Livingstone, D. N. 47
Lloyd, Captain 21, 22, 143, 147
local native doctors 79 See also, doctor babu.
Local Self-Government Bill in Bengal (1885) 93
Lowis Jubilee Sanatorium 39, 86–88, 90

Maclean, G. 32–33
Macrae, R. 45
Madesias labourers 77, 103, 113
mai-baap relationship 190. *See also* planters, relationship with workers
malaria 10, 16, 75, 99
    acquired immunity to 153–156
    acute infestation 154
    association of labour camps with outbreaks of 152
    in Darjeeling foothills 150–151
    hyper-endemicity 154, 165
    infection in mining areas of Bihar 154
    Meenglas Tea Estate, anti-malarial operation at 162–169
    prevention *versus* prophylaxis 156–158
    racial acclimatization and immunity to 153–156
    tropical medicine for treatment of 4
    use of quinine for prevention of 153
Malaria Bureau of India 153, 157, 161
Malaria Committee of the Royal Society. *See* Royal Society's Malaria Committee (1902)
Malaria in India (Hehir) 156
'malaria map' of India 161
managerial farming 14
Mandelli, L. 82

Manson, Patrick 3, 47, 150
Marks, Shula 5
maternity allowance 146
Meches community 25, 99. See also, immunity to malaria, concept of
    Rennie's analysis of the health of 33–34
medical care
    in Duars 83
    ojhas, provided by 81
    rationalization of 80
    for tea planters 68–70, 191
medical college, government-endorsed 79
medical discourse, in tropical colonies 47
medical economy, of the plantations 16, 142–147
medical education in medicine, Western model of 79
medical missionaries 81
medical officials, system of private practice for 73
medical policy in colonial India 6
medical practitioners, employment of 80n109
Medical Registration Act (1914) 70, 75, 79–80
medicine in India 4–7, 181
medicine of warm climates, knowledge and practice of 2–3
Meenglas Tea Estate 126, 171
    anti-malarial operation at 162–169
Megaw, J. W. D. 170
Metelli bazaar 125
Mian Mir, anti-malarial measures at 156–158, 170–172
miasma 15, 37, 45, 83, 100
military hospitals 7
Milligan, J. A. 101
moffusil 52
Mogalkata Tea Estate 63
Monahan, F. J. 112
Montague–Chelmsford Reforms (1920) 94, 132, 135
Morley–Minto Reforms (1909) 93
mosquito-vector transmission 182
municipality of Darjeeling 84, 93–98
municipal reform, in colonial India 94–95
Munro, D. 122
Mussoorie 19, 21, 26, 85

215

native doctors 79–80. *See also* daktar; doctor babus
natural equilibrium, between host and pathogen 161
New Dooars Tea Company 125–126
Nightingale, Florence 45
Nightingale wards, characteristics of 45
non-contractual labour, system of 65, 105, 111, 114
nutritional deficiencies 17

Octavius Steele 63, 72
ojhas (faith-healers) 81, 192
O'Malley, L. S. S. 131
Ootacamund 11–12, 19, 39, 93, 187

Paharia (Nepali)
    immigrants 25–26, 51, 77, 103, 109, 113
    labourers 51, 103
Pali plague 41
parasite-control programmes 8, 10
Pearson, J. T. 29–30
peasant-landholders 62
Permanent Settlement 62
phthisis 31, 33, 42, 178, 187
PLA. *See* Plantation Labour Act (1951)
plantation agriculture, development of 14
plantation economy 16, 51, 54, 102, 106, 116, 119–120, 126, 142, 144, 148, 168, 171, 183, 185
    of east Sumatra 9
plantation enclaves
    anophelines of 162–169
    death rates and fatalities 81
    formation of 54–57
    healthcare and indigenous medical practice in 74–81
    living spaces in 67
    medicine and entrepreneurism in 72–74
    modes of functioning 99
    moral economy of 105–109
    paternalism and plantation medicine 67–71
    research on hookworm in 176–180
    resident medical practitioners within 75

    role in control of epidemics and labour unrest 68
    Tea Gardens Public Health Bill 142
    tropicality, postcoloniality and 192–193
Plantation Labour Act (1951) 190–192
plantation management
    and health care 148
    neglect of the labourers' health 102
    paternalistic rights of 100 See also 'The Measure of a Sahib'
plantation system in India 8
    characteristic of 102
    features of 10
    'moral economy' of 99
    planter-coolie relationship 69, See also planters' attitudes towards labourers; 'The Measure of a Sahib'
planters
    attitudes towards
        bastis 125, 127, 128, 148, 165
        labourers 2, 10, 52, 68
    dispute of *jotedars* 127n27, 133, 135, 137–138
    medical care of 57, 68, 80, 112, 119, 147
    relationship with workers 69, 185, 190–191
    sovereignty within plantation enclaves 125, 148
    See also plantation management
Planters' Grave 82
pneumonia 42
political economy of the plantations 99, 169, 182
preventive health measures 8, 52
preventive medicine 5, 111
prophylaxis 149, 156, 158, 181–182
public health
    bio-medical model of 176
    concept of 7
    education programmes 7
    infrastructure 94–96, 182
    neglect of 5
    policies for 16
    and sanitary reforms 94
public medicine in colonial India, official discourse of 6

Index

quinine 153, 156, 175–176. *See also* prophylaxis

railway unions 146
Ramanna, Mridula 5
Ramasubban, R. 5, 94
Ray, Kabita 5
Ray, Subhajyoti 125
recruitment of labourers 62, 103–104
Rennie, David 27, 33–34, 83, 155
reserve forests 26, 51
resident medical practitioners 75
respiratory diseases 31
revenue collection, agrarian system of 62
revolt of 1857 36
rheumatism 31, 37
Risley, H. H. 115
ritual purity, Brahmanical notions of 76
Rockefeller Foundation (RF)
    International Health Division (IHD) of 178
    mass public health campaigns 179
Rockefeller grant 130
Rockefeller International Health Board 100n1
Ross Institute 10, 170, 174–175
Ross, Ronald 3–4, 157–158, 170, 180
    advocacy of anti-malarial sanitation 158
    mosquito-vector transmission, discovery of 182
Royal Commission for Labour (1931) 130, 142, 146, 167, 175, 179, 181
Royal Society's Malaria Committee (1902) 83, 101, 150, 156, 159
Rupee companies 186
rural sanitation 6

Sagauli, treaty of (1816) 21
sanatorium, development of 90–91
Sanitary Commissioner of India 102, 110–111, 159
sanitary education 6
sanitary enclaves 130
    legislative proposals and 128–131, 139
    and local politics 132–142
    and research on hookworm 176–180
    in western duars 120–128
sanitary reform, for civilian population in India 160
Santhals 55, 77, 103, 113, 116, 155
sardari system of labour 65, 105–107, 111
sardars 65–66, 77
    as mediators 100, 142
    patronage of labourers 55–56, 105
    protection of labourers under 109
    as recruiters 65, 102, 105, 113, 114. *See also* recruitment of labourers
    relationship with labourers 106, 107, 114, 144
seasoning, concept of 34, see also acquired immunity to malaria, concept of
self-help remedies 70
Senchal cantonment 34
shailashahar (mountain-town), construction of 86
Sharma, Jayeeta 58
Sikkim 14–15, 21–22, 24–25, 93, 97, 188
Simla 11, 19, 21, 39, 85, 91, 93, 97, 159, 187
Simla trots 41
sleeping sickness 2
    tropical medicine for treatment of 4
smallpox
    medical policy towards control of 6
    vaccination 109
social space, aspects of 85–86
species sanitation 171, 180, 182
spirit-ousters 71, 81
spleen index of tea estates 171
    in Mal tea district of Duars 166
    in Nagrakata tea district of Duars 166
Sterling companies 186
Story, Arthur 70, 72–74, 83
Strong, F. W. 131
Symington, John 73

Tagore, Rabindranath 88
Tarai fever 82
Tea Committee 57
tea cultivation. *See* tea plantations
tea districts 13–14, 74
    of northern Bengal 53
    of Terai and Duars 17
Tea Districts Labour Association 65, 143
tea economy 15–17
tea estates 16

217

British medical officers within 139
  management of 131
  spleen index of
    Mal tea district of Duars 166
    Nagrakata tea district of Duars 166
  therapeutic facilities in 82
tea gardens 57–58, 63
  expansion in
    Darjeeling 59
    Duars 66
  lease of 63
'The Measure of a Sahib' 191–192
Tea Gardens Public Health Bill 132–133, 138, 141–142
tea industry in Darjeeling 58–59
tea plantations 15–16
  in Darjeeling 13, 25, 51
  death rates and fatalities 81, 123–124, 131
  development of 21
  disease management system 119
  in Duars 62, 64
  expansion of 53, 57–66
  grant of lease of land for 58
  health care system in 120
  labour's partnership in 188–191
  management of 107, 148
  medical economy of 16, 142–147
  political economy of 182
  research on hookworm in 176–180
  resident medical practitioners within 75
  village *chaukidars* 121
Tea Planters' Benevolent Institution 145
Tebhaga movement (1946–47) 146, 188
tenant-sharecroppers 146
Terai Planters Club 170
Terai region 15
  plantations in 62
  representation as an unhealthy regions 82
Terai Tea Planters' Association 47, 62, 65, 141
thymol 176, 181
  after-effects of 177
ticca 107, 120, 190
Tilley, Helen 180
Tinker, Hugh 94, 96, 132, 136

Titalya, treaty of (1817) 21
Tondoo Tea Estate 126
Toong Soong Basti 92
trade unions 146, 190–192
Tribes and Castes of Bengal (Risley) 115
tropical climates for European, suitability of 2
tropical diseases 1–2, 15, 19, 34, 48, 118, 149–150, 173, 181, 193
tropical hygiene 3–4
tropical medicine
  colonialism and 2–4
  and entrepreneurial patronage 172–176
  institutionalization of 2, 4
  and logic of location 180–183
  plantations, sanatoriums and 13–15
tropics, idea of, 1
trypanosomiasis 4, 154, 156
tuberculosis 31

Unani medicine
  hakims 74
  practitioners of 7

vaccination 7, 9, 66, 126
  Indian cultural and social resistance to 6
  for small-pox 109
vector-control programmes 7, 8, 10
venereal diseases 8
Victoria Hospital 187
Village Chaukidari Act (1870) 121
vital statistics, system of 56, 65–66, 92, 103–105, 113, 118, 120–121, 123–125, 128, 130–131
voluntary anti-malaria cooperative societies 169

Waste Land Rules, in Darjeeling district (1859) 58, 60, 62
Watson, Malcolm 158, 162, 164, 170, 180
Watts, Sheldon 157
Webb, G. G. 67n59, 82, 113n60
Wernicke-Stolke family 23
Western Duars tract 14–15, 54–55, 62–63, 103, 118, 120–128, 141
Western education 85
Western medical values 86

Western medicine
   benefits of 5
   in colonial India 16
   practitioners of 70, 74
   See also indigenous medicine
Western sanitary models 6, 94
Western therapeutics 7
   institutionalization of 4–5
'white Australia', notion of 48

white towns 1, 8, 49
witchcraft, practice of 81
workers' welfare, in Duars plantations 102

yellow fever, tropical medicine for treatment of 4

zamindars (landlord) 62, 85, 134, 182